Sexualities
&
Communication
in Everyday Life

Sexualities & Communication in Everyday Life

A Reader

Editors
Karen E. Lovaas • Mercilee M. Jenkins
San Francisco State University

SAGE Publications
Thousand Oaks ▪ London ▪ New Delhi

For information:

Sage Publications, Inc.
2455 Teller Road
Thousand Oaks, California 91320
E-mail: order@sagepub.com

Sage Publications Ltd.
1 Oliver's Yard
55 City Road
London, EC1Y 1SP
United Kingdom

Sage Publications India Pvt. Ltd.
B-42 Panchsheel Enclave
Post Box 4109
New Delhi 110-017 India

Printed in the United States of America.

Sexualities and communication in everyday life: a reader / edited by
Karen E. Lovaas and Mercilee M. Jenkins.
    p. cm.
Includes bibliographical references and index.
ISBN 1-4129-1443-4 (pbk.)
  1. Sex—Social aspects. 2. Communication and sex. 3. Sexual minorities. 4. Sex (Psychology)
5. Identity (Psychology) I. Lovaas, Karen. II. Jenkins, Mercilee M. III. Title.

HQ21.S47512 2007
306.76—dc22

2006006479

This book is printed on acid-free paper.

06 07 08 09 10   10 9 8 7 6 5 4 3 2 1

Acquiring Editor:	Todd R. Armstrong
Editorial Assistant:	Camille Herrera
Project Editor:	Astrid Virding
Copyeditor:	Catherine M. Chilton
Typesetter:	C&M Digitals (P) Ltd.
Indexer:	Naomi Linzer
Cover Designer:	Michelle Lee Kenny
Book Cover Illustrator:	© Erich Hunt

Contents

We dedicate this volume to two amazing people:
David Warrior, with whom Lee started compiling a reader on sexual identity and communication 14 years ago. Although it wasn't possible to complete the original volume due to his death from AIDS, he remains an inspiration.
and
Sally Miller Gearhart, mentor to both of us, activist, scholar, creative writer, beloved teacher, and friend, without whom this area of study would be greatly diminished.

Foreword

Sexualities and Communication in Everyday Life: A Reader is an anthology of readings on the construction and performance of sexualities in private and public discourses. It is an interdisciplinary selection of foundational theoretical essays and contemporary research that can be used in courses related to sexuality and gender in communication departments, as well as across the curriculum in the humanities and social sciences. The readings are a combination of recent journal articles, original pieces solicited for this anthology, and excerpts from key works. Although the majority of selections are drawn from the field of communication, the contributors represent a range of disciplines, including political science, sociology, English literature, anthropology, psychology, gender studies, and nursing; two are poets, essayists, and activists; another, a filmmaker. The resulting time range is from Audre Lorde's "The Uses of the Erotic," originally published in 1978, to the commissioned pieces published for the first time in this volume.

Development of *Sexualities and Communication in Everyday Life: A Reader* was motivated by the editors' difficulties in finding suitable textbooks and readers for courses related to sexualities and communication. There are a number of strong texts related to sexuality in fields other than communication; we refrain from attempting to list them here for fear of omitting important contributions or appearing to rank them. In the past, we have selected books and articles from many of these areas, as well as from the journals of numerous disciplines and our own field of communication. We tried and were unable to find a textbook that offered a good foundation and broad introduction to the growing field of sexualities and communication, as well as interdisciplinary perspectives and approaches. In selecting articles for the reader, we considered, first of all, significance, as in the potential to advance our understanding of sexual identities and communication and suggest new research directions. Our years of teaching courses related to sexual identities and gender motivated us to select works aligned with these primary pedagogical objectives:

- Assist students in understanding the intersections of sexual identity with other identity constructions such as gender, race and ethnicity, class, age, and ability-disability.
- Introduce students to some of the concepts and implications of queer theory.
- Challenge students to move beyond stereotypical, dichotomous views of homosexual and heterosexual identities and communication styles.
- Facilitate students' awareness of and ability to recognize heteronormativity and confront and reduce heterosexism and homophobia.

We come to this project with academic backgrounds and interests that overlap and diverge. Karen Lovaas's academic background is American Studies and Communication, with an emphasis in social and cultural identities.

Mercilee Jenkins' academic areas of emphasis are gender and communication, ethnographic research, and performance studies. Dr. Jenkins designed the course Sexual Identity and Communication at San Francisco State University in 1989 and has been teaching it since 1991, and Dr. Lovaas has been teaching the same course since 1999. We both also teach an undergraduate course and graduate seminar in gender and communication.

The Sexual Identity and Communication course has changed dramatically since 1989. Initially, the text used was James Chesebro's *GaySpeak: Gay Male and Lesbian Communication* (1981). We focused on the rhetoric of gay liberation and the politics of language reform, mirroring the early days of women's studies and gender and communication. Students came mostly from the LGBT minor offered on campus. Student viewpoints on the origins of sexual identity shifted back and forth from constructionist to essentialist, as identity politics gave way to the politics of difference. The class grew to include many more heterosexual students when it became part of the general education program and communication major. Ringer's *Queer Words, Queer Images* was used as soon as it was published in 1994, and more attention in the course was directed to the media and the classroom setting. It was still necessary, however, to create a reader that better tailored the readings to fit the objectives of the course, particularly in regard to issues related to sexuality and interpersonal relationships.

We believe that this anthology addresses the major content and comprehension challenges we experienced in the classroom. The accessible introduction and interdisciplinary foundation in Part I prepare students for the content in the other three sections. Questions following each reading can serve as written homework assignments to engage students prior to or following classroom discussion. They also work to check for reading comprehension or as prompts for small group or full class discussions. It's an exciting time in the fields of communication, lesbian-gay-bisexual-transgender studies, and queer theory, tempting us to produce a much longer textbook. However, in creating this book, we were also mindful of the reality of what one can reasonably accomplish within a single semester or quarter.

We hope that *Sexualities and Communication in Everyday Life: A Reader* will serve an important purpose in meeting the needs of courses that deal with sexualities and communication, motivating those individuals and departments interested in developing such classes but concerned about the lack of an appropriate text, and providing excellent supplementation for related courses such as those in gender and communication or intercultural communication. In addition, the readings may encourage student scholars and academicians to do more research on sexualities and communication and to incorporate sexuality in other work that looks at social and cultural identities such as race, class, and gender.

ACKNOWLEDGMENTS

The terrific support of many colleagues, partners, and friends made this volume possible. In addition to the contributors to this volume, we greatly appreciate the work of our reviewers, Sandra L. Faulkner, Syracuse University; E. Patrick Johnson, Northwestern University; Valerie Palmer-Mehta, University of Alabama; R. Jeffrey Ringer, St. Cloud State University; Ralph R. Smith, Missouri State University; Lesa Lockford, Bowling Green State University, whose insightful comments informed the development of this collection.

We express our deepest thanks to:

Todd Armstrong, our editor at Sage, for his steady encouragement and superb guidance throughout this project; Deya Sayoud, Camille Herrera, and Sarah Quesenberry, for their helpful editorial assistance; Astrid Virding, for her vigilant and thoughtful shepherding of this book through the production process; Catherine Chilton, for her careful copyediting;

Paul Sherwin, Dean of the College of Humanities at San Francisco State University, for his institutional assistance—that is, his marvelous habit of saying yes whenever possible;

Our colleagues in the Department of Speech and Communication Studies—in particular, Gerianne Merrigan, Department Chair, for her unwavering support; Donna Smith, Department Administrator, for her fine assistance with many projects; Gust Yep, for his outstanding contributions to this subject; and Amy Kilgard, for her proofreading skills and Oscar-worthy collegiality;

Our editorial and teaching assistants at San Francisco State University, Marina Whitchurch and Patrick Moe, for their creativity, generosity, and excellence; Michael Underhill, one of Lee's first students in Sexual Identity and Communication and her teaching assistant and editorial assistant for earlier versions of this reader; and

our students in Sexual Identity and Communication at San Francisco State University, who have given the anthology its test runs over the last few semesters, who make teaching this subject a joy, and who continually demonstrate the value of doing this work.

Individually:

Karen expresses her enduring gratitude to her dear partner Erich for loving and believing in her, and her other handsome, longtime live-in companion (feline), Kobo, for his comforting hereness. In addition, she credits the rousing example of her 86½-year-old mother, who recently recovered from breaking her arm while demonstrating an Irish jig.

Lee wishes to thank Sushawn Robb for her partnership in work and love, and Tillie, her cat muse, for her devoted companionship. She offers special thanks to Ron Pelias and Noreen Barnes, longtime friends and colleagues, who inspire her best efforts.

Introduction

Setting the Stage

KAREN E. LOVAAS AND MERCILEE M. JENKINS

Identities are troubling because they embody so many paradoxes about what we have in common and what separates us; about our sense of self and our recognition of others; about conflicting belongings in a changing history and a complex modern world; and about the possibility of social action in and through our collective identities. And few identities are so paradoxical as sexual identities. Sexual identities have a special place in the discourse of identity. They are like relay points for a number of interconnected differences, conflicts and opportunities.
—Jeffrey Weeks (1995, pp. 86-87)

Sexuality is simultaneously a domain of restriction, repression, and danger as well as a domain of exploration, pleasure, and agency.
—C. S. Vance (1984, p. 1)

*S*exualities and Communication in Everyday Life: A Reader is an interdisciplinary collection of readings on the construction and performance of sexualities in private and public discourse, including excerpts from foundational work, recent journal articles, and original pieces solicited for this anthology. Our primary aim is to expand the study of communication to include sexualities and their intersections with gender, race and ethnicity, class, age, nationality, and ability-disability. As teachers of this subject matter, we have assembled this reader to accomplish four main goals, which are (a) to explore sexualities and communication within social and historical contexts, primarily from a queer perspective; (b) to analyze the impacts of sexism, homophobia, and heterosexism on sexualities and social interaction; (c) to enhance our capacities for self-reflection, respectful dialogue, and critical social engagement; and (d) to create a safe classroom environment for a combination of heterosexual, gay, lesbian, bisexual, transgender, queer, and undecided or questioning students who differ in their knowledge and viewpoints on these topics.

Sexualities have been studied across several disciplines, ranging from the biological to the social sciences and humanities. In this introductory chapter, we provide a brief overview of the

1

historical foundation for the study of sexualities and communication, a review of research conducted in this area, a discussion of the theoretical perspectives that we consider essential to understanding and evaluating this work, and an outline of the structure of the book.

EVOLUTION OF SCHOLARSHIP

> As defined by the ancient civil and canonical codes, sodomy was a category of forbidden acts; their perpetrator was nothing more than the juridical subject of them. The nineteenth-century homosexual became a personage, a past, a case history, and a childhood, in addition to being a type of life, a life form. . . . Homosexuality appeared as one of the forms of sexuality when it was transposed from the practice of sodomy onto a kind of interior androgyny, a hermaphrodism of the soul. The sodomite had been a temporary aberration; the homosexual was now a species.
>
> —Michel Foucault (1980, p. 43)

It comes as a great surprise to many people that sexuality as a social identity is a recent invention. Same-sex and cross-sex sexual behaviors were transformed into categories of identity in the late 19th century. Prior to this time, people were not generally identified by their sexual practices. Katz (chapter 1) unravels the history of how the terms *heterosexual* and *homosexual* came into being and places them in perspective as "one historically specific way of organizing the sexes and their pleasure" (see p. 24, this volume). The meaning of *heterosexual* evolved from Kiernan's 1892 definition as an "abnormal manifestation of the sexual appetite . . . desire for two different sexes" to Krafft-Ebing's 1893 use of "hetero-sexual" to signify desire between different sexes that is implicitly procreative and,

thus, "normal," as opposed to "homo-sexual" or same-sex desire, which is "pathological" because it is nonreproductive.

Along with sexology, fields such as religion, medicine, and psychiatry came to play a large part in defining what was considered "normal" and "natural" versus "deviant" and "sinful." Western societies have experienced waves of tolerance and repression regarding sexuality from ancient to modern times, sometimes crystallizing into "moral panics" regarding fears about perceived threats to society, such as "white slavery"[1] in the mid-19th century and AIDS in the 1980s. Moral panics are not driven primarily by emerging factual information about a particular situation but by political forces seeking to reform society (see chapter 2; also Rubin, 1993). Alternative ways of categorizing sexual identities and gender found in other cultures, such as in some Native American tribes (see, e.g., Roscoe, 1991), were not only suppressed but often led to persecution of the offending individuals and the societies that supported them (chapter 9; see also Gunn Allen, 1986; Williams, 1986).

Once homosexuality became a category of people, as opposed to the view that some people engage in same-sex sexual practices, much more research was initially done on male than on female homosexuals. This was, in part, due to the dominance of male researchers and their lack of access to what is usually the more private female sphere. It also reflects the power relationships that characterize patriarchal societies: Men's lives are deemed more important; therefore, more research was done on them. Thus our laws were written to prohibit sodomy, and the word *homosexual* tends to conjure up thoughts about gay men, not lesbians. However, as Adrienne Rich (1980) points out in her classic article on "compulsory heterosexuality," the eroticization of women's oppression in heterosexual relationships and the corresponding condemnation or erasure of lesbian relationships has had a profound effect on the lives of all women and our struggles for freedom and independence (see also

Faderman, 1984; Sahli, 1979; Smith-Rosenberg, 1975).

Kinsey and his team of researchers (Kinsey, Pomeroy, & Martin, 1948; Kinsey, Pomeroy, Martin, & Gebhard, 1953) were the first to demonstrate that a significant portion of the population has had same-sex experiences. There is no simple relationship, however, between how people identify themselves in terms of their sexuality and what they actually do in terms of sexual practices. In other words, what people do sexually and what sexual labels they are willing to claim can be very different. For example, I may identify as straight, although I have had numerous same-sex partners, or I may consider myself a lesbian, although I have had many cross-sex partners. The stigma attached to any sexuality other than heterosexual may affect the labels we choose, but our own self-concepts and the fluidity of our experiences also defy easy, static categorization.

The nature of sexuality as essential or socially constructed has been an ongoing debate with significant social and political implications (Kirsch & Weinrich, 1991; Udis-Kessler, 1990). Critiques of the current biological argument include Fausto-Sterling's (2000) compelling analysis of how the construction of sexuality relates to gender politics (see also, e.g., Birke, 1999; Hubbard, 1990). Sexual identities may be more productively regarded, we believe, as "necessary fictions" we live by (chapter 2), made up of sets of ritualized behaviors we are compelled to repeat, that is, a kind of performativity[2] that inscribes who we are on our bodies (chapter 3).

Many current scholars take a critical approach to the disciplining, criminalizing, punishing, and treating or curing of sexual deviance. No longer are studies of drug addicts, prostitutes, and homosexuals lumped together in deviant psychology and sociology courses. Due to the efforts of gay and lesbian liberation movements in Europe and the United States and psychologists such as Evelyn Hooker, the American Psychological Association stopped including homosexuality as an abnormality in the *Diagnostic and Statistical Manual of Mental Disorders* in 1976. We are, however, a long way from a radical theory of sexuality, as proposed by Gayle Rubin (1993), that would recognize and honor diverse sexualities rather than privileging a few and marginalizing the rest. Those who transgress the binaries of gender and sexual identities are living lives that point the way for new theoretical developments. Transgendered people contest the assumed biological determinates of gender, as well as exposing some of the ways gender is performed in our society (Barnes, 1992; Bornstein, 1994, 1998; Feinberg, 1996; Hutchins & Kaahumani, 1991; Knight, 1992; Namaste, 2000; Stryker, 2004; Wilchins, 1997). Bisexuals resist the necessity of identifying people by their sexual partners and explore the implications of this resistance for the negotiation of their interpersonal relationships (chapter 16; see also Beemyn & Eliason, 1996; Garber, 1995). Intersexed individuals challenge the medical establishment's right to surgically enforce gender conformity and are fighting for the right of self-determination (Chase, 2003). Finally, those who love gender outlaws resist easy categorization by their choice of partners as they explore new ways of being sexual (Hale, 2003).

SEXUALITIES AND COMMUNICATION RESEARCH

Scholarship and teaching related to sexualities and communication have evolved substantially over the last 25 years from a few scattered articles and books to a substantial body of interdisciplinary theory and research. We identify six major strands of research that have developed as scholarship and social issues have changed: (a) the rhetoric of liberation politics (i.e., lesbian feminism, gay liberation, AIDS activism, and the conservative backlash); (b) innovations in language structure and use; (c) analyses of mainstream and alternative media representations; (d) identity formation and interpersonal relationships, including family, friends, and lovers; (e) classroom communication and queer pedagogy; and (f) critical and performative approaches to understanding identity politics in relation to power. (See Henderson, 2000, and Yep, 2003, for other summaries of communication research related to sexual identities.) Woven through these strands is a liberatory impulse that supports individuals, groups, and communities taking matters into their own hands to create social change, whether by inventing new vocabulary (chapter 6; see also Chesebro, 1981; Ringer, 1994), recognizing unconventional relationships (chapter 7), or presenting subversive performances (chapters 3 and 18) that challenge the dichotomous status quo.

Communication research related to sexualities in the 1970s and early 1980s focused on the rhetoric of lesbian feminism and gay liberation and the politics of language reform, mirroring the early days of women's studies and gender and communication research. *GaySpeak: Gay Male and Lesbian Communication,* edited by Chesebro (1981), was the first anthology published dealing with these topics. A preoccupation with identity politics in theory and practice grew stronger as the AIDS epidemic became a primary concern (Chesebro, 1994; Darsey, 1991; Myrick, 1996; Patton, 1990), even as definitions of those identities and communities grew more diverse and complex (Cohen, 2003). As the stakes became higher (literally a matter of life and death), traditional forms of rhetoric gave way to transgressive performances by such groups as ACT UP and Queer Nation as necessary means to call attention to community needs (chapter 18; see also Hilferty, 1991; Kistenberg, 1995; Signorile, 1993; Slagle, 1995). Communication scholars study a broader range of rhetorics now, including the conservative backlash against gays (chapter 13; see also Smith & Windes, 2000) and public representations of transgendered people (chapter 14; see also, e.g., Boyd, 1999).

Changes in language structure and use have continued to mark struggles within and outside the academy. It is indeed a long way from "the love that dare not speak its name" to the multifaceted, often controversial uses of the word *queer*. New generations of gay, lesbian, bisexual, and trans youth are inventing their own vocabularies to define themselves (chapter 6), and scholars continue to do the same in an effort to recognize differences in the experiences of diverse queer people and to name those experiences, societal structures, and identifications; for example, homophobia, heterosexism, heteronormativity, pomosexual, ambiphillic, and "quare" (chapter 4). The extent to which queers exist as distinctive speech communities is taken up by one of our contributors in regard to the socialization and identity formation of gay males (chapter 6; see also Livia, 2001; Livia & Hall, 1997).

Studies of lesbians and gays in the media began by examining representations (or the lack of representations) of them in film, television, newspapers, and so on (Alwood, 1996; Gross & Woods, 1999; Kielwasser & Wolf, 1992; Ringer, 1994; Russo, 1987; Signorile, 1993), including the media response to the AIDS crisis (see, e.g., Albert, 1999; Netzhammer & Shamp, 1994). Currently media researchers investigate such issues as how media programming and advertising maintain and reinforce hegemonic heterosexuality and at the same time exploit a gay niche market. Communication research increasingly involves queer readings and analyses of media (chapter 15; see also, e.g., Burston & Richardson, 1995; Doty, 1993). As alternative media outlets have expanded, so has research examining the functions of those representations in sexually diverse communities (Gross & Woods, 1999).

Research on interpersonal communication initially focused on stage models of sexual identity development as a means of understanding how individuals come to identify as gay (Troiden, 1989) or lesbian (Faderman,

1984) or bisexual (Fox, 1991). Self-disclosure, in particular coming out to family, friends, and coworkers, is seen as a part of this process and has been the topic of numerous anthologies of coming-out stories, as well as scholarly research (e.g., Edgar, 1994; Strommen, 1989). A similar stage model for transsexuals was proposed by Bolin (1988), and Eliason (chapter 8) has applied Marcia's (1987) identity formation model to the development of heterosexual identity. Although the identity development models seem to imply that one arrives at a fixed identity, researchers have also explored how adults may make the transition from one sexual identity to another later in life, such as from a heterosexual to a lesbian identity (Kitzinger & Wilkinson, 1995). The majority of these studies and personal accounts describe the experiences of white middle class U.S. citizens, but increasingly scholars are exploring growing up as gay or lesbian in other cultures or in multicultural contexts (e.g., Almaguer, 1995; Carrier, 1989; Tremble, Schneider, & Appathurai, 1989; Trujillo, 1991; Yep, Lovaas, & Ho, 2001).

Many aspects of relational communication have been examined in relation to LGBT communities (see, e.g., DeCecco, 1988; Fitzpatrick, Jandt, Myrick, & Edgar, 1994; Huston & Schwartz, 1996; Peplau, 1993; Ringer, 1994). However, as Elia (2003) points out in his review of interpersonal communication textbooks, this work is often excluded or relegated to a separate section. Topics of particular interest in LGBT studies, perhaps due to the stigma attached to identifying as LGBT and the impact of the AIDS crisis (Edgar, Fitzpatrick, & Freimuth, 1992), are valuing friendship (Faderman, 1981; Nardi, 1995), creating and sustaining families we choose (Weston, 1991), and the importance of community (D'Emilio, 1983), as well as the contested nature of those communities, which is due partly to gender, class, and racial differences (Joseph, 2002). Humor, a key survival mechanism for nondominant groups that can

help create community and foster group identities even when it might seem derogatory or insulting (Murray, 1983; Painter, 1980), has been most associated in LGBT communities with "camp" or "camping it up" (Newton, 1979). Camp sensibility (Sontag, 1982) plays with social constructions and exposes them as artificial through heightened performances or exaggeration of gender and sexuality stereotypes (chapter 18; see also Bergman, 1993; Robertson, 1996).

An important context for interaction in groups and public presentations of self is the classroom. Creating a queer-friendly classroom is an ongoing topic of communication research, reflecting personal and ethical concerns (DeVito, 1981; Khayatt, 1999; Lovaas, Baroudi, & Collins, 2002; Ringer, 1994). How, when, and why do we come out in the classroom? How do we bring this material to the classroom in a responsible and respectful way? How do we recognize the diversity of our students and honor their sometimes conflicting attitudes and experiences? The complex feelings and experiences of students and faculty in regard to their own and others' sexualities are addressed by three of our contributors in personal performance texts (chapters 16, 17, and 20).

Recent communication scholarship includes more thoroughgoing critiques of heteronormativity (e.g., Sears & Williams, 1997; Yep, 2003) and integrates work informed by queer theory, intersectionality, and performativity (Butler, 1990, 1993; Foucault, 1980), contributing to a more sophisticated understanding of the gender, sex, and sexuality matrix. That is, how do ideas about gender, sex, and sexuality interrelate, produce, and reproduce each other? The shift from identity politics to the politics of difference (Slagle, 1995) encourages examination of diversity and dissent within our communities about topics such as gay marriage (chapter 12). At the same time, we are taking a universalizing versus minoritizing view of sexuality (Sedgwick, 1990; Lovaas, Elia, & Yep, in press). That is, how societies regulate sexualities is of concern not only to sexual minorities but to everyone. Scholars increasingly problematize the category of heterosexuality and examine its social construction in relationship to institutions such as marriage and pornography (chapter 11).

The rich opportunities for scholarship offered by the intersectionality of gender, sexuality, race and ethnicity, class, age, and ability-disability are partially realized in the movement toward ethnographic research and performance studies (see, e.g., Uyehara, 1998). Performances of ethnographic material, such as personal narratives of LGBT community members, bring experiences and expressions that have not been encoded in the dominant discourse to a broad audience (chapters 16 and 20). We have found, as have other authors (Henderson, 2000; Yep, 2003), that performance studies, scholarship, and practice are leading the way in conceptualizing new ways of thinking about sexuality in all its various meanings as it plays out in our lives (see, e.g., Alexander, 2004; Corey & Nakayama, 1997; Johnson, 2003; Nakayama & Corey, 2003).

THEORETICAL FOUNDATIONS

In this section, we lay out the theoretical assumptions underlying this anthology and define key terms found in the collection. The most important theories that frame our approach to understanding sexualities and communication are *social constructionism, feminisms, performativity, intersectionality,* and *queer theory.*

Social Constructionism

We begin with social constructionism, which is a theoretical approach that argues that the best way of understanding the nature of social reality is by viewing it as the result of subjective social processes by which we attach meaning to objects and events, creating knowledge. History, location, culture, language, and circumstance are all important factors influencing these processes. A prominent work is Berger and Luckmann's 1966 book, *The Social Construction of Reality.* As they explain, "the relationship between knowledge and its social base is a dialectical one, that is, knowledge is a social product and knowledge is a factor in social change" (p. 87).

In relation to sexualities, a constructionist looks at how meanings are assigned to bodies, practices, objects, and communities associated with sexuality. Like gender and race, sexuality is a social construct that provides a way of making sense of ourselves and our interactions. This includes a consideration of the science of biology as something other than a pure description of objective fact. How we understand and express sexuality is neither fixed nor universal; it varies across time, place, and cultural group. These understandings are linked to how society is structured, which shapes the ways in which people have greater or lesser access to power and resources.

Viewing sexualities as social constructions allows us to recognize our participation in producing, reproducing, and challenging them. We are not passive recipients of past manners of "doing" sexuality, we are active— although often unconscious—agents in constructing sexuality through our practices.

A social constructionist view of sexualities is a reaction against explanations that locate sexuality as "naturally" emerging from biology, a perspective often referred to as *essentialist.* During different eras, science has tended to focus on particular sites within the body as causing differences in human characteristics and behaviors. Currently, much of this attention is on what role brain structures, genes, and hormones may have in creating one's sense of oneself as being or having a gender, being or having a sexual orientation. Social constructionists argue that the existence of some physical differentiations among people are much less significant than the social meanings and distinctions that are assigned to those differentiations.[3] Thus our gender and sexual identities are less a direct product of anatomical differences between those born male, female, or intersexed than they are a cocreation of self and society. As Simone de Beauvoir (1949/1989) said, "One is not born a woman, but rather becomes one" (p. 267). Similarly, according to this perspective, our sexual identities are less about an innate attraction for one sex or the other than complex, largely learned productions of self in concert with society. The historical emergence of identity formations that center on one's sexuality is described in the excerpts from *The Invention of Heterosexuality* by Jonathan Katz (chapter 1).

Feminisms

In deconstructing gender and recognizing the ways in which "the personal is the political," feminist scholars have made a significant contribution to the study of sexualities and communication since its inception. Early work across many disciplines identified and challenged the patriarchal linguistic structure and language used to keep women, as well as other nondominant groups, in their place and muted or silenced (Ardener, 1975; Kramarae, 1981; Penelope, 1990; Spender, 1989). The academic canon in literature was critiqued as lacking in representations of white women and people of color. The "methodolatry" (Daly & Caputi, 1987), or worship of the logical positive scientific method, was rejected in favor of interpretive theories and research methods that relied on ethnographic techniques to involve active participation from those studied rather than the passive responses assumed of "subjects." In addition, lesbian feminists were the first to challenge the institution of heterosexuality as compulsory for women (Rich, 1980).

In spite of all these positive contributions, some forms of first- and second-wave feminism[4] assumed that all women could be seen as one group; the experiences of women of color were often overlooked or discounted. A womanist (Walker, 1984) critique of this approach emerged early on (see also, Grahn, 1984; Gunn-Allen, 1986; hooks, 1990; Lorde, 1984; Moraga & Anzaldúa, 1983; Trinh, 1984; Trujillo, 1991). Garber (2001) maintains that working class lesbian feminists or womanists of color were the first to expose the complex interplay of their experienced identities through their poetry and thus form the feminist roots of queer theory and intersectionality.

Intersectionality

Gender and sexual identities are but two examples of the social categories by which we organize our social lives. Other social identities frequently discussed include race, ethnicity, socioeconomic class, nationality, ability-disability, religion, and age.

Angela Davis's *Women, Race, and Class* (1981), Barbara Smith's *Home Girls* (1983), and Audre Lorde's *Sister Outsider* (1984) were three of the germinal books to examine the interlocking systems of oppression casting African American women's experience. In 1990, Patricia Hill Collins used the phrase "matrix of domination," and the following year, Kimberle Crenshaw employed "intersectionality," a term now widely adopted within and across disciplines. Rather than understanding gender, sexuality, race, class, nation, and other social locations as independent sites, intersectionality recognizes their mutual production and reproduction (see chapters 4, 10, 21, 22, and 23).

Performativity

Out of what are our sexual identities made? One powerful way of thinking about how we create gender and sexual identities, if not as a simple reflection of biological "realities," is a fairly recent concept referred to as *performativity*. Not entirely unlike performance, performativity refers to how, through the repeated use of verbal and nonverbal symbols associated with conventional ways of recognizing and talking about identities such as gender and sexuality, we actually produce those identity categories. Like social constructionism, performativity assumes that there is not a single, objective social reality readily acknowledged by all. Rather, our social worlds are constantly being made and remade through all kinds of symbolic interactions.

The theorist most closely identified with performativity is Judith Butler (see chapter 3). Butler's performativity is linked to linguistic theories such as J. L. Austin's speech act theory. In *How to Do Things With Words* (1955), Austin contrasts the performative utterance, or words that do things, with constative words that describe things. Declarations such as "I now pronounce you husband and wife" perform an action rather than reporting on a situation in the world. Butler argues that we are continuously engaged in enacting and citing, with our words and bodies, the existing norms and conventions of our surrounding social world. In doing so, we make these behaviors appear real, natural, normal, and inevitable. This is not to suggest that we become mere replicas of each other, clones of the current ideologies about gender, sex, and sexuality. Each of us performs our gender and sexual identities but not in exactly the same ways others do.

Queer Theory

The articulation of sexual identities is not a relatively simple process of assigning labels to phenomena that have always been present but could not be openly recognized without names by which to define them. We must recognize the sociohistorical contexts in which they arise. A critical view of identities acknowledges the role of history and simultaneously reinforces the importance of human agency. According to Jeffrey Weeks (chapter 2), identities in general and sexual identities in particular

are "necessary fictions," expressing a number of paradoxes. This way of looking at sexual identities is similar to what is found in a recent body of work challenging many notions about sex and gender that are widely considered "common sense": queer theory.

First, let's briefly discuss the word *queer*. Queer has functioned as a cruel epithet but has also been claimed as a proud avowal of identity by people expressing a range of sexualities, including individuals who define themselves as simultaneously queer and straight. The term is now found in much popular and academic discourse regarding sexuality. What is queer? "Queer is by definition whatever is at odds with the normal, the legitimate, the dominant. There is nothing in particular to which it necessarily refers. It is an identity without an essence" (Halperin, 1995, p. 62).

What does a queer theoretical perspective offer scholars and activists engaged in work related to sexual identities? Queer theorists view identities as fluid, paradoxical, political, multiple. They actively push our thinking about sexuality out of the dichotomy of homosexual versus heterosexual and invite us to notice the far more complex ways in which we explore and narrate our sexualities. A primary focus of queer theory is disrupting heteronormativity. Heteronormativity, like heterosexism, refers to the beliefs and practices that privilege heterosexuals and heterosexuality. It is a useful term for expressing the ways in which heterosexuality has become more than one of a number of modes of expressing one's sexuality; it exposes heterosexuality as a social institution that sanctions heterosexuality as the only "normal," "natural" expression of sexuality. Unlike any other sexual orientation, heterosexuality is assumed to need no explanation.

Queer theory is not without its detractors. It has been accused of primarily emerging from and representing a middle class white gay male perspective (e.g., Alexander, 2003; Angelides, in press; Anzaldúa, 1991; Barnard, 2003; Hennessy, 2000; Jeffreys, 2003;

Morton, 1996; Namaste, 2000). E. Patrick Johnson's challenge to racism and classism in queer theory (chapters 4 and 21) is an important intervention in the field.

ORGANIZATION OF THE READER

The book is divided into four sections: Part I: Foundations for Thinking About Sexualities and Communication; Part II: Performing and Disciplining Sexualities in Interpersonal Contexts; Part III: Performing and Disciplining Sexualities in Public Discourses; and Part IV: Transforming Sexualities and Communication: Visions and Praxis.

Contributions of the Articles

The five pieces in Part I of the book, "Foundations for Thinking About Sexualities and Communication," provide a grounding for the remainder of the anthology by introducing a few of the most important thinkers examining sexuality from a variety of disciplines and establishing the importance of understanding sexualities within specific sociohistorical contexts.

The first two selections highlight the historicity and politics of the notion of sexualities. We begin with two excerpts from Jonathan Katz's *The Invention of Heterosexuality* (1995). Many people are stunned to learn how recently the Western system of classifying sexual practices and consolidating them into polarized sexual identities evolved. Here Katz explains how and when the terms *heterosexuality, homosexuality*, and *bisexuality* were first used and why it does not make sense to automatically apply them to previous historical eras.

The second selection is an excerpt from Jeffrey Weeks' (1995) *Invented Moralities: Sexual Values in an Age of Uncertainty.* Weeks gives a clear account of the complexities of social identities in general and sexual identities specifically. In this passage, he argues that sexual identities are best viewed as

paradoxical and examines what he considers four key paradoxes of sexual identities.

The next two selections deal with two of the most exciting and influential theoretical innovations in the scholarship on sexualities in recent decades: performativity and queer theory. One of the most cited and influential authors associated with contemporary gender and queer theories is Judith Butler. Sara Salih (2002) explains gender performativity, an extremely useful concept for describing how gender identity categories are reproduced in our everyday lives and typically function to privilege heterosexuality. She discusses concerns that have been raised about performativity, first put forth in *Gender Trouble* (1990), and how Butler responded to those and further clarified her thinking on the subject in *Bodies that Matter* (1993).

The readings on Butler are followed by an extended excerpt from E. Patrick Johnson's 2001 article, "'Quare' Studies, or (Almost) Everything I Know About Queer Studies I Learned From My Grandmother." In this frequently cited article, Johnson critiques the inadequate treatment of race and class in much of queer theory. He urges us to discover new means of integrating the challenge that queer theory poses to the established view of identity categories with a recognition of the unequal varying material conditions of people's lives in relation to their race and class. Johnson proposes the term *quare* as a better way of conceptualizing sexuality as it intersects with other social identity formations and their material consequences.

The final reading in Part I is Audre Lorde's "The Uses of the Erotic: The Erotic as Power" (1984). Poet, essayist, and activist Lorde exposes the corruption of the erotic as female inferiority and reclaims it as a source of inner knowledge and joy. Although it addresses the woman reader, Lorde's chapter speaks to us across the lines of sex, gender, sexual identity, and race in its lovely invocation of the erotic as the seat of human empowerment and transformation.

Part II of the anthology, "Performing and Disciplining Sexualities in Interpersonal Contexts," includes seven essays from recent germane research. We begin with selections addressing issues related to sexual identity development in gay male, lesbian, and heterosexual adolescents and young adults as the foundation for interpersonal relationships. The study of relational communication has focused largely on heterosexual romantic relationships and how they can be conducted or performed most effectively. Authors included in this section take a critical look at the heteronormative relational model and how all of us are disciplined to conform to its requirements. In addition, two authors consider the importance of cultural context as it shapes our definitions of who we are in terms of our relational and erotic desires.

The first three chapters examine sexual identity development as it manifests itself in interpersonal relationships and everyday interactions. We start with William Leap's chapter, "Language, Socialization, and Silence in Gay Adolescence" (first published in 1999), which demonstrates the importance of language in the self-managed socialization of gay male teenagers. Leap maintains that gay adolescents are active agents in their own identity development and manage to claim queer space in everyday heteronormative situations.

Lisa Diamond's chapter, "'Having a Girlfriend Without Knowing It': Intimate Friendships Among Adolescent Sexual-Minority Women" (first published in 2002), looks at the "passionate relationships" of 80 young women interviewed for her study. Her qualitative analysis of the interview data calls into question both prevalent ideas about the differences between friendships and common assumptions about differences between straight women and lesbians.

As Michele Eliason (1995; chapter 8) points out in "Accounts of Sexual Identity Formation in Heterosexual Students," there has not been much research to date on how people who identify as heterosexual come to perceive their sexual identity. Eliason uses Marcia's established identity model to examine how a group of undergraduate college students view their sexual identities in terms of how they have evolved and the degree to which sexual identities affect daily life.

The next two chapters deepen our understanding of the complex interplay of multiple identities including sexuality, gender, race, ethnicity, and nationality as we perform who we are in any particular situation. Terry Tafoya's "M. Dragonfly: Two-Spirit and the Tafoya Principle of Uncertainty" (originally published in 1997) puts forth the paradox that in considering sexuality constructs cross-culturally, we can have context or definition, but never both at the same time. That is, when we attempt to pin down a definition of sexuality, we lose a sense of the specific cultural context, and vice versa. This is not to say that we should give up all labels but that we should understand them "as loosely descriptive social constructs rather than as intrinsic traits that are predictive of the sum of an individual's erotic and affectional desires."

Myron Beasley presents an autoethnograhic narrative of his experiences of negotiating his identities and desires as he travels overseas in "Migrancy and Homodesire." His border-crossing stories are provocative counters to the dominant narratives of straight, white Americans.

The last two articles focus on a particular type of interpersonal relationship, marriage, which has taken center stage as a cultural institution now being contested from a variety of perspectives. Elizabeth Bell, in "Performing 'I Do': Weddings, Pornography, and Sex," takes the radical position that weddings and pornography are complementary rather than oppositional cultural performances of sex that serve to control sexual behavior in society. Bell's analysis of their similarities in structure and function imparts new insight into commonly held beliefs and attitudes about how marriage and pornography both serve the State.

Same-sex marriage is a hotly debated political issue at present. In chapter 12 in Part II, "A Critical Appraisal of Assimilationist and Radical Ideologies Underlying Same-Sex Marriage in LGBT Communities in the United States" (originally published in 2003), Gust Yep, Karen Lovaas, and John Elia look at how same-sex marriage is being discussed in queer communities. They consider the implications of the sexual ideologies underlying the debate for relationship construction.

The six articles in Part III, "Performing and Disciplining Sexualities in Public Discourses," ably demonstrate that public discourses expressing conflicting ideologies regarding gender and sexual identities have a direct impact on our everyday lives and interactions. Identities such as "gay" and "ex-gay" are created through talk, which, when broadcast in the form of "talk shows," reaches millions of people. These popularized opinions have life and death consequences for those identified as LGBT, as we struggle to live our lives faced with a hostile legal system and questionable civil rights. There is, however, a challenge to the dominant conservative rhetoric in the form of LGBT transgressive public performances, which delight in turning hegemonic discourse on its head, celebrating difference, and redefining what it means to be real.

The first three selections in Part III analyze the construction of sexual identities and gender in a range of media contexts, including talk radio, news, and situation comedies. Paul Turpin's "Performing a Rhetoric of Science: Dr. Laura's Portrayal of Homosexuality" is a case study of oppositional rhetoric. He analyzes the two sides of the Dr. Laura controversy, sparked by her statements about homosexuality broadcast on her nationally syndicated talk-radio show.

John Sloop's chapter, "Disciplining the Transgendered: Brandon Teena, Public Representation, and Normativity" (originally published in 2000) is a critical rhetorical analysis of how Brandon Teena's life, death,

and identity have been portrayed in media representations. Sloop argues that the various discourses about Brandon Teena's rape and murder are rich "sites" in which to explore public perceptions of the meanings of sex and gender. The struggle over the meanings of these terms in mass media can tell us a great deal about contemporary gender and sexual politics.

Christopher Castiglia and Christopher Reed (2003) look at the connections between the evolution of television programming and sexual identities in "'Ah, Yes, I Remember It Well': Memory and Queer Culture in *Will and Grace*." They argue that TV sitcoms, and specifically the show *Will and Grace*, are an excellent arena for surveying the role of gay memory in the construction of subcultural sexual identity.

The next two chapters investigate the performance of bisexuality in educational settings, a kind of public platform that continues to be a significant topic in sexual identity and communication research. John Warren and Nicholas Zoffel's chapter, "Living in the Middle: Performances Bi-Men," is a thoughtful reflection on bisexual identity as liminal space. Their narratives are vivid portrayals of the complexities of negotiating bisexual identity in college settings.

Jennifer Tuder sets her performance of bisexual identity, "Holly Kowalski: Sex Across the Curriculum," in the contemporary high school. After beginning to give a generic-sounding speech on the importance of "being kind to people with different sexualities," Holly launches into a confessional address about her own sexuality that is more likely to resonate with her fellow students' social realities.

We move from performances in the classroom to performances in the streets in the last chapter of Part III, "Queering the (Sacred) Body Politic: Considering the Performative Cultural Politics of the Sisters of Perpetual Indulgence." Cathy Glenn offers an insightful analysis of one intentionally outrageous group's efforts to use "camp" performance to promote social change. Her chapter also serves as a transition to our closing section.

Part IV: Transforming Sexualities and Communication: Visions and Praxis contains five examples of work that is pushing the field of sexualities and communication forward. Some of the authors do this by moving into new topical territory, others by connecting academic work with community activism and exhorting all of us to consider our responsibility to advance social justice. The first two selections advance the field by tackling issues and venturing into contexts rarely explored in the academic literature.

In "The Spirituality of Sex and the Sexuality of Spirit: BDSM Erotic Play as Soulwork and Social Critique," Robert G. Westerfelhaus discusses the increasingly voiced perspective that sadomasochism can be a spiritual practice in the context of the larger ongoing reevaluation of modernism. The chapter gives a short history of the evolution of the BDSM (bondage and discipline, dominance and submission, and sadism and masochism) community in the United States before examining some contemporary accounts of BDSM practices as spiritual experiences.

As "Menopause and Desire, or 452 Positions on Love" (2005), the title of Mercilee Jenkins's performance piece, suggests, middle age is not necessarily the end of desire for women, even for those who have had mastectomies. She shares her experiences as a bisexual woman who has lived through the height of the AIDS crisis in San Francisco, including the death of one of her most beloved students; survived breast cancer; and confronted the commodification of women's breasts on Bourbon Street while maintaining an optimistic view of the future as a feminist who is still trying to make the world a better place.

The spirit of social justice underlies the whole of this anthology, but the final three readings have the most explicit focus on social change. First, we return to E. Patrick Johnson's

article on quare studies (2001), the beginning of which appears in Part I of this anthology. In the article's conclusion, he explains that quare studies is a call to make "theory work for its constituency" (see p. 297, this volume). The relationship between theory and everyday praxis should be bidirectional, bridging academy, home, church, and community.

Next, in "Activism and Identity Through the Word: A Mixed-Race Woman Claims Her Space" (2003), Wendy Thompson describes the relationship between her experiences crossing racial and sexual boundaries, her evolving identity, her writing, her art, and her activism. In doing so, she challenges us to consider how our identities and political commitments intersect.

We conclude the reader with an excerpt from the "Making Alliances" section of Gloria Anzaldúa's collection of interviews, *Interviews/Entrevistas* (2000). Anzaldúa acknowledges the complexities of human identities, the challenges of bridging differences, and leaves us with a sense of her own hopefulness about queer, multicultural alliances.

SETTING THE STAGE

We hope that *Sexualities and Communication in Everyday Life* sets the stage for new ways of thinking about sexualities and communication. If sexual identities are "necessary fictions" we perform daily, what other potential individual narratives and dialogues await us? Will we ever cease to identify ourselves and each other in terms of sexuality and gender, and, if so, would that be a good thing? There are always consequences for our choices, as many authors in this volume demonstrate, but the first step is awareness of agency. We all play a part, as all of our practices work to support existing scripts or to devise new ones. What will happen if more of us acknowledge the diversity of our experiences, which defy easy categorization, and talk together about the complex dynamics of our desires? How we perform and negotiate these frequently silenced—and, simultaneously, commercially packaged—chords of everyday life are stimulating resources for reflection and action. Places everyone. Curtain up.

NOTES

1. The term "white slavery" refers to a moral panic in Europe and the United States at the end of the 19th century premised on the belief that White European and American women were being forcibly taken to Africa, South America, or Asia to become prostitutes or sexual slaves. These unfounded fears led to a number of anti-white-slavery campaigns (Dozema, 2000).

2. Performativity is defined in the "Theoretical Foundations" section and further elaborated in the excerpt from Salih in chapter 3.

3. Although they acknowledge the construct-edness of social categories, some members of marginalized groups behave "as if" the group were homogeneous as a means to a specific political goal. This temporary employment of essentialism as a political tool is called "strategic essentialism." See Spivak (1990) and Hall (1996).

4. First-wave feminism refers to the Women's Movement that developed momentum in Europe and the United States in the mid-19th century, resulting in improved legal and civil rights for women and ultimately including the right to vote in the early 20th century. Second-wave feminism refers to the reemergence of the women's movement in the 1960s and 1970s, which was sparked by the social protest movements of that era.

REFERENCES

Albert, E. (1999). Illness and deviance: The response of the press to AIDS. In L. Gross & J. D. Woods (Eds.), *Columbia reader on lesbian and gay men in media, society, and politics* (pp. 393–402). New York: Columbia University Press.

Alexander, B. (2003). Querying queer theory again (or, queer theory as drag performance). In G. A. Yep, K. E. Lovaas, & J. P. Elia (Eds.), *Queer theory and communication: From disciplining queers to queering the discipline(s)* (pp. 349–352). New York: Harrington Park Press.

Alexander, B. (2004). Bu(o)ying condoms: A prophylactic performance of sexuality (or performance as prophylactic agency). *Cultural Studies/Critical Methodologies, 4*(4), 501–525.

Almaguer, T. (1995). Chicano men: A cartography of homosexual identity and behavior. In M. S. Kimmel & M. A. Messner (Eds.), *Men's lives* (pp. 418–431). Boston: Allyn & Bacon.

Alwood, E. (1996). *Straight news: Gays, lesbians, and the news media.* New York: Columbia University Press.

Angelides, S. (in press). Historicizing (bi)sexuality: A rejoinder for gay/lesbian studies, feminism, and queer theory. *Journal of Homosexuality.*

Anzaldúa, G. (1991). To(o) queer the writer: *Loca, escrita y chicana.* In B. Warland (Ed.), *Inversions: Writing by dykes and lesbians* (pp. 249–259). Vancouver, BC: Press Gang.

Anzaldúa, G. E. (2000). Making alliances. In A. Keating (Ed.), *Interviews/entrevistas* (pp. 203–209). New York: Routledge.

Ardener, S. (Ed.). (1975). *Perceiving women.* London: Malaby Press.

Austin, J. L. (1955). *How to do things with words.* Cambridge, MA: Harvard University Press.

Barnard, I. (2003). *Queer race: Cultural interventions in the racial politics of queer theory.* New York: Peter Lang.

Barnes, N. C. (1992). Kate Bornstein's gender and genre bending. In L. Senelick (Ed.), *Gender in performance: The presentation of difference in the performing arts* (pp. 311–323). Hanover, NH: University Press of New England.

Beauvoir, S. de. (1989). *The second sex [Le deuxième sexe]* (H. M. Parshley, Trans.). New York: Vintage Books. (Original work published 1949).

Beemyn, B., & Eliason, M. (Eds.). (1996). *Queer studies: A lesbian, gay, bisexual, and transgender anthology.* New York: New York University Press.

Berger, P. L., & Luckmann, T. (1966). *The social construction of reality: A treatise in the sociology of knowledge.* Garden City, NY: Doubleday.

Bergman, D. (1993). *Camp grounds: Style & homosexuality.* Amherst: University of Massachusetts Press.

Birke, L. (1999). *Biology, bodies and feminism.* Edinbugh, Scotland: Edinburgh University Press.

Bolin, A. (1988). *In search of Eve: Transsexual rites of passage.* South Hadley, MA: Bergin & Garvey.

Bornstein, K. (1994). *Gender outlaw: On men, women, and the rest of us.* New York: Routledge.

Bornstein, K. (1998). *My gender workbook.* New York: Routledge.

Boyd, N. A. (1999). Bodies in motion: Lesbian and transsexual histories. In M. Duberman (Ed.), *A* queer world: The Center for Lesbian and Gay Studies reader (pp. 134–152). New York: New York University Press.

Burston, P., & Richardson, C. (Eds.). (1995). A queer romance: Lesbians, gay men and popular culture. London: Routledge.

Butler, J. (1990). Gender trouble: Feminism and the subversion of identity. New York: Routledge.

Butler, J. (1993). Bodies that matter: On the discursive limits of "sex." New York: Routledge.

Carrier, J. M. (1989). Gay liberation and coming out in Mexico. In G. Herdt (Ed.), Gay and lesbian youth (pp. 225–252). New York: Haworth Press.

Castiglia, C., & Reed, C. (2003). "Ah, yes, I remember it well": Memory and queer culture in Will and Grace. Cultural Critique, 56, 158–188.

Chase, C. (2003). Hermaphrodites with attitude: Mapping the emergence of intersex political activism. In R. J. Corber & S. Valocchi (Eds.), Queer studies: An interdisciplinary reader (pp. 31–45). Oxford, England: Blackwell.

Chesebro, J. W. (1981). GaySpeak: Gay male and lesbian communication. New York: Pilgrim Press.

Chesebro, J. W. (1994). Reflections on gay and lesbian rhetoric. In R. Jeffrey Ringer (Ed.), Queer words, queer images (pp. 77–90). New York: New York University Press.

Cohen, C. J. (2003). Contested membership: Black gay identities and the politics of AIDS. In R. J. Corber & S. Valocchi (Eds.), Queer studies: An interdisciplinary reader (pp. 46–60). Oxford, England: Blackwell.

Collins, P. (1990). Black feminist thought. Boston: Unwin Hyman.

Corey, F. C., & Nakayama, T. K. (1997). Sextext. Text and Performance Quarterly, 17, 58–68.

Crenshaw, K. (1991). Mapping the margins: Intersectionality, identity politics, and violence against women of color. Stanford Law Review, 43(6), 1241–1299.

Daly, M., & Caputi, J. (1987). Websters' first new intergalactic wickedary of the English language. Boston: Beacon Press.

Darsey, J. (1991). From "gay is good" to the scourge of AIDS: The evolution of gay liberation rhetoric, 1977-1990. Communication Studies, 42, 43–66.

Davis, A. Y. (1981). Women, race, and class. New York: Random House.

D'Emilio, J. (1983). Sexual politics, sexual communities: The making of a homosexual minority in the United States 1940-1970. Chicago: University of Chicago Press.

DeCecco, J. (1988). Gay relationships. New York: Harrington Press.

DeVito, J. A. (1981). Educational responsibilities to gay male and lesbian students. In J. W. Chesebro (Ed.), GaySpeak: Gay male and lesbian communication (pp. 197–207). New York: Pilgrim Press.

Diamond, L. M. (2002). "Having a girlfriend without knowing it": Intimate friendships among adolescent sexual-minority women. Journal of Lesbian Studies, 6(5), 5–16.

Doezema, J. (2000). Loose women or lost women? The re-emergence of the myth of "white slavery" in contemporary discourses of "trafficking in women." Gender Issues 18(1), 23-50.

Doty, A. (1993). Making things perfectly queer: Interpreting mass culture. Minneapolis: University of Minnesota Press.

Edgar, T. (1994). Self-disclosure behaviors of the stigmatized: Strategies and outcomes for the revelation of sexual orientation. In J. Ringer (Ed.), Queer words, queer images (pp. 221–237). New York: New York University Press.

Edgar, T., Fitzpatrick, M. A., & Freimuth, V. S. (1992). AIDS: A communication perspective. Hillsdale, NJ: Erlbaum.

Elia, J. P. (2003). Queering relationships: Toward a paradigmatic shift. Journal of Homosexuality, 45(2/3/4), 61–86.

Eliason, M. J. (1995). Accounts of sexual identity formation in heterosexual students. Sex Roles, 32(11/12), 821–834.

Faderman, L. (1981). Surpassing the love of men: Romantic friendship and love between women from the Renaissance to the present. New York: William Morrow.

Faderman, L. (1984). The "new gay" lesbians. Journal of Homosexuality, 10(3/4), 85–95.

Fausto-Sterling, A. (2000). Gender systems: Toward a theory of human sexuality. In Sexing the body: Gender politics and the construction of sexuality (pp. 233–255). New York: Basic Books.

Feinberg, L. (1996). Transgender warriors: Making history from Joan of Arc to RuPaul. Boston: Beacon Press.

Fitzpatrick, M. A., Jandt, F. A., Myrick, F. L., & Edgar, T. (1994). Gay and lesbian couple relationships. In R. J. Ringer (Ed.), Queer words, queer images (pp. 265–277). New York: New York University Press.

Foucault, M. (1980). The history of sexuality. Vol. 1: An introduction. New York: Vintage.

Fox, A. (1991). Development of a bisexual identity. In L. Hutchins & L. Kaahumanu (Eds.), Bi any *other name: Bisexual people speak out* (pp. 29–36). Boston: Alyson.

Garber, L. (2001). *Identity poetics: Race, class, and the lesbian-feminist roots of queer theory.* New York: Columbia University Press.

Garber, M. (1995). *Vice versa: Bisexuality and the eroticism of everyday life.* New York: Simon and Schuster.

Grahn, J. (1984). *Another mother tongue: Gay words, gay world.* Boston: Beacon Press.

Gross, L., & Woods, J. D. (Eds.). (1999). *The Columbia reader on lesbians and gay men in media, society, and politics.* New York: Columbia University Press.

Gunn Allen, P. (1986). *The sacred hoop: Recovering the feminine in American Indian traditions.* Boston: Beacon Press.

Hale, C. J. (2003). Leatherdyke boys and their daddies: How to have sex without women or men. In R. J. Corber & S. Valocchi (Eds.), *Queer studies: An interdisciplinary reader* (pp. 61–70). Oxford, England: Blackwell.

Hall, S. (1996). *Cultural identity and diaspora.* In P. Mongia (Ed.), *Contemporary postcolonial theory: A reader* (pp. 110–121). London: Arnold.

Halperin, D. (1995). *Saint Foucault: Towards a gay hagiography.* New York: Oxford University Press.

Henderson, L. (2000). Queer communication studies. In W. B. Gudykunst (Ed.), *Communication yearbook 24* (pp. 465–484). Thousand Oaks, CA: Sage.

Hennessy, R. (2000). *Profit and pleasure: Sexual identities in late capitalism.* New York: Routledge.

Hilferty, R. (Writer/Director). (1991). *Stop the church* [Documentary]. San Francisco: Frameline.

hooks, b. (1990). *Yearning: Race, gender and cultural politics.* Cambridge, MA: South End Press.

Hubbard, R. (1990). *The politics of women's biology.* New Brunswick, NJ: Rutgers University Press.

Huston, M., & Schwartz, P. (1996). Gendered dynamics in the romantic relationships of lesbians and gay men. In J. T. Wood (Ed.), *Gendered relationships* (pp. 163–176). Mountain View, CA: Mayfield.

Hutchins, L., & Kaahumani, L. (Eds.). (1991). *Bi any other name: Bisexual people speak out.* Los Angeles: Alyson.

Jeffreys, S. (2003). *Unpacking queer politics: A lesbian feminist perspective.* Cambridge, England: Polity Press.

Jenkins, M. (2005). Menopause & desire, or 452 positions on love. *Text and Performance Quarterly, 25*(3), 254–281.

Johnson, E. P. (2001). "Quare" studies, or (almost) everything I know about queer studies I learned from my grandmother. *Text and Performance Quarterly, 21*(1), 1–25.

Johnson, E. P. (2003). *Appropriating blackness: Performance and the politics of authenticity.* Durham, NC: Duke University Press.

Joseph, M. (2002). *Against the romance of community.* Minneapolis: University of Minnesota Press.

Katz, J. N. (1995). *The invention of heterosexuality.* New York: Penguin Books.

Khayatt, D. (1999). Sex and pedagogy: Performing sexualities in the classroom. *GLQ: A Journal of Lesbian and Gay Studies, 5*(1), 107–113.

Kielwasser, A. P., & Wolf, M. A. (1992). Mainstream television, adolescent homosexuality, and significant silence. *Critical Studies in Mass Communication, 9,* 350–373.

Kinsey, A. C., Pomeroy, W. B., & Martin, C. E. (1948). *Sexual behavior in the human male.* Philadelphia, PA: Saunders.

Kinsey, A. C., Pomeroy, W. B., Martin, C. E., & Gebhard, P. H. (1953). *Sexual behavior in the human female.* Philadelphia, PA: Saunders.

Kirsch, J. A. W., & Weinrich, J. D. (1991). Homosexuality, nature and biology: Is homosexuality natural? Does it matter? In J. C. Gonsiorek & J. D. Weinrich (Eds.), *Homosexuality: Research implications for public policy* (pp. 13–31). Newbury Park, CA: Sage Publications.

Kistenberg, C. (1995). *AIDS, social change, and theatre.* London: Taylor & Francis.

Kitzinger, C., & Wilkinson, S. (1995). Transitions from heterosexual to lesbianism: The discursive production of lesbian identities. *Developmental Psychology, 31,* 95–104.

Knight, M. H. (1992). Gender interference in transsexuals' speech. In K. Hall, M. Bucholtz, & B. Moonwomon (Eds.), *Locating power: Proceedings of the second Berkeley women and language conference* (pp. 312–317). Berkeley, CA: Berkeley Women and Language Group.

Kramarae, C. (1981). *Women and men speaking.* Rowley, MA: Newbury House.

Leap, W. (1999). Language, socialization, and silence in gay adolescence. In M. Bucholtz, A. C. Liang, & L. Sutton (Eds.), *Reinventing identities: From category to practice in language and gender* (pp. 259–272). New York: Oxford University Press.

Livia, A. (2001). The future of queer linguistics. In K. Campbell-Kibler, R. J. Podesva, S. J. Roberts, & A. Wong (Eds.), *Language and sexuality: Contesting meaning in theory and practice* (pp. 87–97). Stanford, CA: CSLI.

Livia, A., & Hall, K. (1997). *Queerly phrased: Language, gender and sexuality.* New York: Oxford University Press.

Lorde, A. (1984). *Sister outsider.* Trumansburg, NY: The Crossing Press.

Lovaas, K. E., Baroudi, L., & Collins, S. M. (2002). Transcending heteronormativity in the classroom: Using queer and critical pedagogies to alleviate trans-anxieties. *Journal of Lesbian Studies, 6*(3/4), 177–190.

Lovaas, K. E., Elia, J. P., & Yep, G. A. (in press). Shifting ground(s): Surveying the contested terrain of LGBT studies and queer theory. *Journal of Homosexuality.*

Marcia, J. (1987). Identity in adolescence. In J. Adelson (Ed.), *Handbook of adolescent psychology.* New York: Wiley.

Moraga, C., & Anzaldúa, G. (Eds.). (1983). *Writings by radical women of color.* New York: Kitchen Table Press.

Morton, D. (Ed.). (1996). *The material queer: A LesBiGay cultural studies reader.* Boulder, CO: Westview Press.

Murray, S. O. (1983). Ritual and personal insults in stigmatized subcultures. *Maledicta, 7,* 189–211.

Myrick, R. (1996). *AIDS, communication, and empowerment: Gay male identity and the politics of public health messages.* New York: Harrington Park.

Nakayama, T. K., & Corey, F. C. (2003). Nextext. *Journal of Homosexuality, 45*(2/3/4), 319–334.

Namaste, V. K. (2000). *Invisible lives: The erasure of transsexual and transgendered people.* Chicago: University of Chicago Press.

Nardi, P. M. (1995). The politics of gay men's friendships. In M. S. Kimmel & M. A. Messner (Eds.), *Men's lives* (pp. 337–340). Boston: Allyn & Bacon.

Netzhammer, E. C., & Shamp, S. A. (1994). Guilt by association: Homosexuality and AIDS on prime-time television. In R. J. Ringer (Ed.), *Queer words, queer images: Communication and the construction of homosexuality* (pp. 91–106). New York: New York University Press.

Newton, E. (1979). *Mother camp: Female impersonators in America.* Chicago: University of Chicago Press.

Painter, D. S. (1980). Lesbian humor as a normalization device. In V. Eman & C. Berryman (Eds.), *Communication, language and gender* (pp. 132–148). Rowley, MA: Newberry House.

Patton, C. (1990). *Inventing AIDS.* New York: Routledge.

Penelope, J. (1990). *Speaking freely.* New York: Pergamon Press.

Peplau, L. A. (1993). Lesbian and gay relationships. In L. D. Garnets & D. C. Kimmel (Eds.), *Psychological perspectives on lesbian and gay male experiences* (pp. 395–419). New York: Columbia University Press.

Rich, A. (1980). Compulsory heterosexuality and lesbian existence. *Journal of Women in Culture and Society, 41,* 631–660.

Ringer, R. J. (Ed.). (1994). *Queer words, queer images: Communication and the construction of homosexuality.* New York: New York University Press.

Robertson, P. (1996). *Guilty pleasures: Feminist camp from Mae West to Madonna.* Durham, NC: Duke University Press.

Roscoe, W. (1991). *The Zuni man-woman.* Albuquerque: University of New Mexico Press.

Rubin, G. S. (1993). Thinking sex: Notes for a radical theory of the politics of sexuality. In H. Abelove, M. A. Barale, & D. M. Halperin (Eds.), *The lesbian and gay studies reader* (pp. 3–44). New York: Routledge.

Russo, V. (1987). *The celluloid closet: Homosexuality in the movies.* New York: Perennial Library.

Sahli, N. (1979). Smashing: Women's relationships before the fall. *Chrysalis, 8,* 17–27.

Salih, S. (2002). *Judith Butler.* London: Routledge.

Sears, J. T., & Williams, W. L. (Eds.). (1997). *Overcoming heterosexism and homophobia: Strategies that work.* New York: Columbia University Press.

Sedgwick, E. (1990). *The epistemology of the closet.* Berkeley: University of California Press.

Signorile, M. (1993). *Queer in America: Sex, the media, and the closets of power.* New York: Random House.

Slagle, R. A. (1995). In defense of Queer Nation: From identity politics to a politics of difference. *Western Journal of Communication, 59*(2), 85–102.

Sloop, J. M. (2000). Disciplining the transgendered: Brandon Teena, public representation, and normativity. *Western Journal of Communication, 64*(2), 165–189.

Smith, B. (Ed.). (1983). *Home girls: A Black feminist anthology.* New York: Kitchen Table Press.

Smith, R. R., & Windes, R. R. (2000). *Progay/antigay: The rhetorical war over sexuality.* Thousand Oaks, CA: Sage.

Smith-Rosenberg, C. (1975). The female world of love and ritual: Relations between women in 19th-century America. *Signs, 1,* 1–29.

Sontag, S. (1982). Notes on "camp." In *A Sontag reader* (pp. 105–119). New York: Farrar, Strauss, Giraux.

Spender, D. (1989). *The writing or the sex? Or why you don't have to read women's writing to know it's not good.* New York: Pergamon Press.

Spivak, G. (1990). *The post-colonial critic: Interviews, strategies, dialogues.* New York: Routledge.

Strommen, E. F. (1989). "You're a what?": Family members' reactions to the disclosure of homosexuality. *Journal of Homosexuality, 18*(1/2), 37–58.

Stryker, S. (2004). Transgender studies: Queer theory's evil twin. *GLQ: A Journal of Lesbian and Gay Studies, 10*(2), 212–215.

Tafoya, T. (1997). M. Dragonfly: Two-spirit and the Tafoya principle of uncertainty. In S. Jacobs, W. Thomas, & S. Lang (Eds.), *Two-spirit people: Native American gender identity, sexuality and spirituality* (pp. 192–200). Urbana: University of Illinois Press.

Thompson, W. M. (2003). Activism and identity through the word: A mixed-race woman claims her space. In K. K. Kumashiro (Ed.), *Restoried selves* (pp. 111–118). New York: Harrington Park Press.

Tremble, B., Schneider, M., & Appathurai, C. (1989). Growing up gay or lesbian in a multicultural context. *Journal of Homosexuality, 17*(3/4), 253–267.

Trinh, T. (1984). *Woman, native, other: Writing postcoloniality and feminism.* Bloomington: Indiana University Press.

Troiden, R. R. (1989). The formation of homosexual identities. In G. Herdt (Ed.), *Gay and lesbian youth* (pp. 43–73). New York: Haworth Press.

Trujillo, C. (1991). *Chicana lesbians.* Berkeley, CA: Third Woman Press.

Udis-Kessler, A. (1990). Bisexuality in an essentialist world: Toward an understanding of biphobia. In T. Geller (Ed.), *Bisexuality: A reader and sourcebook* (pp. 51–63). Ojai, CA: Times Change Press.

Uyehara, D. (1998). Hello (sex) kitty: Mad Asian bitch on wheels. In H. Hughes & D. Roman (Eds.), *O solo homo: The new queer performance* (pp. 375–409). New York: Grove Press.

Vance, C. S. (Ed.). (1984). *Pleasure and danger: Exploring female sexuality.* Boston: Routledge & Kegan Paul.

Walker, A. (1984). *In search of our mother's gardens: Womanist prose.* San Diego, CA: Harvest Books.

Weeks, J. (1995). *Invented moralities: Sexual values in an age of uncertainty.* New York: Columbia University Press.

Weston, K. (1991). *Families we choose: Lesbians, gays, kinship.* New York: Columbia University Press.

Wilchins, R. (1997). *Read my lips: Sexual subversion and the end of gender.* Ithaca, NY: Firebrand Books.

Williams, W. L. (1986). *The spirit and the flesh: Sexual diversity in American Indian culture.* Boston: Beacon Press.

Yep, G. A. (2003). The violence of heteronormativity in communication studies: Notes on injury, healing, and queer world making. *Journal of Homosexuality, 45*(2/3/4), 11–60.

Yep, G. A., Lovaas, K. E., & Elia, J. P. (2003). A critical appraisal of assimiliationist and radical ideologies underlying same-sex marriage in LGBT communities in the United States. *Journal of Homosexuality, 45*(1), 45–64.

Yep, G. A., Lovaas, K. E., & Ho, P. C. (2001). Communication in "Asian American" families with queer members: A relational dialectics perspective. In M. Bernstein & R. Reimann (Eds.), *Queer families, queer politics: Challenging culture and the state* (pp. 152–172). New York: Columbia University Press.

PART I

Foundations for Thinking About Sexualities and Communication

1

The Invention of Heterosexuality

The Debut of the Heterosexual

JONATHAN NED KATZ

RICHARD VON KRAFFT-EBING AND THE MIND DOCTORS

In the United States, in the 1890s, "sexual instinct" was generally identified as a *procreative* desire of men and women. But that reproductive ideal was beginning to be challenged, quietly but insistently, in practice and theory, by a new *different-sex pleasure* ethic. According to that radically new standard, the "sexual instinct" referred to men's and women's erotic desire for each other, *irrespective of its procreative potential*. Those two, fundamentally opposed, sexual moralities informed the earliest American definitions of "heterosexuals" and "homosexuals." Under the old procreative standard, the new term *heterosexual* did not, at first, always signify the normal and good.

The earliest-known use of the word *heterosexual* in the United States occurs in an article by Dr. James G. Kiernan, published in a Chicago medical journal in May 1892.[1]

Heterosexual was not equated there with normal sex, but with perversion—a definitional tradition that lasted in middle-class culture into the 1920s. Kiernan linked heterosexual to one of several "abnormal manifestations of the sexual appetite"—in a list of "sexual perversions proper"—in an article on "Sexual Perversion." Kiernan's brief note on depraved heterosexuals attributed their definition (incorrectly, as we'll see) to Dr. Richard von Krafft-Ebing of Vienna.

These heterosexuals were associated with a mental condition, "psychical hermaphroditism." This syndrome assumed that feelings had a biological sex. Heterosexuals experienced so-called male erotic attraction to females *and* so-called female erotic attraction to males. That is, these heterosexuals periodically felt "inclinations to both sexes."[2] The hetero in these heterosexuals referred *not* to their interest in a *different sex*, but to their desire for *two different sexes*. Feeling desire inappropriate, supposedly, for their sex, these heterosexuals were guilty of what we now think of as gender and erotic deviance.

Heterosexuals were also guilty of reproductive deviance. That is, they betrayed inclinations to "abnormal methods of gratification"—modes of ensuring pleasure without reproducing the species. They also demonstrated "traces of the normal sexual appetite"—a touch of the desire to reproduce.

Dr. Kiernan's article also included the earliest-known U.S. publication of the word *homosexual*. The "pure homosexuals" he cited were persons whose "general mental state is that of the opposite sex." These homosexuals were defined explicitly as gender benders, rebels from proper masculinity and femininity. In contrast, his heterosexuals deviated explicitly from gender, erotic, and procreative norms. In their American debut, the abnormality of heterosexuals appeared to be thrice that of homosexuals.[3]

Though Kiernan's article employed the new terms *heterosexual* and *homosexual*, their meaning was ruled by an old, absolute reproductive ideal. His heterosexual described a mixed person and compound urge—at once sex-differentiated, eros-oriented, and reproductive. In Kiernan's essay, heterosexuals' ambivalent procreative desire made them absolutely abnormal. This first exercise in heterosexual definition described an unequivocal pervert.

KRAFFT-EBING'S PSYCHOPATHIA SEXUALIS

The new term *hetero-sexual* next appeared early in 1893, in the first U.S. publication, in English, of *Psychopathia Sexualis, with Especial Reference to Contrary Sexual Instinct: A Medico-Legal Study*, by Richard von Krafft-Ebing, "Professor of Psychiatry and Neurology at the University of Vienna."[4] This book would appear in numerous later U.S. editions, becoming one of the most famous, influential texts on "pathological" sexuality.[5] Its disturbing (and fascinating) examples of a sex called sick began quietly to define a new idea of a sex perceived as healthy.[6]

In this primer, the "pathological sexual instinct" and "contrary sexual instinct" are major terms referring to non-procreative desire. Their opposite, called, simply, "sexual instinct," is reproductive. But that old procreative norm was no longer as absolute for Krafft-Ebing as it was for Kiernan. Conspicuously *absent* from the Viennese doctor's large tome on all varieties of sick sex is any reference to what some other doctors called "conjugal onanism," or "frauds in the accomplishment of the generative function"—birth control.[7]

In the heat of different-sex lust, declares Krafft-Ebing, men and women are not usually thinking of baby making: "In sexual love the real purpose of the instinct, the propagation of the species, does not enter into consciousness."[8] An unconscious procreative "purpose" informs his idea of "sexual love." His sexual instinct is a predisposition with a built-in reproductive aim. That instinct is procreative—whatever the men and women engaged in heterosexual acts are busily desiring. Placing the reproductive aside in the unconscious, Krafft-Ebing created a small, obscure space in which a new pleasure norm began to grow.

Krafft-Ebing's procreative, sex-differentiated, and erotic "sexual instinct" was present by definition in his term *heterosexual*—his book introduced that word to many Americans. A hyphen between Krafft-Ebing's "hetero" and "sexual" newly spliced sex-difference and eroticism to constitute a pleasure defined explicitly by the different sexes of its parties. His heterosexual, unlike Kiernan's, does not desire two sexes, only one, different, sex.

Krafft-Ebing's term *hetero-sexual* makes no *explicit* reference to reproduction, though it always *implicitly* includes reproductive desire. Always therefore, his hetero-sexual implicitly signifies erotic normality. His twin term, *homo-sexual*, always signifies a same-sex desire, pathological because non-reproductive.

Contrary to Kiernan's earlier attribution, Krafft-Ebing consistently uses hetero-sexual to mean normal sex. In contrast, for Kiernan, and some other late–nineteenth- and early–twentieth-century sexologists, a simple reproductive standard was absolute: The hetero-sexuals in Krafft-Ebing's text appeared guilty of procreative ambiguity, thus of perversion.

These distinctions between sexual terms and definitions are historically important, but complex, and may be difficult for us to grasp. Our own society's particular, dominant heterosexual norm also helps to cloud our minds to other ways of categorizing.

Readers such as Dr. Kiernan might also understand Krafft-Ebing's hetero-sexuals to be perverts by association. For the word *heterosexual*, though signifying normality, appears often in the Viennese doctor's book linked with the non-procreative perverse—coupled with "contrary sexual instinct," "physical hermaphroditism," "homo-sexuality," and "fetichism."

For example, Krafft-Ebing's first use of "hetero-sexual" occurs in a discussion of several case histories of "hetero- and homo-sexuality" in which "a certain kind of attire becomes a fetich."[9] The hetero-sexual premieres, with the homo-sexual, as clothes fetishist.

The second hetero-sexual introduced has a "handkerchief fetich." Krafft-Ebing quotes a report on "this impulse in hetero-sexual individuals" by Dr. Albert Moll, another influential early sexologist. The Victorian lady's handkerchief apparently packed an erotic wallop for a number of that era's men. An intense attraction to ladies' hankies might, it seems, even temporarily undermine patriarchal power. A "passion for [women's] handkerchiefs may go so far that the man is entirely under their [women's] control," Dr. Moll warns his endangered fellows.

This reversal of the customary male-female power relationship might not be displeasing to the Victorian woman who found herself—and her hanky—the object of a male fetishist's interest. Moll quotes such a woman:

> "I know a certain gentleman, and when I see him at a distance I only need to draw out my handkerchief so that it peeps out of my pocket, and I am certain that he will follow me as a dog follows its master. Go where I please, this gentleman will follow me. He may be riding in a carriage or engaged in important business, and yet, when he sees my handkerchief he drops everything in order to follow me,—i.e., my handkerchief."[10]

In the above examples, the term *heterosexual* signifies a normal different-sex eroticism, though associated closely with fetishism and the nonprocreative perverse. In the following examples, Krafft-Ebing's normal hetero-sexual is associated, as it most often is, with the "perversion" he calls "homo-sexuality" and "contrary sexual instinct."

BEFORE HETEROSEXUALITY

Looking Backward

If the word *heterosexual* did not exist in the United States until 1892, how did Americans talk and think about, and socially organize the sexes' differences and their sexuality? Did they employ equivalent terms, or wield an altogether different language? Is it possible that, before the debut of the term *heterosexual*, nineteenth-century Americans arranged sex-differences, eroticism, and reproduction in ways substantially different from the way we do? Dare we imagine that they constituted a qualitatively distinct sexual system—a society not appropriately described by our modern term *heterosexual*?

From the present, looking back on past eras before the use of the term *heterosexual*, we can, of course, find well-documented examples of different-sex erotic acts and emotions. Yet, from the standpoint of those who lived, loved, and lusted in the past, those same acts and emotions may not have referred in any essential way to the same combination of sex and gender difference and eroticism that we call heterosexuality. Ways of ordering the sexes, genders, and sexualities have varied radically. That variation challenges our usual assumption that an unchanging, essential heterosexuality takes qualitatively different historical forms. The word *heterosexual*, I propose, itself signifies one timebound historical form—one historically specific way of organizing the sexes and their pleasures.

Earthly Love and Heavenly Love

One example of a nonheterosexual society is ancient Greece, as analyzed by the late French historian Michel Foucault, a discussion that includes his most explicit, extensive comments on heterosexuality.[11]

Foucault repeatedly warns present-day readers of the danger of projecting our heterosexual and homosexual categories on the past. The specific past he refers to is ancient Greece, as represented in those texts that discuss free men's problematic, pleasurable intimacies with women and with boys.

In a passage appraising a famous speech by Pausanias in Plato's *Symposium*, Foucault says that one finds there

a theory of two loves, the second of which—Urania, the heavenly love—is directed [by free men] exclusively to boys. But the distinction that is made *is not between a heterosexual love and a homosexual love* [emphasis added]. Pausanias draws the dividing line between "the love which the baser sort of men feel"—its object is both women and boys, it only looks to the act itself (*to diapratteshai*)—and the more ancient, nobler, and more reasonable love that is drawn to what has the most vigor and intelligence, which obviously can only mean [for free men] the male sex.[12]

Pausanias, Foucault stresses, employed a hierarchical distinction between free men's lower, *earthly love*, focused on acts, and free men's higher, *heavenly love*, defined by a feeling for the beauty of boys, a superior object. That distinction between earthly and heavenly love is substantially different from our contrast between heterosexual and homosexual.

Discussing ancient Greek society, Foucault generalizes, "The notion of homosexuality is plainly inadequate as a means of referring to an experience, forms of valuation, and a system of categorization so different from ours." Our homosexual/heterosexual polarity does not match these ancient Greek men's views. Our distinction is based on sexed difference and sexuality:

The Greeks did not see love for one's own sex and love for the other sex as opposites, as two exclusive choices, two radically different types of behavior. The dividing lines did not follow that kind of boundary.[13]

According to Foucault, ancient Greek writers might sometimes recognize that one man's inclinations usually favored women, another man's boys. But those emotional tendencies were not embedded within the same social organization of sexed difference and eroticism that gives rise to our own heterosexual/homosexual pair. Neither Greek men's inclination for women, nor their desire for boys, was any "more likely than the other, and the two could easily coexist in the same individual."[14] He asks:

Were the Greeks bisexual then? Yes, if we mean by this that a Greek [free man] could, simultaneously or in turn, be enamored by a boy or a girl. . . . But if we wish to turn our attention to the way in which they conceived of this dual practice, we need to take note of the fact that they did not recognize two kinds of "desire," two different or competing "drives," each claiming a share of men's hearts or appetites. We can talk about their "bisexuality," thinking of the free choice they allowed themselves between the two sexes, but for them this option was not offered to a dual, ambivalent, and "bisexual" structure of desire. To their way of thinking what made it possible to desire a man or a woman was simply the appetite that nature had implanted in man's heart for "beautiful" human beings, whatever their sex. . . .[15]

We can take a retrospective look at the ancestry of our own society's sexual terms and organization—their "genealogy," Foucault calls it. But we should not, he suggests, employ our terms *bisexuality, homosexuality,* and *heterosexuality,* in a way to suggest that these were the concepts past subjects used.

Foucault fears his readers' projection on the past of their own society's sexual categories and arrangements because such projections unconsciously and unjustifiably affirm the *similarity* of present and past. His readers will thereby be prevented from perceiving *dissimilarity* and *change*—the historically specific character of ancient prescriptions about free men's pleasure, and the historically particular social organization of eroticism that gave rise to them.

The French historian's sexual relativity theory points us to a basic "presentist" bias in readers' and scholars' vision of sexualities and pleasures past—that is, we necessarily view them from a particular position in the present.

It's significant that Foucault thought it necessary to provide even fairly sophisticated, intellectual readers with repeated cautions against anachronistic projections—a well-known historical blunder.[16] His and others' reiterated warnings against anachronism in sexual history analysis testify not so much to the primitive level of sex history interpreters, or their readers, as to the continuing, enormous power of our present dominant concepts of sexuality. Without realizing it, usually, we are all deeply embedded in a living, institutionalized heterosexual/homosexual distinction.

Maximized Procreation and Sodomitical Sin

For a second example of a society not ordered along heterosexual lines we can turn

to a culture nearer home—the New England colonies in the years 1607 to 1740.[17]

In these formative years, the New England organization of the sexes and their erotic activity was dominated by a reproductive imperative. These fragile, undeveloped agriculture economies were desperate to increase their numbers, and their labor force. So the early colonial mode of procreation was structured to optimize the production of New Englanders. The New England settlers married earlier than Old Englanders, and their ordering of maximized reproduction created a colonial birth rate higher than in England or Europe at the time.

This intensive populating was incited by religious exhortations to multiply, and by legal retributions for acts thought to interfere with procreation (such as sodomy, bestiality, and masturbation) or the dominant reproductive order (such as adultery). In early colonial Boston, after confessing to adultery with twelve men, the eighteen-year-old Mary Latham was hanged with one of her lovers. At least two other early new Englanders were hanged for extramarital acts, thereby serving, according to one historian, "as graphic reminders" of the punishment that could befall those "violating the sexual exclusivity" of marriage. Although all the early New England colonies prescribed death for adultery, very few executions actually occurred under these statutes. (Perhaps, since the crime was "one of the most common," the death penalty would have done more to disrupt the procreative economy than to support it). But more than three hundred women and men found guilty of adultery in early New England were seriously punished with twenty to thirty-nine lashes. (A married man was severely punished only if he committed adultery with a woman pledged or married to another man. An engaged or married woman was considered to have committed adultery whatever the marital status of her partner.)[18]

Sodomy should be punished by death, declared the Reverend John Rayner, even though it might not involve the same "degree of sinning against the family and posterity" as some other "capital sins of uncleanness." William Plaine deserved death for sodomy in England, and for inciting the youth of Guilford, in the New Haven Colony, to "masturbations," John Winthrop explained. For Plaine's crimes frustrated the marriage ordinance and hindered "the generation of mankind."[19]

The death penalty for sodomy prevailing in all the colonies, and the public execution of a few men for this crime, violently signified the profound sinfulness of any eros thought hostile to reproduction. The operative contrast in this society was between fruitfulness and barrenness, not between different-sex and same-sex eroticism.

Women and men were constituted within this mode of procreation as essentially different and unequal. Specifically, the procreative man was constructed as seminal, a seed source. The procreative woman as constituted as seed holder and ripener, a relatively "weaker vessel." For a man to "waste his seed" in nonprocreative, pleasurable acts was to squander a precious, limited procreative resource, as crucial to community survival as the crops the colonists planted in the earth. Although women were perceived to have "seed," a woman's erotic acts with another woman were not apparently thought of as wasting it, or as squandering her seed-ripening ability. So these were lesser violations of the procreative order.

Men and women were, however, regarded as equal in lust. As the Reverend Thomas Shepard sermonized: "Every natural man and woman is born full of sin," their hearts brimming with "atheism, sodomy, blasphemy, murder, whoredom, adultery, witchcraft, [and] buggery. . . ." As a universal temptation, not a minority impulse, a man's erotic desire for another man did not constitute him as a particular kind of person, a buggerer or sodomite.[20] Individuals might lust consistently toward one sex or another and be recognized,

sometimes, as so lusting. But this society did not give rise to a subject defined essentially by an attraction to a same sex or an appetite for a different sex.

Within the early New England organization of pleasure, carnal desire commonly included the mutual lust of man and woman and the occasional lust of man for man. A dominant colonial figure of speech opposed lust for an earthly "creature" to love for an other-worldly God. In these colonies, erotic desire for members of a same sex was not constructed as deviant because erotic desire for a different sex was not construed as a norm. Even within marriage, no other-sex erotic object was completely legitimate, in and of itself.

In this New England, the human body's capacity to function as means of earthly pleasure represented a deeply problematic distraction from a heavenly God, a diversion to which men's and women's bodies were equally prone. Within New England's dominant mode of procreation the body's "private parts" were officially constituted as generative organs, not as hetero pleasure tools.

In a sermon on the "sins of Sodom," the Reverend Samuel Danforth linked "sodomy" and idleness. Using energy in reproductive acts, an important form of production, kept one from wasting energy in unproductive sin. In contrast, since the first quarter of the twentieth century, our society's dominant order of different-sex pleasure has encouraged the use of energy in a variety of heteroerotic activities. This stimulation of hetero pleasures completely apart from procreation constructs a heterosexuality increasingly congruent with homosexuality. In early New England, sodomy stood as perverse paradigm of energy wasted in unproductive pleasure.

The reproductive and erotic acts of New England's women and men were among those productive activities thought of as fundamentally affecting the community's labor force, its security and survival. In contrast, in the twentieth century, the erotic activity of women and men was officially located in the realm of private life, in the separate sphere of dating, courtship, romantic love, marriage, domesticity and family. Until Kate Millett and other feminists questioned this ideological separation of the sexual and political spheres, heterosexuality was thought to inhabit a private realm of intimacy distinct from the often alienated public world of work.

In early New England the eroticism of women and men was publicly linked to sodomy and bestiality in a realm of tempting sinful pleasures. Colonial lust was located in an arena of judgments, an avowedly moral universe. Heterosexuality is located, supposedly, in the realm of nature, biology, hormones, and genes—a matter of physiological fact, a truth of the flesh. Only secretly is heterosexuality a value and a norm, a matter of morality and taste, of politics and power.

The "traditional values" of early colonial New England, its ordering of the sexes, their eroticism, and their reproduction, provides a nice, quintessentially American example of a society not dominated by a heterosexual/homosexual distinction.

The Early–Nineteenth-Century Organization of True Love

Nineteenth-century America, from about 1820 to 1850, is a third society not organized according to our heterosexual law. Neither, it turns out, was it the prudish society of stereotype. The evidence offered recently by historians challenges the common notion of nineteenth-century middle-class society as sexually repressed. The rise of the pro-heterosexual principle can't be explained, then, simply as a sharp break with an antisexual Victorian past. Though recent historians don't always distinguish adequately between early and late nineteenth-century developments, their analyses can help us understand the social origins of the heterosexual as a historically specific term and relationship.

In early–nineteenth-century America, I'll argue, the urban middle class was still struggling to distinguish itself from the supposedly decadent upper orders and supposedly sensual lower orders. The middling sort claimed sexual purity as a major distinguishing characteristic. No middle-class sexual ethic then validated different-sex lust apart from men's and women's love and reproduction. Only in the late nineteenth century did the middle class achieve the power and stability that freed it to publicly affirm, in the name of nature, its own "heterosexuality." The making of the middle class and the invention of heterosexuality went hand in hand.[21]

Ellen Rothman, in her *Hands and Hearts: A History of Courtship in America*, contests the antisexual Victorian stereotype.[22] She analyzes the diaries, love letters, and reminiscences of 350 white, Protestant, middle-class American women and men living in the settled areas of the North who came of courting age between 1770 and 1920. She concludes that courting couples in the early nineteenth century defined "romantic love so that it included sexual attraction but excluded coitus." That particular courtship custom she names the "invention of petting."[23] This common courting convention, she maintains, allowed the middle class quite a lot of private erotic expression short of intercourse. She stresses: "Couples courting in the 1820s and 1830s were comfortable with a wide range of sexually expressive behavior."[24]

In her book *Searching the Heart: Women, Men, and Romantic Love in Nineteenth-Century America*, Karen Lystra also marshals lots of sexy verbal intercourse from nineteenth-century love letters, arguing forcefully against the twentieth-century stereotype of the Victorians. She analyzes the intimate letters of one hundred middle-class and upper-class white couples, and sexual-advice literature of the 1830s through the 1890s.[25] She demonstrates that, under the powerful legitimizing influence of "love," middle- and upper-class women and men, in their *private* behavior and conversations with each other, affirmed a wide range of erotic feelings and activities—though not usually intercourse before marriage.

Summing up the Victorians' "approval of sex when associated with love," Lystra declares,

> The highest values of individual expression and autonomous self-hood were heaped upon the erotic. Victorians did not denigrate sex; they guarded it.[26]

She emphasizes, "Sex had a place of honor and prominence in Victorian culture."[27] She reiterates: "Victorians reveled in the physicality of sex when they believed that the flesh was an expression of the spirit."[28] The idea of eroticism as "a romantically inspired religious experience, a sacrament of love" was, she says, "perhaps the most culturally significant meaning attached to Victorian sexuality."[29] Her sex-positive view of the Victorians is also borne out, she claims, by research in more than fifty nineteenth-century advice books. Mainstream advisers of that day, she claims, encouraged an active eroticism *as an expression of love*.[30]

For a small group of sexual enthusiasts, the radicals of their day, true love was a free love. John D'Emilio and Estelle B. Freedman's *Intimate Matters: A History of Sexuality in America* describes free lovers daringly justifying erotic expression *even outside of marriage*.[31] Free lovers challenged the respectable idea that legal matrimony was necessary to license the erotic intercourse of the sexes. Free love, free lovers argued—not the church, not the state—freely legitimated conjugal unions. Arch-romantics that they were, however, free lovers did not advocate eros unaccompanied by love. Just as this era's mainstream strongly condemned sensuality detached from legal matrimony and love, so its free lovers condemned sensuality detached from romance.[32]

Steven Seidman, a historically oriented sociologist, qualifies somewhat the revisionist historians' view of nineteenth-century eroticism. A note in his own study, *Romantic Longings: Love in America, 1830-1980*, rejects Lystra's argument that the eroticism of Victorian women and men was unambiguously legitimated as symbol of love.[33] Although "all" nineteenth-century sexual advisors, Seidman admits,

> acknowledged the beneficial role of sex in marriage, love was construed as essentially spiritual. Sex, at best, symbolized a spiritual union or functioned as a spiritual act. *In none of these discourses . . . was eroticism ever framed as essential to the meaning of intimacy or as a basis of love* [emphasis added].

Lystra's stress on the Victorians' active appreciation of eroticism is, he thinks, "grossly overstated."[34]

Certainly, an eroticism needing to be sanctified by love was originally unhallowed. Among middle-class Victorians, "sensuality" was a dirty word. Lystra occasionally admits this: "Sex was wholeheartedly approved as an act of love and wholeheartedly condemned by the Victorian mainstream when bodily pleasures were not privileged acts of self-disclosure"—that is, when erotic pleasure was not the expression of love.[35] Lust *not* sanctified by love, she concedes here, was utterly condemned.[36] Her interpretation of nineteenth-century sensuality as legitimized by love does dispel the usual stereotype, though she constructs a counter-myth of erotic Victorians.

In his own book, Seidman usefully stresses the historically specific character of the heterosexual/homosexual opposition. During most of the nineteenth century, he says, "the term *heterosexuality* and what we today take as its natural antithesis, *homosexuality*, were absent" from discourses on gender and eroticism.[37] The heterosexual and homosexual were not thought of "as mutually exclusive categories of desire, identity and love."[38] Only in the early twentieth century did "the concepts of heterosexuality and homosexuality" emerge "as the master categories of a sexual regime that defined the individual's sexual and personal identity and normatively regulated intimate desire and behavior."[39]

As noted, the revisionist historians of nineteenth-century American sexuality typically fail to distinguish carefully between early and late developments. A closer look at early–nineteenth-century society clarifies its difference from that late–nineteenth-century order which gave rise to the heterosexual category.

The early nineteenth century prescribed particular ideals of manhood and womanhood, founding a cult of the true man and true woman. The "Cult of True Womanhood" is said by historian Barbara Welter to mandate "purity"—meaning asexuality—for respectable, middle-class women.[40] More recent historians contest this interpretation of "purity." Karen Lystra, for example, quotes numbers of letters in which women's and men's erotic expression is referred to as "pure" by association—that is, by lust's link with "love." Purifying lust was, in fact, an important function of the middle-class true-love ideal. In this view, the special purity claimed for this era's true women referred not to asexuality but to middle-class women's better control than men over their carnal impulses, often conceived of as weaker than men's. True men, thought to live closer to carnality, and in less control of it, ideally aspired to the same rational regulation of concupiscence as did respectable true women.[41]

The ideal of true men and true women was closely linked to another term, "true love," used repeatedly in this era. Holding strictly to true love was an important way in which the middle class distinguished itself from the allegedly promiscuous upper class and animalistic lower class. Those lust-ridden lower classes included a supposedly vicious foreign element (often Irish, Italian, and Asian) and a supposedly sensual dark-skinned racial group shipped to America from Africa as slaves.[42]

True love was a hierarchical system, topped by an intense spiritual feeling powerful enough to justify marriage, reproduction, and an otherwise unhallowed sensuality. The reigning

sexual standard distinguished, not between different- and same-sex eroticism, but between true love and false love—a feeling not sufficiently deep, permanent, and serious enough to justify the usual sensual courtship practices, or the usual well-nigh immutable marriage.

Given the powerful legitimating influence of true love, many of the letter writers quoted by Lystra, Rothman, and the other revisionists spend much energy trying to prove the trueness of their love. Assuring one's beloved of love's truth was, in fact, a major function of these letters.[43]

In this era, the human body was thought of as directly constituting the true man and true woman, and their feelings. No distinction was made between biologically given sex and socially constructed masculinity and femininity. Under true love's dominion, the human body was perceived as means of love's expression. Under the early–nineteenth-century rule of reproduction (as in early New England), penis and vagina were means of procreation—"generative organs"—not pleasure parts. Only after marriage could they mesh as love parts.

Human energy, thought of as a closed and severely limited system subject to exhaustion, was to be used in work, in producing children, and in sustaining love and family, not wasted on unproductive, libidinous pleasures.

The location of love's labors, the site of engendering and procreating and feeling, was the sacred sanctum of early–nineteenth-century true love, the home of the true man and true woman. This temple of pure, spiritual love was threatened *from within* by the monster masturbator, that archetypal early Victorian cult figure of illicit-because-loveless, non-procreative lust.[44]

The home front was threatened *from without* by the female prostitute, another archetypal figure of lust divorced from love. (Men who slept with men for money do not seem to have been common, stock figures of the early–nineteenth-century middle-class imagination, probably because there weren't many of them, and they weren't thought of as a major threat to the love of men and women).[45]

Only rarely was reference made to those other illicit erotic figures, the "sodomite" and "sapphist" (unlike the later "homosexual," these were persons with no "heterosexual" opposite, terms with no antonyms). State sodomy laws defined a particular, obscure act, referred to in a limited legalese, not a common criminal, medical, or psychological type of person, not a personal, self-defined "identity" and, until the nineteenth century's end, not a particular sexual group.[46]

Because the early–nineteenth-century middle-class mind was not commonly focused on dreams of legitimate different-sex pleasures, neither was it haunted by nightmares of perverted same-sex satisfactions. The sexual pervert did not emerge as an obsession of society's newborn, fledgling normal sexuals until the nineteenth century's last decades. Though the early–nineteenth-century middle-class might be worried by erotic thoughts unhitched from love, this group was not yet preoccupied by an ideal of an essential, normal, different-sex sexuality.

In early–nineteenth-century America no universal eros was thought to constitute the fundamental nucleus of all passionate intimacies. In this pre-Freudian world, love did not imply eros. So respectable Victorian women and men referred often and explicitly to their "passionate" feelings with little thought that those intense emotions were a close relation of sensuality. Proper middle-class women might often speak of their intense "passion" for each other without feeling compromised by eroticism.[47] Unlike post-Freudian passion, early–nineteenth-century passion inhabited a universe separate and distinct from the hothouse world of sensuality.

Given the early–nineteenth-century distinction between the moral character of passionate love and the immoral character of sensual lust, intense, passion-filled romantic friendships could flourish erotically between members of the same sex without great fear that they

bordered on the sodomitical or sapphic. Those terms' rare use suggests the lack of any public link between sensuality and same-sex passion. Same-sex romantic friendships might even enjoy an uncomplicated existence unknown to many different-sex relations—haunted as these might be by the very gender difference that constituted the sexes as opposite—therefore as potential love and marriage objects for each other, therefore as potential sensual partners. "Until the 1880s," say the historians of American sexuality, John D'Emilio and Estelle B. Freedman, most same-sex "romantic friendships were thought to be devoid of sexual content." The "modern terms *homosexuality* and *heterosexuality* do not apply to an era that had not yet articulated these distinctions."[48]

Spiritual love and passion inhabited an abode far from the earthly, earthy home of sexuality. True love was enacted legitimately only within marriage, the legal mode of proper procreation. Intercourse, as sign of love's "consummation," held a special, deep significance. The intercourse of penis and vagina, men and women commonly agreed, was the one move they could not make before marriage and still remain respectable. Intercourse distinguished the true and virtuous woman from the fallen. Refraining from intercourse was the final test of the true man's manliness, his status as genteel, Christian gentleman.

The early–nineteenth-century middle-class fixation on penis-vagina coitus implied that numerous pleasurable acts *not* involving the "penetration" of this specific female part by this specific male part were *not* thought of as prohibited, or even as "sexual." Quite a lot of erotic activity then passed as permissible in a love relationship precisely because it wasn't "intercourse."

This cult of intercourse was formulated most clearly by the more restrictionist ideologists of sex, as discussed by Lystra: the promoters of a procreative ethic. But they were waging a losing battle. The number of "legitimate" births per middle-class family shows a continuous sharp decline during the nineteenth century.[49] By the late nineteenth century the old true-love standard was giving way to a new, different-sex erotic ideal termed *normal* and *heterosexual*. A close look at that late–nineteenth-century era suggests how it came to terms.

The Late–Nineteenth-Century Construction of Sexual Instinct

Each of the revisionist historians of nineteenth-century sexuality presents one or several memorable examples of lust-loving, male-female couples. The most enthusiastic sensualists they offer typically date to the late nineteenth century, though often serving generalizations about "Victorian" sexuality or "nineteenth-century" eroticism.

One of Ellen Rothman's featured couples is Lester Ward and Lizzie Vought. In 1860, in Myersburg, Pennsylvania, the nineteen-year old Lester (later, a well-known sociologist) began keeping a diary of his and Lizzie's courtship. This record suggests that Lizzie was as active in the couple's sexual explorations as her diarist boyfriend.[50]

In 1861, when Lester and "the girl" (as he called her) were often separated, his diary indicates that Lizzie made sure that, when they could, the two got together in private. After a Saturday spent with the girl and friends, Lester stayed on to spend "a happy night" with Lizzie:

> Closely held in loving arms we lay, embraced, and kissed all night (not going to bed until five in the morning). We have never acted in such a way before. All that we did I shall not tell here, but it was all very sweet and loving and nothing infamous.[51]

Lester's "I shall not tell here," his refusal to put into words all of the couple's erotic doings, and his defensive "nothing infamous," are telling. Even this easygoing enthusiast of

bodily love evidently felt the judgmental power of a strict standard of sexual propriety.

Six months later the still-courting couple first "tasted the joys of love and happiness which only belong to a married life." The phrasing suggests that their initial coupling was perceived as breaking a well-known intercourse ban.

About a year later, in 1862, Lester and Lizzie married. Lester Ward's diary, says Rothman, suggests that this couple experienced little emotional conflict over their sexual explorations, even their atypical premarital intercourse.[52] Lester and Lizzie stand in Rothman's text for a revised vision of Victorians as privately erotic, publicly reticent.

In 1860, the same year that Lester Ward began his diary, an eloquent, embattled exponent of the new male-female lustiness, Walt Whitman, was publishing his third edition of *Leaves of Grass*. That year's version first included a section, "Children of Adam," publicly evoking and promoting the procreational-erotic intercourse of men and women. As a pioneering sex radical, Whitman broke with the early–nineteenth-century idea that women's passion for motherhood included no eros. Whitman's poems publicly proclaimed women's lusty, enthusiastic participation with men in the act of conceiving robust babies. Another of Whitman's new sections, "Calamus," vividly detailed acts of erotic communion between men.

As research by Michael Lynch stresses, Whitman borrowed terms from his day's pop psychologists, the phrenologists, naming and evoking hot "amative" relations between men and women, and sizzling "adhesive" intimacies between men.[53] In the perspective of heterosexual history, Whitman's titling of these amative and adhesive intimacies was an attempt to position male-female and male-male eroticisms together as a "natural," "healthy" division of human erotic responses. (Along with most other writers of the time, Whitman almost completely ignored eros between women—a powerful indication of phallic rule: erotic acts not involving a penis were insignificant.) Though now perhaps better known as man-lover, Whitman is also a late-Victorian trailblazer of a publicly silenced, often vilified lust between the sexes.[54]

Historian Peter Gay's first two hefty volumes on *The Bourgeois Experience* in nineteenth-century Western Europe and the U.S. constitute a mammoth defense—980 pages of text and notes—of the middle class, its *Education of the Senses* and its *Tender Passion* (as these volumes are subtitled). Gay sets out to restore the Victorian middle class's erotic reputation, so often characterized as "repressed" or "hypocritical."

Personalizing Gay's presentation of the Victorians as ardent champions of eros (even sex athletes) is his discussion of the "Erotic Record" documenting the 1877 courtship, later marriage and enthusiastic adultery of Mabel Loomis and David Todd. The story of Mabel and her men is, significantly, a late–nineteenth-century tale, though Gay doesn't emphasize this point.

This end-of-the-century story includes Mabel's thirteen-year, graphically detailed, doubly adulterous affair with Austin Dickinson (Emily's married brother) in Amherst, the outwardly staid, inwardly steaming New England college town.[55] Peter Gay employs the tale of Mabel and David and Austin to counter the typecasting of Victorians as prudes. Like other revisionists, he insists that the nineteenth century middle class was secretly sexual, though publicly prudish.[56]

Evidence offered by Gay and the other revisionists suggests that, as the nineteenth century went on, the private pleasure practices of the middle class were diverging more and more from the public ideal of true love. By the end of the century, as the middle class secured its social place, its members felt less need to distinguish their class's sexual purity from the eroticism of the rich and the sensuality of the poor, the colored, and the foreign.[57] In the late nineteenth century, as the white Protestant middle class pursued its earthly happiness, its attitude toward work shifted in favor of pleasurable consumption. By century's end the ideal of true love conflicted more and more with middle-class sensuous activity. Lust was bustin' out all over.

Peter Gay mentions Mabel Loomis Todd's need "to find expressive equivalents for her erotic emotions, manifested by her diary keeping."[58] That need of Mabel's was, I think, typical of her class. In the late nineteenth century, Mabel's personal letters and diaries provided a private place for putting into words and justifying—literally, coming to terms with—middle-class practices which could not be talked of publicly without censure. Like Mabel, the late–nineteenth-century middle class needed to name and justify the private erotic practices that were growing more prevalent, and more open, by century's end. That class's special interest would find expression in the proclamation of a universal heterosexuality. The invention of heterosexuality publicly named, scientifically normalized, and ethically justified the middle-class practice of different-sex pleasure.[59]

Coming to Terms

The heterosexual and homosexual did not appear out of the blue in 1892. Those two sex-differentiated, erotic categories were in the making from the 1860s to the end of the century. In late–nineteenth-century Germany, England, France, and Italy, and in America, our modern, historically specific idea of the heterosexual began to be constructed; the experience of a proper, middle-class, different-sex lust began to be publicly named and documented.

In the initial strand of the heterosexual category's history we may be surprised to discover the prominent part played by early theorists and defenders of same-sex love. In 1862 in Germany, one of these pioneers, the writer Karl Heinrich Ulrichs, began to produce new sexual names and theories defending the love of the man who loved men, the *Uranier* (or "Urning"). The Urning's opposite, the true man (the man who loved women), he called a *Dionäer* (or "Dioning"). His theory later included the *Urninde*, the woman "with a masculine love-drive"—his phrase for the woman with male feelings—that is, the woman who loved women.

The Urning's erotic desire for a true man, Ulrichs argued, was as natural as the "Dioning-love" of true man and true woman. His Dioning and Urning are the foreparents of the heterosexual and homosexual. Starting in 1864, Ulrichs presented his theories in twelve books with the collective title *Researches on the Riddle of Love Between Men*, written and printed at his own expense.[60]

In Ulrichs's eroticized update of the early Victorian true man, the real man possessed a male body and a male sex-love for women. The Urning was a true man with the feelings of a true woman. The Urning possessed a male body and the female's sex-love for men.

As we've seen, the Victorian concept of the "true" mechanically linked biology with psychology. Feelings were thought of as female or male in exactly the same sense as penis or clitoris: anatomy equaled psychology, sex physiology determined the sex of feelings. Sex-love for a female was a male feeling, sex-love for a male was a female feeling. A female sex-love could inhabit a male body, a male sex-love could inhabit a female body.

According to this theory there existed only *one* sexual desire, focused on the other sex. (In today's terms, there was only one different-sex "sexual orientation," not two distinct "heterosexual" and "homosexual" desires.) Within this conceptual system, a (male) Urning felt a woman's erotic love for men, a (female) Urninde experienced a man's attraction to women. In each case, the desire for a different-sex was felt by a person of the "wrong" sex. Their desire was therefore "contrary" to the one, normative "sexual instinct." Ulrichs

accepted this one-instinct idea, but argued that the emotions of Urnings were biologically inborn, therefore natural for them, and so their acts should not be punished by any law against "unnatural fornication."

In a letter to Ulrichs on May 6, 1868, another early sex-law reformer, the writer Karl Maria Kertbeny, is first known to have privately used four new terms he had coined: "*Monosexual; Homosexual; Heterosexual; und Heterogenit*"—the debut of homosexual and heterosexual, and two now forgotten terms.[61] Though Kertbeny's letter did not define his foursome, his other writings indicate that "Monosexual" refers to masturbation, practiced by both sexes. "Heterogenit" refers to erotic acts of human beings with animals. "Homosexual" refers to erotic acts performed by men with men and women with women. And "Heterosexual" refers to erotic acts of men and women, as did another of his new terms, "Normalsexualität," normal sexuality.

Heterosexuality and normal sexuality he defined as the innate form of sexual satisfaction of the majority of the population. That emphasis on numbers as the foundation of the normal marks a historic break with the old qualitative, procreative standard.

But Kertbeny's heterosexual, and his normal sexual, are by no means normative. Both the heterosexual and normal sexual are characterized by their "unfettered capacity for degeneracy"—he who coins the terms loads the dice.[62] The sex "drive" of normal sexuals is said to be stronger than that of masturbators, bestialists, or homosexuals, and this explains normal sexuals' laxity, license, and "unfetteredness." Kertbeny's heterosexual men and women participate with each other

in so-called natural [procreative] as well as unnatural [nonprocreative] coitus. They are also capable of giving themselves over to same-sex excesses. Additionally, normally-sexed individuals are no less likely to engage in self-defilement [masturbation] if there is insufficient opportunity to satisfy one's sex drive. And they are equally likely to assault male but especially female minors . . .; to indulge in incest; to engage in bestiality . . .; and even to behave depravedly with corpses if their moral self-control does not control their lust. And it is only amongst the normally-sexed that the special breed of so-called "bleeders" occurs, those who, thirsting for blood, can only satisfy their passion by wounding and torturing.[63]

Kertbeny's heterosexuals and normal sexuals are certainly no paragons of virtue. Considering psychiatrists' later cooptation of the term *heterosexual* to affirm the superiority of different-sex eroticism, Kertbeny's coinage of *heterosexual* in the service of homosexual emancipation is one of sex history's grand ironies.

Kertbeny first publicly used his new term *homosexuality* in the fall of 1869, in an anonymous leaflet against the adoption of the "unnatural fornication" law throughout a united Germany.[64] The public proclamation of the homosexual's existence preceded the public unveiling of the heterosexual. The first public use of Kertbeny's word heterosexual occurred in Germany in 1880, in a published defense of homosexuality, in a book by a zoologist on *The Discovery of the Soul*.[65] *Heterosexual* next made four public appearances in 1889, all in the fourth German edition of Krafft-Ebing's *Psychopathia Sexualis*.[66] Via Krafft-Ebing, *heterosexual* passed in three years into English, as I've noted, first reaching America in 1892. That year, Dr. Kiernan's article on "Sexual Perversion" spoke of Krafft-Ebing's "heterosexuals," associating them with nonprocreative perversion.[67]

Influenced, partly, by Ulrich's years of public agitation for sodomy-law reform and the rights of Urnings, in 1869 psychiatrists began to play their own distinct role in the public naming and theorizing of sexual normality and abnormality. Although medical-legal articles on sexual crime appeared in the 1850s, only at the end of the 1860s did medical professionals begin to assert a new proprietary claim to a special expertise on sex-difference

and eroticism, and begin to name the object of their concern. A mini-history of the psychiatric labeling of "abnormal sexuality" suggests how these doctors' explicit specifying of "sexual perversion" furthered their implicit theorizing of "normal sexuality."[68]

In August 1869, a German medical journal published an article by Dr. K.F.O. Westphal that first named an emotion he called "Die conträre Sexualempfindung" ("contrary sexual feeling"). That emotion was "contrary" to the proper, procreative "sexual feeling" of men and women.[69] Westphal's contrary sexual feeling was the first, and became one of the best known, contenders in the late–nineteenth-century name-that-perversion contest.

In 1871, an anonymous review of Westphal's essay in the London *Journal of Mental Science* first translated the German *contrary sexual feeling* into English as "inverted sexual proclivity." That urge inverted the proper, procreative "sexual proclivity" of men and women.[70]

In 1878, an article in an Italian medical review, by a Dr. Tamassia, first used the phrase "inversione sessuale." Translated into English, "sexual inversion" became a second prominent contender in the fin de siècle aberration-labeling sweepstakes.[71]

In 1897, the medically trained Havelock Ellis first used "sexual inversion" in a publicly printed English work. As liberal sex reformer, Ellis tried to appropriate medical terms and concepts for the cause of sexual expression.[72]

Before the invention of "heterosexuality," the term "contrary sexual feeling" presupposed the existence of a non-contrary "sexual feeling," the term "sexual inversion" presupposed a noninverted sexual desire. From the start of this medicalizing, "contrary" and "inverted" sexuality were problematized, "sexual feeling" was taken for granted. This inaugurated a hundred-year tradition in which the abnormal and the homosexual were posed as riddle, the normal and heterosexual were assumed.

In the last decades of the nineteenth century, the new term *heterosexual* moved into the world, sometimes linked with nonprocreative "perversion," sometimes with "normal," procreative, different-sex eroticism. The theorizing of Sigmund Freud played an influential role in stabilizing, publicizing, and normalizing the new heterosexual ideal.

NOTES

1. Dr. James G. Kiernan, "Responsibility in Sexual Perversion," *Chicago Medical Recorder 3* (May 1892), 185–210; "Read before the Chicago Medical Society, March 7, 1892," but it's difficult to imagine him reading his footnote on Krafft-Ebing. Kiernan's note on 197–98 cites Krafft-Ebing's classifications in *Psychopathia Sexualis*, "Chaddock's translation" (no date). The U.S. publication in 1893 of C. G. Chaddock's translation of Krafft-Ebing's *Psychopathia Sexualis followed* Kiernan's article (see note 4 below). So there's some confusion about the exact source of Kiernan's brief note on Krafft-Ebing's terms "hetero-sexual" and "homo-sexual." Perhaps Kiernan saw a prepublication version of Chaddock's translation. It's also possible that Kiernan had seen some earlier article by Krafft-Ebing or the English translation by F. J. Rebman of the 10th German edition of Krafft-Ebing's *Psychopathia Sexualis*, published in London in 1889 (I have not inspected that edition). Kiernan seems to have based his brief gloss on Krafft-Ebing's definition of the heterosexual and homosexual on a superficial reading of pages 222–23 of the 1893 edition of Chaddock's translation of *Psychopathia Sexualis*, paragraphs numbered 1–4.

2. Mental hermaphrodites experienced, sometimes, the "wrong" feelings for their biological sex; their erotic desire was improperly inverted. A moral judgment founded the ostensibly objective, scientific concept of psychical hermaphroditism. Kiernan's idea of "physical hermaphroditism" is not exactly the same as the attraction we now label "bisexual," referring as we do to the sex of the subject and the two different sexes to which he or she is attracted. Psychical hermaphroditism referred to mental gender, while our bisexuality refers to the sex of a sex partner. Mental hermaphroditism might lead to both sexes as erotic partners, but the term laid the cause in the mental gender of the subject (like the concept of inversion).

Our bisexuality does not involve any necessary link to mental gender. I am grateful to Lisa Duggan for this clarification.

3. But heterosexuals' appearance of triple the abnormality of homosexuals was deceiving. For Kiernan, the gender deviance of homosexuals *implied* that they were also, simultaneously, rebels from a procreative norm and an erotic norm. But it's significant that Kiernan explicitly stresses homosexuals' gender rebellion, not their erotic or reproductive deviancy. George Chauncey, Jr., discusses the late-nineteenth-century stress on gender inversion in "From Sexual Inversion to Homosexuality: Medicine and the Changing Conceptualization of Female Deviance," *Salmagundi* 56–59 (Fall-Winter 1983), 114–46.

4. R. von Krafft-Ebing, *Psychopathia Sexualis, with Especial Reference to Contrary Sexual Instinct: A Medico-Legal Study*, trans. Charles Gilbert Chaddock (Philadelphia: F. A. Davis, 1893), from the 7th and revised German ed.; preface dated November 1892. Hereafter cited as Krafft-Ebing. The U.S. Copyright Office received and registered this edition on February 16, 1893 (Copyright Office to Katz, May 25, 1990).

This book's year of publication is confused, because its copyright page and its preface are dated 1892, while its title page lists the year of publication as 1893. *The National Union Catalogue of Pre-1956 Publications* says this edition was first published in 1892, and the first citation of "hetero-sexual" listed in the *Oxford English Dictionary* (1976 Supplement, p. 85) is to this edition of Krafft-Ebing, attributed to 1892. That year is incorrect. Although it was evidently prepared by November 1892, the date of its preface, it was not officially published until 1893.

For Krafft-Ebing and his *Psychopathia* see Peter Gay, *The Bourgeois Experience: Victoria to Freud, Volume II, The Tender Passion* (NY: Oxford University Press, 1986), 221, 223–24, 226, 229, 230–32, 286, 338, 350; Gert Hekma, "A History of Sexology: Social and Historical Aspects of Sexuality," in Jan Bremmer, ed., *From Sappho to De Sade: Moments in the History of Sexuality* (first published 1989; NY: Routledge, 1991), 173–93; and Arnold I. Davidson, "Closing Up the Corpses: Diseases of Sexuality and the Emergence of the Psychiatric Style of Reasoning," in George Boolos, ed., *Meaning and Method: Essays in Honor of Hilary Putnam* (NY: Cambridge University Press, 1990), 295–325. I am also greatly indebted to talks with Harry Oosterhuis and an advance copy of his paper

"Richard von Krafft-Ebing's Step-Children of Nature: Psychiatry and the Making of Modern Sexual Identity," presented as a talk at the Second Carleton Conference on the History of the Family, May 12, 1994, in Ottawa, Canada.

5. Krafft-Ebing's focus, as a psychiatrist, on disturbed mental states contrasts with the earlier nineteenth-century focus of neurologists on disturbed brains. I thank Lisa Duggan for this comment.

6. In this text the doctor's descriptions of sex sickness and sex health replaced the old, overtly moral judgments about bad sex and good sex, introducing the modern medical model of sexuality to numbers of Americans.

7. See, for example, L. F. E. Bergeret, *The Prevention Obstacle, or Conjugal Onanism. The Dangers and Inconveniences to the Individual, to the Family, and to Society, of Frauds in the Accomplishment of the Generative Functions*, trans. from the third French edition by P. De Marmon (NY: 1870; photographic reprint NY: Arno Press, 1974).

8. Krafft-Ebing 9.

9. Krafft-Ebing 169.

10. Krafft-Ebing 174.

11. Michel Foucault's comments are scattered throughout the second and third volumes of his *History of Sexuality*. See *The Use of Pleasure: Volume 2 of The History of Sexuality*, trans. by Robert Hurley (NY: Pantheon, 1985); and *The Care of the Self: Volume 3 of The History of Sexuality*, trans. by Robert Hurley (NY: Pantheon, 1986).

Foucault's basic approach to ancient Greece and Rome is supported eloquently by David M. Halperin in *One Hundred Years of Homosexuality and Other Essays on Greek Love* (NY: Routledge, 1990); John J. Winkler, *The Constraints of Desire: The Anthropology of Sex and Gender in Ancient Greece* (NY: Routledge, 1990); and in David M. Halperin, John J. Winkler, and Froma I. Zeitlin, eds., *Before Sexuality: The Construction of Erotic Experience in the Ancient Greek World* (Princeton: Princeton University Press, 1990).

Foucault's and the social constructionist interpretation of ancient Greek and Roman society is contested in John Boswell's "Revolutions, Universals, and Sexual Categories," in Martin Duberman, Martha Vicinus, and George Chauncey, eds., *Hidden from History: Reclaiming the Gay and Lesbian Past* (NY: New American Library, 1989), 17–36. Social constructionism is also contested in numbers of the essays in Edward Stein,

ed., *Forms of Desire: Sexual Orientation and the Social Constructionist Controversy* (NY: Garland, 1990).

12. Foucault, *The Use of Pleasure* II, 188–89.

13. Foucault, *The Use of Pleasure* II, 187.

14. Foucault, *The Use of Pleasure* II, 188.

15. This historian suggests that we may legitimately use our own society's term and concept "bisexuality" (or, implicitly, "homosexuality" or "heterosexuality") when we want to translate and describe for ourselves, in our terms; the emotions of individuals apart from their particular historical structure, their concepts, and their language (Foucault, *The Use of Pleasure* II, 188).

16. The first volume of Foucault's *History of Sexuality* was first published in France in 1976, and the second and third volumes in 1984.

17. See Jonathan Ned Katz, "The Age of Sodomitical Sin, 1607–1740," an essay in *Gay/Lesbian Almanac: A New Documentary* (NY: Harper & Row, 1983), 23–65; and documents, 66–136. Also see Michael Warner, "New English Sodom," in Jonathan Goldberg, ed., *Queering the Renaissance* (Durham, N.C.: Duke University Press, 1994), 330–58; Goldberg's "Sodomy in the New World: Anthropologies Old and New," in Michael Warner, ed., *Fear of a Queer Planet: Queer Politics and Social Theory* (Minneapolis: University of Minnesota Press, 1993), 3-18; Goldberg's "Part Three: 'They Are All Sodomites': The New World," in his *Sodometries: Renaissance Texts, Modern Sexualities* (Stanford, CA: Stanford University Press, 1992), 179–249; and John D'Emilio and Estella B. Freedman, "Part I. The Reproductive Matrix, 1600-1800," in their *Intimate Matters: A History of Sexuality in America* (NY: Harper & Row, 1988), 3–54. And note the sources cited in all these texts.

18. See Lyle Koehler, *A Search for Power: The "Weaker Sex" in Seventeenth-Century New England* (Urbana: University of Illinois Press, 1980), 146–52.

19. Katz, *G/LA* 31.

20. The term "Sodomite" was used in these colonies, but it referred directly to persons from Sodom and their whole array of sins, not to a person defined essentially by the act of sodomy. My interpretation of the uses of the term "Sodomite" in these colonies differs with the analysis of Michael Warner in his "New English Sodom."

21. On the making of the American middle class, for starters see: Mary P. Ryan, *Cradle of the Middle Class: The Family in Oneida County,*

New York, 1790–1865 (Cambridge, MA: Harvard University Press, 1981); Karen Halttunen, *Confidence Men and Painted Women: A Study of Middle-Class Culture in America, 1830–1870* (New Haven: Yale University Press, 1982); Stuart M. Blumin, "The Hypothesis of Middle-Class Formation in Nineteenth-Century America: A Critique and Some Proposals," *American Historical Review 90* (1985), 299–338; and Blumin's *The Emergence of the Middle Class Social Experience in the American City, 1760–1900* (NY: Cambridge University Press, 1989). Also see Paul Boyer, *Urban Masses and Moral Order in America 1820–1920* (Cambridge, MA: Harvard University Press, 1978).

22. Ellen K. Rothman, *Hands and Hearts: A History of Courtship in America* (NY: Basic Books, 1984).

23. Rothman 54.

24. Rothman 51.

25. Karen Lystra, *Searching the Heart: Women, Men, and Romantic Love in Nineteenth-Century America* (NY: Oxford University Press, 1989).

26. Lystra 85.

27. Lystra 85.

28. Lystra 84.

29. Lystra 59.

30. Lystra 101–02, 113, 117, 118.

31. D'Emilio and Freedman xviii, 111–16, 120, 138, 156–57.

32. Rothman's, Lystra's, D'Emilio and Freedman's, and Peter Gay's work (discussed later) point to the absence in the nineteenth-century U.S. of any public ideology that naturalized, medicalized, and justified different-sex eroticism in and of itself, apart from different-sex love. A normal, official, medically modeled, physiological heterosexuality had not yet been declared.

33. Steven Seidman, *Romantic Longings: Love in America, 1830-1980* (NY: Routledge, 1991), 208–09.

34. Seidman 208–09.

35. Lystra 84.

36. Lystra never adequately explores this nasty underside of nineteenth-century true love—the idea (and the strong feeling) that sensuality divorced from true love was deeply, fundamentally problematic. Because Lystra separates her chapters on sexuality from her chapters on the tensions experienced by couples in love, her couples appear to enjoy eros without suffering any substantial, prolonged anguish, guilt, shame, or conflict about their erotic feelings or activities. A few pages by Lystra on tensions in the sexual relations of women and men fail to balance her stress on couples' ability to unambiguously justify sexual expression by love (see 69–76). In contrast, Rothman suggests throughout her book that the task of vindicating an otherwise unjustified carnal lust did cause deep anxiety about love's sufficiency and intense consternation about love's faltering (see Rothman 52–53, 130, 135–37, 230, 233–41).

37. Seidman 22–23.

38. Seidman 8.

39. Seidman 189. But, then, Seidman uses the heterosexual term as if it *did* have a functional, operative life in mid-nineteenth-century society (see 22–23).

40. Barbara Welter, "The Cult of True Womanhood: 1820–1860," *American Quarterly 18* (Summer 1966), 151–74; Welter's analysis is extended here to include True Men and True Love.

41. True women and men were distinguished from false women and men, called by a variety of derogatory names. Those who failed to live up to true woman's and true man's character and calling, or who deviated from these strict sex standards, were castigated as false-sexed creatures. For criticizing the traditional female role, Mary Wollstonecraft, Frances Wright, and Harriet Martineau were condemned by a minister in 1838 as "only semi-women, mental hermaphrodites" (see Katz, *G/LA*, 140). In 1852 the *New York Herald* referred to "mannish women," and a Mr. Mandeville referred to women activists as a "hybrid species, half man and half woman, belonging to neither sex." The following year the *Herald* referred to "unsexed women," and such epithets were hurled at feminists and other nonconforming women and men well into the twentieth century (see Peter Gay, *The Bourgeois Experience: Victoria to Freud, Volume I, Education of the Senses* [NY: Oxford University Press, 1984], 190, 191).

42. For the middle class's relation to the working class, see D'Emilio and Freedman, xvi, 46, 57, 130, 142, 152, 167, 183–84. Also see Seidman, 59–60, 117–18.

43. The term "true love" simultaneously asserted love's *existence* and love's *value*. True love and false love signified an essential contrast between an authentic and unauthentic affection. True love made no reference to any distinction between different-sex and same-sex eroticism.

44. Seidman 23, 37; D'Emilio and Freedman 68–69, 71, 72.

45. D'Emilio and Freeman 130–38. The term "male prostitute" seems to have referred in the nineteenth century to the man who employed women

prostitutes, not specifically and only to the man who prostituted himself to men for money. I am grateful to Timothy Gilfoyle for this information.

46. Michael Lynch, "New York Sodomy, 1796–1873," paper presented at the New York Institute for the Humanities, February 1, 1985.

47. "Passionlessness" is one historian's confused and confusing name for the emotions that nineteenth-century women and men referred to constantly as "passion"—and honored for their depth and intensity. See Nancy F. Cott, "Passionlessness: An Interpretation of Victorian Sexual Ideology, 1790–1850," *Signs* 4 (1978), 219–36.

48. D'Emilio and Freedman 121.

49. For the decline of fertility see D'Emilio and Freedman 57–59, 66, 146, 151, 172, 173–74, 189, 201, 247, 251–52, 330–31.

50. Rothman 120–22, 128.

51. Rothman 128–29.

52. Rothman 129.

53. Walt Whitman, *Leaves of Grass, Facsimile Edition of the 1860 Text* (Ithaca, NY: Cornell University Press, 1961).

54. Michael Lynch, "'Here is Adhesiveness': From Friendship to Homosexuality," *Victorian Studies* 29:1 (Autumn 1985), 67–96. Although Whitman never refers to erotic acts between women, he had apparently heard of a problematic intimacy between women which he compared to his own tense relationships with Peter Doyle and Fred Vaughan. See Edward F. Grier, ed., *Walt Whitman, Notebooks and Unpublished Prose Manuscripts*, II (NY: New York University Press, 1984), 890, n. 77. The reference is to Jenny Bullard, of New Ipswich, New Hampshire, described as "handsome, bountiful, generous, cordial, strong, careless, laughing, large, regardless of dress or personal appearance and [who] appreciates and likes Leaves of Grass." Bullard is said to have lived with two women and never to have married.

55. Although Gay doesn't mention Emily Dickinson's letters to Sue Gilbert, these document Emily's own earlier, intense, passionate relationship with the female friend who was to become her brother Austin's unhappy wife. See Lillian Faderman, "Emily Dickinson's Letters to Sue Gilbert," *Massachusetts Review* 18:2 (Summer 1977), 197–225.

56. Gay 89.

57. Kathy Peiss's *Cheap Amusements: Working Women and Leisure in Turn-of-the-Century New York* (Philadelphia: Temple University Press, 1986), Peiss's "'Charity Girls'

and City Pleasures: Historical Notes on Working Class Sexuality, 1880-1920," in Ann Snitow, Christine Stansell, and Sharon Thompson, eds., *Powers of Desire: The Politics of Sexuality* (NY: Monthly Review Press, 1983), 74–87; and Joanne J. Meyerowitz's *Women Adrift: Independent Wage Earners in Chicago, 1880-1930* (Chicago: University of Chicago Press, 1988), argue that "heterosexuality" had its roots in working-class leisure practices in urban areas. I do not disagree. I am arguing that the middle class reevaluated working-class, "foreign," and African-American sexual culture when it publicly adopted the term and idea of heterosexuality to justify its own class practices. Also see Christine Stansell, *City of Women: Sex and Class in New York, 1789-1860* (NY: Alfred A. Knopf, 1986).

58. Gay 77.

59. My understanding of the historical specifics of normalization is modeled on Foucault's analytical investigations.

The "sexualization" of late–nineteenth- and twentieth-century U.S. culture is a theme of numbers of books and articles; see, for example, D'Emilio and Freedman, "Part III: Toward a New Sexual Order, 1880-1930" and "Part IV: The Rise and Fall of Sexual Liberalism, 1920 to the Present," 171–343; Rothman, "Part III: 1870-1920," 179–284; Seidman, "Part Two: Modern Times (1890–1960)," 65–120; Kevin White, ch. 4, "Male Ideology and the Roots of the Sexualized Society, 1910-1930," in *The First Sexual Revolution: The emergence of Male Heterosexuality in Modern America* (NY: New York University Press, 1993), 57–79; and Peter Gardella, *Innocent Ecstasy: How Christianity Gave America an Ethic of Sexual Pleasure* (NY: Oxford University Press, 1985).

60. Hubert Kennedy, *Ulrichs: The Life and Works of Karl Heinrich Ulrichs, Pioneer of the Modern Gay Movement* (Boston: Alyson, 1988), 50, 56–58, 155. On Ulrichs also see Manfred Herzer, "Kertbeny and the Nameless Love," *Journal of Homosexuality* 12:1 (1985), 16. In general, see Gert Hekma, "'A Female Soul in a Male Body': Sexual Inversion as Gender Inversion in Nineteenth-Century Sexology," in Gilbert Herdt, ed., *Third Sex, Third Gender: Beyond Sexual Dimorphism in Culture and History* (NY: Zone Books, 1994), 213–39.

61. The original German text of Kertbeny's letter to Ulrichs of May 6, 1868, is printed in facsimile and in typed transcription with a brief introduction in German and a bibliography by Manfred Herzer in the periodical *Capri: Zeitschrift für*

schunile Geschichte 1 (1987), 25–35. I am grateful to Herzer for sending me a copy and to Michael Lombardi-Nash for translating this letter for me and for sending me copies of his translation of works by Karl Heinrich Ulrichs; and to Paul Nash for sponsoring those copies. Copies of these and other translations may be bought from Urania Manuscripts, 6858 Arthur Court, Jacksonville, FL 32211. Kertbeny and his work are discussed in Manfred Herzer, "Kertbeny and the Nameless Love," and Jean-Claude Féray and Manfred Herzer, "Homosexual Studies and Politics in the Nineteenth Century: Karl Maria Kertbeny," trans. by Glen w. Peppel, *Journal of Homosexuality* 19:1 (1990), 23–47. The meaning of Kertbeny's terms is also discussed in Manfred Herzer to Katz, April 16, 1989. I stress my gratitude for the letters and wonderful research of Manfred Herzer. I am also indebted to the pioneering work of John Lauritsen and David Thorstad on the history of the homosexual emancipation movement in nineteenth-century Germany—see their pamphlet *The Early Homosexual Rights Movement (1864-1935)* (NY: Times Change Press, 1974)—and to James D. Steakley's *The Homosexual Emancipation Movement in Germany* (NY: Arno Press, 1975).

62. Féray and Herzer 34–35.

63. Féray and Herzer 36.

64. Féray and Herzer 25, 34–35.

65. Féray and Herzer 25, 37; and Herzer to Katz, April 16, 1989.

66. Herzer, "Kertbeny and the Nameless Love," 6, 21 n. 6. The term "heterosexual" appears in the 4th edition of R. von Krafft-Ebing, *Psychopathia sexualis . . .* (Stuttgart: Ferdinand Enke, 1889), 96, 99. "Heterosexual" appears four times in three different phrases: "*heterosexuale Empfindung*" (heterosexual sensation); "*heterosexuale Gefühle*" (heterosexual feeling); and "*heterosexualer Verkehr*" (heterosexual intercourse): Herzer to Katz, July 6, 1983, and April 16, 1989. I thank James Steakley for help with the German.

67. See my discussion of Kiernan's article in Chapter 2 of *The Invention of Heterosexuality*.

68. Havelock Ellis, *Studies in the Psychology of Sex*, Volume II, Part II, *Sexual Inversion* (NY: Random House, 1936), 2–4.

69. Dr. Karl Friedrich Otto Westphal, "*Die conträre Sexualempfindung*," *Archiv für Psychiatrie und Nervenkrankheiten* 2:1 (Aug.

1869), 73–108. I am indebted to James D. Steakley for the correct date of this major article. I comment on Westphal in *Gay/Lesbian Almanac: A New Documentary* (NY: Harper & Row, 1983), 147, 183, 188–90, 682 n. 14. Also see Vern Bullough, *Sexual Variance in Society and History* (NY: John Wiley and Sons, 1976), 639, 670 n. 12. Additional comment on Westphal and the psychiatric terms and concepts appears in Arnold I. Davidson, "Closing Up the Corpses: Diseases of Sexuality and the Emergency of the Psychiatric Style of Reasoning," in George Boolos, ed., *Meaning and Method: Essays in Honor of Hilary Putnam* (NY: Cambridge University Press, 1990), 295–325; in Féray and Herzer; Gert Hekma, "A History of Sexology: Social and Historical Aspects of Sexuality," in Jan Bremmer, ed., *From Sappho to De Sade: Moments in the History of Sexuality* (NY: Routledge, 1989), 173–93; also see Hekman's bibliography, 196–211; Herzer, "Kertbeny and the Nameless Love"; and Kennedy, *Ulrichs*. Peter Gay, *The Bourgeois Experience, Victoria to Freud, Volume II, The Tender Passion* (NY: Oxford University Press, 1986), 223–30, refers to Havelock Ellis's mini-history of these terms, first published in his *Sexual Inversion* in the English edition of 1897 and U.S. edition of 1900 (I believe Gay means 1901, the date of the first American edition of the *Sexual Inversion* volume); see Ellis, *Sexual Inversion*, 2-4. Also see Michel Foucault, *The History of Sexuality, Volume I, An Introduction* (NY: Pantheon, 1978), 43.

70. Ellis, *Sexual Inversion*, 3.

71. In 1879, Dr. Allen w. Hagenbach's American medical journal discussion of masturbation first referred to the case of an effeminate young man with a "morbid" attraction to persons of his own sex (though that attraction was not yet given a proper name; see Vern Bullough, "Homosexuality and the Secret Sin in Nineteenth Century America," *Journal of the History of Medicine* 28 [1973], 143–54). The first British medical journal article on the subject of same-sex attraction was published in 1881 (though the subject was German, the doctor Viennese). In 1883, the sexual emancipationist John Addington Symonds used "sexual inversion" in his *privately printed* publication, *A Problem in Greek Ethics* (see Ellis, *Sexual Inversion*, 3).

72. Ellis, *Sexual Inversion*, 3.

Discussion Questions

1. According to Katz, when was the word *heterosexual* first used in the United States? What did *heterosexual* and *homosexual* mean, according to Kiernan?

2. How did Krafft-Ebing's use of the term *hetero-sexual* differ from Kiernan's?

3. Why is Karl Heinrich Ulrichs referred to as a pioneer in the study of sexuality?

4. What are some of the different ways people organized human sexuality prior to what Katz discusses as the "invention of heterosexuality"?

5. What did you learn from this reading? Which, if any, assumptions of yours does it challenge?

6. If the word *heterosexual* were not in the dictionary, what difference might that make in how you live your life?

7. How has the terminology we use in talking about sexuality changed since the period of time Katz reviewed? Do you believe that the labels we use to talk about sexuality and sexual identities will continue to evolve?

2

Necessary Fictions

Sexual Identities and the Politics of Diversity

JEFFREY WEEKS

We live today in societies that are in many ways less "alienated" than in the past: that is to say societies in which there is greater indeterminacy in our position within them and in which we are more free to decide on movements and identity. They are also societies in which social reproduction depends less and less on repetitive practices and requires the constant production of social myths.
> —Ernesto Laclau, *New Reflections on the Revolution of our Time*

Human beings are, necessarily, actors who cannot become something before they have pretended to be it; and they can be divided, not into the hypocritical and the sincere, but into the sane who know they are acting and the mad who do not.
> —W. H. Auden, "The Age of Anxiety"

The prologues are over. It is a question, now,
Of final belief. So, say that final belief
Must be in a fiction. It is time to choose.
> —Wallace Stevens, "Asides on the Oboe"

IDENTITY TROUBLE

Sexuality has become a constitutive element in postmodern politics. The politics of the right is preoccupied with sex education, abortion, the threat of the "gay agenda," the dangers of single parenting and the underclass and the need to shore up the family and its "traditional"

SOURCE: This chapter originally appeared as part of *Invented Moralities*. Copyright © 1995 Columbia University Press. Reprinted by permission.

assignment of gender and childrearing responsibilities. The politics of the left is challenged by the claims of women and erotic minorities for rights, and faced by the need to translate its discourse of fairness and equality into an understanding and endorsement of sexual change. In both directions we see a conventional politics having to confront and come to terms with an increasing erotic and cultural diversity. Nor is this challenge limited to the boundaries of the traditional polity. When the neo-foundationalist rhetoric of "liberation and purity" (Bhatt 1995) can mobilize men and women of Asian origin in the slums of Bradford *and* the villages of Punjab, or when the universalisms of Roman Catholicism and Islam can attempt to enter into dialogue on the dangers of abortion and homosexuality, as in the International Conference on Population and Development in 1994, though with limited success (O'Brien 1994), a new focus has clearly entered into global political discourse: one concerned with the boundaries of identity and the fact of cultural difference, symbolized by the pleasures and dangers of sexual choice.

In this new and unprecedented situation it is not surprising that it is the radical agenda of those who extol the virtues of choice, personal autonomy and the value of diversity who have become the target of hostile moral attack. The radical sexual movements that have sprung up since the 1970s have been the site for some of the most sustained interrogation of values and ethics during the past generation (Seidman 1992). Questions about sexual practices, relationships and lifestyles raised by feminism, lesbian and gay politics and to a lesser extent by other "erotic minorities" have in turn fed into mainstream culture, in the form of fashion, representation, sexual techniques, political strategies and moral debate. The responses to these influences have been mixed: from stylistic absorption or dialogue to explicit opposition and outrage. But there has been a sustained common element in the subsequent flurries. In one way or another, they have all

raised issues about identity: who we are, why we are, in what ways should we live, how we should love, have sex. . . .

The problematic nature of sexual identity has become the fulcrum of wider debates about the meaning and direction of sexual values, and of the politics of the erotic. This is not because of the power of radical ideas alone, or possibly at all; rather the radical questions raised by recent sexual politics have fed into a much wider uncertainty about the stability and fixity of our sexual belongings and identifications, and hence of who we are and should or could be. For this reason, in this chapter I want to explore in some detail this radical agenda, first by looking again at the question of identity, and then by exploring the trouble that radical sexual politics can cause. Let me begin with a personal anecdote.

Several years ago I was a member of a conference panel on precisely this problem of identity. A fellow panellist, Jackie Kay, read as her contribution one of her poems, "Close Shave" (1991, p. 56). It was a poignant poem of deep but frustrated love and sexual attraction, between a miner, the epitome (in British culture at least) of male strength, communal spirit and family pride (a "man's man"), and another man, the local barber:

> The only time I forget is down the pit
> right down in the belly of it,
> my lamp shining like a third eye,
> my breath short and fast like my wife's
> when she is knitting. Snip, snap.
> . . . It doesn't bear thinking.

What doesn't bear thinking is an open declaration of love from a (married) man for another man:

> . . . It's my daughters that worry me.
> Course I can never tell the boys down
>   the pit.
> When I'm down here I work fast so it
>   hurts.

There is, perhaps, little that is unusual or special about the detail of this account: we know of the cost of the homosexual closet on countless lives; we are familiar with the conflicts between desire and duty that flit across all our social adventures. Many of us know that hurts. But there is, I think, something unusual, special, not so familiar yet at the same time deeply representative, about the circumstances in which the poem was written and published. It was submitted for a poetry competition in South Wales, the mythical (though now largely desolated) heart of mining culture. To the surprise of the judges, the person who came forward to receive the prize was a woman. Not only a woman, but a black woman, a feminist; and a black feminist with a rich Scottish accent.

Here for me was a nice metaphor for the complexity of modern identities, revealing in one physical presence a rich diversity of presences, neither one excluding the other. An empathy and subtle identification were expressed across the divides of class, gender, ethnicity and sexuality, while simultaneously a very specific and enabling identity was also asserted: Scottish, black, female and feminist, alive to historical resonances and political alignments, bringing to mind the fact that in the 1984-5 miners' strike in Britain lesbian and gay groups forged an unexpected solidarity with miners in South Wales; and had their support reciprocated in resistance to subsequent anti-gay legislation from the British state (Jackson 1994). Identities and identifications can simultaneously affirm and obliterate differences.

Contemporary identities are, it is now almost commonplace to say, hybrid, made of many fragments of history and of social, and personal experience; they are heterogeneous, establishing many possible identifications across the boundaries of many potential differences; they are often political in the broadest sense, making links which defy the neat categorizations of social policy and social science, and challenging settled power relations (Rutherford 1990). Yet they are personally knitted together into narratives which give coherence to individual lives, support and promote social agency, and express certain values: values which we share with those with whom we identify, and which differentiate us from countless others with whom we do not, often cannot, identify.

Because of these complexities, identities are troubling. We search for them, claim them, assert and affirm them, usually with all the passion and personal conviction we can command. They provide a bedrock for our most fundamental being and most prized social belongings. Yet we are often forced to question them, or have them questioned for us, remake and reinvent them, search for new and more satisfying personal "homes," all the time. As I write, in these turbulent globalized, post-Cold War, "postmodern" times, questions of identity, personal and collective, are flashpoints for some of the most poisoned and violent disputes across the world: "intercommunal strife," "ethnic cleansing," the reassertion of "lost" or more likely invented national or tribal traditions have become tokens of our apparent inability to live with diversity, to tolerate the existence of different identities. Simultaneously, new political and cultural identities have proliferated, around race and ethnicity, gender and sexuality, HIV and AIDS, among other collective identities, which have emerged to confirm and promote common human interests, to challenge frozen hierarchies of power and, implicitly or explicitly, to argue for autonomy, diversity and choice. But they in turn generate new types of controversy, around "identity politics," "political correctness," the threat to the "natural order" of sexuality and the like. Not all identities are harmless and enabling. Identities can be battlegrounds. So is the trouble worthwhile?

THE PARADOXES OF IDENTITY

Identities are troubling because they embody so many paradoxes: about what we have in common and what separates us; about our sense of self and our recognition of others; about conflicting belongings in a changing history and a complex modern world; and about the possibility of social action in and through our collective identities. And few identities are so paradoxical as sexual identities.

Sexual identities have a special place in the discourse of identity. They are like relay points for a number of interconnected differences, conflicts and opportunities. For the past few centuries, at least, sex may have been central to the fixing of the individual's place in the culture, but it has not been simply a categorization and placing for a *sexualized* identity (as male or female, normal or pervert, heterosexual or homosexual), rather for a whole set of social positionings. Concepts of national identity have been intricately bound up with notions of appropriate gendered or sexualized behaviour (Parker et al. 1992). The injunctions of nineteenth-century imperial propagandists to the young innocent—to "be a man" and eschew masturbation, homosexuality or nameless other secret sins, or to embody motherhood and purity for the sake of the race—brought together class, race, gender and sexuality into a potent brew which locked normality and sexuality into a fixed hierarchy that few could escape from even if not so many lived up to it.

The settling of class identities in the first wave of industrialization in the nineteenth century also froze the fluidity of gender differences and sexual behaviour. "Respectability" betokened more than a middle-class modesty and discretion; it became a way of life where sexual desire and gendered activity were regulated by approved and approvable behaviour (Weeks 1981/1989). Alfred Kinsey was neither the first nor the last to notice the distinct class accents to human sexual behaviour (Kinsey et al. 1948). Similarly, the generation of a racialized "Western identity," with its distinct sexual classifications and typologies, in turn depended upon the identification of the colonized of the world as distinctly "other," more

primitive, more priapic or blatant, and certainly less "civilized," which in turn served to confirm "our" superiority, and the truth of "our" sexualities.

Unsurprisingly, racial differences have been marked by gendered and sexualized boundaries. Gates (1993, p. 234), for example, notes the ways in which American black nationalism became sexualized in the 1960s "in such a way as to engender a curious subterranean connection between homophobia and nationalism," so that an assertion of a fiercely heterosexual masculinity became a token of black male belonging, with often dire results (see also Mercer and Julien 1988). Sexuality is woven into the web of all the social belongings we embrace, and that is why the emergence over the past two hundred years, and in a rush since the 1960s, of alternative or oppositional sexualized identities— lesbian and gay, "queer," bisexual, transvestite and transsexual, sadomasochistic, an exotic parade dancing into history with a potentially infinite series of scripts and choreographies—is seen as subversive by sexual conservatives. They breach boundaries, disrupt order and call into question the fixity of inherited identities of all kinds, not just sexual, which is also the reason, no doubt, for identities being so problematic to those committed to sexual change. If they are asserted too firmly there are dangers of fixing identifications and values that are really necessarily always in flux; yet if their validity is denied, there is an even greater danger of disempowering individuals and groups from the best means of mobilizing for radical change (Weeks 1991).

Identities are paradoxical, and they raise paradoxes. I want to illustrate this by exploring four key paradoxes.

Paradox 1: Sexual identity assumes fixity and uniformity while confirming the reality of unfixity, diversity and difference. Many of us in the west like to say who we are by telling of our sex: "I am gay/straight"; "I am male/ female." It places us securely in recognized discourses, embodying assumptions, beliefs, practices and codes of behaviour. Yet the truth is rather more complex. "Possibility and many-sideness," Rosenblum (1987, p. 149) has argued, "are built into the very idea of identity formation." This is especially true of sexual identities. Academically and theoretically, we increasingly recognize both the diverse desires, needs and passions of individuals and the diversity of (often conflicting) social obligations and belonging, pulling us in a variety of directions. Is being a member of an ethnic or racial minority community more important than a sexual identification? Do class or community loyalties take precedence over identification with the aims of a political movement such as feminism? Such anguishings have characterized the sexual politics of the past thirty years. We fear the uncertainty, the abyss, the unknown, the threat of dissolution that not having a fixed identity entails. So we often try to fix identities, by asserting that what we are now is what we have really, truly always been, if only we had known.

But consider the realities. We all know lifelong heterosexuals who suddenly come out as lesbian or gay. We know self-identified gays who equally suddenly opt for a heterosexual lifestyle. We also know of many cultures in the world where such questions are meaningless. Where, then, is the essential person? In her book on cross-dressing, *Vested Interests*, Marjorie Garber (1992) tells of the spokesperson for the International Foundation for Gender Education, one Yvonne Cook. Yvonne is a biological male who cross-dresses, and identifies as a woman, as a lesbian. She dates a biological woman who cross-dresses as a man. Which label corresponds to the real her—or him? Here sexual identities seem endlessly fluid, taken up and used rather than realized, a glittering performance or complicated game rather than a truth claim.

Since the nineteenth century the placing of individuals into clearly demarcated sexual categories, and hence identities, has gone hand in hand with the presentation of plentiful

evidence detailing the fluidity and uncertainty of desire and cultural loyalties (Weeks 1985). It is difficult to fit neatly into the social categories which define and limit possible identifications. The binary divisions that many of us in Western countries take for granted, between men and women, heterosexual and homosexual, normal and perverse, provide barriers against, in the words of Epstein and Straub (1991, p. 14), "the uncontrollable elasticity and terrifying lack of boundaries within or between bodies." They simplify the complexity of desires, they order the potential multiplicity of our identifications. But those barriers are often fragile, inadequate blocks to the flux of contemporary life, and the range of possible ways of being. The repressed usually returns, sometimes in distorted and damaging ways (such as the homophobia of the "repressed homosexual"), sometimes in liberating and creative ways, in the elective communities where dissident or oppositional sexual identities, at least, are forged and confirmed. Then identities can become enabling. Yet, I would argue, they are still only ever provisional. We can put on a good performance with them. But we should never believe they are final, or embody some unique truth about ourselves. "Unfixity," write Laclau and Mouffe, "has become the condition of every social identity" (1985, p. 85)—and especially, I would add, of every sexual identity.

Paradox 2: Identities are deeply personal but tell us about multiple social belongings. All cultures seem to depend on their members having a secure sense of self, and a placing in the order of things. But there is no reason to think that the modern individual is a reflex product of his or her "instincts." Self-identity, at the heart of which is sexual identity, is not something that is given as a result of the continuities of an individual's life or the fixity and force of his or her desires. It is something that has to be worked on, invented and reinvented in accord with the changing rhythms, demands, opportunities and closures of a complex world; it depends on the effectiveness of the biographical narratives we construct for ourselves in a turbulent world, on our ability to keep a particular narrative going (Plummer 1995).

We apparently need a sense of the essential self to provide a grounding for our actions, to ward off existential fear and anxiety and to provide a springboard for action (Giddens 1991; Cohen 1994). So we write into our personal narratives the elements which confirm what we say we are. And here our bodily feelings and presence become central. In a world of apparently constant flux, where the fixed points keep moving or dissolving, we hold on to what seems most tangible, the truth of our bodily needs and desires, or, in the age of AIDS, our vulnerabilities. It is not suprising that the making and remaking of the body then becomes so basic to our assertion of identities. We worry about its health and the forces that can undermine it (smoking in relative private becomes more tabooed than having sex in public, our cholesterol levels more important than our protein intake); we run and do exercises to ward off its infirmity and temporality (even as we collapse from exhaustion, sore feet or painful muscles); we adorn it in clothes that affirm our sense of individuality (but which also provide a badge of our belonging to one subgroup or another, or our enslavement to the whims of the marketplace); we assert the imperatives of its desires and potentiality for pleasure (though they as often wrack us with their contradictory messages as confirm a single bodily truth). For the body is seen as the final court of judgement on what we are or can become. Why else are we so worried if sexual desires, whether homosexual or heterosexual, are inborn or acquired? For what other reason are we so concerned whether gendered behaviour corresponds with physical attributes? Only because everything else is so uncertain do we need the judgement that our bodies apparently dictate.

Of course, the fact of different, and highly gendered, bodies matters; on the physiological differences of biological men and women has been built an empire of division. But the body is a fickle master or mistress: its needs change; it falls prey to want or plenty; to sickness and physical decay; its sources of pleasures can be transformed, whether through chance, training, physical alteration, mental control—or, increasingly, the demands of a new regime of "safer sex." Even the apparently most decisive of differences between biological men and women, reproductive capacity, is now subject to major medical intervention and potential manipulation. So in the postmodern world are we not really, as some speculate, cyborgs, mythic creatures half human, half machine, beyond gender, sexual categorization and fixed social positioning? As Haraway put it, "By the late twentieth century, our time, a mythic time, we are all chimeras, theorized and fabricated hybrids of machine and organism" (1991, p. 150).

The body is no more immune to the power of culture, and its transforming possibilities, than our mental attitudes or social identifications. The body, as Giddens suggests, "in late modernity becomes increasingly socialised and drawn into the reflexive organization of social life" (1991, p. 198). Yet we necessarily use the body as the focus of our sense of biographical continuity, while implicitly acknowledging our social belongings and cultural baggage. The body, marked by gender, race, age, subject to pleasure, pain and ultimate extinction, is the site for the inscription of difference, the battleground for conflicting cultural meanings.

The sexual persona, like the whole personality, is, in Connell's formulation (1987, p. 220), a social practice seen from "the perspective of the life history," and the sources of that personal history are inevitably cultural. The sociosexual identities we adopt, inhabit and adapt work in so far as they order and give meaning to individual needs and desires, but they are not emanations of those needs and desires. Indeed they have no necessary connection at all to the contingencies of the body. The sources of the narratives that keep us going, that make sense of our individual peculiarities, are deeply historical, dependent on social bonds that provide the map for personal meaning and cultural identification. And those bonds are multiple: we come from different nations, classes, statuses, religions, racial and ethnic groupings, different genders and generations and geographical areas, each of which provides a sliver of experience, a residue of a personal history, which we try to integrate into our personal biographies, to shape our individual identity. Sexual identity involves a perpetual invention and reinvention, but on ground fought over by many histories.

Paradox 3: Sexual identities are simultaneously historical and contingent. The idea that sexual identities are not simple expressions of bodily truth but are historical phenomena—and therefore constantly changing—is a relatively recent one, pioneered largely by feminist and lesbian and gay scholars (see for example, Duberman, Vicinus and Chauncey 1989). Its origins were largely political, demonstrating the historicity and potential ephemerality of the categories we take for granted as natural and inevitable, even as their power was acknowledged. Behind this position is a clear assumption that, as Laclau puts it, "the constitution of a social identity is an act of power and that identity as such is power" (1990, p. 30). Sexual identities embody power relations, products of imposition *and* agency, and are rooted in many histories.

We still know most about the constitution of Western homosexual identities over the past few hundred years than about any other, particularly the overarching categorization of heterosexuality and heterosexual identities (but see essays in Peiss and Simmons 1989; Katz 1995). Nor is this surprising, for the dominant or hegemonic form of any social position becomes the given, the taken for granted, part of the air we breathe, from which everything else becomes a deviation at best or a perversion at worst. As such it tends to escape thorough investigation—though this is now changing. We are increasingly accustomed to seeing sexuality as a spectrum along which lie many potential sexual desires and many different identities. But that easy pluralism obscures the fact that historically sexual identities have been organized into violent hierarchies, where some positions are marked as superior (more natural, healthier, more true to the body than others). The shaping of a distinctive categorisation of "the homosexual" over the past century or so in the leading Western countries (but not, until recently, others) has been an act of power, whose effect, intended or not, has been to reinforce the normality of heterosexuality. As Eve Sedgwick has put it:

> The importance—an importance—of the category "homosexual" . . . comes not necessarily from its regulatory relation to a nascent or already constituted minority of homosexual people or desires, but from its potential for giving whoever wields it a structuring definitional leverage (1985, p. 86).

The emergence since the eighteenth century, she argues, of an institutionalized homophobia and homosexual panic brutally separates men from men, but more crucially serves to confirm and consolidate male (heterosexual) power not only over other men but over women, for "the domination offered by the strategy is not only over a minority population, but over the bonds that structure all social form" (1985, p. 97). In other words, the apparently neutral description of men as either homosexual or heterosexual conceals the intricate play of power, of domination and subordination, which minoritizes the homosexual experience, and consolidates male power in a new, effective pattern. In the same fashion, the categorization, in psychology, sexology and a variety of other social practices, of some women as homosexual and others as very definitely not, breaks the continuum of all women, and hence serves further to consolidate the sexual power of men (Smith-Rosenberg 1985).

The fact that such arguments are still not only controversial in themselves but contested even as a starting point for debate is a testimony to the power of the categories that have become sedimented in our consciousness during the twentieth century, and to our cultural preference for neat divisions of people and identities: you are either this or that. But the process of trying to divide people into heterosexual or homosexual groups has been a complex one, and one that is, in Sedgwick's phrase, still "radically incomplete" (Sedgwick 1990, p. 159), especially when they can be seen not to apply in other cultures, or even universally within our own. There are two related points that must be made here.

The first is that the discursive construction of categories of sexual subjects is a constant process, and involves a struggle over definitions on a sexual-political terrain that is ever shifting. The agents of sexual regulation, whether state, churches or other institutions such as those of medicine or psychology are involved in an effort of definition that is never ending, and the reason for this is quite simply that sexual identities, including (perhaps especially) heterosexual ones, are profoundly unstable. Take two recent sexual-political events in, respectively, Britain and the United States. The notorious Clause 28 of the British Local Government Act passed in 1988 banned the "promotion of homosexuality as a pretended family relationship" by local authorities. Whatever the political context in which it took place (Weeks 1981/1989), its only rationale could have been an assumption that without such an act, the influence of an activist lesbian and gay movement promoting "positive images" of homosexuality could radically overflow the boundaries between heterosexual and homosexual, to the detriment of the principles of normality (Smith 1990). In the *Bowers v. Hardwick* decision by the US Supreme Court in 1986 a Georgian man,

arrested for having sex with another man in his own home, had his appeal that this was an infringement of his right to privacy overturned. In effect this denied the right to privacy to homosexuals in their sexual behaviour (Brill 1990). This decision, it has been argued:

> not only set the constitution's imprimatur on punishment of "homosexual sodomy" but equated that act with "homosexuality" and indeed with "homosexuals"—a group now not only defined but known by its sodomitical essence (Halley 1991, p. 356).

In effect, by identifying certain classes of illegal sexual activity ("sodomy") with a particular type of personage, it ruled such people out of the normal protection of the constitution.

The interesting point about these two separate cases is that the logic of the actions, one by a court, the other by parliament, were justified on quite different grounds. In the American example, the Supreme Court took a radical step towards taking for granted an immutable homosexual essence, defined by particular sexual practices. In the British case, the argument was different: essentially that, because homosexuality was not necessarily inherent, but could be acquired by overexposure to homosexual proselytizing, it was the task of government to limit "promotion." But in both cases, despite the contrary arguments, the clear aim and intention was to construct a class of legal subjects denied certain legal protection in order to delimit their rights and claims—in the interests of sustaining a heterosexual value system that was seen as simultaneously natural and inevitable, and fragile and undetermined by the homosexual experience.

The second point is that these categorizations and imposed definitions cannot and do not exhaust the actual lived experience of sexuality or the proliferation of oppositional identities. In the case of homosexuality, there is plentiful evidence that cultures of opposition, pleasure and self-identification were emerging before and then against the opprobrious categorizations that emerged in the law, medicine, sexology and so on in the course of the nineteenth century (see, e.g., Bray 1982). It is a characteristic of what Dollimore has called the "perverse dynamic" (1991, p. 160) that a political and sexual ordering is always internally disordered by the very perversities it produces, and sets up against itself. The power to define may have set the limits on what could be said, done or spoken, but those apparently fixed by the definitions nevertheless produced their own resistances and identities. More recently, the emergence of a distinctive identity politics around sexuality has articulated a growing recognition that the power to define itself combines a multiplicity of powers and hierarchies, not only around gender and sexuality, but also around race and ethnicity, class and status, which in turn has produced new frontiers in sexual politics, and new forms of resistance. Sexual identities are enmeshed in relations of domination and subordination, where many histories intertwine. These examples are simply recent ones of the constant historical work needed to mark distinctions in order to sustain what is seen as a necessary, and certainly dominant, order.

Yet if histories (rather than History) and various forms of power relations (rather than a single Power) provide the context for sexual identities, our assumption of them is not determined by the past but by the contingencies, chances and opportunities of the historic present. As I have already suggested, there is no necessary relationship between a particular organization of desire and a social identity. Many people who practise various forms of homosexual activity fail to recognize themselves in labels such as "homosexual," lesbian and gay, queer, or whatever the available identity is at any particular time, even in the West, where such descriptions and self-descriptions are hegemonic. In other parts of the world, homosexual practices, where they are not banned totally, are integrated into various

patterns of relations, without giving rise to Western-style identities, though other forms of identity do of course exist (Herdt 1994).

This has become particularly crucial in the age of AIDS. It has sometimes been said that HIV and AIDS, in their spread across the world, tell the truth about identity, revealing in infection what is concealed in social life. But it is more accurate to say that HIV reveals the truth about often concealed sexual activities. The assumption that evidence of certain practices reveals the prevalence of identities is not only a fallacy but a dangerous one when it comes to health and safer-sex education, because it assumes that people will recognize themselves in social identities that are peculiar to very specific parts of the world. The development in British AIDS work of a well-intentioned label of "men who have sex with men" is an attempt to recognize that existing labels do not exhaust homosexual activity. Consequently, there are men who often have unsafe sex with other men who do not regard themselves as at risk of a "gay plague" because they do not see themselves as gay. Campaigns directed at these "MWHSWM" have, however, been less than successful because they do not address people in terms that they can themselves recognize (King 1993). Most men who have sex with other men, who refuse a gay self-description, probably see themselves as bisexual or even heterosexual, or are locked into identifications, such as those of minority ethnic groups, where a gay identity is either lacking or tabooed.

Available identities are taken up for a variety of reasons: because they make sense of individual experiences, because they give access to communities of meaning and support, because they are politically chosen (Weeks 1985). These identities can, however, equally be refused, precisely because they do not make sense to an individual, or because they have no cultural purchase. Identities necessarily differentiate. They also have differential weight for individuals and collectives at

different times. The positive assertion of sexualized identities is more likely to be a result of
a sense of exclusion, denial or threat than an
easy acceptance of one's lot. By and large the
heterosexual majority have not felt it necessary, until the challenges of recent years,
aggressively to assert their heterosexual identities, simply because they set the norm. It was
not until the twentieth century that women
asserted their sense of themselves as sexual
beings, because while before that women may
have been regarded as "the sex," their sexuality was generally during the nineteenth century
not seen as autonomous but responsive to that
of men (Bland 1996). Similarly, the differential
emergence of distinctive male homosexual and
lesbian identities can be related to the separate
experiences and histories of men and women
(Weeks 1977/1990).

The creation of an identity involves finding a
delicate balance between the hazards and
opportunities of contemporary life and an identification with some sort of history, an "imaginary reunification," in Stuart Hall's phrase, of
past and present: "identities are the names we
give to the different ways we are positioned,
and position ourselves, in the narratives of the
past" (quoted in Gates 1993, p. 231).

The challenge is always one of shaping
usable narratives that can make sense of the
present through appropriating a particular
history. Not surprisingly, one of the first signs
of the public emergence of new identities is the
appearance of works that detail the "roots" of
those hitherto obscured from recorded or
respectable history: history as a way of legitimizing contingency.

*Paradox 4: Sexual identities are fictions—but
necessary fictions.* Sexual identities are historical inventions, which change in complex
histories. They are imagined in contingent circumstances. They can be taken up and abandoned. To put it polemically, they are fictions.
This is not of course how they are seen or
experienced, or what we wish to believe.

Worse, in the age of uncertainty through
which we are currently struggling, to say this
often seems a betrayal of what we need most
desperately to hold on to, an arid intellectual-
ism which leaves minorities without hope, and
the vulnerable defenceless. As HIV disease visibly and remorselessly spread in the male gay
communities of the West from the early 1980s,
it was the existence of strong lesbian and gay
communities and identities which provided the
essential context for combating the virus: in
providing social networks for support and
campaigning, in developing a grammar for
safer sex, in promoting a language of resistance and survival. The homophobia that was
encouraged by AIDS demanded, and in fact
greatly strengthened, lesbian and gay identities; without them, it often seemed in the
embattled 1980s, there was nothing. To say
that all this was a fiction seemed perverse.

But to say that something is a historical fiction is not to denigrate it. On the contrary, it is
simply to recognize that we cannot escape our
histories, and that we need means to challenge
their apparently iron laws and inexorabilities
by constructing narratives of the past in order
to imagine the present and future. Oppositional
sexual identities, in particular, provide such
means and alternatives, fictions that provide
sources of comfort and support, a sense of
belonging, a focus for opposition, a strategy for
survival and cultural and political challenge.
Such a view of identity does two things. First of
all it offers a critical view of all identities,
demonstrating their historicity and arbitrari-
ness. It denaturalizes them, revealing the coils
of power that entangle them. It returns identities to the world of human beings, revealing
their openness and contingency.

Second, because of this, it makes human
agency not only possible, but also essential.
For if sexual identities are made in history, and
in relations of power, they can also be remade.
Identities then can be seen as sites of contestation. They multiply points of resistance and
challenge, and expand the potentialities for

change. Identities, particularly those identities which challenge the imposing edifice of Nature, History, Truth, are a resource for realizing human diversity. They provide means of realizing a progressive individualism, our "potential for individualization" (Melucci 1989, p. 48) and a respect for difference.

Frank Kermode (1967) has made a useful distinction between myths and fictions. Myth, he argues:

> operates within the diagrams of ritual, which presupposes total and adequate explanations of things as they are and were: it is a sequence of radically unchangeable gestures. Fictions are for finding things out, and they change as the needs of sense-making change. Myths are the agents of stability, fictions are the agents of change (p. 210).

From this viewpoint, the dominant (hetero)sexual identities in our culture have some of the qualities of myths: they speak for an assumed naturalness, eternity and truth which belie their historical and contingent nature. The radical, oppositional identities which have arisen in and against the hegemonic ones can be seen as fictions: they offer narratives of individual life, collective memory and imagined alternatives which provide the motivation and inspiration for change. In that sense, they are not only fictions—they are necessary fictions. Without them we would have no basis to explain our individual needs and desires, nor a sense of collective belonging that provides the agency and means for change.

The danger is that these historical inventions, these fictional unities, become closed, the exclusive home of those who identify with them. The semi-ethnic lesbian and gay identities that developed in the USA in the 1970s and 1980s (Epstein 1990; Herdt 1992) provide a graphic example of the dangers as well as the opportunities. They provided the possibilities of individual and collective growth, but they also drew boundaries around the homosexual experience. In extreme cases such developments can themselves become barriers to change. But if their historicity, openness, flexibility and conditional nature—fictional qualities—are acknowledged fully, they provide the opportunity for thinking about not only who you are, but also about who you want to become. They reveal the power relations that inhibit change, by making power visible. And once we accept that sexuality takes its form from historically specific power relations, then it becomes possible to imagine new forms of desire which are not blocked by a sense of powerlessness and inevitability. Oppositional sexual identities in their collective form provide vistas for different futures. By interrogating and challenging normalizing and imposed forms of identity, it becomes possible to invent oneself anew.

Identities in this sense are less about expressing an essential truth about our sexual being; they are more about mapping out different values: the values of autonomy, relationships, of belonging, of difference and diversity. They provide continuous possibilities for invention and reinvention, open processes through which change can happen. As Foucault put it, specifically referring to gay identities, but with a wider echo:

> There ought to be an inventiveness special to a situation like ours. . . . We must think that what exists is far from filling all possible spaces. To make a truly unavoidable challenge to the question: what can we make work, what new game can we invent? (1989, p. 209).

That, of course, means that sexual identities are more than troubling on a personal level; they also cause trouble on a social level. I agree with Judith Butler's summing up of the paradox of identity:

> I'm permanently troubled by identity categories, consider them to be invariable stumbling-blocks, and understand them, even promote them, as sites of necessary trouble (1991, p. 14).

It is the necessary trouble caused by the paradoxes of identity that makes the politics of sexuality so fraught with tensions but so important for rethinking the nature of our social and cultural values.

REFERENCES

Auden, W. H. 1937/1979, *Selected Poems*, London, Faber and Faber.

Bhatt, C. 1995, *Liberation and Purity: Race, New Religious Movements and the Ethics of Postmodernity*, London, UCL Press.

Bland, L. (1995). *Banishing the beast: Sexuality and the early feminists*. New York: New Press.

Bray, A. 1982, *Homosexuality in Renaissance England*, London, GMP.

Brill, A. 1990. *Nobody's Business: The Paradoxes of Privacy*. Reading, MA, Addison-Wesley.

Butler, J. 1991, "Imitation and gender insubordination," in D. Fuss (ed), *Inside/Out: Lesbian Theories, Gay Theories*, New York and London, Routledge.

Cohen, A. P. 1994, *Self Consciousness: An Alternative Anthropology of Identity*, London and New York, Routledge.

Connell, R. 1987, *Gender and Power*, Cambridge, Polity Press.

Dollimore, J. 1991, *Sexual Dissidence: Augustine to Wilde, Freud to Foucault*, Oxford, Clarendon Press.

Duberman, M. B., Vicinus, M. and Chauncey, G. (eds) 1989, *Hidden from History: Reclaiming the Lesbian and Gay Past*, New York, New American Library.

Epstein, J. and Straub, K. (eds) 1991, *BodyGuards: The Cultural Politics of Gender Ambiguity*, London and New York, Routledge.

Epstein, S. 1990, "Gay politics, ethnic identity: the limits of social constructionism," in E. Stein (ed), *Forms of Desire: Sexual Orientation and the Social Constructionist Controversy*, New York and London, Garland Publishing.

Foucault, M. 1989, *Foucault Live (Interviews, 1966-84)*, ed. Sylvere Lotringer, New York, Semiotext(e) Foreign Agents Series.

Garber, M. 1992, *Vested Interests: Cross-Dressing and Cultural Anxiety*, London and New York, Routledge.

Gates, H. L. Jr. 1993, "The black man's burden," in M. Warner (ed), *Fear of a Queer Planet: Queer Politics and Social Theory*, Minneapolis and London, University of Minnesota Press.

Giddens, A. 1991, *Modernity and Self-Identity: Self and Society in the Late Modern Age*, Cambridge, Polity Press.

Halley, J. E. 1991, "Misreading sodomy: a critique of the classification of 'homosexuals' in Federal Equal Protection Law," in J. Epstein and K. Straub (eds), *BodyGuards: The Cultural Politics of Gender Ambiguity*, London and New York, Routledge.

Haraway, D. 1991, *Simians, Cyborgs, and Women: The Reinvention of Nature*, London, Free Association Books.

Herdt, G. (ed) 1992, *Gay Culture in America: Essays from the Field*, Boston, Beacon Press.

Herdt, G. (ed) 1994, *Third Sex, Third Gender: Beyond Sexual Dimorphism in Culture and History*, New York and Paris, Zone Books.

Jackson, M. 1994, *Fucking with Miners: The Story of Lesbians and Gays Support the Miners*, London, privately circulated.

Katz, J. N. 1995, *The Invention of Heterosexuality*, New York, NAL/Dutton.

Kay, J. 1991, *The Adoption Papers*, Newcastle upon Tyne, Bloodaxe Books.

Kermode, F. 1967, *The Sense of an Ending: Studies in the Theory of Fiction*, London, Oxford and New York, Oxford University Press.

King, E. 1993, *Safety in Numbers: Safer Sex and Gay Men*, London, Cassell.

Kinsey, A., Pomeroy, W. B. and Martin, C. 1948, *Sexual Behavior in the Human Male*, Philadelphia, W. B. Saunders Company.

Laclau, E. 1990, *New Reflections on the Revolution of our Time*, London and New York, Verso.

Laclau, E. and Mouffe, C. 1985, *Hegemony and Socialist Strategy: Towards a Radical Democratic Politics*, London and New York, Verso.

Melucci, A. 1989, *Nomads of the Present: Social Movements and Individual Needs in Contemporary Society*, London, Radius.

Mercer, K. and Julien, I. 1988, "Race, sexual politics and black sexuality: a dossier," in R. Chapman and J. Rutherford (eds), *Male Order: Unwrapping Masculinity*, London, Lawrence and Wishart.

O'Brien, C. C. 1994, "A great defeat for the Vatican," *The Independent*, 16 September 1994.

Parker, A., Russo, M., Sommer, D. and Yaeger, P. (eds) 1992, *Nationalisms and Sexualities*, London and New York, Routledge.

Peiss, K. and Simmons, C., with Padgug, R. 1989, *Passion and Power: Sexuality in History*, Philadelphia, Temple University Press.

Plummer, K. 1995, *Telling Sexual Stories*, London and New York, Routledge.

Rosenblum, N. 1987, *Another Liberalism: Romanticism and the Recontruction of Liberal Thought*, Cambridge, MA, Harvard University Press.

Rutherford, J. (ed) 1990, *Identity: Community, Culture, Difference*, London, Lawrence and Wishart.

Sedgwick, E. K. 1985, *Between Men: English Literature and Male Homosocial Desire*, New York, Columbia University Press.

Sedgwick, E. K. 1990, *Epistemology of the Closet*, Berkeley and Los Angeles, University of California Press.

Seidman, S. 1992, *Embattled Eros: Sexual Politics and Ethics in Contemporary America*, London and New York, Routledge.

Smith, A-M. 1990, "A symptomatology of an authoritarian discourse: the parliamentary debates on the prohibition of the promotion of homosexuality," *New Formations: A Journal of Culture/Theory/Politics* 10, Spring 1990.

Smith-Rosenberg, C. 1985, "The female world of love and ritual," in *Disorderly Conduct: Visions of Gender in Victorian America*, New York and Oxford, Oxford University Press.

Stevens, W. 1990, *The Palm at the End of the Mind: Selected Poems and a Play*, ed. H. Stevens, London, Vintage Books.

Weeks, J. 1977/1990, *Coming Out: Homosexual Politics in Britain from the Nineteenth Century to the Present*, London, Quartet.

Weeks, J. 1981/1989, *Sex, Politics, and Society: The Regulation of Sexuality since 1800*, Harlow, Longman.

Weeks, J. 1985, *Sexuality and its Discontents: Meanings, Myths and Modern Sexualities*, London and Boston, Routledge and Kegan Paul.

Weeks, J. 1991, *Against Nature: Essays on History, Sexuality and Identity*, London, Rivers Oram Press.

Discussion Questions

1. Why, according to Weeks, are identities "troubling"?

2. What makes sexual identities particularly paradoxical?

3. Weeks argues that the categories and definitions of sexuality "cannot and do not exhaust the actual lived experience of sexuality or the proliferation of oppositional identities." Do you agree or disagree? How does your own experience support or challenge this claim?

4. In what ways can sexual identities be seen as "necessary fictions"? Do you think that the same logic applies to other social identities?

5. In what ways can you see your own sexual identity as a necessary fiction?

3

On Judith Butler and Performativity

SARA SALIH

"Science" and "naturalness" are discursive constructs and, although it might seem strange to refute the authority of "science" after quoting apparently "scientific" data, the point Butler is making is clear: the body is not a "mute facticity" (GT: 129), i.e. a fact of nature, but like gender it is produced by discourses such as the ones Butler has been analyzing. As with gender, to suggest that there is no body prior to cultural inscription will lead Butler to argue that sex as well as gender can be performatively reinscribed in ways that accentuate its factitiousness (i.e. its constructedness) rather than its facticity (i.e. the fact of its existence). Such reinscriptions, or re-citations as Butler will call them in *Bodies That Matter*, constitute the subject's agency within the law, in other words, the possibilities of subverting the law against itself. Agency is an important concept for Butler, since it signifies the opportunities for subverting the law against itself to radical, political ends.

PERFORMATIVITY

Butler has collapsed the sex/gender distinction in order to argue that there is no sex that is not always already gender. All bodies are gendered from the beginning of their social existence (and there is no existence that is not social), which means that there is no "natural body" that pre-exists its cultural inscription. This seems to point towards the conclusion that gender is not something one *is*, it is something one *does*, an act, or more precisely, a sequence of acts, a verb rather than a noun, a "doing" rather than a "being" (GT: 25). Butler elaborates this idea in the first chapter of *Gender Trouble*:

> Gender is the repeated stylization of the body, a set of repeated acts within a highly rigid regulatory frame that congeal over time to produce the appearance of substance, of a natural sort of being. A political genealogy of gender ontologies, if it is

successful, will deconstruct the substantive appearance of gender into its constitutive acts and locate and account for those acts within the compulsory frames set by the various forces that police the social appearance of gender.

Gender is not just a process, but it is a particular type of process, "a set of repeated acts *within a highly rigid regulatory frame*" as Butler puts it. I have italicized that last phrase in order to stress that, as with the wardrobe analogy that I introduce later in this chapter, Butler is *not* suggesting that the subject is free to choose which gender she or he is going to enact. "The script," if you like, is always already determined within this regulatory frame, and the subject has a limited number of "costumes" from which to make a constrained choice of gender style.

The idea of performativity is introduced in the first chapter of *Gender Trouble* when Butler states that "gender proves to be performance— that is, constituting the identity it is purported to be. In this sense, gender is always a doing, though not a doing by a subject who might be said to pre-exist the deed" (GT: 25). She then quotes the claim Nietzsche makes in *On the Genealogy of Morals* that "there is no 'being' behind doing, acting, becoming; 'the doer' is merely a fiction imposed on the doing—the doing itself is everything" (1887: 29), before adding her own gendered corollary to his formulation: "there is no gender identity behind the expressions of gender; that identity is performatively constituted by the very 'expressions' that are said to be its results" (GT: 25).

This is a statement that has confused many people. How can there be a performance without a performer, an act without an actor? Actually, Butler is not claiming that gender is a performance, and she distinguishes between performance and performativity (although at times in *Gender Trouble* the two terms seem to slide into one another). In an interview given in 1993 she emphasizes the importance of this distinction, arguing that, whereas

performance presupposes a preexisting subject, performativity contests the very notion of the subject (GP: 33). In this interview Butler also explicitly connects her use of the concept "performativity" to the speech act theory of J. L. Austin's *How To Do Things With Words* (1955) and Derrida's deconstruction of Austin's ideas in his essay "Signature Event Context" (1972). Both of these texts are discussed in detail in Chapter 4 of *Judith Butler*, where I look at Butler's theorizations of language, but here it should be noted that, although neither Austin nor Derrida is in evidence in *Gender Trouble*, Butler implicitly draws from their linguistic theories in her formulations of gender identity.

How is linguistic performativity connected to gender? Towards the beginning of *Gender Trouble* Butler states that "[w]ithin the inherited discourse of the metaphysics of substance, gender proves to be performative, that is, constituting the identity it is purported to be" (GT: 24–5). Gender is an act that brings into being what it names: in this context, a "masculine" man or a "feminine" woman. Gender identities are constructed and constituted by language, which means that there is no gender identity that precedes language. If you like, it is not that an identity "does" discourse or language, but the other way around—language and discourse "do" gender. There is no "I" outside language since identity is a signifying practice, and culturally intelligible subjects are the effects rather than the causes of discourses that conceal their workings (GT: 145). It is in this sense that gender identity is performative.

At this point, we might return to the wardrobe analogy I explored in an earlier chapter of *Judith Butler* (p. 50), where I argued that one's gender is performatively constituted in the same way that one's choice of clothes is curtailed, perhaps even predetermined, by the society, context, economy, etc. within which one is situated. Readers familiar with Daphne du Maurier's novel *Rebecca* (1938) will remember that the nameless narrator shocks her husband by turning up at a party in an identical dress to that worn by his dead wife on a similar occasion. In preparation for the party, the narrator, assisted by the malign Mrs. Danvers, believes that she is choosing her costume and thereby creating herself, whereas it turns out that Mrs. Danvers is in fact recreating the narrator as Rebecca. If Mrs. Danvers is taken to exemplify authority or power here, *Rebecca* may provide an example of the way in which identities, far from being chosen by an individual agent, precede and constitute those "agents" or subjects (just as Rebecca literally precedes the narrator).

SURFACE/DEPTH

Butler's argument that there is no identity outside language leads her to reject the commonly accepted distinction between surface and depth, the Cartesian dualism between body and soul. In the third chapter of *Gender Trouble* she draws from Foucault's book *Discipline and Punish*, in which he challenges "the doctrine of internalization," the theory that subjects are formed by internalizing disciplinary structures. Foucault replaces this with "the model of inscription": as Butler describes it, this is the idea that "[the] law is not literally internalized, but incorporated, with the consequence that bodies are produced which signify that law on and through the body" (GT: 134–5). Because there is no "interior" to gender "the law" cannot be internalized, but is written on the body in what Butler calls "the corporeal stylization of gender, the fantasied [*sic*] and fantastic figuration of the body" (GT: 135). Butler repeatedly refutes the idea of a pre-linguistic inner core or essence by claiming that gender acts are not performed by the subject, but they performatively constitute a subject that is the effect of discourse rather than the cause of it: "*that the gendered body is performative suggests that it has no ontological status apart from the various acts which constitute its reality,*" she writes (GT: 136; my

emphasis). Once again we return to the notion that there is no doer behind the deed, no volitional agent that knowingly "does" its gender, since the gendered body is inseparable from the acts that constitute it. All the same, in the account of parody and drag that follows this description it does at times sound as though there *is* an actor or a "doer" behind the deed, and Butler later admits that in *Gender Trouble* she "waffled" between describing gender in terms of linguistic performativity and characterizing it as straightforward theatre. Her theories are clarified in *Bodies That Matter* where Butler emphasizes the Derridean and Austinian underpinnings of performativity that are as yet only implicit in *Gender Trouble*.

PARODY AND DRAG

"If the inner truth of gender is a fabrication and if a true gender is a fantasy instituted and inscribed on the surface of bodies, then it seems that genders can be neither true nor false, but are only produced as the truth effects of a discourse of primary and stable identity," Butler writes in the third chapter of *Gender Trouble* (GT: 136). In that case, it must be possible to "act" that gender in ways which will draw attention to the constructedness of heterosexual identities that may have a vested interest in presenting themselves as "essential" and "natural," so that it would be true to say that all gender is a form of parody, but that some gender performances are more parodic than others. Indeed, by highlighting the disjunction between the body of the performer and the gender that is being performed, parodic performances such as drag effectively reveal the imitative nature of *all* gender identities. "*In imitating gender, drag implicitly reveals the imitative structure of gender itself—as well as its contingency,*" Butler claims; "part of the pleasure, the giddiness of the performance is in the recognition of a radical contingency in the relation between sex and gender" (GT: 137–8; her emphasis).

Gender is a "corporeal style," an act (or a sequence of acts), a "strategy" which has cultural survival as its end, since those who do not "do" their gender correctly are punished by society (GT: 139–40); it is a repetition, a copy of a copy and, crucially, the gender parody Butler describes does not presuppose the existence of an original, since it is the very notion of an original that is being parodied (GT: 138). Gender performatives that do not try to conceal their genealogy, indeed, that go out of their way to accentuate it, displace heterocentric assumptions by revealing that heterosexual identities are as constructed and "unoriginal" as the imitations of them.

Gender does not happen once and for all when we are born, but is a sequence of repeated acts that harden into the appearance of something that's been there all along. If gender is "a regulated process of repetition" taking place in language, then it will be possible to repeat one's gender differently, as drag artists do (and you might also recall my wardrobe analogy—the ripped clothes and the sequins representing my attempts to "do" my gender in subversive and unexpected ways). As I argued previously, you cannot go out and acquire a whole new gender wardrobe for yourself, since, as Butler puts it, "[t]here is only a taking up of the tools where they lie, where the very 'taking up' is enabled by the tool lying there" (GT: 145). So you have to make do with the "tools," or in my example, the "clothes" that you already have, radically modifying them in ways which will reveal the "unnatural" nature of gender.

There are two problems with this formulation: one is that the *manner* of taking up the tool will be determined as well as enabled by the tool itself—in other words, subversion and agency are conditioned, if not determined, by discourses that cannot be evaded. This leads to the second problem, which is that, if subversion itself is conditioned and constrained by discourse, then how can we tell that it is subversion at all? What is the difference between subversive parody and the sort of "ordinary" parody that Butler claims everyone is unwittingly engaged in anyway? All gender is parodic, but Butler warns that "[p]arody by itself is not subversive," and she poses the important question as to which performances effect the various destabilizations of gender and sex she describes, and where those performances take place (GT: 139). There are some forms of drag that are definitely *not* subversive, but serve only to reinforce existing heterosexual power structures—in *Bodies*, Butler cites Dustin Hoffman's performance in *Tootsie* as an example of what she calls "high het entertainment," and we might also add the more recent film *Mrs. Doubtfire* in which Robin Williams gives a cross-dressed performance as a nanny. Neither of these drag performances are subversive, since they serve to reinforce existing distinctions between "male" and "female," "masculine" and "feminine," "gay" and "straight."

The question as to what constitutes "subversive," as opposed to ordinary everyday gender parody, is left open in the conclusion to *Gender Trouble*, "From Parody to Politics," where Butler asserts that it *is* possible to disrupt what are taken to be the foundations of gender, anticipating *what* such parodic repetitions will achieve, without suggesting exactly *how* this can take place. Butler's claim on the penultimate page of *Gender Trouble* that "[t]he task is not whether to repeat, but how to repeat, or, indeed to repeat and, through a radical proliferation of gender, *to displace* the very gender norms that enable the repetition itself" (GT: 148) presents a similar problem: she has already asserted that to describe identity as an effect is not to imply that identity is "fatally determined" or "fully artificial and arbitrary," and yet at times it sounds as though the subject she describes is in fact trapped within a discourse it has no power to evade or to alter. In which case, "how to repeat" will already be determined in advance, and what looks like agency is merely yet another effect of the law disguised as something different.

All the same, this is certainly not a view Butler expresses, and she seems optimistic about the possibilities of denaturalizing, proliferating and unfixing identities in order to reveal the constructed nature of heterosexuality. A proliferation of identities will reveal the ontological possibilities that are currently restricted by foundationalist models of identity (i.e. those theories which assume that identity is simply *there* and fixed and final). This is not, then, "the death of the subject," or if it is, it is the theoretical death of an old, fixed subject, and the birth of a new, constructed one characterized by subversive possibility and agency. "Construction is not opposed to agency; it is the necessary scene of agency," Butler affirms (GT: 147; see also CF: 15), and this leads her to refute another assumption popular among critics who are hostile to so-called "postmodern" formulations of identity: "[t]he deconstruction of identity is not the deconstruction of politics; rather, it establishes as political the very terms through which identity is articulated" (GT: 148). Identity is intrinsically political, while construction and deconstruction (note that they are not antithetical) are the necessary—in fact the *only*—scenes of agency. Subversion must take place from within existing discourse, since that is all there is.

However, a number of important questions remain. We have already encountered a potential difficulty in the attempt to differentiate between subversive and ordinary parody, and we still have not answered the question as to what or who exactly is "doing" the parodying. Indeed, if there is no pre-discursive subject, is it possible to talk in terms of parody and agency at all, since both might seem to presuppose an "I", a doer behind the deed? How helpful is the notion of parodic gender anyway? Does it really reveal the lack of an original that is being imitated, or does it merely draw attention to the factitiousness of the drag artist? Some of these questions and criticisms are dealt with in the next section.

THE TROUBLE WITH *GENDER TROUBLE*

The fact that Butler's description of gender identity has raised so many questions is a testament to its force, and at least some of *Gender Trouble's* importance lies in the debates it has generated amongst philosophers, feminists, sociologists and theorists of gender, sex and identity, who continue to worry over the meaning of "performativity," whether it enables or forecloses agency, and whether Butler does indeed sound the death knell of the subject. In a written exchange with Butler, which took place in 1991 and was published in 1995 as *Feminist Contentions: A Philosophical Exchange*, the political philosopher Seyla Benhabib asserts that feminist appropriations of Nietzsche, which Benhabib dubs "the 'death of the subject' thesis," can only lead to self-incoherence. If there is no gender identity behind the expressions of gender, asks Benhabib, then how can women change the "expressions" (by which she apparently means "acts") by which they are constituted? "If we are no more than the sum total of the gendered expressions we perform, is there ever any chance to stop the performance for a while, to pull the curtain down, and let it rise only if one can have a say in the production of the play itself?" (Benhabib et al. 1995: 21). Butler claims that the Self is a masquerading performer, writes Benhabib, and

> we are now asked to believe that there is no self behind the mask. Given how fragile and tenuous women's sense of selfhood is in many cases, how much of a hit and miss affair their struggles for autonomy are, this reduction of female agency to "a doing without the doer" at best appears to me to be making a virtue out of necessity. (Benhabib et al. 1995: 22)

The claim that the subject is necessary, if only as a fiction, has been made by other theorists, who are also likely to collapse "performativity" into "performance." Indeed, this elision leads Benhabib to assume that there is a subjective entity lurking behind "the curtain"—a notion that we know Butler refutes. Butler replies to Benhabib's (sometimes literal) misreadings in her essay "For a Careful Reading," which is also included in *Feminist Contentions*, where she corrects the reduction of performativity to theatrical performance.

Two sociologists, John Hood Williams and Wendy Cealy Harrison, also question Butler's assertion that there is no doer behind the deed, although their critique is based on a clearer understanding of performativity than Benhabib's. Although they think it is helpful to deconstruct the idea of the ontological status of gender, they wonder whether a new ontology is founded on the equally foundationalist conception of gender performativity (Hood Williams and Cealy Harrison 1998: 75, 88). Feminist critic Toril Moi similarly objects that Butler has instated "power" as her "god" (1999: 47), and this does indeed raise the question as to whether one essential subject (stable, coherently sexed and gendered) has merely been replaced by another (unstable, performative, contingent). Furthermore, we might consider the ways in which the characterization of power as proliferating and self-subverting draws attention away from its oppressive and violent nature, a point that is made by the feminist theorist Teresa de Lauretis in her book, *Technologies of Gender* (though not in relation to Butler) (1987: 18). We have also seen that Butler's theories of discursively constructed melancholic gender identities might imply that the subject she describes is, like the Lacanian subject, negatively characterized by lack, loss and its enthrallment to a pervasive and unavoidable law.

Hood Williams and Cealy Harrison also question the theoretical wisdom of combining speech act theory and psychoanalytic theory, since they argue that there is nothing citational about psychoanalytic accounts of identity (1998: 90). They find the assertion that there is no "I" behind discourse curious for a theorist who is so interested in psychoanalysis, as psychoanalysis is centrally concerned with the "I" and the process of its constitution (Hood Williams and Cealy Harrison 1998: 83). Furthermore, they describe Butler's reading of Freud as "idiosyncratic" (1998: 85), while the theorist Jay Prosser also questions the accuracy of Butler's analysis of Freud, particularly a mis-citation of a key passage from Freud's *The Ego and the Id*, the theory that the body is a fantasized surface and a projection of the ego. Prosser's book is an "attempt to read individual corporeal experience back into theories of 'the' body" (1998: 7), so for him the question as to whether the body is a phantasmatic surface or a pre-existing depth is crucial. Claiming that formulations of transgendered identity are central to queer studies (and the transgendered individual is indeed important for both Butler and Foucault), Prosser rejects the notion that gender is performative, pointing out that "there are transgendered trajectories, in particular *transsexual* trajectories, that aspire to that which this scheme [i.e. performativity] devalues. Namely, there are transsexuals who seek very pointedly to be nonperformative, to be constative, quite simply, to *be*" (1998: 32).

Butler addresses some of these criticisms in the Preface to the 1999 anniversary edition of *Gender Trouble*, where she acknowledges that the first edition of the book contains certain omissions, in particular, transgender, intersexuality, "[r]acialized sexualities" and taboos against miscegenation. Butler also accepts that her explanation of performativity is insufficient, and she admits that sometimes she does not distinguish between linguistic and theatrical performativity which she now regards as related (GTII: xxvi, xxv).

Butler's next book, *Bodies That Matter*, continues in similar interrogative mode, answering some of the questions arising from *Gender Trouble* and posing new and equally "troubling" ones about "the matter" of the body, its signification and its "citation" in discourse.

PERFORMATIVE BODIES

In one section of *Judith Butler*, we encounter Butler's glancing reference to the performativity of the phallus and look in detail at her account of a discursively constructed body which cannot be separated from the linguistic acts that name it and constitute it. Here we will turn to a statement Butler makes in the Introduction to *Bodies*, that, when it comes to the matter of bodies, the *constative claim is always to some degree performative* (BTM: 11). Remember the interpellative call of the policeman who hails the man in the street, or the doctor or nurse who exclaims "It's a girl!" when the image of a foetus is seen on a scan. Earlier, I placed Butler's formulations of performative identities in the context of J. L. Austin's linguistic theories. In *Bodies That Matter* Butler once again draws from these lectures on linguistics, *How To Do Things With Words*. Austin distinguishes between two types of utterances, those that describe or report on something, and those that, in saying, actually perform what is being said. An example of the first, which Austin calls *constative utterances*, might be the statement, "It's a sunny day," or "I went shopping" (Austin also calls these *perlocutionary acts*); by saying "I went shopping," I am not doing it, I am merely reporting an occurrence. On the other hand, if I am a heterosexual man standing in front of a registrar in a Register Office and I utter the words "I do" in answer to the question, "Do you take this woman to be your wife?", then I am actually performing the action by making the utterance: statements like these are called *performative utterances* or *illocutionary acts*. "To name the ship *is* to say (in the appropriate circumstances) the words 'I name &c.' When I say, before the registrar or altar &c., 'I do', I am not reporting on a marriage, I am indulging in it" (Austin 1955: 6).

To claim, as Butler does, that sex is always ("to some degree") performative is to claim that bodies are never merely described, they

are always constituted in the act of description. When the doctor or nurse declares "It's a girl/boy!", they are not simply reporting on what they see (this would be a constative utterance), they are actually assigning a sex and a gender to a body that can have no existence outside discourse. In other words, the statement "It's a girl/boy!" is performative. Butler returns to the birth/ultrasound scene in the final chapter to *Bodies*, "Critically Queer," where, as before, she argues that discourse precedes and constitutes the "I," i.e. the subject:

> To the extent that the naming of the "girl" is transitive, that is, initiates the process by which a certain "girling" is compelled, the term or, rather, its symbolic power, governs the formation of a corporeally enacted femininity that never fully approximates the norm. This is a "girl", however, who is compelled to "cite" the norm in order to qualify and remain a viable subject. Femininity is thus not the product of a choice, but the forcible citation of a norm, one whose complex historicity is indissociable from relations of discipline, regulation, punishment. (BTM: 232)

"It's a girl!" is not a statement of fact but an interpellation that initiates the process of "girling," a process based on perceived and *imposed* differences between men and women, differences that are far from "natural." To demonstrate the performative operations of interpellation, Butler cites a cartoon strip in which an infant is assigned its place in the sex-gender system with the exclamation "It's a lesbian!" "Far from an essentialist joke, the queer appropriation of the performative mimes and exposes both the binding power of the heterosexualizing law *and its expropriability*," writes Butler (BTM: 232; her emphasis). We will return to expropriability and citation shortly; here the point to note is that, since sexual and gendered differences are performatively installed by and in discourse, it would be possible to designate or confer identity on the basis of an alternative set of discursively constituted attributes. Clearly, to announce that an infant is a lesbian is not a neutral act of description but a performative statement that interpellates the infant as such. "It's a girl!" functions in exactly the same way: it is a performative utterence that henceforth compels the "girl" to cite both sexual and gendered norms in order to qualify for subjecthood within the heterosexual matrix that "hails" her.

"It is in terms of a norm that compels a certain 'citation' in order for a viable subject to be produced that the notion of gender performativity calls to be rethought," Butler claims (BTM: 232). The term "citation," highlighted in Butler's statement by its quotation marks, has been used throughout *Bodies* in a specifically Derridean sense that both differentiates it from, and aligns it with, performativity. The citation of sex and gender norms will be dealt with in the next section.

CITATIONAL SIGNS

In the previous section I quoted Butler's assertion that femininity is not a choice but the forcible citation of a norm. What exactly does it mean to cite sex or gender, and how does Butler use this term in *Bodies That Matter*? The *Oxford English Dictionary* definition of the verb "to cite" reveals interesting etymological links with interpellation (although these are not connections Butler acknowledges). The word comes from the Latin *citare*, to set in motion or to call, and its meanings are listed as: 1) to summon officially to appear in a court of law; 2) to summon or arouse; 3) to quote; 4) to adduce proof; and 5) to call to mind, mention, refer to. The third, fourth and fifth dictionary definitions are closest to Butler's use of the term, but "summoning" could also indicate the theoretical links between citation and interpellation.

Butler uses "citation" in a specifically Derridean sense to describe the ways in which ontological norms are deployed in discourse,

sometimes forcibly and sometimes not. Derrida's essay "Signature Event Context" is a response to Austin's claim that performative utterances are only "successful" if they remain within the constraints of context and authorial intention. According to Austin, in order for a statement to have performative force (in other words, in order for it to enact what it names), it must 1) be uttered by the person designated to do so in an appropriate context; 2) adhere to certain conventions; and 3) take the intention(s) of the utterer into account. For example, if a brain surgeon stands at a church altar facing two people of the same sex and announces "I pronounce you man and wife," the statement will have no performative force in the Austinian sense, since we can assume that the brain surgeon is not ordained and therefore is not the person authorized to marry the pair. Similarly, a priest who whispers "I pronounce you man and wife" to his two teddy bears late at night before going to sleep is not conducting a marriage ceremony, even though he is authorized to do so, but is playing a game or having a fantasy. Clearly, *his* statement will have as little force as the unordained brain surgeon's, since 1) the context is inappropriate; 2) as with same-sex couples, in the UK and the US there is currently no law or convention regulating or permitting the marriage of toys; and 3) it is presumably not the priest's intention to marry his teddy bears to one another.

Austin spends some time attempting to distinguish felicitous from infelicitous performatives. What is important at this stage is that Derrida seizes on the "weakness" Austin discerns in the linguistic sign: after all, Austin would not attempt to differentiate between felicitous and infelicitous performatives if he did not know that statements are liable to be taken out of context and used in ways that their original utterers did not intend. Derrida asserts that what Austin regards as a pitfall or a weakness is in fact a feature of *all* linguistic signs that are vulnerable to appropriation, reiteration and, to return to the subject of this section, *re-citation*. This is what Derrida calls "the essential iterability of [a] sign" which cannot be contained or enclosed by any context, convention or authorial intention (1972: 93). Rather, Derrida asserts that signs can be transplanted into unforeseen contexts and cited in unexpected ways, an appropriation and relocation that he calls citational grafting: all signs may be placed between quotation marks ("sex," "race"), cited, grafted, and reiterated in ways that do not conform to their speaker's or writer's original intentions and this means that, as Derrida puts it, the possibility of failure is intrinsic and necessary to the sign, indeed it is *constitutive* of the sign (1972: 97, 101–3).

These ideas will be familiar from *Gender Trouble* where, as I noted, Derrida is an implicit rather than a stated presence, and where failure, citation and re-citation are crucial to Butler's discussions of subversive gender performatives. In *Bodies*, Butler sees potential for subversion in Derrida's characterizations of the citational sign, and she now charts a move in her own theory from performativity to citationality, since rethinking performativity through citationality is deemed useful for radical democratic theory (BTM: 191; see also 14). Specifically, Butler asserts that Derrida's citationality will be useful as a queer strategy of converting the abjection and exclusion of non-sanctioned sexed and gendered identities into political agency.

In the final chapter of *Bodies*, Butler suggests that what she has called "the contentious practices of 'queerness'" exemplify the political enactment of performativity as citationality (BTM: 21). Butler is referring to subversive practices whereby gender performatives are "cited," grafted onto other contexts, thereby revealing the citationality and the intrinsic— but necessary and *useful*—failure of all gender performatives. Butler gave examples of these practices in *Gender Trouble*, where she focused on parody and drag as strategies of subversion

and agency. In *Bodies* she returns to drag as an example of what she calls "queer trouble," and she finds other occasions for "Nietzschean hopefulness" in the iterability and citationality of the sign. We will return to these ways of "making trouble" in the next section but one.

THE MATTER OF RACE

Can race, like sex, sexuality and gender be cited and re-cited in ways that reveal the vulnerability of the terms of the law to appropriation and subversion? Is race an interpellated performance, and is a racial identity something that is "assumed" rather than something one simply "is"? Would it be possible once again to alter the terms of de Beauvoir's statement and affirm that "one is not born but rather one becomes black/white"? Or could the word "race" be substituted for "sex" in Butler's description of *Bodies That Matter* as "a poststructuralist rewriting of discursive performativity as it operates in the materialization of sex"? (BTM: 12).

Discussions of race were largely absent from *Gender Trouble*, and in *Bodies* Butler is careful to make the "addition" of considerations of racial identity to her analyses of identity formation (BTM: 18). Accepting that normative heterosexuality is not the only regulatory regime operating in the production of the body, Butler asks what other "regimes of regulatory production contour the materiality of bodies" (BTM: 17), and she asserts that "[t]he symbolic—that register of regulatory ideality—is also and always a racial industry, indeed, [it is] the reiterated practice of *racializing* interpellations" (BTM: 18; original emphasis). Butler rejects models of power that see racial differences as subordinate to sexual difference, and she argues that both racial and heterosexual imperatives are at work in reproductive and sexing practices.

Interpellations do not just "call us" into sex, sexuality and gender, but they are also "racializing" imperatives that institute racial difference as a condition of subjecthood. Sexual and racial differences are not autonomous or discrete axes of power (BTM: 116–17) and Butler repeatedly emphasizes that sex and gender are in no way prior to race. "What appear within such an enumerative framework as separable categories are, rather, the conditions of articulation *for* each other," she states; "How is race lived in the modality of sexuality? How is gender lived in the modality of race? How do colonial and neo-colonial nation-states rehearse gender relations in the consolidation of state power?" (BTM: 117).

These are the questions Butler sets herself, but in spite of this the "matter" of race is not convincingly integrated into her discussions (which is why I am dealing with the question in a separate, penultimate section here). Although she analyzes how sex, sexuality and gender are interpellated, assumed and performatively constituted, there are no parallel discussions of performative race or *how* exactly race is interpellated by what Butler calls "racializing norms." Moreover, some critics might feel that it is important to preserve the distinction between the "raced" body and the gendered/sexed/sexualized one. Remember the "It's a lesbian!" joke: there the humor is derived from the fact that sexuality is not visible at birth, whereas by contrast race very often (although certainly not always) is. The African-American theorist Henry Louis Gates Jr. effectively crystallizes this issue when he makes the following statement in his essay "The Master's Pieces":

> It's important to remember that "race" is *only* a sociopolitical category, nothing more. At the same time—in terms of its practical performative force—that doesn't help me when I'm trying to get a taxi on the corner of 125th and Lenox Avenue. ("Please sir, it's only a metaphor.") (1992: 37–8)

Gates' wry observation shows that the visibly "raced" body (black or white) cannot be theorized in exactly the same way as the sexualized, sexed or gendered body, although this is not to dispute Butler's assertion that all these vectors of power operate simultaneously and through one another.

It may be significant that Butler's most extended discussion of race centers on a novella by Nella Larsen, *Passing*, in which one of the protagonists attempts to "pass" for white. Here the body is *not* visibly black, and Clare (the woman who is "passing" for white) is only "outed" (Butler's term, BTM: 170) when her white husband encounters her among a group of black people. Butler uses *Passing* to confirm her point that race and sexuality are imbricated and implicated, since she discerns an overlapping of the "mute homosexuality" between the two women protagonists and Clare's "muted" blackness, which, like homosexual desire, attempts to conceal itself (BTM: 175). Moreover, just as heterosexuality requires homosexuality in order to constitute its coherence, so "whiteness" requires "blackness" to offset itself and confirm its racial boundaries. Heterosexuality and whiteness are simultaneously destabilized in *Passing*, as queering—i.e. the desire between the two women—upsets and exposes both racial and sexual passing (BTM: 177). (For a discussion of race and melancholia, see Butler's interview "On Speech, Race and Melancholia," 1999). Butler's analysis of Larsen's novella similarly "queers" psychoanalytic theory by exposing its assumption of the primacy of sexuality and whiteness. In fact, Butler sees *Passing* as a challenge to psychoanalytic theory, "a theorization of desire, displacement, and jealous rage that has significant implications for rewriting psychoanalytic theory in ways that explicitly come to terms with race" (BTM: 182).

The other analysis of race in *Bodies* occurs in Butler's discussion of Jennie Livingston's *Paris Is Burning* (BTM: 121–40), a film about drag balls in Harlem that are attended by/ performed by African-American or Latino/Latina "men." Again, Butler sees the film as exemplifying her assertion that sexual difference does not precede race or class in the constitution of the subject, so that the symbolic is also a racializing set of norms and the subject is produced by racially informed conceptions of "sex" (BTM: 130). Butler's analyses of *Paris Is Burning* and *Passing* lead her to conclude that the theoretical priority of homosexuality and gender must give way to a more complex mapping of power that places both terms in their specific racial and political contexts (BTM: 240).

Butler herself has been scrupulous in *not* suggesting that any one term takes priority over another, even though the organization of *Bodies* might suggest otherwise—if not the priority of sex over race, at least the separability of the terms. Since race is largely dealt with in discrete chapters (and, for that matter, these chapters are "literary" rather than "theoretical" in their focus), as I noted before, "the matter," so to speak, remains somewhat at a distance from Butler's other theoretical discussions. We may be left with questions concerning the relationship between race and the lesbian phallus, or how Butler's description of "girling" might be applied to race, since neither the lesbian phallus nor interpellation/performativity are specifically discussed in the context of race. All the same, to talk in terms of "racializing norms" is indeed to suggest that race, like gender, sex and sexuality, is constructed rather than natural, assumed in response to the interpellative "call" of discourse and the law, even though Butler is somewhat unspecific as to how exactly this "call to race" takes place.

QUEER TROUBLE

In spite of the tragic outcome of both texts, Butler highlights the moments of promising instability in *Paris Is Burning* and *Passing*. In Butler's analysis, *Paris Is Burning* represents the resignification of normative heterosexual kinship (an issue to which Butler will return in

Antigone's Claim), while *Passing* similarly reveals how hegemonic racial and sexual norms may be destabilized by subjects who do not fit neatly in the categories of white heterosexuality. Such norms are far from monolithic or stable, but, as we saw in a previous section, they may be reiterated and cited in ways that undermine heterosexual hegemony. (For an alternative reading of *Paris Is Burning*, see bell hooks' essay, "Is Paris Burning?" [1996].)

However, if all linguistic signs are citational, citationality in and of itself is not a subversive practice, and it follows that some signs will continue to work in the service of oppressive heterosexuality norms (and this is something we already know from Butler's description of femininity as "a *forcible* citation of the norm" [BTM: 232; my emphasis]). Clearly, there are "good" (subversive) citations and "bad" (forced) citations, and the task will be to distinguish between them—which is not always easy as we shall see. Another problem is that discourse and the law operate by concealing their citationality and genealogy, presenting themselves as timeless and singular, while performativity similarly "conceals or dissimulates the conventions of which it is a repetition" (BTM: 12). Again, it will be necessary to distinguish between those performatives which consolidate the heterosexual norm and those that work to reveal its contingency, instability and citationality.

In a previous example, I described an unordained brain surgeon who conducts a marriage ceremony that, in Austinian terms, will have no performative (or indeed legal) force because it falls outside recognized and sanctioned conventions. Butler, on the other hand, might assert that the utterance of "I pronounce you, etc." by someone who is not authorized to do so is a subversive political strategy, since it is a recitation of an unstable heterosexual norm that is always vulnerable to appropriation. There are alternative, equally subversive ways of citing heterosexual signs that are *all* vulnerable to appropriation: the lesbian phallus is one such "recitation," and Butler gives other examples, some of which are theatrical. As in *Gender Trouble*, parody and drag are modes of queer performance that subversively "allegorize" (to use Butler's term) heterosexual melancholy, thereby revealing the allegorical nature of *all* sexual identities. Although Butler is careful to distinguish performance from performativity in *Bodies*, she also asserts that theatre provides crucial opportunities for queer politics. "[A]n important set of histories might be told in which the increasing politicization *of* theatricality for queers is at stake," she writes. "Such a history might include traditions of cross-dressing, drag balls, street walking, butch-femme spectacles . . . kiss-ins by Queer Nation; drag performance benefits for AIDS" (BTM: 233).

What Butler calls "the increasing theatricalization of political rage in response to the killing inattention of public policy-makers on the issue of AIDS" is epitomized by the appropriation of the term "queer," an interpellative performative that has been converted from an insult into a linguistic sign of affirmation and resistance (BTM: 233). And yet, although she continues to find subversive potential in the contingency and resignifiability of the sign, Butler is also aware that citation is not necessarily subversive and she points out that certain "denaturalizations" of the heterosexual norm actually enforce heterosexual hegemony (BTM: 231). Such parodies may certainly be "domesticated" so that they lose their subversive potential and function merely as what Butler calls "high het entertainment," and Butler cites Julie Andrews in *Victor*, *Victoria*, Dustin Hoffmann in *Tootsie* or Jack Lemmon in *Some Like It Hot* as examples of drag performances that have been produced by the heterosexual entertainment industry for itself (further examples might include Julian Clarry and Eddie Izzard) (BTM: 126). Such performances only confirm the boundaries between "straight" and "not straight" identities, providing what Butler calls "a ritualistic release

for a heterosexual economy that must constantly police its own boundaries against the invasion of queerness" (BTM: 126).

As before, it is difficult to disentangle subversive citations and performatives from the power structures they oppose, since subversion is necessarily and inevitably implicated in discourse and the law. However, this constitutes the promise as well as the problematic of performativity, and Butler argues that making use of existing "resources" for subversive ends will require vigilance and hard work. "How will we know the difference between the power we promote and the power we oppose?", she writes. The problem, of course, is that one *can't* know this in advance, so that subversive recitation will always involve a certain amount of risk. It is a risk that Butler well understands, as she once again submits her work to the scrutiny of readers who are likely to interpret and deploy her ideas in unforeseen ways. The effects of one's words are incalculable, since performatives and their significations do not begin or end (BTM: 241). Perhaps it will be appropriate to end with a "citation" of Butler's concluding acknowledgment of the vulnerability of her own terms to appropriation and redeployment:

> it is one of the ambivalent implications of the decentering of the subject to have one's writing be the site of a necessary and inevitable expropriation. But this yielding of ownership over what one writes has an important set of political corollaries, for the taking up, reforming, deforming of one's words does open up a difficult future terrain of community, one in which the hope of ever fully recognizing oneself in the terms by which one signifies is sure to be disappointed. This not owning of one's words is there from the start, however, since speaking is always in some ways the speaking of a stranger through and as oneself, the melancholic reiteration of a language that one never chose, that one does not find as an instrument to be used, but that one is, as it were, used by, expropriated in, as the unstable and continuing condition of the "one"

and the "we", the ambivalent condition of the power that binds. (BTM: 241–2)

This statement could be interpreted as a gesture of humility or a disclaimer of responsibility on Butler's part, and there may be contexts in which it is problematic to claim that one does not use language but is, rather, used by it. ("I didn't write those words! They wrote me.") Butler returns to the issues of speech acts, linguistic responsibility and the "reach of . . . signifiability" (BTM: 241) when she analyzes hate speech, "obscenity" and censorship in her next book, *Excitable Speech*.

REFERENCES

Austin, J. L. [1955] *How to Do Things With Words*, Cambridge, Mass.: Harvard University Press, 1962.

Benhabib, Seyla, Judith Butler, Drucilla Cornell and Nancy Fraser (1995) *Feminist Contentions: A Philosophical Exchange*, London: Routledge.

Butler, Judith (1990; Anniversary edition 1999) *Gender Trouble: Feminism and the Subversion of Identity*, New York: Routledge.

—— (1992) "Contingent Foundations: Feminism and the Question of Postmodernism," in Judith Butler and Joan Scott (eds.) *Feminists Theorize the Political*, London: Routledge, pp. 3–21.

—— (1993) *Bodies That Matter: On the Discursive Limits of "Sex,"* New York: Routledge.

—— (1994) "Gender as Performance: An Interview with Judith Butler," *Radical Philosophy: A Journal of Socialist and Feminist Philosophy* 67 (Summer): 32–9.

—— (1997) *Excitable Speech: A Politics of the Performative*, New York: Routledge.

—— (1999) "On Speech, Race and Melancholia: An Interview with Judith Butler," *Theory, Culture and Society* 16 (2): 163–74.

—— (2000) *Antigone's Claim: Kinship Between Life and Death*, New York: Columbia University Press.

de Beauvoir, Simone [1949] *The Second Sex (La Deuxième Sex)*, trans. H. M. Parshley, London: Everyman, 1993.

de Lauretis, Teresa (1987) *Technologies of Gender: Essays on Film, Theory and Fiction*, Bloomington: Indiana University Press.

Derrida, Jacques [1972] "Signature Event Context" ("Signature Evénement Contexte"), in Peggy Kamuf (ed.) *A Derrida Reader: Between the Blinds*, New York: Columbia University Press, 1999, pp. 80–111.

Foucault, Michel [1975] *Discipline and Punish: The Birth of the Prison (Surveiller et Punir: Naissance de la Prison)*, trans. Alan Sheridan, London: Penguin, 1977.

Freud, Sigmund [1923] *The Ego and the Id (Das Ich und das Es)*, The Pelican Freud Library Vol. 11, London: Penguin, 1991, pp. 339–407.

Gates, Henry Louis Jr. (1992) "The Master's Pieces: On Canon-Formation and the African-American Tradition," in H. L. Gates (ed.) *Loose Canons: Notes on the Culture Wars*, Oxford: Oxford University Press, pp. 17–42.

Hood Williams, John and Wendy Cealy Harrison (1998) "Trouble With Gender," *The Sociological Review* 46 (1): 73–94.

hooks, bell (1996) "Is Paris Burning?" in bell hooks *Reel to Real: Race, Sex, and Class at the Movies*, London: Routledge, pp. 214–26.

Larsen, Nella [1928, 1929] *Quicksand and Passing*, Deborah E. MacDowell (ed.), New Brunswick, New Jersey: Rutgers University Press, 1986.

Moi, Toril (1999) *What Is a Woman? and Other Essays*, Oxford: Oxford University Press.

Nietzsche, Friedrich [1887] *On the Genealogy of Morals (Zur Genealogie der Moral)*, trans. Douglas Smith, Oxford: Oxford University Press, 1996.

Prosser, Jay (1998) *Second Skins: The Body Narratives of Transsexuality*, New York: Columbia University Press.

Discussion Questions

1. What, according to Salih's discussion of Judith Butler's work, is gender? What does it mean to say that gender is performative? How is performativity different than performance?

2. What are some of the questions that have been raised about Butler's conception of gender performativity?

3. Do you think that performativity is a useful way of thinking about other social identities, such as race, ethnicity, and class? Why or why not?

4. How well does Weeks' notion of sexual identities as necessary fictions complement Butler's concept of sex and gender as performative?

5. After reading this chapter, what do you believe is possible in regard to subverting hegemonic norms of gender, sex, and sexual identity?

4

"Quare" Studies, or (Almost) Everything I Know About Queer Studies I Learned From My Grandmother [Part I]

I love queer. Queer is a homosexual of either sex. It's more convenient than saying "gays" which has to be qualified, or "lesbians and gay men." It's an extremely useful polemic term because it is who we say we are, which is, "Fuck You."

—Spike Pittsberg
(quoted in C. Smith 280)

I use queer to describe my particular brand of lesbian feminism, which has much to do with the radical feminism I was involved with in the early '80s. I also use it externally to describe a political inclusivity—a new move toward a celebration of difference across sexualities, across genders, across sexual preference and across object choice. The two link.

—Linda Semple
(quoted in C. Smith 280)

I'm more inclined to use the words "black lesbian," because when I hear the word queer I think of white, gay men.

—Isling Mack-Nataf
(quoted in C. Smith 280)

SOURCE: This chapter was originally published as a part of "Quare" Studies, or (Almost) Everything I Know About Queer Studies I Learned From My Grandmother, in *Text and Performance Quarterly* (vol. 21, no. 1, pp. 1-25). Copyright © 2001 National Communication Association. Reprinted by permission.

69

I define myself as gay mostly. I will not use queer because it is not part of my vernacular—but I have nothing against its use. The same debates around naming occur in the "black community." Naming is powerful. Black people and gay people constantly renaming ourselves is a way to shift power from whites and hets respectively.

—Inge Blackman
(quoted in C. Smith 280)

Personally speaking, I do not consider myself a "queer" activist or, for that matter, a "queer" anything. This is not because I do not consider myself an activist; in fact, I hold my political work to be one of my most important contributions to all of my communities. But like other lesbian, gay, bisexual, and transgendered activists of color, I find the label "queer" fraught with unspoken assumptions which inhibit the radical political potential of this category.

—Cathy Cohen ("Punks" 451)

"QUARE" ETYMOLOGY (WITH APOLOGIES TO ALICE WALKER)

Quare (Kwâr), *n.* 1. meaning *queer;* also, opp. of *straight;* odd or slightly off kilter; from the African American vernacular for queer; sometimes homophobic in usage, but always denotes excess incapable of being contained within conventional categories of *being;* curiously equivalent to the Anglo-Irish (and sometimes "Black" Irish) variant of queer, as in Brendan Behan's famous play, *The Quare Fellow.*

—*adj.* 2. a lesbian, gay, bisexual, or transgendered person of color who loves other men or women, sexually or nonsexually, and appreciates black culture and community.

—*n.* 3. one who *thinks* and *feels* and *acts* (and, sometimes, "acts up"); committed to struggle against all forms of oppression—racial, sexual, gender, class, religious, etc.

—*n.* 4. one for whom sexual and gender identities always already intersect with racial subjectivity.

5. quare is to queer as "reading" is to "throwing shade."[1]

I AM going out on a limb. This is a precarious position, but the stakes are high enough

to warrant risky business. The business to which I refer is reconceptualizing the still incubating discipline called queer studies. Now, what's in a name? This is an important question when, as James Baldwin proclaims in the titles of two of his works, I have "no name in the street" or, worse still, "nobody *knows* my name" (emphasis added). I used to answer to "queer," but when I was hailed by that naming, interpellated in that moment, I felt as if I was being called "out of my name." I needed something with more "soul," more "bang," something closer to "home." It is my name after all!

Then I remembered how "queer" is used in my family. My grandmother, for example, used it often when I was a child and still uses it today. When she says the word, she does so in a thick, black, southern dialect: "That sho'll is a quare chile." Her use of "queer" is almost always nuanced. Still, one might wonder, what, if anything, could a poor, black, eighty-something, southern, homophobic woman teach her educated, middle-class, thirty-something, gay grandson about queer studies? Everything. Or *almost* everything. On the one hand, my grandmother uses "quare" to denote something or someone who is odd, irregular, or slightly off kilter—definitions in keeping with traditional understandings and uses of "queer." On the other hand, she also deploys "quare" to connote something excessive— something that might philosophically translate into an excess of discursive and epistemological meanings grounded in African American cultural rituals and lived experience. Her knowing or not knowing vis-à-vis "quare" is predicated on her own "multiple and complex social, historical, and cultural positionality" (Henderson 147). It is this culture-specific positionality that I find absent from the dominant and more conventional usage of "queer," particularly in its most recent theoretical reappropriation in the academy.

I knew there was something to "quare," that its implications reached far beyond my grandmother's front porch. Little did I know, however, that its use extended across the Atlantic. Then, I found "quare" in Ireland.[2] In *Quare Joyce*, Joseph Valente writes,

> I have elected to use the Anglo-Irish epithet *quare* in the title as a kind of transnational/ transidiomatic pun. *Quare*, meaning odd or strange, as in Brendan Behan's famous play, *The Quare Fellow*, has lately been appropriated as a distinctively Irish variant of *queer*, as in the recent prose collection *Quare Fellas*, whose editor, Brian Finnegan, reinterprets Behan's own usage of the term as having "covertly alluded to his own sexuality." (4, emphasis in original)

Valente's appropriation of the Irish epithet "quare" to "queerly" read James Joyce establishes a connection between race and ethnicity in relation to queer identity. Indeed, Valente's "quare" reading of Joyce, when conjoined with my grandmother's "quare" reading of those who are slightly off kilter, provides a strategy for reading racial and ethnic sexuality. Where the two uses of "quare" diverge is in their deployment. Valente deploys quare to devise a queer literary exegesis of Joyce. Rather than drawing on "quare" as a *literary* mode of reading/theorizing, however, I draw

upon the *vernacular* roots implicit in my grandmother's use of the word to devise a strategy for theorizing racialized sexuality.

Because much of queer theory critically interrogates notions of selfhood, agency, and experience, it is often unable to accommodate the issues faced by gays and lesbians of color who come from "raced" communities. Gloria Anzaldúa explicitly addresses this limitation when she warns that "queer is used as a false unifying umbrella which all 'queers' of all races, ethnicities and classes are shored under" (250). While acknowledging that "at times we need this umbrella to solidify our ranks against outsiders," Anzaldúa nevertheless urges that "even when we seek shelter under it ["queer"], we must not forget that it homogenizes, erases our differences" (250).

"Quare," on the other hand, not only speaks across identities, it *articulates* identities as well. "Quare" offers a way to critique stable notions of identity and, at the same time, to locate racialized and class knowledges. My project is one of recapitulation and recuperation. I want to maintain the inclusivity and playful spirit of "queer" that animates much of queer theory, but I also want to jettison its homogenizing tendencies. As a disciplinary expansion, then, I wish to "quare" "queer" such that ways of knowing are viewed both as discursively mediated and as historically situated and materially conditioned. This reconceptualization foregrounds the ways in which lesbians, bisexuals, gays, and transgendered people of color come to sexual and racial knowledge. Moreover, quare studies acknowledges the different "standpoints" found among lesbian, bisexual, gay, and transgendered people of color— differences that are also conditioned by class and gender.[3]

Quare studies is a theory of and for gays and lesbians of color. Thus, I acknowledge that in my attempt to advance quare studies, I run the risk of advancing another version of

identity politics. Despite this, I find it necessary to traverse this political mine field in
order to illuminate the ways in which some
strands of queer theory fail to incorporate
racialized sexuality. The theory that I advance
is a "theory in the flesh" (Moraga and
Anzaldúa 23). Theories in the flesh emphasize
the diversity within and among gays, bisexuals, lesbians, and transgendered people of
color while simultaneously accounting for
how racism and classism affect how we experience and theorize the world. Theories in the
flesh also conjoin theory and practice through
an embodied politics of resistance. This politics of resistance is manifest in vernacular
traditions such as performance, folklore, literature, and verbal art.

This essay offers an extended meditation on
and intervention in queer theory and practice.
I begin by mapping out a general history of
queer theory's deployment in contemporary
academic discourse, focusing on the lack of
discourse on race and class within the queer
theoretical paradigm. Following this, I offer an
analysis of one queer theorist's (mis)reading of
two black gay performances. Next, I propose
an intervention in queer theory by outlining
the components of quare theory, a theory that
incorporates race and class as categories of
analysis in the study of sexuality.

"RACE TROUBLE": QUEER STUDIES OR THE STUDY OF WHITE QUEERS

At a moment when queer studies has gained
momentum in the academy and forged a space
as a legitimate disciplinary subject, much of
the scholarship produced in its name elides
issues of race and class. While the epigraphs
that open this essay suggest that the label
"queer" sometimes speaks across (homo)sexu-
alities, they also suggest that the term is not
necessarily embraced by gays, bisexuals, lesbians, and transgendered people of color.
Indeed, the statements of Mack-Nataf,

Blackman, and Cohen reflect a general suspicion that the label often displaces and rarely
addresses their concerns.[4]

Some queer theorists have argued that their
use of "queer" is more than just a reappropriation of an offensive term. Cherry Smith, for
example, maintains that the term entails a
"radical questioning of social and cultural
norms, notions of gender, reproductive sexuality and the family" (280). Others underscore
the playfulness and inclusivity of the term,
arguing that it opens up rather than fixes identities. According to Eve Sedgwick, "What it
takes—all it takes—to make the description
'queer' a true one is the impulsion to use it in
the first person" (9). Indeed, Sedgwick suggests,
it may refer to

> pushy femmes, radical faeries, fantasists,
> drags, clones, leatherfolk, ladies in tuxedos,
> feminist women or feminist men, masturba-
> tors, bulldaggers, divas, Snap! queens, butch
> bottoms, storytellers, transsexuals, aunties,
> wannabes, lesbian-identified men or les-
> bians who sleep with men, or . . . people
> able to relish, learn from, or identify with
> such. (8)

For Sedgwick, then, it would appear that
"queer" is a catchall term not bound to any
particular identity, a notion that moves us
away from binaries such as homosexual/
heterosexual and gay/lesbian. Michael Warner
offers an even more politicized and polemical
view:

> The preference for "queer" represents,
> among other things, an aggressive impulse
> of generalization; it rejects a minoritizing
> logic of toleration or simple political
> interest-representation in favor of a more
> thorough resistance to regimes of the nor-
> mal. For academics, being interested in
> Queer theory is a way to mess up the desex-
> ualized spaces of the academy, exude some
> rut, reimagine the public from and for
> which academic intellectuals write, dress,
> and perform. (xxvi)

The foregoing theorists identify "queer" as a site of indeterminate possibility, a site where sexual practice does not necessarily determine one's status as queer. Indeed, Lauren Berlant and Michael Warner argue that queer is "more a matter of aspiration than it is the expression of an identity or a history" (344). Accordingly, straight-identified critic Calvin Thomas appropriates Judith Butler's notion of "critical queerness" to suggest that "just as there is more than one way to be 'critical,' there may be more than one (or two or three) to be 'queer'" (83).

Some critics have applied Butler's theory of gender to identity formation more generally. Butler calls into question the notion of the "self" as distinct from discursive cultural fields. That is, like gender, there is no independent or pure "self" or agent that stands outside socially and culturally mediated discursive systems. Any move toward identification, then, is, in her view, to be hoodwinked into believing that identities are discourse free and capable of existing outside the systems those identity formations seek to critique. Even when identity is contextualized and qualified, Butler still insists that theories of identity "invariably close with an embarrassed 'etc.'" (*Gender* 143). Butler's emphasis on gender and sex as "performative" would seem to undergird a progressive, forward-facing theory of sexuality. In fact, some theorists have made the theoretical leap from the gender performative to the racial performative, thereby demonstrating the potential of her theory for understanding the ontology of race.[5]

But to riff off of the now popular phrase "gender trouble," *there is some race trouble here with queer theory*. More particularly, in its "race for theory" (Christian), queer theory has often failed to address the material realities of gays and lesbians of color. As black British activist Helen (Charles) asks,

> What happens to the definition of "queer" when you're washing up or having a wank?

> When you're aware of misplacement or displacement in your colour, gender, identity? Do they get subsumed . . . into a homogeneous category, where class and other things that make up a cultural identity are ignored? (101–102)

What, for example, are the ethical and material implications of queer theory if its project is to dismantle all notions of identity and agency? The deconstructive turn in queer theory highlights the ways in which ideology functions to oppress and to proscribe ways of knowing, but what is the utility of queer theory on the front lines, in the trenches, on the street, or any place where the racialized and sexualized body is beaten, starved, fired, cursed—indeed, where the body is the site of trauma?[6]

Beyond queer theory's failure to focus on materiality, it also has failed to acknowledge consistently and critically the intellectual, aesthetic, and political contributions of nonwhite and non–middle-class gays, bisexuals, lesbians, and transgendered people in the struggle against homophobia and oppression. Moreover, even when white queer theorists acknowledge these contributions, rarely do they self-consciously and overtly reflect on the ways in which their whiteness informs their critical queer position, and this is occurring at a time when naming one's positionality has become almost standard protocol in other areas of scholarship. Although there are exceptions, most often white queer theorists fail to acknowledge and address racial privilege.[7]

Because transgendered people, lesbians, gays, and bisexuals of color often ground their theorizing in a politics of identity, they frequently fall prey to accusations of "essentialism" or "anti-intellectualism." Galvanizing around identity, however, is not always an unintentional "essentialist" move. Many times, it is an intentional strategic choice.[8] Cathy Cohen, for example, suggests that "queer theorizing which calls for the elimination of fixed categories seems to ignore the ways in which some traditional social identities and communal ties can, in fact, be important to one's survival" ("Punks" 450). The "communal ties" to which Cohen refers are those which exist in communities of color across boundaries of sexuality. For example, my grandmother, who is homophobic, nonetheless must be included in the struggle against oppression in spite of her bigotry. While her homophobia must be critiqued, her feminist and race struggles over the course of her life have enabled me and others in my family to enact strategies of resistance against a number of oppressions, including homophobia. Some queer activist groups, however, have argued fervently for the disavowal of any alliance with heterosexuals, a disavowal that those of us who belong to communities of color cannot necessarily afford to make.[9] Therefore, while offering a progressive and sometimes transgressive politics of sexuality, the seams of queer theory become exposed when that theory is applied to identities around which sexuality may pivot, such as race and class.

As a counter to this myopia and in an attempt to close the gap between theory and practice, self and Other, Audre Lorde proclaims:

> Without community there is no liberation, only the most vulnerable and temporary armistice between an individual and her oppression. But community must not mean a shedding of our differences, nor the pathetic pretense that these differences do not exist. . . . *I urge each one of us here to reach down into that deep place of knowledge inside herself and touch the terror and loathing of any difference that lives there. See whose face it wears. Then the personal as the political can begin to illuminate all our choices.* (112–13, emphasis in original)

For Lorde, a theory that dissolves the communal identity—in all of its difference—around which the marginalized can politically organize is not a progressive one. Nor is it one that gays, bisexuals, transgendered people, and lesbians of color can afford to adopt, for to do so would be to foreclose possibilities of change.

"YOUR BLUES AIN'T LIKE MINE": THE INVALIDATION OF "EXPERIENCE"

As a specific example of how some queer theorists (mis)read or minimize the work, lives, and cultural production of gays, lesbians, bisexuals, and transgendered people of color and to lay the groundwork for a return to a focus on embodied performance as a critical praxis, I offer an analysis of one queer theorist's reading of two black gay performances. In *The Ethics of Marginality,* for example, queer theorist John Champagne uses black gay theorists' objections to the photographs of Robert Mapplethorpe to call attention to the trouble with deploying "experience" as evidentiary.[10] Specifically, Champagne focuses on a speech delivered by Essex Hemphill, a black gay writer and activist, at the 1990 OUTWRITE conference of gay and lesbian writers. In his speech, Hemphill critiqued Mapplethorpe's photographs of black men.[11] Champagne takes exception to Hemphill's critique, arguing that Hemphill's reading is "Monolithic" and bespeaks "a largely untheorized relation between desire, representation, and the political" (59). What I wish to interrogate, however, is Champagne's reading of Hemphill's apparent "emotionality" during the speech.

In Champagne's account, Hemphill began to cry during his speech, to which there were two responses: one of sympathy/empathy and one of protest. Commenting on an overheard conversation between two whites in the audience, Champagne writes, "Although I agreed with much of the substance of this person's comments concerning race relations in the gay and lesbian community, I was suspicious of the almost masochistic pleasure released in and through this public declaration of white culpability" (58). I find it surprising that Champagne would characterize what appears to be white self-reflexivity about racial and class privilege as "masochistic" given how rare such self-reflexivity is in the academy and else-where. After characterizing as masochistic the two whites who sympathetically align them-selves with Hemphill, Champagne aligns him-self with the one person who displayed vocal disapproval by booing Hemphill's speech:

> I have to admit that I admired the bravura of the lone booer. I disagreed with Hemphill's readings of the photographs and felt that his tears were an attempt to shame the audience into refusing to interrogate the terms of his address. If, as Gayatri Spivak has suggested, we might term the politics of an explanation the means by which it secures its particular mode of being in the world, the politics of Hemphill's reading of Mapplethorpe might be described as the politics of tears, a politics that assures the validity of its produced explanation by appealing to some kind of "authentic," uni-versal, and (thus) uninterrogated "human" emotion of experience. (58–59)

Champagne's own "bravura" in *his* reading of Hemphill's tears illuminates the ways in which many queer theorists, in their quest to move beyond the body, ground their critique in the discursive rather than the corporeal. I suggest that the two terrains are not mutually exclusive, but rather stand in a dialogical/dialectical relationship to one another. What about the authenticity of pain, for example, that may supercede the cognitive and emerges from the heart—not *for* display but *despite* display? What is the significance of a black *man* crying in public? We must grant each other time and space not only to talk *of* the body but *through* it as well.[12] In Champagne's formulation however, bodily experience is anti-intellectual, and Hemphill's black bodily experience is manipulative. This seems to be an unself-reflexive, if not unfair, assumption to make when, for the most part, white bodies are discursively and corporeally naturalized as universal. Historically, white bodies have not been trafficked, violated, burned, and dragged behind trucks because they embody racialized

identities. In Champagne's analysis, bodily whiteness goes uninterrogated.[13]

In order to posit an alternative reading of Hemphill's tears, I turn to bell hooks' insights regarding the ways in which whites often mis-read emotionality elicited through black cul-tural aesthetics. "In the context of white institutions, particularly universities," hooks writes, "that mode of address is questionable precisely because it moves people. Style is equated in such a setting with a lack of sub-stance" (21). hooks believes that this transfor-mation of cultural space requires an "audience [to] shift . . . paradigms," and, in that way, "a marginal aspect of black cultural identity [is] centralized" (22). Unlike Champagne's own diminution of the "subversive powers [and politics] of style" (127–28), hooks affirms the transgressive and transformative potential of style, citing it as "one example of counter-hegemonic cultural practice," as well as "an insertion of radical black subjectivity" (22). Despite Champagne's statements to the con-trary, his reading of Hemphill constitutes him-self as a "sovereign subject" within his theory of anti-subjectivity, a positionality that renders him "overseer" of black cultural practices and discourse. On the other hand, Hemphill's tears, as a performance of black style that draws upon emotionality, may be read as more than simply a willful act of manipulation to sub-stantiate the black gay "experience" of subju-gation and objectification. More complexly, it may be read as a "confrontation with differ-ence which takes place on new ground, in that counter-hegemonic marginal space where rad-ical black subjectivity is *seen,* not overseen by an authoritative Other claiming to know us better than we know ourselves" (hooks 22). In his reading of Hemphill, Champagne positions himself as "authoritative Other," assuming, as he does, the motivation behind Hemphill's tears.[14]

Champagne also devotes an entire chapter to *Tongues Untied,* a film by black gay film maker, Marlon Riggs. Once again critiquing what he sees as the film's problematic reliance on "experience" as evidentiary, Champagne offers a queer reading of Riggs' film to call into question the filmic representation of blackness and class:

> In *Tongues Untied,* one of the consequences of failing to dis-articulate, in one's reading, the hybrid weave of discursive practices deployed by the film might be the erasure of what I would term certain discontinuities of class, race, and imperialism as they might interweave with the necessarily inadequate nominations "Black" and "gay." For example, much of the film seems to employ a set of discursive practices historically familiar to a middle-class audience, Black and non-Black alike. The film tends to privilege the (discursive) "experience" of middle-class Black gay men, and is largely articulated from that position. The film privileges poetry, and in particular, a poetry that seems to owe as much historically to Walt Whitman and William Carlos Williams as to Langston Hughes or Countee Cullen; moreover, the film's more overtly political rhetoric seems culled from organized urban struggles in the gay as well as Black communities, struggles often headed by largely middle-class people.
>
> Another moment in the film that suggests a certain middle-class position is arguably one of the central images of the film, a series of documentary style shots of what appears to be a Gay Pride Day march in Manhattan. A group of Black gay men carry a banner that reads "Black Men Loving Black Men Is a Revolutionary Act," apparently echoing the rhetoric of early middle-class feminism. Furthermore, the men who carry this banner are arguably marked as middle-class, their bodies sculpted into the bulging, muscular style so prominent in the gay ghettos of San Francisco and New York. (68–69)

Champagne's critique is problematic in several ways. First, it is based on the premise that *Tongues Untied* elides the issue of class in its focus on race and homosexuality. However, Champagne then goes on to demonstrate the ways in which the film speaks to a middle-class sensibility. What is missing here is an explanation as to why black middle-class

status precludes one from socially and politically engaging issues of race and sexuality. Because Champagne does not provide such an explanation, the reader is left to assume that a black middle-class subject position, as Valerie Smith has suggested, "is a space of pure compromise and capitulation, from which all autonomy disappears once it encounters hegemonic power" (67). Second, in his class-based analysis, Champagne reads literary selections, material goods, and clothing aesthetics as "evidence" of the film's middle-class leanings. However, he fails to recognize that the *appearance* of belonging to a particular class does not always reflect one's actual class status. In the black community, for instance, middle-class status is often performed—what is referred to in the vernacular as acting "boojee" (bourgeois). The way a black person adorns herself or publicly displays his material possessions may not necessarily reflect his or her economic status. Put another way, one might *live* in the projects but not necessarily *appear* to.[15] Champagne, however, misreads signs of class in the film in order to support his thesis that middle-class status in the film is symptomatic of deeply rooted sexual conservatism and homophobia. Incredibly, he links this conservatism not only to that of anti-porn feminists, but also to political bigots like Jesse Helms.[16]

I am perplexed as to why the film cannot privilege black, middle-class gay experience. Is *Tongues Untied* a red herring of black gay representation because it does not do the discursive work that Champagne wishes it to do? Is it *The Cosby Show* in "gay face" because it portrays black middle-class life (and I'm not so sure that it does)? Positioning the film in such a light seems to bespeak just the kind of essentialism that Champagne so adamantly argues against. That is, he links class and epistemology to serve the purpose of his critique, yet dismisses race-based ways of knowing. Why is class privileged epistemologically while "raced" ways of knowing are dismissed? Champagne states that "to point out that

Riggs' film seems to privilege the (discursive) experience of largely middle-class urban Black gay men and to employ conventions of filmmaking familiar to a middle-class audience is not, in and of itself, a criticism of the video" (69). This disclaimer notwithstanding, Champagne goes on to do a close (mis)reading of various moments and aesthetics of the film—from specific scenes to what he argues is the film's "experimental documentary" style—to substantiate his class critique.

Unlike Champagne's deployment of queer theory, the model of quare studies that I propose would not only critique the concept of "race" as historically contingent and socially and culturally constructed/performed, it would also address the material effects of race in a white supremacist society. Quare studies requires an acknowledgment by the critic of her position within an oppressive system. To fail to do so would, as Ruth Goldman argues, "[leave] the burden of dealing with difference on the people who are themselves different, while simultaneously allowing white academics to construct a discourse of silence around race and other queer perspectives" (173). One's "experience" within that system, however discursively mediated, is also materially conditioned. A critic cannot ethically and responsibly speak from a privileged place, as Champagne does, and not own up to that privilege. To do so is to maintain the force of hegemonic whiteness, which, until very recently, has gone uninterrogated.[17]

"QUARING" THE QUEER: TROPING THE TROPE

Queer studies has rightfully problematized identity politics by elaborating on the processes by which agents and subjects come into being; however, there is a critical gap in queer studies between theory and practice, performance and performativity. Quare studies can narrow that gap to the extent that it pursues an epistemology rooted in the body.

As a "theory in the flesh" quare studies necessarily engenders a kind of identity politics, one that acknowledges difference within and between particular groups. Thus, identity politics does not necessarily mean the reduction of multiple identities into a monolithic identity or narrow cultural nationalism. Rather, quare studies moves beyond simply theorizing subjectivity and agency as discursively mediated to theorizing how that mediation may propel material bodies into action. As Shane Phelan reminds us, the maintenance of a progressive identity politics asks "not whether we share a given position but whether we share a commitment to improve it, and whether we can commit to the pain of embarrassment and confrontation as we disagree" (156).

Quare studies would reinstate the subject and the identity around which the subject circulates that queer theory so easily dismisses. By refocusing our attention on the racialized bodies, experiences, and knowledges of transgendered people, lesbians, gays, and bisexuals of color, quare studies grounds the discursive process of mediated identification and subjectivity in a political praxis that speaks to the material existence of "colored" bodies. While strategically galvanized around identity, quare studies should be committed to interrogating identity claims that exclude rather than include. I am thinking here of black nationalist claims of "black authenticity" that exclude, categorically, homosexual identities. Blind allegiance to "isms" of any kind is one of the fears of queer theorists who critique identity politics. Cognizant of that risk, quare studies must not deploy a totalizing and homogeneous formulation of identity. Rather, it must foster contingent, fragile coalitions as it struggles against common oppressive forms.

A number of queer theorists have proposed potential strategies (albeit limited ones) that may be deployed in the service of dismantling oppressive systems. Most significantly, Judith Butler's formulation of performativity has had an important impact not only on gender and sexuality studies, but on queer studies as well. While I am swayed by Butler's formulation of gender performativity, I am disturbed by her theory's failure to articulate a meatier politics of resistance. For example, what are the implications of dismantling subjectivity and social will to ground zero within oppressive regimes? Does an emphasis on the discursive constitution of subjects propel us beyond a state of quietism to address the very real injustices in the world? The body, I believe, has to be theorized in ways that not only describe the ways in which it is brought into being, but what it *does* once it *is* constituted and the relationship between it and the other bodies around it. In other words, I desire a rejoinder to performativity that allows a space for subjectivity, for agency (however momentary and discursively fraught), and, ultimately, for change.

Therefore, to complement notions of performativity, quare studies also deploys theories of performance. Performance theory not only highlights the discursive effects of acts, it also points to how these acts are historically situated. Butler herself acknowledges that the conflation of "performativity to performance would be a mistake" (*Bodies* 234). Indeed, the focus on performativity alone may problematically reduce performativity and performance to one interpretative frame to theorize human experience. On the other hand, focusing on both may bring together two interpretative frames whose relationship is more dialogical and dialectical.

In her introduction to *Performance and Cultural Politics,* Elin Diamond proposes such a relationship between performance and performativity:

> When being is de-essentialized, when gender and even race are understood as fictional ontologies, modes of expression without true substance, the idea of performance comes to the fore. But performance both affirms and denies this evacuation of substance. In the sense that the "I" has no interior secure ego or core identity, "I" must always enunciate itself: there is only performance of a self, not an external representation of an interior truth. But in the sense that I do my performance in public, for spectators who are interpreting and/or performing with me, there are real effects, meanings solicited or imposed that produce relations in the real. Can performance make a difference? A performance, whether it inspires love or loathing, often consolidates cultural or subcultural affiliations, and these affiliations might be as regressive as they are progressive. The point is, as soon as performativity comes to rest on *a* performance, questions of embodiment and political effects, all become discussible. Performance . . . is precisely the site in which concealed or dissimulated conventions might be investigated. When performativity materializes as performance in that risky and dangerous negotiation between doing (a reiteration of norms) and a thing done (discursive conventions that frame our interpretations), between somebody's body and the conventions of embodiment, we have access to cultural meanings and critique. Performativity . . . must be rooted in the materiality and historical density of performance. (5, emphasis in original)

I quote Diamond at length here because of the implications her construals of performance and performativity have for reinstating subjectivity and agency through the performance of identity. Although fleeting and ephemeral, these performances may activate a politics of subjectivity.

The performance of self is not only a performance/construction of identity for/toward an "out there" or merely an attachment or "taking up" (Butler, *Gender* 145) of a predetermined, discursively contingent identity. It is also a performance of self for the self in a moment of self-reflexivity that has the potential to transform one's view of self in relation to the world. People have a need to exercise control over the production of their images so that they feel empowered. For the disenfranchised, the recognition, construction, and maintenance of self-image and cultural identity function to sustain, even when social systems fail to do so. Granted, formations/performances of identity may simply reify oppressive systems, but they may also contest and subvert dominant meaning systems. When gays, lesbians, bisexuals, and transgendered people of color "talk back," whether using the "tools of the master" (Lorde 110) or the vernacular on the street, their voices, singularly or collectively, do not exist in some vacuous wasteland of discursivity. As symbolic anthropologist Victor Turner suggests, their performances

> are not simple reflectors or expressions of culture or even of changing culture but may themselves be active *agencies* of change, representing the eye by which culture sees itself and the drawing board on which creative actors sketch out what they believe to be more apt or interesting "designs for living." . . . Performative reflexivity is a condition in which a sociocultural group, or its most perceptive members, acting representatively, turn, bend, or reflect back upon themselves, upon the relations, actions, symbols, meanings, codes, roles, statuses, social structures, ethical and legal rules, and other sociocultural components which make up their public selves. (24, my emphasis)

Turner's theory of performative cultural reflexivity suggests a transgressive aspect of performative identity that neither dissolves identity into a fixed "I" nor presumes a monolithic "we." Rather, Turner's assertions suggest that social beings "look back" and "look forward" in a manner that wrestles with the ways in which that community exists in the world and theorizes that existence. As Cindy Patton warns, not everyone who claims an identity does so in the ways critics of essentialist identity claim they do (181).

Theories of performance, as opposed to theories of performativity, also take into account the context and historical moment of performance (Strine 7). We need to account for the temporal and spatial specificity of performance not only to frame its existence, but also to name the ways in which it signifies. Such an analysis would acknowledge the discursivity of subjects, but it would also "unfix" the discursively constituted subject as always already a pawn of power. Although many queer theorists appropriate Foucault to substantiate

the imperialism of power, Foucault himself acknowledges that discourse has the potential to disrupt power:

> Discourses are not once and for all subservient to power or raised up against it, any more than silences are. We must make allowances for the complex and unstable process whereby discourse can be both an instrument and an effect of power, but also a hindrance, a stumbling-block, a point of resistance and a starting point for an opposing strategy. Discourse transmits and produces power; it reinforces it, *but also undermines and exposes it, renders it fragile and makes it possible to thwart it.* (100–101, my emphasis)

Although people of color may not have theorized our lives in Foucault's terms, we have used discourse in subversive ways because it was necessary for our survival. Failure to ground discourse in materiality is to privilege the position of those whose subjectivity and agency, outside the realm of gender and sexuality, have never been subjugated. The tendency of many lesbians, bisexuals, gays, and transgendered people of color is to unite around a racial identity at a moment when their subjectivity is already under erasure.

Elaborating more extensively on the notion of performance as a site of agency for lesbian, gay, bisexual, and transgendered people of color, Latino performance theorist José Muñoz proposes a theory of "disidentification" whereby queers of color work within and against dominant ideology to effect change:

> Disidentification is the third mode of dealing with dominant ideology, one that neither opts to assimilate within such a structure nor strictly opposes it; rather, disidentification is a strategy that works on and against dominant ideology. Instead of buckling under the pressures of dominant ideology (identification, assimilation) or attempting to break free of its inescapable sphere (counteridentification, utopianism), this "working on and against" is a strategy that tries to transform a cultural logic from

within, always laboring to enact permanent structural change while at the same time valuing the importance of local and every-day struggles of resistance. (11–12)

Muñoz's concept of "disidentification" reflects the process through which people of color have always managed to survive in a white supremacist society: by "working on and against" oppressive institutional structures.

The performance strategies of African Americans who labored and struggled under human bondage exemplify this disidentificatory practice. For instance, vernacular traditions that emerged among enslaved Africans—including folktales, spirituals, and the blues—provided the foundation for social and political empowerment. These discursively mediated forms, spoken and filtered through black bodies, enabled survival. The point here is that the inheritance of hegemonic discourses does not preclude one from "disidentifying," from putting those discourses in the service of resistance. Although they had no institutional power, enslaved blacks refused to become helpless victims and instead enacted their agency by cultivating discursive weapons based on an identity as oppressed people. The result was the creation of folktales about the "bottom rail becoming the top riser" (i.e., a metaphor for the slave rising out of slavery) or spirituals that called folks to "Gather at the River" (i.e., to plan an escape).

These resistant vernacular performances did not disappear with slavery. Gays, lesbians, bisexuals, and transgendered people of color continued to enact performative agency to work on and against oppressive systems. Quare singers such as Bessie Smith and Ma Rainey, for instance, used the blues to challenge the notion of inferior black female subjectivity and covertly brought the image of the black lesbian into the American imaginary.[18] Later, through his flamboyant style and campy costumes, Little Richard not only fashioned himself as the "emancipator" and "originator"

of rock-n-roll, he also offered a critique of hegemonic black and white masculinity in the music industry. Later still, the black transgendered singer Sylvester transformed disco with his high soaring falsetto voice and gospel riffs. Indeed, Sylvester's music transcended the boundary drawn between the church and the world, between the sacred and profane, creating a space for other quare singers, like Blackberri, who would come after him. Even RuPaul's drag of many flavors demonstrates the resourcefulness of quares of color to reinvent themselves in ways that transform their material conditions. Quare vernacular tools operate outside the realm of musical and theatrical performance as well. Performance practices such as vogueing, snapping, "throwing shade," and "reading" attest to the ways in which gays, lesbians, bisexuals, and transgendered people of color devise technologies of self-assertion and summon the agency to resist.[19]

Taken together, performance and quare theories alert us to the ways in which these disidentificatory performances serve material ends, and they do this work by accounting for the context in which these performances occur. The stage, for instance, is not confined solely to the theater, the dance club, or the concert hall. Streets, social services lines, picket lines, loan offices, and emergency rooms, among others, may also serve as useful staging grounds for disidentificatory performances. Theorizing the social context of performance sutures the gap between discourse and lived experience by examining how quares use performance as a strategy of survival in their day-to-day experiences. Such an analysis requires that we, like Robin Kelley, reconceptualize "play" (performance) as "work." Moreover, quare theory focuses attention on the social consequences of those performances. It is one thing to do drag on the club stage but quite another to embody a drag queen identity on the street. Bodies are sites of discursive effects, but they are sites of social ones as well.

I do not wish to suggest that quare vernacular performances do not, at times, collude with sexist, misogynist, racist, and even homophobic ideologies. Lesbian, bisexual, gay, and transgendered people of color must always realize that we cannot transgress for transgression's sake lest our work end up romanticizing and prolonging our state of struggle and that of others. In other words, while we may occasionally enjoy the pleasures of transgressive performance, we must transgress responsibly or run the risk of creating and sustaining representations of ourselves that are anti-gay, anti-woman, anti-transgender, anti-working class, and anti-black. Despite this risk, we must not retreat to the position that changes within the system are impossible. The social movements of the past century are testament that change is possible.

Ultimately, quare studies offers a more utilitarian theory of identity politics, focusing not just on performers and effects, but also on contexts and historical situatedness. It does not, as bell hooks warns, separate the "politics of difference from the politics of racism" (26). Quare studies grants space for marginalized individuals to enact "radical black subjectivity" (hooks 26) by adopting the both/and posture of "disidentification." Quare studies proposes a theory grounded in a critique of naïve essentialism and an enactment of political praxis. Such theorizing may *strategically* embrace identity politics while also acknowledging the contingency of identity, a double move that Angelia Wilson adroitly describes as "politically necessary and politically dangerous" (107).

NOTES

1. See Johnson, "SNAP! Culture" 125–128.
2. I have long known about the connection between African Americans and the Irish. As noted in the film *The Commitments*, "The Irish are the blacks of Europe." The connection is there—that is, at least until the Irish became "white." For a sustained discussion of how Irish emigrants obtained "white" racial privilege, see Ignatiev.

3. For more on "standpoint" theory, see Collins.
4. In *Bodies That Matter,* Judith Butler anticipates the contestability of "queer," noting that it excludes as much as it includes but that such a contested term may energize a new kind of political activism. She proposes that

> it may be that the critique of the term will initiate a resurgence of both feminist and anti-racist mobilization within lesbian and gay politics or open up new possibilities for coalitional alliances that do not presume that these constituencies are radically distinct from one another. The term will be revised, dispelled, rendered obsolete to the extent that it yields to the demands which resist the term precisely because of the exclusions by which it is mobilized. (228–29)

To be sure, there are gay, bisexual, lesbian and transgendered people of color who embrace "queer." In my experience, however, those who embrace the term represent a small minority. At the "Black Queer Studies at the Millennium Conference" held at the University of North Carolina on April 7–9, 2000, for example, many of the conference attendees were disturbed by the organizers' choice of "queer" for the title of a conference on black sexuality. So ardent was their disapproval that it became a subject of debate during one of the panels.

5. See, for example, Hall and Gilroy, "'Race.'"
6. I thank Michelé Barale for this insight.
7. While it is true that some white queer theorists are self-reflexive about their privilege and incorporate the works and experiences of gays, bisexuals, lesbians and transgendered people of color into their scholarship, this is not the norm. Paula Moya calls attention to how the theorizing of women of color is appropriated by postmodernist theorists: "[Judith] Butler extracts one sentence from [Cherríe] Moraga, buries it in a footnote, and then misreads it in order to justify her own inability to account for the complex interrelations that structure various forms of human identity" (133).

David Bergman also offers a problematic reading of black gay fiction when he reads James Baldwin through the homophobic rhetoric of Eldridge Cleaver and theorizes that black communities are more homophobic than white ones (163–87). For other critiques of simplistic or dismissive readings of the works of gays, bisexuals, lesbians, and transgendered people of color see Ng, (Charles), and Namaste. One notable exception is Ruth Goldman's "Who Is That *Queer* Queer," in which she, a white bisexual, calls other white queer theorists to task for their failure to theorize their whiteness: "those of us who are white tend not to dwell on our race, perhaps because this would only serve to normalize us—reduce our queerness, if you will" (173).

8. For more on "strategic" essentialism, see: Case 1–12; de Lauretis; and Fuss 1–21.

9. For a sustained discussion of queer activists' disavowal of heterosexual political alliances, see Cohen, "Punks" 440–52.

10. Champagne draws from Joan Scott's "The Evidence of Experience," where she argues that "experience" is discursively constituted, mediated by and through linguistic systems and embedded in ideology. Like all discursive terrains, the ground upon which "experience" moves is turbulent and supple, quickly disrupting the foothold we think we might have on history and the "evidentiary." Scott writes,

> Experience is at once always already an interpretation *and* is in need of interpretation. What counts as experience is neither self-evident nor straightforward; it is always contested, always therefore political. The study of experience, therefore, must call into question its originary status in historical explanation. This will happen when historians take as their project not the reproduction and transmission of knowledge said to be arrived at through experience, but the analysis of the production of that knowledge itself. (37, emphasis in original)

Scott is particularly concerned here with histories that draw on "experience" as evidentiary in order to historicize difference. "By remaining within the epistemological frame of orthodox history," Scott argues, "these studies lose the possibility of examining those assumptions and practices that excluded considerations of difference in the first place" (24–25).

11. Robert Mapplethorpe's photographs of black gay men continue to be a source of controversy in the black gay community. Reactions to the photos range from outrage to ambivalence to appreciation. I believe the most complex reading of Mapplethorpe is found in Isaac Julien and Kobena Mercer's "True Confessions: A Discourse on Images of Black Male Sexuality." They write:

> While we recognize the oppressive dimension of these images of black men as Other, we are also attracted: We want to look but don't always find the images we want to see. This ambivalent mixture of attraction and repulsion goes for images of black gay men in porn generally, but the inscribed or preferred meanings of these images are not fixed; they can at times, be pried apart into alternative readings when different experiences are brought to bear on their interpretation. (170)

12. I thank Soyini Madison for raising this issue.

13. I do not mean to deny that white gay, lesbian, bisexual, and transgendered people have been emotionally, psychologically, and physically harmed. The recent murder of Matthew Shepard is a sad testament to this fact. Indeed, given how his attackers killed him, there are ways in which we may read Shepard's murder through a racial lens. What I am suggesting, however, is that racial violence (or the threat of it) is enacted upon black bodies in different ways and for different reasons than it is on white bodies.

14. Emotionality as manipulative or putatively repugnant may also be read through the lens of gender. Generally understood as a "weak" (read "feminine") gender performance, emotional display among men of any race or sexual orientation represents a threat to heteronormativity and, therefore, is often met with disapproval.

15. I do not wish to suggest that the appearance of poverty or wealth never reflects that one is actually poor or wealthy. What I am suggesting, however, is that in many African American communities, style figures more substantively than some might imagine. Accordingly, there exists a politics of taste among African Americans that is performed so as to dislodge fixed perceptions about who one is or where one is from. In many instances, for example, performing a certain middle-class style has enabled African Americans to "pass" in various and strategically savvy ways. For more on the performance of style in African American communities see B. Smith's "Home" and Beam's "Leaving." For a theoretical perspective on the politics of taste, see Bourdieu.

16. Champagne writes that

> like the white antiporn feminists whose rhetoric they sometimes share, intellectuals like Riggs and Hemphill may in fact be

expressing in *Tongues Untied* a (middle-) class-inflected sense of disgust related to sexuality—obviously, not related to all sexuality, but to a particularly culturally problematic kind. It is perhaps thus not a coincidence at all that the rhetoric deployed by Hemphill in his reading of Mapplethorpe should be so similar to that of Dworkin, Stoltenberg, and even Jesse Helms. (79)

17. For examples of white critics who interrogate "whiteness," see Frankenberg, Hill, and Roediger.

18. For an analysis of Bessie Smith's explicitly lesbian blues songs, see Harrison 103–104.

19. See Riggs "Black Macho" and Johnson "SNAP!" and "Feeling."

WORKS CITED

Anzaldúa, Gloria. "To(o) Queer the Writer: *Loca, escrita y chicana.*" *Inversions: Writing by Dykes and Lesbians.* Ed. Betsy Warland. Vancouver: Press Gang, 1991. 249–259.

Baldwin, James. *Nobody Knows My Name: More Notes of a Native Son.* New York: Vintage, 1993.

———. *No Name in the Street.* New York: Dial, 1972.

Beam, Joseph. "Making Ourselves from Scratch." *Brother to Brother: New Writings by Black Gay Men.* Ed. Essex Hemphill. Boston: Alyson, 1991. 261–262.

———. "Leaving the Shadows Behind." *In the Life.* Ed. Joseph Beam. Boston: Alyson, 1986. 13–18.

Bergman, David. *Gaiety Transfigured: Gay Self-Representation in American Literature.* Madison: U of Wisconsin P, 1991.

Berlant, Lauren, and Michael Warner. "What Does Queer Theory Teach Us about X?" *PMLA* 110 (1995): 343–349.

Black Is . . . Black Ain't. Dir. Marlon Riggs. Independent Film Series, 1995.

Bourdieu, Pierre. *Distinction: A Social Critique of the Judgement of Taste.* Trans. Richard Nice. Cambridge: Harvard UP, 1984.

Butler, Judith. *Bodies That Matter: On the Discursive Limits of "Sex."* New York: Routledge, 1993.

———. *Gender Trouble: Feminism and the Subversion of Identity.* New York: Routledge, 1990.

Case, Sue-Ellen. *The Domain Matrix: Performing Lesbian at the End of Print Culture.* Bloomington: Indiana UP, 1996.

Champagne, John. *The Ethics of Marginality: A New Approach to Gay Studies.* Minneapolis: U of Minnesota P, 1995.

(Charles), Helen. "'Queer Nigger': Theorizing 'White' Activism." *Activating Theory: Lesbian, Gay, Bisexual Politics.* Eds. Joseph Bistrow and Angelia R. Wilson. London: Lawrence and Wishart, 1993. 97–117.

Christian, Barbara. "The Race for Theory." *Cultural Critique* 6 (1985): 51–63.

Cohen, Cathy. *The Boundaries of Blackness: AIDS and the Breakdown of Black Politics.* Chicago: U of Chicago P, 1999.

———. "Punks, Bulldaggers, and Welfare Queens: The Radical Potential of Queer Politics?" *GLQ: A Journal of Lesbian & Gay Studies* 3 (1997): 437–465.

Collins, Patricia Hill. "The Social Construction of Black Feminist Thought." *Words of Fire: An Anthology of African-American Feminist Thought.* Ed. Beverly Guy-Sheftall. New York: New Press, 1995. 338–357.

The Commitments. Dir. Alan Parker. Lauren Films, 1991.

de Lauretis, Teresa. "The Essence of the Triangle, or Taking the Risk of Essentialism Seriously: Feminist Theory in Italy, the U.S. and Britain." *differences* 1.2 (1989): 3–37.

Diamond, Elin, ed. Introduction. *Performance & Cultural Politics.* New York: Routledge, 1996. 1–9.

Foucault, Michel. *The History of Sexuality, Vol. 1.* Trans. Robert Hurley. New York: Random House, 1980.

Frankenberg, Ruth, ed. *Displacing Whiteness: Essays in Social and Cultural Criticism.* Durham: Duke UP, 1997.

Fuss, Diana. *Essentially Speaking: Feminism, Nature & Difference.* New York: Routledge, 1989.

Gilroy, Paul. "'Race,' Class, and Agency." *There Ain't No Black in the Union Jack: The Cultural Politics of Race and Nation.* London: Hutchinson, 1987. 15–42.

Goldman, Ruth. "Who Is That *Queer* Queer?" *Queer Studies: A Lesbian, Gay, Bisexual and Transgender Anthology.* Eds. Brett Beemyn and Mickey Eliason. New York: NYU P, 1996. 169–182.

Hall, Stuart. "Subjects in History: Making Diasporic Identities." *The House That Race Built.* Ed. Wahneema Lubiano. New York: Pantheon, 1997. 289–299.

Harrison, Daphne Duval. *Black Pearls: Blues Queens of the 1920's.* New Brunswick: Rutgers UP, 1998.

Henderson, Mae. "Speaking in Tongues." *Feminist Theorize the Political*. Eds. Judith Butler and Joan V. Scott. New York: Routledge, 1992. 144–165.

Hill, Mike, ed. *Whiteness: A Critical Reader*. New York: NYU P, 1997.

hooks, bell. *Yearning*. Boston: South End, 1990.

Ignatiev, Noel. *How the Irish Became White*. New York: Routledge, 1995.

Johnson, E. Patrick. "Feeling the Spirit in the Dark: Expanding Notions of the Sacred in the African American Gay Community." *Callaloo* 21 (1998): 399–418.

———. "SNAP! Culture: A Different Kind of 'Reading.'" *Text and Performance Quarterly* 3 (1995): 121–142.

Julien, Isaac, and Kobena Mercer. "True Confessions: A Discourse on Images of Black Male Sexuality." *Brother to Brother: New Writings by Black Gay Men*. Ed. Essex Hemphill. Boston: Alyson, 1991. 167–173.

Kelley, Robin D.G. "Looking to Get Paid: How Some Black Youth Put Culture to Work." *Yo Mama's Disfunktional!: Fighting the Culture Wars in Urban America*. Boston: Beacon, 1997. 43–77.

Lorde, Audre. *Sister Outsider*. Freedom, CA: Crossing, 1984.

Moraga, Cherríe, and Gloria Anzaldúa, eds. *This Bridge Called My Back: Writings by Radical Women of Color*. New York: Kitchen Table, 1983.

Moya, Paula M.L. "Postmodernism, 'Realism,' and the Politics of Identity: Cherríe Moraga and Chicano Feminism." *Feminist Genealogies, Colonial Legacies, Democratic Futures*. Eds. M. Jacqui Alexander and Chandra Talpade Mohanty. New York: Routledge, 1997. 125–50.

Muñoz, José Esteban. *Disidentifications: Queers of Color and the Performance of Politics*. Minneapolis: U of Minnesota P, 1999.

Namaste, Ki. "'Tragic Misreadings': Queer Theory's Erasure of Transgender Identity." *Queer Studies: A Lesbian, Gay, Bisexual and Transgender Anthology*. Eds. Brett Beemyn and Mickey Eliason. New York: NYU P, 1996. 183–203.

Ng, Vivien. "Race Matters." *Lesbian and Gay Studies: A Critical Introduction*. Eds. Andy Medhurst and Sally R. Munt. London: Cassell. 215–231.

Patton, Cindy. "Performativity and Social Distinction: The End of AIDS Epidemiology." *Performativity and Performance*. Eds. Andrew

Parker and Eve Kosofsky Sedgwick. New York: Routledge, 1995. 173–196.

Phelan, Shane. *Getting Specific*. Minneapolis: U of Minnesota P, 1994.

Riggs, Marlon. "Black Macho Revisited: Reflections of a SNAP! Queen." *Brother to Brother: New Writings by Black Gay Men*. Ed. Essex Hemphill. Boston: Alyson, 1991. 253–257.

Roediger, David. *Towards the Abolition of Whiteness*. London: Verso, 1994.

Scott, Joan V. "Experience." *Feminists Theorize the Political*. Eds. Judith Butler and Joan W. Scott. New York: Routledge, 1992. 22–40.

Sedgwick, Eve Kosofsky. "Queer and Now." *Tendencies*. Durham: Duke UP, 1993. 1–20.

Smith, Barbara. "Home." *Home Girls: A Black Feminist Anthology*. Ed. Barbara Smith. New York: Kitchen Table, 1983. 64–72.

Smith, Cherry. "What Is This Thing Called Queer?" *Material Queer: A LesBiGay Cultural Studies Reader*. Ed. Donald Morton. Boulder: Westview, 1996. 277–285.

Smith, Valerie. *Not Just Race, Not Just Gender: Making Feminist Readings*. New York: Routledge, 1998.

Strine, Mary. "Articulating Performance/Performativity: Disciplinary Tasks and the Contingencies of Practice." National Speech Communication Association Conference. San Diego, CA. November 1996.

Thomas, Calvin. "Straight with a Twist: Queer Theory and the Subject of Heterosexuality." *The Gay '90's: Disciplinary and Interdisciplinary Formations in Queer Studies*. Eds. Thomas Foster, Carol Siegel, and Ellen E. Berry. New York: NYU P, 1997. 83–115.

Turner, Victor. *The Anthropology of Performance*. New York: Performing Arts Journal, 1986.

Valente, Joseph. "Joyce's (Sexual) Choices: A Historical Overview." *Quare Joyce*. Ed. Joseph Valente. Ann Arbor: U of Michigan P, 1998. 1–18.

Walker, Alice. *In Search of Our Mothers' Gardens: Womanist Prose*. San Diego: Harcourt Brace Jovanovich, 1983.

Warner, Michael. Introduction. *Fear of a Queer Planet: Queer Politics and Social Theory*. Ed. Michael Warner. Minneapolis: U of Minnesota P, 1993. vii–xxxi.

Wilson, Angelia R. "Somewhere Over the Rainbow: Queer Translating." *Playing With Fire: Queer Politics, Queer Theories*. Ed. Shane Phelan. New York: Routledge, 1997. 99–111.

Discussion Questions

1. What does Johnson mean by "quare"? What are the origins of the word, and what kind of work does it do? In what, if any, contexts can you see yourself using "quare," and why?

2. Briefly, what is Johnson's critique of queer theory?

3. How does Johnson feel about performativity?

4. How do quare studies differ from queer theory?

5

The Uses of the Erotic

The Erotic as Power

AUDRE LORDE

*A*udre Lorde died in November, 1992. Audre Lorde was author of more than a dozen books of poetry and prose, recipient of national and international awards, and a founding member of Kitchen Table: Women of Color Press. Her most recent poetry includes Undersongs: Chosen Poems Old and New Revised *(1992) and* Our Dead Behind Us *(1986); in* Zami: A New Spelling of My Name *(1982) she writes her own bio-mythography, and her recent essays and speeches can be found in* A Burst of Light *(1988) and* Sister Outsider *(1984), which includes the chapter reprinted here. Anti-ascetic in her demands that desire be made conscious and sensuality affirmed, Lorde responds in this 1978 essay to Second Wave Feminists' debates over whether or not pornography creates and maintains sexual oppression. By disentangling women's eroticism from its cultural misuse and calling*

for a realization of the erotic as the most self-responsible source of women's power, Lorde, locating that power in women's acknowledgment of desire, blurs the boundaries between the erotic, on the one hand, and political, creative, and everyday activities, on the other. And in issuing her call to all women, regardless of their sexual identity, Lorde erases erotic differences between straight, bisexual, and lesbian desire in order to promote such desire as a creative force for revolutionary change.

There are many kinds of power, used and unused, acknowledged or otherwise. The erotic is a resource within each of us that lies in a deeply female and spiritual plane, firmly rooted in the power of our unexpressed or unrecognized feeling. In order to perpetuate itself, every oppression must corrupt or distort those various sources of power within the culture of the oppressed that can provide energy

SOURCE: This chapter was originally a paper presented at the Fourth Berkshire Conference on the History of Women, Mount Holyoke College, August 25, 1978, and was later published as a chapter in *Sister Outsider*. Copyright © 1984 Audre Lorde and The Crossing Press, a division of Ten Speed Press, Berkeley, CA. Reprinted by permission.

for change. For women, this has meant a suppression of the erotic as a considered source of power and information within our lives.

We have been taught to suspect this resource, vilified, abused, and devalued within Western society. On the one hand, the superficially erotic has been encouraged as a sign of female inferiority; on the other hand, women have been made to suffer and to feel both contemptible and suspect by virtue of its existence.

It is a short step from there to the false belief that only by the suppression of the erotic within our lives and consciousness can women be truly strong. But that strength is illusory, for it is fashioned within the context of male models of power.

As women, we have come to distrust that power which rises from our deepest and nonrational knowledge. We have been warned against it all our lives by the male world, which values this depth of feeling enough to keep women around in order to exercise it in the service of men, but which fears this same depth too much to examine the possibility of it within themselves. So women are maintained at a distant/inferior position to be psychically milked, much the same way ants maintain colonies of aphids to provide a life-giving substance for their masters.

But the erotic offers a well of replenishing and provocative force to the woman who does not fear its revelation, nor succumb to the belief that sensation is enough.

The erotic has often been misnamed by men and used against women. It has been made into the confused, the trivial, the psychotic, the plasticized sensation. For this reason, we have often turned away from the exploration and consideration of the erotic as a source of power and information, confusing it with its opposite, the pornographic. But pornography is a direct denial of the power of the erotic, for it represents the suppression of true feeling. Pornography emphasizes sensation without feeling.

The erotic is a measure between the beginnings of our sense of self and the chaos of our strongest feelings. It is an internal sense of satisfaction to which, once we have experienced it, we know we can aspire. For having experienced the fullness of this depth of feeling and recognizing its power, in honor and self-respect we can require no less of ourselves.

It is never easy to demand the most from ourselves, from our lives, from our work. To encourage excellence is to go beyond the encouraged mediocrity of our society is to encourage excellence. But giving in to the fear of feeling and working to capacity is a luxury only the unintentional can afford, and the unintentional are those who do not wish to guide their own destinies.

This internal requirement toward excellence which we learn from the erotic must not be misconstrued as demanding the impossible from ourselves nor from others. Such a demand incapacitates everyone in the process. For the erotic is not a question only of what we do; it is a question of how acutely and fully we can feel in the doing. Once we know the extent to which we are capable of feeling that sense of satisfaction and completion, we can then observe which of our various life endeavors brings us closest to that fullness.

The aim of each thing which we do is to make our lives and the lives of our children richer and more possible. Within the celebration of the erotic in all our endeavors, my work becomes a conscious decision—a longed-for bed which I enter gratefully and from which I rise up empowered.

Of course, women so empowered are dangerous. So we are taught to separate the erotic demand from most vital areas of our lives other than sex. And the lack of concern for the erotic root and satisfactions of our work is felt in our disaffection from so much of what we do. For instance, how often do we truly love our work even at its most difficult?

The principal horror of any system which defines the good in terms of profit rather than in terms of human need, or which defines human need to the exclusion of the psychic and emotional components of that need—the principal horror of such a system is that it robs our work of its erotic value, its erotic power and life appeal and fulfillment. Such a system reduces work to a travesty of necessities, a duty by which we earn bread or oblivion for ourselves and those we love. But this is tantamount to blinding a painter and then telling her to improve her work, and to enjoy the act of painting. It is not only next to impossible, it is also profoundly cruel.

As women, we need to examine the ways in which our world can be truly different. I am speaking here of the necessity for reassessing the quality of all the aspects of our lives and of our work, and of how we move toward and through them.

The very word *erotic* comes from the Greek word *eros,* the personification of love in all its aspects—born of Chaos, and personifying creative power and harmony. When I speak of the erotic, then, I speak of it as an assertion of the lifeforce of women; of that creative energy empowered, the knowledge and use of which we are now reclaiming in our language, our history, our dancing, our loving, our work, our lives.

There are frequent attempts to equate pornography and eroticism, two diametrically opposed uses of the sexual. Because of these attempts, it has become fashionable to separate the spiritual (psychic and emotional) from the political, to see them as contradictory or antithetical. "What do you mean, a poetic revolutionary, a meditating gunrunner?" In the same way, we have attempted to separate the spiritual and the erotic, thereby reducing the spiritual to a world of flattened affect, a world of the ascetic who aspires to feel nothing. But nothing is farther from the truth. For the ascetic position is one of the highest fear, the gravest immobility. The severe abstinence of the ascetic becomes the ruling obsession. And it is one not of self-discipline but of self-abnegation.

The dichotomy between the spiritual and the political is also false, resulting from an incomplete attention to our erotic knowledge. For the bridge which connects them is formed by the erotic—the sensual—those physical, emotional, and psychic expressions of what is deepest and strongest and richest within each of us, being shared: the passions of love, in its deepest meanings.

Beyond the superficial, the considered phrase, "It feels right to me," acknowledges the strength of the erotic into a true knowledge, for what that means is the first and most powerful guiding light toward any understanding. And understanding is a handmaiden which can only wait upon, or clarify, that knowledge, deeply born. The erotic is the nurturer or nursemaid of all our deepest knowledge.

The erotic functions for me in several ways, and the first is in providing the power which comes from sharing deeply any pursuit with another person. The sharing of joy, whether physical, emotional, psychic, or intellectual, forms a bridge between the sharers which can be the basis for understanding much of what is not shared between them, and lessens the threat of their difference.

Another important way in which the erotic connection functions is the open and fearless underlining of my capacity for joy. In the way my body stretches to music and opens into response, hearkening to its deepest rhythms, so every level upon which I sense also opens to the erotically satisfying experience, whether it is dancing, building a bookcase, writing a poem, examining an idea.

That self-connection shared is a measure of the joy which I know myself to be capable of feeling, a reminder of my capacity for feeling. And that deep and irreplaceable knowledge of my capacity for joy comes to demand from all of my life that it be lived within the knowledge that such satisfaction is possible, and does not have to be called *marriage,* nor *god,* nor *an afterlife.*

This is one reason why the erotic is so feared, and so often relegated to the bedroom alone, when it is recognized at all. For once we begin to feel deeply all the aspects of our lives, we begin to demand from ourselves and from our life-pursuits that they feel in accordance with that joy which we know ourselves to be capable of. Our erotic knowledge empowers us, becomes a lens through which we scrutinize all aspects of our existence, forcing us to evaluate those aspects honestly in terms of their relative meaning within our lives. And this is a grave responsibility, projected from within each of us, not to settle for the convenient, the shoddy, the conventionally expected, nor the merely safe.

During World War II, we bought sealed plastic packets of white, uncolored margarine, with a tiny, intense pellet of yellow coloring perched like a topaz just inside the clear skin of the bag. We would leave the margarine out for a while to soften, and then we would pinch the little pellet to break it inside the bag, releasing the rich yellowness into the soft pale mass of margarine. Then taking it carefully between our fingers, we would knead it gently back and forth, over and over, until the color had spread throughout the whole pound bag of margarine, thoroughly coloring it.

I find the erotic such a kernel within myself. When released from its intense and constrained pellet, it flows through and colors my life with a kind of energy that heightens and sensitizes and strengthens all my experience.

We have been raised to fear the *yes* within ourselves, our deepest cravings. But, once recognized, those which do not enhance our future lose their power and can be altered. The fear of our desires keeps them suspect and indiscriminately powerful, for to suppress any truth is to give it strength beyond endurance. The fear that we cannot grow beyond whatever distortions we may find within ourselves keeps us docile and loyal and obedient, externally defined, and leads us to accept many facets of our oppression as women.

When we live outside ourselves, and by that I mean on external directives only rather than from our internal knowledge and needs, when we live away from those erotic guides from

within ourselves, then our lives are limited by external and alien forms, and we conform to the needs of a structure that is not based on human need, let alone an individual's. But when we begin to live from within outward, in touch with the power of the erotic within ourselves, and allowing that power to inform and illuminate our actions upon the world around us, then we begin to be responsible to ourselves in the deepest sense. For as we begin to recognize our deepest feelings, we begin to give up, of necessity, being satisfied with suffering and self-negation, and with the numbness which so often seems like their only alternative in our society. Our acts against oppression become integral with self, motivated and empowered from within.

In touch with the erotic, I become less willing to accept powerlessness, or those other supplied states of being which are not native to me, such as resignation, despair, self-effacement, depression, self-denial.

And yes, there is a hierarchy. There is a difference between painting a back fence and writing a poem, but only one of quantity. And there is, for me, no difference between writing a good poem and moving into sunlight against the body of a woman I love.

This brings me to the last consideration of the erotic. To share the power of each other's feelings is different from using another's feelings as we would use a kleenex. When we look the other way from our experience, erotic or otherwise, we use rather than share the feelings of those others who participate in the experience with us. And use without consent of the used is abuse.

In order to be utilized, our erotic feelings must be recognized. The need for sharing deep feeling is a human need. But within the European-American tradition, this need is satisfied by certain proscribed erotic comings-together. These occasions are almost always characterized by a simultaneous looking away, a pretense of calling them something else, whether a religion, a fit, mob violence, or even playing doctor. And this misnaming of the need and the deed give rise to that distortion which results in pornography and obscenity—the abuse of feeling.

When we look away from the importance of the erotic in the development and sustenance of our power, or when we look away from ourselves as we satisfy our erotic needs in concert with others, we use each other as objects of satisfaction rather than share our joy in the satisfying, rather than make connection with our similarities and our differences. To refuse to be conscious of what we are feeling at any time, however comfortable that might seem, is to deny a large part of the experience, and to allow ourselves to be reduced to the pornographic, the abused, and the absurd.

The erotic cannot be felt secondhand. As a Black lesbian feminist, I have a particular feeling, knowledge, and understanding for those sisters with whom I have danced hard, played, or even fought. This deep participation has often been the forerunner for joint concerted actions not possible before.

But this erotic charge is not easily shared by women who continue to operate under an exclusively European-American male tradition. I know it was not available to me when I was trying to adapt my consciousness to this mode of living and sensation.

Only now, I find more and more women-identified women brave enough to risk sharing the erotic's electrical charge without having to look away, and without distorting the enormously powerful and creative nature of that exchange. Recognizing the power of the erotic within our lives can give us the energy to pursue genuine change within our world, rather than merely settling for a shift of characters in the same weary drama.

For not only do we touch our most profoundly creative source, but we do that which is female and self-affirming in the face of a racist, patriarchal, and anti-erotic society.

Discussion Questions

1. How does Lorde describe the erotic? How does her understanding of the erotic as power challenge traditional conceptions of both of those terms? How does Lorde distinguish eroticism from pornography?

2. Lorde's paper was addressed specifically to women. Do you believe that there are significant differences in how groups of people experience the erotic in their lives? Are we all equally capable of discovering and using this form of power in our lives? Why or why not?

3. This chapter closes the foundational section of the reader. Why do you think that the editors chose to place it here?

PART II

Performing and Disciplining Sexualities in Interpersonal Contexts

6

Language, Socialization, and Silence in Gay Adolescence

WILLIAM LEAP

This chapter explores a component of the "coming-out" experience that remains largely overlooked in the literature on gay adolescence: How do gay teenagers go about acquiring the language of gay culture? My discussion of this question builds on three assumptions: (1) that something called "gay culture"[1] (as distinct from gay "lifestyle" or erotic interests) really exists; (2) that "gay culture" includes distinctive "ways of talking" within its inventory of symbolics and semiotics; and (3) that these "ways of talking" are sufficiently rich and complex to justify being termed gay *language*, rather than an argot, "secret code," or rhetorical style.[2]

By exploring the convergence of language, identity construction, and gay socialization, this chapter joins other recent studies exploring the close connections between language and culture that underlie, for example, recollections of childhood in a "lesbian living room" (Morgan & Wood 1995), dialogue between entertainer and audience at a black drag club (Barrett 1995, 1999), menu-planning

SOURCE: This chapter was originally published as "Language, Socialization, and Silence in Gay Adolescence" in *Reinventing Identities: The Gendered Self in Discourse* (Mary Bucholtz, A. C. Liang, and Laurel A. Sutton, eds.). Copyright © 1999 Oxford University Press. Reprinted by permission.

Author's Note: This chapter builds on a discussion of gay English and language socialization that first appeared in Leap (1994) and that I develop further in Leap (1996). I presented versions of this work as an invited lecture at Pennsylvania State University's Lesbian/Gay Studies Series (February 1995) and in a session on lesbian and gay discourse held at the annual meeting of the American Association for Applied Linguistics (Long Beach, CA, March 1995). Mary Bucholtz gave a close reading to the chapter in preliminary draft, and her guidance helped immeasurably in the development of the final argument. My thanks, as well, to Liz Sheehan (American University), Tony D'Augeli (Penn State), Rick Arons (St. John's), and the other editors of this volume for their useful contributions to this project.

for a lesbian seder (Moonwomon 1996), or the in-flight disclosure of gay identities between an airline passenger and an airline steward (Leap 1993). These studies show how participation in lesbian- and gay-centered text-making in different social settings builds familiarity with the rules of lesbian- and gay-centered grammar and discourse and with other cultural practices relevant to those domains. They also demonstrate how participation in such social moments assumes some degree of familiarity with lesbian- and gay-centered language and cultural practices. In the absence of such information, text-making becomes highly dependent on situated (rather than prediscursive) meanings, on negotiation and inference, on "double (that is, hearer- as well as speaker-based) subjectivity" (Goodwin 1989:12), and in some instances on conditions of risk (Leap 1996:72–73). None of these processes is uniquely lesbian or gay in its basis, but all the same, text-making conducted on such terms has clear implications for lesbian and gay experience. Particularly vulnerable in this regard are young persons who are just beginning to lay claim to lesbian or gay identities and who turn to lesbian- and gay-centered text-making as a format for acting on those claims. Text-making in these cases ranges from the disclosure of same-sex desires to close friends or adult authority figures to the construction of silence as agemates use an individual's ambiguous sexuality as a focus for teasing and taunting. Overlapping with the construction of textual silence, of course, is the almost epidemic-like incidence of attempted suicide reported for American teenagers struggling to come to terms with their homosexuality.[3]

Understandably, when gay men look back on their adolescence, they often speak of this period of their gender career as a time of loneliness and isolation, conditions that one gay man summarized powerfully with the phrase "a vast desert of nothing" (Leap 1996:127).[4] But some gay men also describe this period as a time when they set out to make sense out of newly discovered feelings, emotions, and interest; when they assembled information that would help them better understand those discoveries; and when they tried to locate other individuals who might share (or understand or at least not dismiss) these concerns. And—of particular importance to this chapter—gay men talk about attempts to find a language through which they can describe, interpret, and account for the new directions now taking shape within their lives.

Some examples of such statements appear below. They were chosen from a larger set of texts I collected during a recent study of gay language socialization (reported, in part, in Leap 1994, 1996:125–139).[5] Each example describes a young man's attempts to make sense out of a male-centered sexual identity, even though the details of that identity were just beginning to be disclosed. And each example shows how language became a resource during this process.

Jim (a 22-year-old gay white man who was born in Buffalo, New York, and lived there until he started college in Washington, D.C.) told me:

> I was never sat down by my mom and dad and told the heterosexual version of the birds and the bees. Um, you know, when you get to the time where you are twelve, thirteen, or fourteen, you begin to be sexually aware, you really look, strive for sources of information.
>
> I started looking for information about homosexuality . . . and eventually I branched off into the *Encyclopaedia Britannica* we had in the house. I looked up in the index as far as sexual goes: penis, phallus, every single adjective, synonym of that. . . . I eventually went to the public library, school library and that wasn't easy because it was public and you had to build up your confidence. . . .
>
> I tried to do as much as possible, reading, whatever I thought might have gotten somewhere. For example, if I came across a column like for example Ann Landers might have mentioned it, I'd be her fan for a couple of months so maybe she'd bring it up again.

Sam (a 21-year-old gay white man who was born and raised in central Ohio and attended college in Washington, D.C.) told me:

> *Brothers* (a cable television sitcom) had an effeminate stereotyped gay man. That was a good example of how not to talk. I didn't believe gay people talked like that. *Consenting Adult* related a view which I knew was true and was looking for: a normal guy can be gay. *Deathtrap*—my mom was disgusted by the kissing scene. I was distracted.

Wallace (a gay white man in his early 30s who grew up in the Washington, D.C. suburbs and is a professional actor with several companies in the Washington area) noted in an interview published in the *Washington Post* (Brown & Swisher 1994):

> I grew up in Maryland, right outside of D.C. and spent my childhood listening to *West Side Story* and *A Chorus Line*. Those cast albums and movie musicals on TV were sort of secret messages from a world we didn't experience in our suburban, private school upbringing. That saved us.

Robert (a 27-year-old gay white man who was born in northern Florida, finished graduate school in North Carolina, and is now on the faculty of a junior college in northern Virginia) told me:

> Later in high school, my junior year, I guess, people started calling me faggot. I don't know if it was a joke or what, but they called me that. A lot. Even my teammates, they'd toss me a towel and say, "Hey faggot, catch this," or someone'd say, "Hey faggot, the coach needs to talk to you."
>
> (Q: Did you get angry? Did this upset you?)
>
> You know, it's funny. I didn't get mad at all. I was uncomfortable, but I was not mad. See, I knew by then that I was gay so—without even knowing it, they were right! They were telling the truth. I couldn't get mad at them for telling the truth.

Joe (a 24-year-old gay white man and a campus and community activist) told me:

> I have been gay since the womb: I started experimenting with sex when I was very young and when I found others doing the same thing I knew there was something to all of this—but I didn't know exactly what it was.
>
> (Q: So when did you come out?)
>
> You mean, telling anybody about all this experimentation? Not 'til I was a teenager. I met an older woman, middle-aged, who had lots of gay friends. She introduced me to some other, gay men and they took me under their wing. That is how I learned the rest of it, the social thing, the networks.

Sam continues:

> (Q: Did you know or know about gay people in [your hometown] when you were in high school?)
>
> No, not at first, but by the time I ended ninth grade, I had learned about five people: one aged thirty-five, three older than that, and one my own age. He became my best friend in high school.
>
> (Q: How did you find these people?)
>
> Pure luck. . . . I wanted to find someone like me. Found him by pure luck. Met him in the eighth grade. I told him in the ninth grade. He told me he was bisexual in the tenth. Both of us were scared. Having been friends, we did not want to jeopardize each other's secret. We talked a lot. No topic was safe. Though really, it was me doing the talking. He was the novice, someone for me to talk to.

Jim continues:

> I, later in my senior year, when I was seventeen or eighteen. I had an English teacher, too. It was real interesting, our relationship, because he was very pull-students-aside-and-get-into-their-lives kind of thing. I do not know for what reason, but he did that with me. He was very helpful in that he knew I was gay and kind of brought me out a bit more. I remember that, for some reason, he approached me, and said: How does your mother feel about this? And I said: Wow! And I told him, and the dam was lifted, and all the information I needed in my life was there, me seeking advice from him, that sort of thing.

CHARTING A PATH THROUGH THE "DESERT OF NOTHING"

Although life stories are subjectives (and in some sense fictional) documents, they do provide a *detail* of gay experience that cannot be retrieved from statistical surveys or other broadly based forms of data-gathering.[6] And in the present case, many details in these narratives speak directly to the importance of language and language learning for gay socialization and for the construction of gay identity during adolescence.

The close connection between language, identity, and heteronormativity provides the background for the present discussion, and I begin my analysis with some general comments on this connection.

Heteronormativity Versus the Gay Imaginary

By *heteronormativity*, I mean the principles of order and control that position heterosexuality as the cornerstone of the American sex/gender system and obligate the personal construction of sexuality and gender in terms of heterosexual norms. Heteronormativity assumes, for example, that there are two sexes and therefore two genders. Heteronormativity then requires that all discussions of gendered identity and opportunity be framed strictly in terms of this dichotomy, forcing gendered actors to be labelled as either "women" or "men," regardless of the identification that the actors might give to themselves.

An abundance of institutions, "a pervasive cluster of forces" (Rich 1980:640), in Western society conspire to give heteronormativity its natural and normal facade. Importantly, however, while heteronormativity is certainly powerful and pervasive in late modern Western societies, it is not entirely totalizing. Alternative constructions of sexuality and gender are possible within this system, although particular alternatives do not always intersect smoothly with normative claims to authority. Hence the regulation of heteronormativity unfolds through distinctions between acceptable and unacceptable sexual/gendered identities and practices and through an ordering of the social worth of individuals on the basis of their allegiance to such distinctions.

In this way, heteronormativity co-occurs with, and profits from, the social presence of the *subaltern* (an "identity-in-differential" which is set apart from both the ideal and the elite [Spivak 1988:284]), the *queer* ("a unity . . . of shared dissent from the dominant organization of sex and gender" composed of lesbian, gay, and other lifestyles "whose icons are heavily associated by cultural outsides with the culture of gay life, politics and practices" [Whittle 1994:27]); the *stigmatized* (persons who, through various means, must contend with a "spoiled identity" [Goffman 1963]), as well as other stances situated on the margins of late modern society.

Language holds a prominent place in the intersection of the heteronormative and the marginal. In English and other Western languages, conversation, narration, and other forms of text-making provide contexts within which heteronormative messages are produced and reproduced in everyday life. Morphemic and lexical contrasts, processes of reference and inference, and other structural details provide the framework through which heteronormative messages become inscribed in, remembered within, and retained beyond the textured moment.

Unavoidably, language keeps heteronormative stances in the foreground of daily activity and keeps alternative forms of reference in the background, the margins, and the shadows. Such arrangements ensure that normative assumptions become expectable, reasonable, and acceptable components of the local cultural inventory and that alternative stances remain less familiar, more mysterious, and less desirable.

But even while it imposes such limitations on social reference, language-based normativity does not always disrupt the working of the personal imaginary. Individuals still construct their own sense of sexual/gendered possibilities and apply their own meanings to those constructions, even if they do not find referential support for these imagined constructions with normatively sanctioned sex/gender discourse. Hence the pervasive presence of silence within heteronormative domains, a silence that reflects an absence of articulation but not necessarily an absence of personal voice. And hence the delight in the discovery of labels, even when the points of reference are not intended to be complimentary or to have any positive implications.

By my reading of his statement cited above, this is the point of Robert's reactions to his peers' taunting and teasing in the high school locker room. Robert's teammates called him *faggot*, but rather than becoming angry at this name-calling, Robert diffuses the statements by acknowledging the truthfulness of their reference. He admits that he *was* gay, after all, and says that he could not be upset at his colleagues for telling the truth. We must not be sidetracked by Robert's seemingly naive rewriting of logical argument. Instead, we must consider how Robert's interpretation of these statements gives him a way of living through moments when he was the target of invective, moments when he had no alternative but either to "confirm" his manhood through a fistfight or some other form of competitive force, thereby directing the team's teasing toward the vanquished party, or simply to maintain his silence. As he told me in our interview, the latter seemed the more reasonable option for a young man growing up in a small Southern town.

Such choices are familiar parts of the gay adolescent social landscape: They are found not only in the narratives collected here but also in more overtly functional work representing gay adolescent experience. Robert Reinhardt's character Billy in his novel *A History of Shadows* (1986), for example, would understand Robert's decision. Like

Robert, in the novel Billy remembers thinking that he "was the only homosexual in the world." He continues:

> Well, that's not quite true. . . . But I felt I was the only homosexual. It's hard being something for which one doesn't even have a name. And I didn't for a long time. I used to wonder, what am I? I saw the boys in my class and longed for them, but I couldn't figure out what the vague aching was, and I couldn't recognize it in others. I couldn't see that anyone looked at me with the same longing.
>
> I found out about sex in the streets. The first name I had for what I was, was "cock-sucker.". . . (It) was an awful word the way they used it, but it meant that my condition was nameable. I knew I was awful, but I finally had a name for all those odd feelings. I wasn't nothing. I was awful, but I wasn't nothing. (Reinhardt 1986:25)

My condition was nameable. I finally had a name for those odd feelings. I wasn't nothing. Here, the relief in finding a label for "those odd feelings" outweighs the negative content surrounding this usage. And once again, rather than being overwhelmed by negative sentiment, Billy found a way to pull something useful from the statements and to disregard the remainder of the message. Wallace did the same thing, as he reports in the passage cited above, when he began to locate "secret messages from a world we didn't experience" in cast albums and Broadway musicals. Sam did the same thing when he rejected the stereotyped homosexual's use of language on *Brothers* because he "didn't believe gay people talked like that." And Jim did the same thing when he searched through Ann Landers's columns for her occasional comments on homosexuality.

All of these narratives speak to a process that Julia Kristeva (1982) describes in some detail. Even though I may willingly subordinate myself to some object that "precedes and possesses me," an object over which I have no control, "sublimation" allows me to "dissolve

[it] in the raptures of a bottomless memory."[7] Then, "as soon as I perceive [the now-sublimated object], as soon as I name it, the sublime triggers—as it has always triggered— a spree of perceptions and words that expands memory boundlessly. I then forget the point of departure and find myself removed to a secondary universe, set off from the other where I 'am'—delight and loss" (1982:10–11). Kristeva's description speaks to a re-creation of awareness, a construction of a personal imaginary, that does not challenge the dominant and oppressive heteronormativity but does enable individuals to make their own way in spite of heterosexual norms. For Robert and Billy, for Sam and Wallace and Jim, and for the other men contributing life stories to this chapter, the journey of self-discovery moves them through the "desert of nothing." Expressions of personal agency are central to this journey, and—as I will show below— familiarity with a gay-centered language is central to expressions of personal agency. But first, I must say more about personal agency.

Self-Managed Socialization

A striking feature in the life stories I have collected from gay men has been the consistent presence of the first-person active voice. That is, narrators position themselves as narrative agents, not merely as objects, in their stories. They describe personal struggles to take charge of their gay socialization and present the socialization process itself as a self-initiated, self-managed experience, even while they discuss the frustration and pain it causes.

It is tempting to view such claims as a consequence of the life-story genre: that is, stories that describe events in the speaker's own life are likely to position the speaker as the central character. But genre alone is an inadequate explanation for this component of textual design, because speakers can always adapt narratives to their own needs (see Sawin, 1999). If the events in these narratives reflect

the tensions between social heteronormativity and the personal gay imaginary as they unfold in adolescent lives, then the pervasiveness of first-person reference must be part of this reflection and its presence must be explained in similar terms.

What then are the narrators telling me when they describe gay adolescence as a time of self-managed socialization? First, these references suggest that gay socialization is quite different from the socialization experiences that unfold elsewhere in the life course. The complex of institutional support that enables the transmission of heteronormative conventions and practices between and within generations (some of which are described in Coates, 1999) has very little parallel within gay adolescence, even with the expanding numbers of gay community centers, youth outreach programs, and religious support groups that have emerged in recent years. Understandably, then, statements like *I knew I was different but didn't have a word for it* and *I thought I was the only such person in the world* continue to assume an almost trope-like status in gay men's descriptions of their teenage years. Nothing like these statements appears in the ethnographic descriptions of normative language socialization (e.g., Heath 1983; Ochs 1988; Schieffelin 1990; Ward 1971) or in the comments on socialization experiences that these researchers have collected from members of the speech communities under study. The predominant socialization processes in those settings have to do with incorporating the individual into the social group, not with enabling individuals to claim space on its margin. Claiming space on the margin is, however, the predominant theme in gay men's socialization narratives, as the examples reviewed here have shown. Support for such efforts could come from external sources such as guidance from friends, family members, teachers, or other authority figures, but the narratives always describe such support as accidental and unplanned occurrences, as interventions over which the individual has no control. Sam refers to his relationship with a sympathetic agemate as "pure luck"; Jim "do[es]n't know for what reason" a high school teacher started asking him helpful questions about his sexuality. The point is that although external support is always possible in gay socialization, the availability of such support is in no sense reliable. This leaves only one resource to provide accessible guidance to the individual as he struggles to understand male-centered desire and gay-centered identity: the individual himself.

For this reason, I find it imperative to read the pervasive references to personal agency, to narrator-as-actor, in these life-story segments not as indications of "what I really did to learn about gay life" but as after-the-fact realization that "this [self-managed socialization] was the only way, at this point in my life, that I could have learned about gay experience." Such an analysis places the narrative's emphasis on first-person agency squarely within the narrative strategy that Arthur Kleinmann (1988:50) terms "retrospective narratization." This emphasis reflects the narrator's sense of "significance and validity in the creation of life story," not his "fidelity to historical circumstances" (51). In this case, it is the depiction of loneliness and emptiness combined with the discussions of self-managed socialization that gives these narratives their intended significance and validity.

Retrieving Gay Messages

Also important is the narrators' descriptions of the sources they consulted while conducting their individualized, personalized search for information about gay experience and about themselves: library books, magazines, newspaper columns, motion pictures, television sitcoms, talk shows, Broadway musicals, gay folklore, jokes, supportive responses from friends and strangers. As already discussed, even derogatory homophobic

statements become useful resources in this process.

The particular items that narrators include in this inventory are not as important as the range and variety of materials. Perhaps no single source provided sufficient information to answer the narrators' questions, or the narrators were not satisfied with deriving information from only one source. Either way, the narratives suggest that seeking out information about gay experience is an important part of self-managed socialization.

But seeking out information assumes that the individual knows where to find appropriate sources or is willing to search sufficiently broadly until he stumbles across the right locations. Events in the narratives cited here position both of these practices within the gay socialization process, and they also imply that, once the searching begins, locating gay-relevant materials is not a difficult task. Indeed, as Alexander Doty (1993) argues, any text in today's mass culture contains (at least potentially) a queer message and hence contains information that could be relevant to gay socialization.

At the same time, Doty continues, "unless the text is *about* queers, it seems to me that the queerness of most mass culture texts is less an essential waiting-to-be-discovered property than the result of acts of production and reception" (1993:ix). It would be valuable to know more about the specifics of the reception process described in these narratives. It seems easy enough (as Jim explained) to scan the index of the *Encyclopaedia Britannica* "as far as sexual goes: penis, phallus, every single adjective, synonym of that." But Sam's rereading of the gay character on *Brothers* and Wallace's "queering" of *West Side Story* speak to a more complex interpretation of textual material. What are the clues, the cues, the signals, the signifiers that call forth gay-centered interpretation of such texts?

Answering these questions is similar to answering questions about the mechanics of *gaydar*, the recognition strategy which Michael Musto describes as "the art of spotting sisters [i.e., other gay men], no matter how concealed, invisible or pretending to be straight they are" (1993:120). Gay men who freely discuss using gaydar are not necessarily explicit regarding the criteria that guide their evaluation of "suspect gay" status; and, when described, such criteria differ greatly from one gay man to the next (see discussion in Leap 1996:49–66). It is likely that the interpretive processes relevant to queer reading in such encounters are closely linked to the processes that underlie location and retrieval of information about gay-centered culture and language during gay adolescence. If so, then interpretive skills that are central to self-managed socialization during gay adolescence continue to be valuable resources throughout the gender career.

Homophobia, Rehearsal, and the Language of the Closet

Particularly important in regard to the movement from adolescence to adulthood are the ways in which a retrieval of gay-centered messages from written and other media texts provides *rehearsal* for encounters with gay-centered messages in social settings. Learning how to recognize and make sense out of gay-centered messages in seemingly heteronormative texts is one part of rehearsal. And so is building a personal repertoire of gay commentary by memorizing words, phrases, and sentences from novels, motion pictures, or plays with explicitly gay themes. *Boys in the Band* (Crowley 1968) and *Consenting Adult* (Hobson 1975) remain two popular sources for this purpose. Equally helpful, reported gay men in their 20s, were the dialogues from television soap operas; for gay men in their 40s, additional sources included memorable lines from the films of Bette Davis and the numerous anecdotes attributed to the private life of Tallulah Bankhead.

These sets of information gave gay adolescents opportunities to anticipate the linguistic skills (both of reception and of production—see the previous comment by Doty) that they would need in conversation with another gay, gay-friendly, or potentially gay-friendly individual. On some occasions, as Sam's discovery of "someone like me" suggests, being prepared for those conversations helped both parties secure a long-lasting friendship or led to other successful outcomes. Unfortunately, modeling real-life exchanges around media-derived images of gay communication and its social dynamics can also yield misleading expectations about a conversation and its effects. Often, the resulting (mis)communication leads to unpleasant consequences, as the following story (from Rhoads 1994) suggests.

Andrew (one of Rhoads's key informants) had sex with his best friend in junior high school, and he "found the experience eye-opening":

> "I thought, 'Oh wow, maybe this isn't so wrong.'". . . He learned all his life that having sex with a man was wrong, but this experience seemed to tell him something different. "I thought it seemed like he enjoyed it and I enjoyed it. So it was something we shouldn't do? I was like, 'Oh this is great. There is someone else who feels like I do.'"
>
> The next day, Andrew's friend (the one with whom he had sex) spread it all over school that Andrew had sexually assaulted him. "It was horrendous: I mean it was my first real encounter with homophobia." (1994:74)

There was little Andrew could do to prevent his "friend" from spreading stories about sexual assault. To deny the charge would be a predictable reaction and would only draw greater attention to the event. Besides, to whom would Andrew voice his denial? Such events require more subtle responses on the part of the gay-accused: silence, secrecy, abjection, erasure, and disguise—each of which gains representation through a language of restraint, a language that parallels the restricted discussions of gay life and gay opportunity in public heteronormative discourse and that transfers those restrictions into the personal linguistic inventory.[8]

Silence, secrecy, disguise, privacy, and restraint are, of course, features that define the experience of "the closet" in Western tradition. Understandably, many gay theorists view "the closet" as a primary obstacle to gay self-determination and consider "coming out of the closet" as the culmination of the move from individuation to disclosure (Davies 1992:76ff.), "the most momentous act in the life of any lesbian or gay person" (Plummer 1995:82), and the primary rite of passage in contemporary gay experience (Rhoads 1994:7–8). The life stories that I have collected contain ample documentation of the damage created when the closet becomes the long-term anchor for a person's gay identity. At the same time, these stories also point out that the closet is not a site of gay denial. Certainly, being "in the closet" discourages explicit expressions of gay identity, but gay socialization is still possible within that enclosure—especially if the socialization process unfolds in personalized, self-managed terms. Closets have keyholes, closet doors have cracks, and closet walls are thin.

So although it is often appropriate to theorize the closet in terms of regulation and repression, it is also possible to theorize this construction as a simpler and less threatening form of gay experience, a subdued alternative to the more explicit demands of a public gay voice. The term *voice* is important here. If the closet is part of gay culture, then the closet, too, has a language—a language that privileges silence over speech, restraint over expression, concealment over cooperation, safety over risk (see also Liang, 1999). And for some gay adolescents, learning the language of the closet is as integral to gay self-managed socialization as are the gay messages in TV sitcoms and rock and roll lyrics, the negotiations of gay disclosure between good friends, or the

other strategies that guide their journey through the "desert of nothing."

LANGUAGE AND SURVIVAL

As my analysis of "the closet" suggests, interpreting gay adolescence in terms of self-managed socialization offers a somewhat different perspective on gay adolescence from that usually presented in the scholarly literature. Certainly, as Rhoads argues:

> Adolescence is a stressful time for everyone. . . . For gay and bisexual men, this period of life is even more traumatic because in addition to the typical stressors such as leaving home, dating and thoughts of career, they must also come to term with their same-sex attractions. (1994:67)

Yet the narratives that Rhoads discusses, like the life stories in Gilbert Herdt and Andrew Boxer's (1993) study of the Horizon Project in Chicago, the life stories in Jim Sears's *Growing Up Gay in the South* (1991), or the life-story segments I have discussed here, are not just narratives of trauma and frustration. They are also survivors' stories. They describe the narrators' efforts—to use Plummer's (1995:50) formulation—to "move from secrecy, suffering and an often felt sense of victimization toward a major change: therapy, survival, recovery or politics." These efforts may still be continuing at the time of narration, the move may be ongoing, but the narrative stance is consistently the same in these collections: Narrators may find homosexuality to be disruptive, painful, and isolating, yet they search out ways to define gay identity to their own satisfaction and to articulate it successfully with other components of adolescent experience.

Worth interrogating, then, are the reasons why other gay teenagers are not successful in such efforts at self-managed socialization and why still others do not underake such efforts in the first place. We can move this interrogation forward by recognizing that gay adolescents are not, in any categorical sense, neurotic, maladjusted, and self-destructive, but they are likely to become so when their search for information about gay experience and their other efforts toward self-discovery are devalued, thwarted, and ridiculed at every turn. We can ask, accordingly, whether our own institutions and communities provide teenagers with the opportunities, incentives, and resources on which self-managed socialization depends; we can ask what support each of us is providing to that end.

NOTES

1. By the term *gay teenagers* I mean male teenagers who are in the process of discovering male-centered desire and constructing personal identity in response to those discoveries.

2. These assumptions are warranted by a number of works of scholarship: Ken Plummer (1995:91–95) traces the factors that prompted the emergence of gay culture in recent years; Gilbert Herdt and Andrew Boxer (1992:3–13, 1993:1–24) explore the ways in which an authentically gay culture provides a moral critique of contemporary U.S. society; Esther Newton (1993) employs historical perspectives to show how gay culture offers complex if often subtle sites for resistance to heteronormativity; Plummer assigns stories and storytelling a prominent place in gay culture; Birch Moonwomon's (1995) distinction between linguistic and societal discourses in such stories argues powerfully in favor of the existence of lesbian and gay language(s), as well as lesbian and gay texts; Leap (1995:xi–xvii, 1996:1–11 and introduction) offers additional arguments to that end.

3. Recent estimates suggest that gay teenagers are twice as likely to attempt suicide as are their heterosexual agemates and that as many as three out of every five gay teenagers give serious thought to suicide at least once during their adolescent years (Gibson 1989; Rhoads 1994:67–68).

4. The remainder of this chapter focuses on gay men's experiences with linguistic and cultural socialization during adolescence. How closely these experiences parallel the socialization experiences of lesbians remains to be determined.

5. The statements below come from a collection of quotations assembled for Leap (1996) and

are reproduced here with permission of the University of Minnesota Press. Statements without a bibliographic citation come from interviews I conducted between 1989 and 1992 with self-identified European American and African American gay men aged 18 to 25 and 40 to 55. My lead-in questions for this discussion established my interest in learning about the respondent's experience with gay adolescence. I intentionally kept the focus of discussion open-ended and unstructured, so that I could hear how the respondent himself would talk about his "discovery" of a "gay self."

6. I recognize the limitations of using life-story narratives as a database for studies of gay socialization. Life stories are not factual documents but a form of fiction—that is, they are constructed, crafted texts; they emerge out of the respondent's subjective (re)framing and (re)claiming of a life experience; and, as retrospective narratives (Kleinmann 1988:50–51), their vision of "the past" is likely to be influenced by the politics of the present. But as I see it, the subjective, reflexive nature of these texts makes them especially valuable to the study of gay life as lived experience. In fact, just as telling these stories allows respondents to experiment with presentations of memory, listening to them allows the audience (in this case, the researcher) to coparticipate in those experiments, and by extension to coparticipate in the events that the respondents' narratives now reclaim. Ellen Lewin (1993, especially pages 9–11) reached similar conclusions when she examined the life-story narratives of lesbian mothers. So did Faye Ginsberg (1989, especially pages 141–145) when she studied abortion-rights controversies in Fargo, North Dakota. A particularly vivid example of researcher coparticipation in retold events is found in Kathleen Wood's (1999) discussion of a lesbian coming-out story told in American Sign Language.

7. The wording here retains Kristeva's pronominal usage.

8. I want the term *language* in the phrase *language of restraint* to be read literally. Silence, abjection, and so on are not arbitrary components of conversational or narrative structure; their presence conforms to linguistic rules derived from the *grammar* (that is, the knowledge of language) that the gay adolescent brings into the speech event and from the *discourse practices* that actualize this knowledge within specific text-making settings. By referring here to a language of restraint, I position the textual occurrences of silence, abjection, and so on as products of a particular aggregation of

linguistic knowledge and linguistic practices, some of which I have described in Leap (1996:24–48). Gay teenagers build familiarity with this aggregation of knowledge and practice, this "language," as a part of their experiences with gay socialization and their everyday encounters with heteronormative living; what happened to Andrew in the example cited here is telling in both regards.

REFERENCES

Barrett, Rusty (1995). Supermodels of the world unite: Political economy and the language of performance among African-American drag queens. In William Leap (ed.), *Beyond the lavender lexicon*. Newark: Gordon & Breach, 207–226.

_____ (1999). Indexing polyphonous identity in the speech of African American drag queens. In Mary Bucholtz, A. C. Liang, and Laurel A. Sutton (eds.), *Reinventing identities: The gendered self in discourse*. Oxford: Oxford University Press, 13–31.

Brown, Joe, & Kara Swisher (1994). Backstage: The one who fit the bill. *Washington Post* (August 6):C2.

Coates, Jennifer (1999). Challenging feminities: The talk of teenage girls. In Mary Bucholtz, A. C. Liang, and Laurel A. Sutton (eds.), *Reinventing identities: The gendered self in discourse*. Oxford: Oxford University Press, 123–144.

Crowley, Matt (1968). *Boys in the band*. New York: Samuel French.

Davies, Peter (1992). The role of disclosure in coming out among gay men. In Ken Plummer (ed.), *Modern homosexualities*. New York: Routledge, 75–85.

Doty, Alexander (1993). *Making things perfectly queer: Interpreting mass culture*. Minneapolis: University of Minnesota Press.

Gibson, Paul (1989). Gay male and lesbian youth suicide. In M. R. Feinlieb (ed.), *Report of the Secretary's Task Force on Youth Suicide*. Washington, DC: U.S. Department of Health and Human Services, 110–142.

Ginsberg, Faye (1989). *Contested lives: The abortion debate in an American community*. Berkeley: University of California Press.

Goffman, Erving (1963). *Stigma: Notes on the management of spoiled identity*. Englewood Cliffs, NJ: Prentice Hall.

Goodwin, Joseph P. (1989). *More man than you'll ever be: Gay folklore and acculturation in Middle America*. Bloomington: Indiana University Press.

Heath, Shirley Brice (1983). *Ways with words: Language, life, and work in communities and classrooms*. Cambridge: Cambridge University Press.

Herdt, Gilbert, & Andrew Boxer (1992). Introduction: Culture, history and life course of gay men. In Gilbert Herdt (ed.), *Gay culture in America: Essays from the field*. Boston: Beacon Press, 1–27.

_____ (1993). *Children of horizons: How gay and lesbian teens are leading a new way out of the closet*. Boston: Beacon Press.

Hobson, Laura Z. (1975). *Consenting adult*. Garden City, NY: Doubleday.

Kleinmann, Arthur (1988). *The illness narratives: Suffering, healing and the human condition*. New York: Basic Books.

Kristeva, Julia (1982). Approaching abjection. In Kristeva, *Powers of horror*. New York: Columbia University Press, 1–31.

Leap, William L. (1993). Gay men's English: Cooperative discourse in a language of risk. *New York Folklore* 19(1–2):45–70.

_____ (1994). Learning gay culture in a "desert of nothing": Language as a resource in gender socialization [Special issue]. *High School Journal* 77(1–2):122–131. "The Gay Teenager."

_____ (1995). Introduction. In William Leap (ed.), *Beyond the lavender lexicon*. Newark: Gordon & Breach, vii–xxix.

_____ (1996). *Word's out: Gay English in America*. Minneapolis: University of Minnesota Press.

Lewin, Ellen (1993). *Lesbian mothers: Accounts of gender in American culture*. Ithaca: Cornell University Press.

Liang, A. C. (1999). Conversationally implicating lesbian and gay identity. In Mary Bucholtz, A. C. Liang, and Laurel A. Sutton (eds.), *Reinventing identities: The gendered self in discourse*. Oxford: Oxford University Press, 293-311.

Moonwomon, Birch (1995). Lesbian discourse, lesbian knowledge. In William Leap (ed.), *Beyond the lavender lexicon*. Newark: Gordon & Breach, 45–64.

_____ (1996). Lesbian conversation as a site for ideological identity construction. Paper presented at the annual meeting of the American Association for Applied Linguistics, Chicago.

Morgan, Ruth, & Kathleen Wood (1995). Lesbians in the living room: Collusion, co-construction and co-narration in conversation. In William Leap (ed.), *Beyond the lavender lexicon*. Newark: Gordon & Breach, 235–248.

Musto, Michael (1993). Gaydar: Using that intu-
itive sixth sense. *Out* 12:120–124.

Newton, Esther (1993). *Cherry Grove, Fire Island.*
Boston: Beacon Press.

Ochs, Elinor (1988). *Culture and language development: Language acquisition and language
socialization in a Samoan village.* Cambridge:
Cambridge University Press.

Plummer, Ken (1995). *Telling sexual stories:
Power, change and social worlds.* London:
Routledge.

Reinhardt, Robert C. (1986). *A history of shadows.*
Boston: Alyson Press.

Rhoads, Richard (1994). *Coming out in college:
The struggle for a queer identity.* Westport,
CT: Bergin & Garvey.

Rich, Adrienne (1980). Compulsory heterosexuality and lesbian existence. *Signs* 5:631–660.

Sawin, Patricia (1999). Gender, context and the
narrative construction of identity: Rethinking
models of "women's narrative." In Mary
Bucholtz, A. C. Liang, and Laurel A. Sutton
(eds.), *Reinventing identities: The gendered self
in discourse.* Oxford: Oxford University Press,
241–258.

Schieffelin, Bambi (1990). *The give and take of
everyday life: Language socialization of Kaluli*

children. Cambridge: Cambridge University
Press.

Sears, Jim (1991). *Growing up gay in the South:
Race, gender and journeys of the spirit.*
Binghamton, NY: Harrington Park Press.

Spivak, Gayatri Chakravorty (1988). Can the subaltern speak? In Cary Nelson & Lawrence
Grossberg (eds.), *Marxism and the interpretation of culture.* Basingstoke, England:
Macmillan, 271–313.

Ward, Martha (1971). *Them children: A study in
language learning.* New York: Holt, Rinehart
& Winston.

Whittle, Stephen (1994). Consuming differences:
The collaboration of the gay body with the cultural state. In Stephen Whittle (ed.), *The margins of the city: Gay men's urban lives.*
Brookfield, VT: Ashgate, 27–41.

Wood, Kathleen (1999). Coherent identities and heterosexist ideologies: Deaf and hearing lesbian
coming-out stories. In Mary Bucholtz, A. C.
Liang, and Laurel A. Sutton (eds.), *Reinventing
identities: The gendered self in discourse.*
Oxford: Oxford University Press, 46–63.

Discussion Questions

1. What are the three assumptions that Leap makes as he begins his discussion of "how gay teenagers go about acquiring the language of gay culture"?

2. How does Leap define *heteronormativity*? What do you think about the usefulness of this term?

3. What, according to Leap, is the role of language in the development of sexual identity?

4. Reflect on your own experience in acquiring competence in sexual identity–centered discourses. In what ways has your socialization been self-managed?

5. Consider whether you believe there is such a thing as "gaydar." Provide a rationale and evidence for your thinking on this subject.

7

"Having a Girlfriend Without Knowing It"

Intimate Friendships Among Adolescent Sexual-Minority Women

LISA M. DIAMOND

INTRODUCTION

Friendships and romantic relationships loom large in most people's recollections of their adolescent years, and for good reason. These two types of relationships take on particular importance during the second decade of life. Researchers have found that youths become increasingly skilled at negotiating reciprocally intimate interactions as they mature, deepening and enriching their close friendships. When they eventually form romantic relationships that combine heightened emotional and physical intimacy, the results can be unusually intense.

Stereotypes and media images of adolescent girls' relationships reflect this view. Young women's same-sex friendships are portrayed as especially intense and important during the high school years, yet their first full-blown love affairs with men are supposedly more so. The assumption underlying this view is that although both friendships and romantic relationships may be emotionally intimate, the sexual "charge" of a romantic relationship gives rise to a heightened intensity that never emerges between platonic friends, no matter how close. Thus, friendships and romantic relationships are presumed to be fundamentally different types of social ties with correspondingly distinct spheres of affect and behavior.

Does this "separate spheres" model apply to all young women? Previous research has

SOURCE: This chapter was originally published as "Having a Girlfriend Without Knowing It," in the *Journal of Lesbian Studies* (vol. 6, no. 1) and simultaneously in *Lesbian Love and Relationships* (Suzanna M. Rose, ed.). Copyright © 2002 Harrington Press, an imprint of The Haworth Press, Inc. Reprinted with permission.

found that some sexual-minority women recall intense but platonic adolescent friendships containing many of the feelings and behaviors typically associated with romantic relationships (Diamond, 2000a). Although these "passionate friendships" might seem to challenge the separate spheres model, the conventional interpretation of such relationships is that they are not, in fact, platonic at all. Rather, they are reinterpreted as unrequited romantic relationships whose special intensity stems from repressed sexual longing.

The main problem with this tidy explanation is that the women describing such friendships frequently refute it. Although some sexual-minority women admit to having harbored secret sexual desires for their closest same-sex friends, others claim that the passion they felt for such friends was exclusively emotional (Diamond, 2000a). Clearly, the separate-spheres perception of platonic friendships as fundamentally distinct from and less intense than romantic relationships does not do justice to these unique relationships. Rather than re-interpreting passionate friendships as repressed romantic relationships in order to shoehorn them into the separate spheres model, we should carefully attend to sexual-minority women's own descriptions and interpretations of these bonds.

Toward this end, I present a qualitative investigation of the most intimate adolescent friendships of 80 adolescent and young adult sexual-minority women who were interviewed as part of a longitudinal study of female sexual identity development. Extensive detail on the methods and results of this ongoing research can be found elsewhere (Diamond, 1998, 2000a, 2000b). My aim here is to provide a more descriptive account of these women's adolescent relationships that highlights the challenges they pose for conventional interpretations of the links and distinctions between sexual and emotional intimacy. Finally, although a small proportion of these women developed passionate friendships with young men, I limit the current discussion to same-sex

friendships (see Diamond, 2000a for a discussion of male-male and male-female passionate friendships).

BACKGROUND AND METHODS OF THE STUDY

Participants were 80 lesbian, bisexual, and "unlabeled" women between 18 and 25 years of age who were interviewed over the phone as part of an ongoing longitudinal study of female sexual identity development. Sampling took place across a wide range of settings, including (a) lesbian, gay, and bisexual community events (i.e., picnics, parades, social events) and youth groups in two moderately-sized cities and a number of small urban and rural communities in central New York state; (b) classes on gender and sexuality issues taught at a large, private university in central New York; and (c) lesbian, gay, and bisexual student groups at a large, private university, a large, public university, and a small, private, women's college in central New York.

The recruitment strategy succeeded in sampling sizable numbers of bisexual women and nonheterosexual women who decline to label their sexual identity, both of which are underrepresented in most research on sexual minorities. However, the sample shares a chronic drawback with other samples of sexual minorities in that it comprises predominantly White, highly educated, middle to upper class individuals. Nearly all of the college-aged participants had enrolled in college at one point, and 75% came from families in which at least one parent had completed college. Sixty-three percent of women came from families in which at least one parent had a professional or technical occupation, and 84% were White.

I conducted scripted, 30-minute telephone interviews with each participant focusing on her most intense adolescent friendship. Participants were asked to described the type and frequency of physical affection in the relationship, whether they became sexually attracted to the friend, whether the friendship ever involved sexual contact, whether they ever became preoccupied or fascinated with their friend, how frequently they spent time with their friend, and how important the friendship was—relative to their other close relationships at the time—as a source of support and emotional security. Finally, participants were asked to reflect on the specific similarities and differences between this friendship and typical romantic relationships.

CHARACTERISTICS OF SEXUAL-MINORITY WOMEN'S CLOSEST ADOLESCENT FRIENDSHIPS

> It was like having a girlfriend without knowing it. We spent 100% of our time together—my other friends used to call her "the Queen" because they knew I wouldn't go anywhere without her. We used to sit on each other's laps, sleep in the same bed and stuff. Sometimes it freaked me out how intense it was, and the amount of physical closeness. My other friends said "Well, do you think about her sexually?" And I didn't, so they said "Then don't worry about it." I tried to go to college near her, but it didn't work out. When we said goodbye, I was crying so hard my whole body was shaking. We talked to each other on the phone every day that first year of college.

This young lesbian's narrative is typical of the descriptions these women provided of their closest adolescent friendships. Most notably, the emotional tenor of these relationships often resembled romantic love, a state described by Leibowitz (1983) as involving feelings of excitement, desire for self-revelation and mutual understanding with the love object, fascination and preoccupation with the love object, possessiveness and idealizing of the love object, and a sense that losing the love object would greatly diminish one's life. Many—and sometimes all—of these features emerged in women's descriptions of their adolescent passionate friendships.

For example, over three-fourths of women reported that they were strongly possessive of

their friend's time and attention and chronically fascinated or preoccupied with their friend's behavior and appearance. As one woman noted, "I was always so tuned in to her—I would notice little things, like if her purse strap fell off her shoulder, and I would just quietly put it back." Another described her preoccupation with her friend as "borderline obsession," and described the type of continuous and intrusive thinking about the friend that characterizes the early stages of romantic infatuation (Tennov, 1979). Possessiveness was also common. Participants reported being oversensitive to the real or imagined threat of the friend's attachment to a boyfriend or to another close friend, and often sought reassurance that the friend continued to prize their friendship above all other bonds.

Given that such feelings and behaviors are so much more typical of romantic relationships than friendships, it is not surprising that women's friends and family members frequently misinterpreted their intense friendships as love affairs. As one young woman described,

> When I left for college she made me a goodbye tape of songs—love songs. A friend of mine found the tape and said "What guy made this for you?" It must have looked weird, because most people don't feel so strongly about their friends. But it didn't seem strange to me at the time—I did love her, that deeply. A day without her was unimaginable.

Perhaps the best example of how such relationships blurred the boundaries between friendship and romantic love is that of two friends who sought out a couples counselor to repair the tension in their relationship that developed during their first year of college-induced separation. At first, the counselor assumed they were a lesbian couple; after receiving a lengthy explanation of the depth and long history of the friendship, the counselor finally remarked, "I see—what you have is like a marriage, so that's how I'll treat it."

Physical affection was another common feature of these bonds. As one woman said, "We were always a lot closer, physically, than I was with my other friends. We would sometimes sleep together in my twin bed, sit on each other's laps—I didn't really do that with anybody else." Another noted that "We were so physical with each other that I feel like it made us more able to read each other's emotional cues. . . . There just seemed to be a lot more massaging, back-rubs, playing with each other's hair, wrestling." Although physical affection is common in many young women's same-sex friendships, the types of affectionate behaviors that characterized these friendships—cuddling side-to-side, cuddling face-to-face, holding hands, gazing into each other's eyes—are particularly intimate behaviors that are usually only observed in parent/child relationships and romantic relationships (Hazan & Zeifman, 1994). Yet three-fifths of women reported routinely engaging in two or more of these behaviors with their friends.

Notably, participants often explicitly indicated that this affectionate contact was not sexually motivated. As one woman described, "It was like this pull to be near her, this longing for nearness, but it wasn't sexual." The distinction between affectionate and sexual motives for physical intimacy is obviously ambiguous, and thus, one might reasonably challenge these women's claims that such affectionate behaviors had no sexual overtones. Yet, it bears noting that by the time these women were interviewed, most had spent a number of years reflecting on these friendships and often actively searching their memories for evidence of repressed same-sex attractions. Although some succeeded in unearthing such memories, many others did not. In fact, some participants felt it was the absence of sexual attraction in the friendship that made them so comfortable with such a high degree of physical intimacy.

Some women, however, eventually became attracted to their friends, usually several years after the friendship had been established. Approximately half of the participants reported that at some point in the friendship, they experienced at least a fleeting moment of sexual desire for their friend. Yet notably, friendships that contained elements of sexual attraction did not contain higher levels of physical affection, possessiveness, preoccupation, or any of these "romantic" feelings and behaviors described above. This provides further evidence that the special intensity of these relationships is not simply subverted sexual interest.

THE DEVELOPMENTAL CONTEXT OF PASSIONATE FRIENDSHIPS

Although women appear capable of forming such bonds throughout the life course (see especially Rothblum & Brehony, 1993; Weinstock & Rothblum, 1996), they may be particularly likely and uniquely meaningful for young women owing to the normative developmental tasks of adolescence. Specifically, peers become increasingly important as sources of support and security during this stage of life (Sullivan, 1953), and same-sex friendships play a critical role in this regard. Sullivan (1953) argued that close same-sex "chumships" are the first peer relationships in which true reciprocal intimacy becomes established, and research has found that young women's same-sex friendships are especially intimate and affectionate, both emotionally and physically (Barth & Kinder, 1988; Buhrmester & Furman, 1987; Bukowski, Gauze, Hoza, & Newcomb, 1993; Savin-Williams & Berndt, 1990; Stoneman, Brody, & MacKinnon, 1986).

Notably, the most intense friendships were described as occurring during early rather than late adolescence. This may be because youths who are less sexually mature are less likely than their older counterparts to perceive a necessary association between sexual and emotional intimacy. As one woman indicated,

At that age—I was 14—we had no sense of what it looked like from the outside, we just thought that we were friends, like any friends. At some point, we became much more physically affectionate, and her mom found out and told us we couldn't see each other. We didn't even understand why. I didn't figure it out until years later. Maybe if we had been older, we would have thought that we either had to back off, or just turn it into a romantic relationship. But at that time, it never even occurred to us.

Furthermore, romantic relationships may begin to compete with passionate friendships for a woman's time and attention during late adolescence, making it difficult to sustain the unique intensity of these bonds. In this regard, it is important to note that most sexual-minority women's adolescent romantic relationships are exclusively heterosexual (Savin-Williams, 1996). Because sexual-minority women tend to experience their first same-sex attractions and to identify as lesbian or bisexual at later ages than their male counterparts (Boxer, Cook, & Herdt, 1989; Savin-Williams, 1990; Sears, 1991), they are less likely than young gay and bisexual men to pursue same-sex romances and more likely to engage in normative cross-sex relationships.

SEXUAL INVOLVEMENT WITH PASSIONATE FRIENDS

The few sexual-minority women that do manage to develop same-sex romantic relationships during the high school years frequently do so with friends (Savin-Williams & Diamond, 2000; Vetere, 1983). Thus, the transformation of a passionate friendship into a sexual relationship is often a woman's first direct experience with same-sex sexuality. Such a relationship often initiates or accelerates a sexual-minority woman's process of sexual questioning and identification. However, not all women who become sexually involved with passionate friends eventually identify as lesbian or bisexual, even when they find this

same-sex experience both emotionally and physically satisfying. This further highlights the importance of studying such friendships on their own terms, rather than interpreting them strictly as adolescent precursors to adult lesbian relationships.

Some participants reported experiencing unexpected, unprecedented same-sex attractions for passionate friends that seemed to emanate directly from the unique emotional intensity of the relationship. Some of these women never again experience same-sex attractions, suggesting that such attractions may sometimes represent emergent properties of intense affectional bonds rather than unequivocal "markers" of lesbian or bisexual orientations. This, of course, directly contradicts conventional models of sexual desire and orientation. As Blumstein and Schwartz (1990) noted, such models contend that it is impossible to experience "some" same-sex attractions for one specific individual.

Yet this is precisely what some women described. One notable case was a woman who had just begun questioning her sexual identity when I first interviewed her:

Just last week I sort of became involved with my best friend, who I'm currently living with, and who I've known since I was 12. We've always been really affectionate, but last Tuesday it just sort of kept going. I stopped it at first—I was sort of freaked out. Finally we just let it happen. I don't know what we're doing—are we dating? We haven't even told anyone. Right now I only have these feelings for her, and I don't know if that'll change, I don't know if I'm a lesbian. I just know I want to be with her, forever.

At the second interview 2 years later, this young woman reported that her clandestine sexual relationship lasted for over a year, during which time neither partner experienced same-sex attractions for any other woman. They finally terminated their sexual involvement after disagreeing on whether to continue hiding the relationship, but continued to live together and to maintain a primary emotional relationship. As she said, "The sexual part is over, but that was never the main thing. She's still the most important person in my life."

Similarly, another respondent who became sexually involved with a passionate friend claimed that "It was like taking the relationship to the next level—in some ways, I guess it felt like the only way I could express how deeply I felt about her." These cases indicate that the emergence of sexual desire or activity within an adolescent's passionate friendship need not indicate that either of the participants is lesbian or bisexual, just as the lack of sexual desire or activity in the passionate friendships of sexual minorities need not indicate that either participant is denying the sexual nature of the relationship. For both sexual-minority and heterosexual adolescents, sexual desire and activity with passionate friends may be an unexpected consequence of the unusual emotional and physical intimacy of the relationship.

PASSIONATE FRIENDSHIPS AND SEXUAL IDENTITY

I do not, however, intend to suggest that a woman's same-sex sexuality has no bearing on her participation or behavior in same-sex passionate friendships. Although this study cannot speak to the overall prevalence of passionate friendships, it is reasonable to expect that they occur with greater frequency among sexual minorities than among heterosexuals. Yet, the basis for such an association is not as self-evident as it might first appear. As noted above, we cannot simply assume that such friendships are motivated by sexual-minority women's same-sex attractions. Furthermore, because affectional components of sexual orientation remain sorely under-researched (Brown, 1995), we do not yet understand the extent to which sexual orientation circumscribes individuals' motivations and capacities to bond emotionally with men and women at different stages of life.

This blind spot is particularly problematic given the fluidity between emotional and sexual feelings reported by many sexual-minority women. A large body of research demonstrates that strong affectional bonds between women often provide a critical foundation for experiences of same-sex sexual desire. Not only do sexual-minority women frequently experience their first same-sex attraction and first same-sex contact with close friends (Gramick, 1984; Kitzinger & Wilkinson, 1995; Savin-Williams & Diamond, 2000; Vetere, 1983), many continue to employ a "friendship script" in courting future lovers (Peplau & Amaro, 1982; Rose, Zand, & Cini, 1993). In fact, some sexual-minority women have trouble distinguishing between close, same-sex friendships and same-sex love affairs, given the primacy of emotional intimacy in both relationships (Rose et al., 1993).

How then might we conceptualize possible associations between sexual identity and participation in passionate friendships? One possibility is that this association is spurious, resulting from an unmeasured third variable: openness to physical and emotional intimacy with women. Such openness might facilitate strong same-sex attachments among all female adolescents, but may have the added effect of accelerating sexual questioning among sexual-minority women. Previous research has documented considerable variation in the ages at which sexual-minority women first experience same-sex attractions and adopt non-heterosexual identities. Some do so in early adolescence, whereas others do so in their 30s or 40s (Golden, 1996; Kitzinger & Wilkinson, 1995; Rust, 1992, 1993; Weinberg, Williams, & Pryor, 1994). The women in the current sample first questioned their sexual identities between 14 and 20 years of age. Given the salience of same-sex friendships for women's sexual questioning, it is plausible that female adolescents who are comfortable pursuing close, affectionate friendships with female friends will more quickly become aware of their same-sex attractions. These and other possibilities should be explored in future research. The key point is that knowing a young woman's eventual identity does not necessarily reveal her history of and motives for close contact with either female or male peers during adolescence.

CONCLUSION

Because both popular and scientific conceptions of interpersonal relationships assume consistent boundaries between friendship and romance, they offer only two possible characterizations of unusually intimate bonds between young women: unacknowledged and unconsummated same-sex romances or "just friends." Neither, however, effectively captures the distinctive nature of young sexual-minority women's most intimate adolescent friendships. While the former mistakenly conflates passion with explicit sexual arousal, the latter fails to communicate the unique importance of these relationships. As Rothblum (1997) noted, the label "friend" is conventionally applied to any individual with whom one is not sexually involved, thereby placing soulmates and casual acquaintances in the same category.

Overall, sexual-minority women's descriptions of their passionate friendships caution against assuming that (a) any female adolescent who eventually identifies as lesbian or bisexual must have been sexually attracted to any female friend with whom she shared an intense emotional bond; (b) friendships become emotionally passionate only when there is an undercurrent of sexual attraction; and (c) the emergence of sexual attraction for a passionate friend, or the initiation of sexual contact with a passionate friend, expresses and is delimited by a woman's sexual orientation. Instead, these women's experiences suggest that interconnections between passion, attraction, sexual activity, and sexual orientation are relatively fluid and situation-dependent. Bonds that violate the "separate spheres" conceptualization of friendships and romantic relationships

are deserving of systematic study because they raise critical questions not only about what "qualifies" a relationship as romantic, intimate or emotionally primary, but what "qualifies" a woman as lesbian or bisexual. Addressing these issues is central to understanding the social and sexual development of sexual-minority and heterosexual women.

REFERENCES

Barth, R. J., & Kinder, B. N. (1988). A theoretical analysis of sex differences in same-sex friendships. *Sex Roles, 19,* 349–363.

Blumstein, P., & Schwartz, P. (1990). Intimate relationships and the creation of sexuality. In D. P. McWhirter, S. A. Sanders, & J. M. Reinisch (Eds.), *Homosexuality/heterosexuality: Concepts of sexual orientation* (pp. 307–320). New York: Oxford University Press.

Boxer, A. M., Cook, J. A., & Herdt, G. (1989). *First homosexual and heterosexual experiences reported by gay and lesbian youth in an urban community.* Paper presented at the Annual Meeting of the American Sociological Association, San Francisco, California.

Brown, L. (1995). Lesbian identities: Concepts and issues. In A. R. D'Augelli & C. Patterson (Eds.), *Lesbian, gay, and bisexual identities over the lifespan* (pp. 3–23). New York: Oxford University Press.

Buhrmester, D., & Furman, W. (1987). The development of companionship and intimacy. *Child Development, 58,* 1101–1113.

Bukowski, W., Gauze, C., Hoza, B., & Newcomb, A. F. (1993). Differences and consistency between same-sex and other-sex peer relationships during early adolescence. *Developmental Psychology, 29,* 255–263.

Diamond, L. M. (1998). Development of sexual orientation among adolescent and young adult women. *Developmental Psychology, 34,* 1085–1095.

Diamond, L. M. (2000a). Passionate friendships among adolescent sexual-minority women. *Journal of Research on Adolescence, 10,* 191–209.

Diamond, L. M. (2000b). Sexual identity, attractions, and behavior among young sexual-minority women over a two-year period. *Developmental Psychology, 36,* 241–250.

Golden, C. (1996). What's in a name? Sexual self-identification among women. In R. C. Savin-Williams & K. M. Cohen (Eds.), *The lives of lesbians, gays, and bisexuals: Children to adults* (pp. 229–249). Fort Worth, TX: Harcourt Brace.

Gramick, J. (1984). Developing a lesbian identity. In T. Darty & S. Potter (Eds.), *Women-identified women* (pp. 31–44). Palo Alto, CA: Mayfield.

Hazan, C., & Zeifman, D. (1994). Sex and the psychological tether. In D. Perlman & K. Bartholomew (Eds.), *Advances in personal relationships: A research annual* (Vol. 5, pp. 151–177). London: Jessica Kingsley Publishers.

Kitzinger, C., & Wilkinson, S. (1995). Transitions from heterosexuality to lesbianism: The discursive production of lesbian identities. *Developmental Psychology, 31,* 95–104.

Leibowitz, M. (1983). *The chemistry of love.* New York: Berkeley Books.

Peplau, L. A., & Amaro, H. (1982). Understanding lesbian relationships. In W. Paul, J. D. Weinrich, J. C. Gonsiorek, & M. E. Hotvedt (Eds.), *Homosexuality: Social, psychological, and biological issues* (pp. 233–248). Beverly Hills: Sage.

Rose, S., Zand, D., & Cini, M. A. (1993). Lesbian courtship scripts. In E. D. Rothblum & K. A. Brehony (Eds.), *Boston marriages* (pp. 70–85). Amherst: University of Massachusetts Press.

Rothblum, E. D. (1997). *Help! My friend is sexually attracted to me!* In J. S. Weinstock (Chair), Lesbian friendships and social change. Symposium conducted at the annual meetings of the Association for Women in Psychology, Pittsburgh, PA.

Rothblum, E. D., & Brehony, K. A. (Eds.). (1993). *Boston marriages.* Amherst: University of Massachusetts Press.

Rust, P. (1992). The politics of sexual identity: Sexual attraction and behavior among lesbian and bisexual women. *Social Problems, 39,* 366–386.

Rust, P. (1993). Coming out in the age of social constructionism: Sexual identity formation among lesbians and bisexual women. *Gender and Society, 7,* 50–77.

Savin-Williams, R. C. (1990). *Gay and lesbian youth: Expressions of identity.* Washington, DC: Hemisphere.

Savin-Williams, R. C. (1996). Dating and romantic relationships among gay, lesbian, and bisexual youths. In R.C. Savin-Williams & K. M. Cohen (Eds.), *The lives of lesbians, gays, and bisexuals: Children to adults* (pp. 166–180). Forth Worth, TX: Harcourt Brace.

Savin-Williams, R. C., & Berndt, T. J. (1990). Friendship and peer relations. In S. S. Feldman & G. R. Elliott (Eds.), *At the threshold: The developing adolescent* (pp. 277–307). Cambridge, MA: Harvard University Press.

Savin-Williams, R. C., & Diamond, L. M. (2000). Sexual identity trajectories among sexual-minority youths: Gender comparisons. *Archives of Sexual Behavior, 29,* 419–440.

Sears, J. T. (1991). *Growing up gay in the South: Race, gender, and journeys of the spirit.* New York: Harrington Park Press.

Stoneman, Z., Brody, G. H., & MacKinnon, C. E. (1986). Same-sex and cross-sex siblings: Activity choices, roles, behaviors, and gender stereotypes. *Sex Roles, 9/10,* 495–511.

Sullivan, H. S. (1953). *The interpersonal theory of psychiatry.* New York: Norton.

Tennov, D. (1979). *Love and limerence: The experience of being in love.* New York: Stein and Day.

Vetere, V. A. (1983). The role of friendship in the development and maintenance of lesbian love relationships. *Journal of Homosexuality, 8,* 51–65.

Weinberg, M. S., Williams, C. J., & Pryor, D. W. (1994). *Dual attraction: Understanding bisexuality.* New York: Oxford University Press.

Weinstock, J. S., & Rothblum, E. D. (Eds.). (1996). *Lesbian friendships: For ourselves and for each other.* New York: NYU Press.

Discussion Questions

1. Have you ever had an intense friendship; that is, a best friend or soul mate? If so, describe your relationship in terms of how you spent your time, what you did, how you felt, how exclusive or inclusive you were of other people, and if you ever had fights or breakups. How similar or different was, or is, this relationship to any romance you have had?

2. Diamond's article challenges the normative assumption that romantic relationships and friendships are separate spheres. Based on your experiences, do you tend to agree or disagree?

3. According to Diamond, what is the relationship between sexual identities and "passionate friendships" among women?

4. What are the implications of this study for how we think about women's sexual identity development?

5. How applicable do you think Diamond's study is for thinking about men's sexual identity development?

8

Accounts of Sexual Identity Formation in Heterosexual Students

MICHELE J. ELIASON

Very little research has focused on the ways in which heterosexual people perceive their sexual identity. This chapter explores heterosexual identity from the standpoint of an established identity model, that of James Marcia. Twenty-six heterosexual undergraduate students (14 men: 3 African-American, 1 Latino, and 10 White, and 12 women: 3 African-American, 1 Latina, and 8 White) wrote two 3-page essays on how their sexual identities formed and how they influence their daily lives. Students could be categorized into all four of Marcia's identity statuses. Additionally, six common themes were noted in their essays: had never thought about sexual identity; society made me heterosexual; gender determines sexual identity; issues of choice versus innateness of sexuality; no alternative to heterosexuality; and the influence of religion.

The vast majority of literature on sexual identity has taken one of two forms: studies of gay or lesbian identity development or studies of heterosexuals' attitudes about lesbian, gay, or bisexual people. These studies often assume that heterosexuals are a monolithic, stable group with predictable attitudes about non-heterosexuals and a consistent and clear sense of their own (hetero)sexual identity. Rarely has research addressed the question of how heterosexuals achieve a sexual identity, or questioned the stability or homogeneity of this identity, or indeed, asked whether most heterosexuals experience themselves as even having a sexual identity.

One of the earliest theoretical models of heterosexuality comes from Freud. Weeks (1985) described the evolution of Freud's theory of sexuality as follows. Freud ultimately felt that a sexual identity was a precarious construct,

SOURCE: This chapter was originally published as "Accounts of Sexual Identity Formation in Heterosexual Students" in *Sex Roles* (vol. 32, no. 11/12). Copyright © 1995 Springer Science and Business Media. Reprinted by permission.

always threatened by repressed desires. Sexual identity formation begins shortly after birth, as the child progresses through psychosexual stages. Freud felt that a key component of sexuality was the early assumption of the child that all humans are genitally alike, with a penis. When faced with people without penises, boys could develop castration anxiety and girls could develop penis envy. These emotions paved the way for the Oedipal complex of the phallic stage, whereby the child learns to repress sexual desire for the mother and to identify with the same-sex parent. If the conflict is successfully resolved, at maturity the individual will select partners of the other gender. Freud thought that humans were born "polymorphously perverse," or capable of sexual attractions to anyone (or thing), and only by a complex and traumatic psychic family drama did heterosexual identity emerge. In his three essays on sexuality in 1905, Freud follows a discussion of homosexuality with this statement. "Thus, from the point of view of psychoanalysis the exclusive sexual interest felt by men for women is also a problem that needs elucidating and is not a self-evident fact based upon an attraction that is ultimately of a chemical nature" (p. 11). Interestingly, homosexual desire is a key component of early sexuality, as the lines of desire and identification blur. de Kuyper (1993) suggested that "normal" resolution of the Oedipal complex results in male homophobia (fear of one's own homosexual desires). Freud is one of the few theorists of this century to point out the constructedness of heterosexuality, but few who followed him pursued this point.

Erik Erikson (1968) was among the first of contemporary theorists to stress the importance of identity development. He suggested that personal identity leads to individuality and consists of authentic truths about one's self. In his developmental stage theory, Erikson proposed that identity is the major crisis of the adolescent (at least for males; Erikson thought that identity and intimacy

were achieved more or less simultaneously for women, since he thought that a woman's identity depended on a relationship to a man). In Erikson's scheme, adolescence or young adulthood would be a crucial time of achieving identity, unlike Freud, who thought that events in early childhood most strongly influenced the emergence of an identity in adolescence. For Erikson, heterosexuality is assumed, and no alternative models of sexual identity are available. Yet, his theory is significant, as he proposed that the adolescent identity crisis must be resolved before healthy intimate relationships are possible.

James Marcia (1987) proposed that identity could exist in different states or statuses, depending on whether exploration and commitment were present. The four identity statuses that he described were:

1. diffusion—the person has no active sense of identity and there has been no exploration and no commitment to any identity.

2. foreclosure—the person has accepted an identity imposed by another or by societal expectations. This person accepts the identity without critique and without exploring options.

3. moratorium—the person is in the active stage of exploring an identity, but has not yet made a commitment.

4. achievement—the process of moratorium has been completed and the person has made a conscious commitment to a particular identity.

Marcia (1987) views identity as

an internal, self-constructed, dynamic organization of drives, abilities, beliefs, and individual history. The better developed this structure is, the more aware individuals appear to be of their own uniqueness and similarity to others and of their own strengths and weaknesses in making their way in the world. The less developed this structure is, the more confused individuals seem about their own distinctiveness and the more they have to rely on external sources to evaluate themselves. (p. 159)

Marcia's methods have been used to study vocational choice, religious beliefs, political philosophies, gender role preferences, family role preferences, moral reasoning, and a variety of personality traits (Archer, 1989; Marcia, 1987). In regards to sexual identity, since heterosexuality is the normative identity and until recently other options were not readily available in families, the media, or communities, foreclosure may be the most common sexual identity status for the heterosexual person.

Feminist scholars have also addressed sexuality, and have linked sexuality to gender politics. For example, Adrienne Rich (1980) demonstrated quite eloquently how heterosexuality is forced upon women by the major institutions of society such as law, religion, medicine, and the media. But in spite of the widespread acknowledgement of Rich's work in feminist writing, few theorists have really taken her ideas to heart and analyzed heterosexuality as a political construct (Wilkinson & Kitzinger, 1993). On the other hand, there is now a substantial body of research and theory about lesbian, gay, and bisexual identity (Bell, Weinberg, & Hammersmith, 1981; Cass, 1984; Eliason, 1995; Troiden, 1988; Weinberg, Williams, & Pryor, 1994).

Penelope (1993) noted that the term heterosexual was not even coined until 1901 (about 30 years after the term "homosexual" was first used). The original definition of heterosexual was "an abnormal or perverted sexual appetite toward the opposite sex" (p. 262). Penelope attempted to relate heterosexual identity to stage theories proposed by developmental psychologists such as Erikson, Gould, and Levinson. She pointed out the fragility of the construct: "heterosexuality qualifies only as a prefabricated way of living that one slips into anonymously. . . . Remove the social

institutions which support it, and the whole fragile edifice will collapse" (p. 264).

Since heterosexuality is considered the norm or default sexual identity, some may question why it is necessary to study it. There are a number of important reasons. In the past, research that did not distinguish among sexual identities lumped all sorts of people together, possibly obscuring the distinctiveness of each type. Secondly, there is growing evidence of the constructedness of all sexuality (Foucault, 1978; Rich, 1980; Weeks, 1986). Rather than assume that heterosexuality is biologically determined, current studies might demonstrate the social meaning of being heterosexual and the myriad ways by which people are socialized to be heterosexual. Another reason to study heterosexuality might be to break down the myth of its monolithic nature and explore the diverse ways of being heterosexual. We know that heterosexuality can go awry, leading to serious societal problems such as rape, incest, and a variety of "sexual dysfunctions." Understanding how heterosexuality develops and is experienced differently by women and men may shed light on some of these problems. There is also ample evidence that a sexual identity gives very little information about actual sexual behavior. Some people who label themselves as heterosexual engage in no sexual activity at all, or have regular same-gender sexual experiences. There is a multitude of ways of expressing and acting upon sexual desire in heterosexuals. The relationships between identity and behavior need to be explored. Finally, in order to completely understand "deviance" from the norm (i.e., sexual minorities), the norm must be well understood.

So how do we begin to study a construct that has been taken-for-granted? The purpose of this study was to explore some of the ways by which a heterosexual identity develops, and how it is perceived to affect daily life. Marcia's identity status model will be applied to accounts of heterosexual identity development, and the narratives will be analyzed for common themes that are specific to sexual identity.

METHODS

Respondents

Twenty-six self-identified heterosexual students in a class entitled "Theorizing Sexual Identities" served as respondents. There were 14 males, ranging in age from 20 to 25; three were African-American, one was Latino, and ten were White. The twelve women ranged in age from 19 to 26 and included three African-Americans, one Latina, and eight White women. The class also included eleven self-identified gay, lesbian, and bisexual students. Their responses are not included in this paper.

The Task

At the first class meeting, students were given an assignment to be completed by the next class. They were to describe how their sexual identity had formed and how it affected their daily lives. They were provided with definitions of gender and sexual identity, but given no other guidance. The last week of class, they were asked to repeat the assignment. The essays varied in length from two to four pages.

RESULTS

Marcia's Identity Statuses

First, each student's entire essay was read carefully and examined for statements indicating identity exploration and identity commitment. Evidence of exploration included comments about whether the student had ever really thought about, read about, talked to someone about sexual identity. Evidence of commitment included mention of making a conscious decision, indicating they would never change identities, or stating no other options were possible. Five of the student

Table 8.1 Themes About Heterosexual Identity Found in Women's and Men's Accounts

Theme	Response (%)	
	Women	Men
Never thought about sexual identity	25	36
Outside forces made me heterosexual	83	86
Gender socialization made me heterosexual	42	38
Heterosexuality is inborn, fixed	17	36
Heterosexuality is a choice	8	7
There are no viable alternatives	8	29
Religion was a factor in identity	33	43

essays were rated by an independent judge who, in each case, arrived at the same identity status category as the author.

Using Marcia's definitions (see above), students were then categorized as identity diffused, foreclosed, moratorium, or achieved. Using this system, one-half of the men's responses were judged as foreclosed, 29% as diffused, 20% as achieved, and none were in moratorium. Of the women's responses, one-third were considered foreclosed, one-third in moratorium, one-sixth diffused and one-sixth identity achieved. The subjects who were rated as diffused (women and men) were those whose narratives focused on gender identity rather than sexual identity. The gender versus sexual identity dilemma is discussed further below.

Common Themes

To explore how these students regarded their sexual identities, the author searched for themes in the narratives. Six common themes were identified in their original narratives about heterosexual sexual identity. These are described in terms of gender in Table 8.1, and discussed below.

Had Never Thought About Sexual Identity. About one-fourth of the women, and more than one-third of the men stated that their sexual identity was just not something they ever thought about, at least in regards to themselves. Many of these comments are consistent with Marcia's status of identity diffusion, whereas others seem to indicate foreclosure. Respondents' comments included:

> The question of how my sexual identity formed really left me stumped

> I have never really thought about it until today

> I know I have developed a sexual identity. The problem is I just didn't notice

> I never gave consideration to my sexual identity, it just came naturally

> I just automatically became a lover of the opposite sex

> My sexual identity developed long before I can remember. I have always been heterosexual

It may be that an even higher number of heterosexuals in the general population would endorse such statements. These students, after all, had enrolled in a class about sexual identity. However, it was clear from their other comments that sexual identity to them meant "other," such as lesbian, gay, or bisexual. Few identified heterosexual as a sexual identity per se. There were a few exceptions. Three of the women reported that they had questioned their sexual identity at some point.

> I was raised heterosexual, but at about puberty, I questioned that at times, but not too seriously

> My sexual experiences have been with both men and women, but with women, I think I was just experimenting. I don't remember any great passion with women

> I have only experienced sexual relationships with men, but no longer rule out the possibility of having a relationship with a woman (this student continued to struggle with issues of her own sexuality throughout the semester and is one of the women who was in moratorium, or in the active stage of questioning her sexual identity).

I Was Made Into a Heterosexual. A finding that was rather surprising (at least to me), was that the majority of respondents, and about equal numbers of women and men, felt that some outside force had made them heterosexual. These comments generally indicated identity foreclosure—accepting an identity thrust upon one from the outside.

> My parents instilled morals and values upon me

> I guess from birth my parents have shaped me with heterosexual thoughts

> I assumed my identity through my parents. I had the privilege of growing up in a household with loving parents

> I grew up in a heterosexual environment and believe I was socialized to be heterosexual

> Thru school, church, literature, friends, and family, I have learned to be who I am

> Society has molded the idea of what I should act like, who I should associate myself with, and who I should have sex with

> I was raised in a conservative family where religion played a major role

> I am heterosexual because that was what was expected of me

> My sexual identity developed not only because of my personal beliefs and preferences, but also because of the pressure my family put on me

> I can say my culture, Latino, was a driving force in the development of my sexual identity

As the semester progressed, these students were often surprised by information provided by lesbian, gay, and bisexual students about their own upbringings; that they had also grown up in homes with loving heterosexual parents, in conservative religions, in small towns, and so on.

Gender = Sexuality. Many respondents thought that their gender socialization was a major determining factor in their sexual identity. Some, despite the lecture on the differences between gender and sexual identity, conflated the terms. These comments may also fit under the category of foreclosure, suggesting that gender pre-determines sexual identity.

> My sexual identity is as a male. My father stressed the fact that as a member of the male population, I should behave as a man should. That is, to be attracted to members of the female population

> I'm not sure if I was brought up in a heterosexual manner, but my gender identity was what made me turn to the opposite sex. Maybe others make the choice, but I think being female, I had it chosen for me

> My life as a woman really comes natural—women want men

> I prefer the sports of men—football, baseball, hockey. I won't cook or clean or the like unless I have to. They aren't male type things

> Whatever I'm doing be it going to class, doing laundry, going drinking, etc., I am always looking at women and acting every way possible as masculine as possible. This does not mean I act the tough guy, but not feminine in any way

> My grandfather . . . would always tell me very sternly that I looked like a "damn little girl" . . . there were many more of these "pro-manly" experiences in my upbringing

Many other students recognized the artificiality, or constructedness of gender. For example,

> [after describing being a tomboy as a child] I realized that I had to become softer to hang out with the popular girls so I played my roles

> A question I asked myself, "do you want to be a man like your father and work with tools or like your mom and serve the family." I chose to act the man

> By dating, I began to see what boys wanted from me. I started wearing tight dresses and wiggling

> I very much feel like I must be aggressive and assertive in all situations

> And that tears and emotional pain are for women. Though I have these feelings, I often feel guilty for displaying them

> Many rate your masculinity or femininity according to your sexual identity

Is Sexuality Innate or a Choice? Men were more likely than women to view their sexuality as an innate, unchanging force:

> God made men to reproduce with women

> I don't ever see my sexuality as changing

> I was born to like women

> It's something I was born with and will always be

> My sexuality has not, nor ever will change

A minority of men used the language of choice in describing their sexuality, but often mixed words denoting the innateness of sexuality with choice.

> My choice of identity has opened the door for a lot of opportunities (but also, "I was born to like women")

> I have found an identity I can live with for the rest of my life

Women had a wider range of ideas about the "cause" of their sexual identity:

> I can honestly say that the rest of my life I will remain heterosexual (author's note: by the end of the semester, this student had decided that she was bisexual.)

> For now, I am happily heterosexual, but who is to say what could happen?

> It's easier in this society to be heterosexual. I don't think I would have the courage to be otherwise

I don't think mine [sexual identity] will ever stay constant. I really like the notion of fluidity

I have chosen heterosexuality because it fits me at this time in my life

I view my sexuality as a continuum that cannot be labeled

There Are No Viable Options to Heterosexuality. This response was more common in men, and is compatible with discussions of the construction of masculinity in our society as a certain variety of heterosexuality (see Herek, 1993, for example). That is, masculinity and heterosexuality are entwined in the socialization process in a much more direct and powerful way than femininity is tied to sexual identity. According to Herek (1993) to be a man or to be masculine is defined as being homophobic.

I knew I was heterosexual mainly because being gay was never an option

It was at school where I developed my early notions on who should be the aggressor and who should be timid and shy. Real men were heterosexual, period

Growing up, whenever boys wanted to tease or hurt another boy, they would refer to him as "faggot" or "queer boy." No way did I want to be labeled this way

As a child I wasn't exposed to anything but heterosexual relationships

I guess I just assumed that one day I would have a wife and kids—there were no other options

Women were less likely to discuss sexual identity in terms of homophobia or gender socialization, but several mentioned the invisibility of alternatives to heterosexuality:

I was raised in a family that doesn't recognize any other form of sexual identity

If you hear something enough times [heterosexuality] you start to believe it

The idea of heterosexuality is so placed in our heads that we don't see how something could be anything else

Religion as an Influence. A significant number of women and men noted that religious beliefs in their childhood were a major source of information about sexual identity. Many especially noted the influence of Catholicism. Some of these comments provide further evidence of identity foreclosure.

I come from a Catholic background . . . my religious background has had a large impact on me and I have had to battle the "good girl–bad girl" notion all my life

I was raised in a conservative family atmosphere where religion played a major role in our lives

I was brought up in a Catholic family with very strong morals and values . . . homosexuals were not "normal" people

If God wanted men to be able to reproduce with men, he would have created Adam and Steve, not Adam and Eve

How Heterosexuality Affects My Life. The second part of the assignment was to describe the ways that heterosexual identity affected the student in everyday life. In general, the White men in the class had difficulty identifying ways that heterosexuality affected their lives:

As for what impact my identity has on my everyday life, I think first of all people are just people. We all want basically the same things

I see my life as being pretty average and therefore, assume people don't prejudge me

I don't always have to think about who I am—life is easy

It doesn't affect my life all that much

I don't think my sexual identity affects me any different than anyone else

I lead a normal heterosexual life

I believe my perceptions on sexual identity have no big impact on my life, other than when I see a "hot" girl it reassures my heterosexuality

My sexual identity affects the clothes I wear and the friends that I have

My sexual preference allows me to walk through life usually without a care

How my sexuality affects my daily life? Well, for starters, I've only had sex with White girls my age. I am attracted to different races and want to experiment but I think it's not right to have a relationship with anybody except Caucasians. I enjoy viewing lesbian acts but don't think they should be able to start families

Women and men of color were often able to point out how sexuality intersects with other human characteristics such as race, gender, class, and so on.

I can say that because I am a Latino in a White society, I have experienced biases of others toward me . . . because of my heterosexual bias, it's hard to know how it [sexual identity and attitudes] developed

If I talk about how my sexuality affects my life, I have to include being female, being White, being working class

I believe my sexual identity affects my life in many ways. I am a black heterosexual male living in America . . . I grew up with the macho image of guys in sports . . . being heterosexual has taught me to be very close-minded in my views. When I was young . . . I hadn't come across any societal boundaries except racial

Being a black woman in this society, you have to deal with society, politics, and especially men. Society labels you if you are not feminine enough

Heterosexuality has influenced my life in many ways. It has kept me naïve of the world

The three women who had questioned their sexual identity appeared to have a stronger sense of what it means to be heterosexual women in this society:

Well, I'm heterosexual and I guess that affects my life in good and bad ways. As far as the good goes, when I want to be invisible or inconspicuous with my relationships, I can. Nobody is going to think of me as different.

I'm not going to have my love relationship mentally sexualized by my friends, family, acquaintances or store clerks. When I watch movies, read books, or listen to music, the relationships illustrated are similar to mine (girl-boy)

. . . I can show affection to my partner in public. Nobody will hate him or our relationship without getting to know him

Because I am attracted to men, I am forced to deal with the male dominated society more closely. I must deal with men and the power struggle and also what I've found to be their reluctance to open up for emotional intimacy

I have not had to fear being faced with the violence and hatred when in public with a [same-sex] partner. Regardless of that, I still have faced many homophobic reactions . . . because I do not fit the stereotypical feminine role

The process of moratorium, or identity exploration, appears to make students much more aware of how their sexual identity affects their life. They are aware of the privilege and taken-for-grantedness of heterosexuality.

Comments at the End of the Semester

The final essays were reviewed to determine whether students had changed their attitudes. Generally, two common themes were identified. First, many students wrote about their changes in attitudes about people with different sexual identities than their own. Second, some reported greater personal awareness of their sexual identity.

I think my sexual identity will always be "black heterosexual male" which is a step up from "black heterosexual homophobic male"

I guess I can say I have changed . . . I have an open mind to all sexual identities that I should of always had but didn't. It's a shame that it took me 20 years to figure this out

Before this class, I saw the gay, bi, lesbian community as different and unique. But now I see them as friends with warm hearted open feelings that have a lot to offer to others

I have become a speaker of the cause. I have made a point to talk to many people about the problems and misconceptions of the lesbian, gay, and bisexual community

Regarding their own sexual identity, students commented:

Before [in the first essay] I said "born to like women" but I really meant "taught to like women." Television, movies, brothers, parents are just some of the things that could have an impact on sexual identity. I think that I was so blind that I did not even realize that this was being taught to me

I learned a lot about other people's sexuality and I think I learned that I take my own sexuality for granted

To be quite honest, before I took this class, I was ignorant not only to other sexualities, but to my own

This class obviously hasn't changed me, but it has awakened me

Before this class, sexuality (any type) was "other." I just couldn't put sexuality and myself together . . . unlike my upbringing, I want my children to know that there are different sexualities, classes, races, cultures, etc.

Since I started this class, I have had many questions about my own sexuality

Even though I am engaged, I had to stop and wonder about being with women—not only sexually but romantically and mentally

An interesting remark shared by four of the White men in the class was that they felt in the minority. One response typifies their concerns:

I did, however, feel separate. The class turned out to be mostly homosexual, a situation that I had never been in . . . this type of separated feeling is what I believe this society needs to get rid of in order to desegregate our two communities

In actuality, there were 26 heterosexual and 11 gay, lesbian, or bisexual students in the class. This perception by some of the White men may mirror White heterosexual men's discomfort in this changing society—a society in which they used to have the advantage. As women, people of color, and people of diverse sexual identities clamor for a place, the White men feel the most threatened because they have the most to lose.

CONCLUSIONS

These students' comments demonstrate wide diversity in the ways they defined their sexual identity, theorized the origins of sexual identity, and felt the effects of sexuality on their everyday lives. Most expressed some notion of identity foreclosure. They had accepted an identity imposed upon them by society, religion, their gender, or their parents' expectations. Others expressed bewilderment—they were identity diffused in regard to sexual identity and had not really thought about it until this class. Three women seemed to be in the process of moratorium, or actively questioning their identity. Their essays all semester were long and full of soul-searching questions. No men appeared to be in moratorium. Of the few students who were identity achieved, there appeared to be a gender difference in their accounts. The men who had carefully considered their sexual identity and committed to heterosexuality had largely done so on the basis of rejecting a gay identity. The women, on the other hand, had considered what it would mean to be a lesbian or bisexual, and had decided that, although it was an option they might choose later, heterosexuality suited their lives at this time. In other words, they did not reject a same-sex orientation altogether.

This sample was small, not allowing for detailed analysis of issues such as race, class, ethnicity, and other human factors that may intersect with sexuality. There is some suggestion in the student narratives that heterosexual sexual identity may differ by race. The students of color in this class generally had more awareness of sexual identity, but often pointed out that race was a more salient identity for them than sexuality. Thus, heterosexual students of color may be different from heterosexual White students in much the same ways that gay, lesbian, or bisexual people of color differ from gay, lesbian, bisexual White people (Chan, 1993; Hemphill, 1991; Loiacano, 1993; Lorde, 1982).

In conclusion, the study of heterosexual sexual identity may potentially have great impact. First, many heterosexual students were unaware of what it means to be heterosexual in this society, and had experienced much uncertainty about themselves. Self-awareness and understanding is necessary before a person can really understand about sexual difference. Many of these students had unknowingly perpetuated stereotypes about lesbian, gay, and bisexual people until they examined their own sexual identity development. Finally, understanding of the processes of heterosexual sexual identity development will be helpful in understanding all forms of sexual diversity.

REFERENCES

Archer, S. (1989). Gender differences in identity development: Issues of process, domain, and timing. *Journal of Adolescence, 12,* 117–138.

Bell, A., Weinberg, M., & Hammersmith, S. (1981). *Sexual preference: Its development in men and women.* Bloomington: Indiana University Press.

Cass, V. (1984). Homosexual identity formation: Testing a theoretical model. *Journal of Sex Research, 20,* 143–167.

Chan, C. (1993). Issues of identity development among Asian-American lesbians and gay men.

In L. Garnets & D. Kimmel (Eds.), *Psychological perspectives on lesbian and gay male experiences.* New York: Columbia University Press.

de Kuyper, E. (1993). The Freudian construction of sexuality: The gay foundations of heterosexuality and straight homophobia. *Journal of Homosexuality, 24,* 137–144.

Eliason, M. J. (1995). Identity formation in lesbian, gay, and bisexual persons: Beyond a minoritizing view. *Journal of Homosexuality, 39.*

Erikson, E. (1968). *Identity, youth and crisis.* New York: Norton.

Foucault, M. (1978). *The history of sexuality, Vol. 1.* New York: Vintage Books.

Freud, S. (1905). *Three contributions to the theory of sex* (Trans. A. A. Brill, 1962). New York: E. P. Dutton.

Hemphill, E. (Ed.). (1991). *Brother to brother: New writings by black gay men.* Boston: Alyson.

Herek, G. (1993). On heterosexual masculinity: Some psychical consequences of the social construction of gender and sexuality. In L. Garnets & D. Kimmel (Eds.), *Psychological perspectives on lesbian and gay male experiences.* New York: Columbia University Press.

Loiacano, D. (1993). Gay identity issues among Black Americans: Racism, homophobia and need for validation. In L. Garnets & D. Kimmel (Eds.), *Psychological perspectives on lesbian and gay male experiences.* New York: Columbia University Press.

Lorde, A. (1982). *Zami: A new spelling of my name.* Freedom, CA: The Crossing Press.

Marcia, J. (1987). Identity in adolescence. In J. Adelson (Ed.), *Handbook of adolescent psychology.* New York: Wiley.

Penelope, J. (1993). Heterosexual identity: Out of the closets. In S. Wilkinson & C. Kitzinger (Eds.), *Heterosexuality.* London: Sage.

Rich, A. (1980). Compulsory heterosexuality and lesbian existence. *Signs, 5,* 631–660.

Troiden, R. (1988). *Gay and lesbian identity: A sociological analysis.* New York: General Hall.

Weinberg, M., Williams, C., & Pryor, D. (1994). *Dual attractions: Understanding bisexuality.* New York: Oxford University Press.

Weeks, J. (1985). *Sexuality and its discontents.* London: Routledge.

Weeks, J. (1986). *Sexuality.* London: Routledge.

Wilkinson, S., & Kitzinger, C. (Eds.). (1993). *Heterosexuality.* London: Sage.

Discussion Questions

1. Write a two- to three-page essay on how your sexual identity is evolving and how it influences your daily life.

2. What are the four stages of Marcia's identity status model?

3. What are the strengths and weaknesses of this model?

4. How well do you think that Marcia's identity status model applies to heterosexual identity development, and why?

5. How well do you think that Marcia's identity status model applies to sexual identity development in general? Is it equally well suited to all sexual identities? Why or why not?

6. Considering chapters 6 and 7 as well as this chapter, what similarities and differences might there be between the identity development of LGBT individuals and heterosexuals?

9

M. Dragonfly

Two-Spirit and the Tafoya Principle of Uncertainty

TERRY TAFOYA

Long ago, a young boy fashioned a toy for his sister, to amuse her and to distract her from her hunger, as they had no food. He wove together corn-husk for wings, and assembled other things of his world, creating something no one had ever quite seen before. That night, as he and his sister slept with their hunger, the toy began to move and fly about his home. This dragonfly, for such it was, assisted the boy, his sister, and his people, providing them food. Even today, the symbol of the dragonfly, its meaning of water and life, is used in pottery and weaving.
—traditional Pueblo story, as retold by Tony Hillerman (1986)

Ana kush i washa (I am speaking to you).

Never before, in two decades of university teaching or presentations, have I used a first-person voice in an academic setting. To a great extent this was because of my early negative experiences while working in the (then) emerging field of antiracism and antidiscrimination as a consultant for the Seattle public school system, where personal statements I made were often discounted by antagonistic audience members as "overly sensitive" or only reflecting my individual experience and not Native American experiences as a whole.

But I am choosing, somewhat reluctantly, to speak because the concept of using one's own voice is a critical issue in understanding two-spirit concerns. I am aware of the irony in

SOURCE: This chapter was originally published as "M. Dragonfly: Two-Spirit and the Tafoya Principle of Uncertainty," in *Two-Spirit People: Native American Gender Identity, Sexuality, and Spirituality* (Sue-Ellen Jacobs, Wesley Thomas, and Sabine Lang, eds.). Copyright © 1997 Board of Trustees of the University of Illinois. Reprinted by permission.

the fact that I am not using my first language to speak and must use English for the benefit of my audience. But this illustrates the interactive nature of speaking in one's voice. To be from a culture of oral tradition means that every time one speaks in a public setting the event is a kind of ceremony. This ceremony involves spectators no less than actors, no differently than those who stand on Pueblo rooftops to watch ceremonies give something of themselves to what they see.

In this chapter I will play with the concept of M. Dragonfly, with its pun on the play *M. Butterfly,* because I think both this chapter and the play speak to much the same issues: presentation of self, perception of self and others, implications for cross-cultural communications, and, perhaps most important of all, the political and socioeconomic power involved in who defines whom with regard to gender and sexuality.[1] *M. Butterfly* is based on a historical event involving a French ambassador who maintained a long-term relationship with a biological Chinese male whom he believed to be a female Chinese Opera star. The play moves from a journalistic recounting of the event to a fictional exploration of how the ambassador made sense of his experience, concluding that, "only a man can truly know how a woman is supposed to act" (Hwang 1989:63).

The statement crystallizes not only the message of the play but also the focus of this effort of creating a working model of conceptualizing what two-spirit means. The ambassador's premise is that those in a dominant position of power and authority are the only ones who "truly know" how those in lesser positions of power and authority "are supposed to act." I suspect those who define themselves as two-spirit are also examining how they "are supposed to act," having been historically instructed by non-Native "experts" about the nature of their role.

The story of the Dragonfly also offers a metaphor of the two-spirit. Not born but created and, once created for a specific purpose,

gaining a life of its own, surpassing the intentions of its creator, and eventually providing something life-affirming and nurturing. The creation of the Dragonfly speaks also to the independence of its actions and behaviors from its creator and its power to instruct its creator. I believe that is also what we are witnessing at this historic moment. Native people are choosing the name *two-spirit* to represent an aspect of themselves. They are also empowering themselves to act independently from the anthropologists who have worked hard to define them (an act of creation in itself) and to take the opportunity to instruct the anthropologists and each other in a manner that may prove to be as life-affirming and nurturing as the work of the Dragonfly.

To choose the name *two-spirit* for oneself, as opposed to "berdache" [*sic*] from the history of non-Native people, is to speak in what Cindy Patton has termed "dissident vernaculars," terms that move

> away from the model of pristine scientific ideas which need "translation" for people lacking in the dominant culture's language skills or concepts. "Dissident vernaculars" also suggests that meanings created by and in communities are upsetting to the dominant culture precisely because speaking in one's own fashion is a means of resistance, a strengthening of the subculture that has created the new meaning. (1990:148)

I have always been a rim-walker, neither one thing or another, in much that I do and am. Let me therefore take privilege and say that I am not speaking as an anthropologist, although I completed all the coursework for a doctorate in anthropology. As one whose paternal relatives reside in a pueblo that banned all anthropologists in the 1920s after Elsie Clews Parsons published unauthorized ethnographic materials of our village, I know all too well that research does not exist in a political vacuum.

Were I speaking as an anthropologist, I might point out that the symbol of the

Dragonfly reflects an entity that begins its life in one form, an aquatic larval stage, and then transforms into something completely different. Were I an anthropologist, I would explore this in remarkable detail and draw parallels of how a two-spirit may begin as a biological male or female but transform into someone quite different. But, not being an anthropologist, I will not mention any of this. Besides, I know of no formal traditional association of the Dragonfly with the two-spirit. Such is the power of words, however, that for all I know the Dragonfly will become a new symbol for "The Movement." According to a personal communication from Will Roscoe, Winfield Coleman, a Cheyenne scholar, has stated that there is a possible connection with the "Dragonfly Lodge" of the Cheyenne to the "berdache." In this connection, the Dragonfly is a symbol of the whirlwind, that which connects Mother Earth and Father Sky, the bridge between female and male principles.

Were I a political writer rather than a simple storyteller, I might also point out the exciting evolution and empowerment of the transgendered community as its members struggle to wrest the control of gender definitions from the hands of the medical establishment, insurance companies, and politicians—not to mention the manufacturers of rest-room signs. The discovery that there are lesbians, bisexuals, or gays emphasizes the fact that gender orientation and sexual orientation are two separate categories. As Weeks points out, "Despite the lack of any scientific basis for such a view, many authors have either treated sexual orientation as a facet of gender, or have confounded gender role behavior and sexual orientation" (as cited in Paul 1993:42).

Many voices and many audiences work together to understand an event. These voices are also internal as I debate with myself about how to phrase something, how much detail to use, or how to frame it through an amusing analogy or snappy symbol. As a trained storyteller, I am constantly evaluating the knowledge base and

reaction of my audience. Indeed, although the inherent message may be intended to be the same, the methodology of delivery to various audiences may be quite different, and the results are also different because the action of accommodating to the audience will frequently mean reenforcing its existing schema or worldview. This is why automatically translating "two-spirit" as a "gay role," or "what we call our homosexuals," makes speaking much easier but may not contribute to the exchange of accurate meaning. Winfield Coleman, in presenting his research on Cheyenne androgynous priests, remarked that when he was last on the Cheyenne reservation, a tribal member said something about, "those . . . what do you call 'em—lesbians?" to which Coleman replied "*Heemaneh*. The term historically used for the two-spirit by the Cheyenne" (Roscoe, personal communication, no date).

But is this really the term used for Cheyenne two-spirits historically, or is it possibly something else? And was the tribal member really forgetful of his language's term for such an individual to the point where he had to be reminded by the anthropological Keeper of Knowledge, or was the tribal member attempting to communicate in a manner he believed Coleman would understand? Or was he, as I feel many members of various tribes are doing, attempting to understand a difference in the traditional role of the *heemaneh* and contemporary individuals who may indeed be lesbian?

Often, for the sake of expediency and other reasons, Native American people may translate something that does not reflect how we perceive something but that works within a specific context. For example, my administrative assistant tried to call one of my relatives, Sobiyax, on the Skokomish Reservation to see if he would be willing to substitute for me at a speaking engagement. Several months earlier, my assistant had asked how I was related to Sobiyax and, not wanting to go into detail, I said, "Oh, he's a cousin," because I knew that would satisfy my non-Indian assistant's curiosity and was minimally accurate. My assistant stated his request to the switchboard operator on the reservation and emphasized that my message was important and that I was "a relative." When the operator paused before replying, he elaborated and told her I was Sobiyax's "cousin." She laughed and said, "That Terry Tafoya, he's no relative, he's just relative."

Within many Native communities and languages there are a variety of identities. For example, in my mother's language, there are twenty-eight specific identity terms for oneself. In the context of my family, the most distant English term of relationship on a personal level is *cousin*. Because of the historical and personal involvement I have with Sobiyax and his family, a more appropriate and respectful term in English would be "my brother," reflecting not only my emotional relationship with him but also our similarity in age. Were he much older, I might call him "Dad" or "Uncle." This is, of course, speaking abstractly. In reality, I would call him by his spiritual name, Sobiyax, and he, as a sign of endearment and intimacy, would call me by one of my spiritual names. And in both cases we would use the spiritual names we had "witnessed" in our respective Naming Ceremonies. The switchboard operator was Sobiyax's eldest sister. Inadvertently, my assistant managed to insult two of my relatives on my behalf without having a clue about what he was doing.

Just so. Names themselves are not the only issue, but the context of their use is an essential consideration. Hayles (1993) suggests that many people with a scientific bias hold what she calls the "gift-wrap idea of language." They see language as a gift wrapping that I use to hand you an idea. You receive the package, unwrap it, and take out the idea. In this view, the wrapping is purely instrumental, a way of getting an idea from me to you. The idea is what counts, not the wrapping. People trained in literature tend to think this view of language is completely wrong. They deeply believe that the language constitutes an idea rather than

expresses it. Because no two verbal formulations can ever be identical, to say something in other words is to say something different (Hayles 1993:48).

Considering that "berdache" is frequently glossed in the literature with such English classifications as hermaphrodite, transvestite, or homosexual, we might do well to question the context in which these terms are used. Paul reminds us that the "labels of bisexual, heterosexual, and homosexual suggest an isomorphism to a person's sexual behavior, sexual fantasies, erotic arousal, and affectional relationships that are not consistent with research evidence" (1993:45; cf. Blumstein and Schwartz, 1977; Masters and Johnson, 1979). In addition, such categories emphasize discontinuities rather than consistencies along the full range of variations in erotic and affectional preferences. Even Freud seemed aware of the complexity of this construction when he wrote: "What is for practical reasons called homosexuality may arise from a whole variety of psychosexual inhibitory processes; the particular process we have singled out is perhaps only one among many, and is perhaps related to only one type of homosexuality" (1914: 101).

Only one type of homosexuality indeed! What is the sexuality of the one who partners a two-spirit? If one accepts the concept of more than two genders, then such a "man" or "woman" is not having a homosexual relationship but is fundamentally engaged in a heterosexual encounter by being involved with a third or fourth (or fifth or sixth) gender. And were I an activist, I might remind the reader of Foucault's suggestion that the so-called scientific categories of gender and sexuality are medical and therefore pathologically focused and "constitute a sexuality that is economically useful and politically conservative" (1978:36). As Janice Irvine, a sexology critic, points out, the underlying theories of only two genders, a heterosexuality versus homosexuality, inform sexological practices in important ways.

Sexology contributes to the collective sexual discourse of the medical and psychiatric professions, a discourse that is itself a means of social control. Categories of "natural" and "deviant" not only operate on the personal level to shape individual experience, but underpin the legal system as well. Whenever a personal preference/orientation becomes a "sexual dysfunction," a "sexual deviancy," or a crime is a political decision often related to its status in the psychiatric community. (1990:104)

Weeks states that standard sexual classifications are "not inborn, pregiven, or 'natural'. . . these classifications are striven for, contested, negotiated, and achieved often in the struggles of the subordinate to the dominate" (as cited in DeCecco & Elia, 1993:5). Were I a historian, I might remind the audience that the hatred and oppression against Native Americans by European invaders and colonialists might have had some influence on what so-called informants would discuss, considering that the interviewer might classify community-sanctioned behavior as a "sexual dysfunction, a sexual deviancy, or a crime." I might point out that the 1513 event of Balboa's executing forty Native people he labeled "sodomites" might instruct the subjects of anthropologists to be somewhat hesitant in their discussions of gender and sexuality in general (Goldberg 1992:180). Greg Sarris, a Pomo scholar and speaking as both a Pomo and an academic, reminds us that "representatives from the dominant culture exploring the resistance of a subjugated people are likely to see little more than what those people choose or can afford to show them" (1993:68). Sarris might suggest that even such "gay-positive" works as those of Walter Williams, which attempt to "give voice" to the Native two-spirit, are typical ethnographic reports that provide a "story of a story," "The reality of the situation is that the self which is identifiable as Indian, and has come to signify Indian in the text, is Indian in contact with non-Indian" (89).

Ultimately, it is probably impossible ever to recapture objectively accurate information on Native concepts of sexuality. Written historic records are likely to tell more about European observers' sexuality than that of those observed. Historically, ethnic animosity against Native people was usually so intense that "rationality [was] usually the first sacrifice, where those one opposes are automatically called perverted, cannibals, thieves, and degenerates" (Tannahill 1980:168). It may be difficult to know when one is reporting and when one is propagandizing. Thus, it is possible that the Spanish used such accusations as "they are all sodomites and practice that abominable vice" (Salmoral 1990:76) to justify their conquering efforts, much in the manner of contemporary anti-gay efforts by Christian extremists. Who knows how many of those accused or noted as hermaphrodite, transvestite, or homosexual were what are now labeled as two-spirit?

Sarris is a powerful advocate for our awareness of not only acknowledging what the experience of the observed and observer may be, as well as their interaction, but also for the interaction of the reader of texts that report these interactions and intersections, moving far afield from the gift-wrap theory of ideas.

In 1985, at the International Academy of Sex Research, I suggested the Tafoya Principle of Uncertainty. I called it that because I discovered that you get tenure faster if you name something after yourself. In physics, the Heisenberg Principle of Uncertainty states that one can know the speed of an electron or its location, but one cannot know both simultaneously. In other words, to know its location, the electron needs to be in a fixed placed and not moving; to measure its velocity, the electron must be moving and not in a fixed place.

The Tafoya Principle of Uncertainty states that in cross-cultural research one can have context or definition but not both at the same time. The more one attempts to establish a context for a situation or process, the more one will blur a clean, simple definition for a situation or process and the more one will lose a sense of context. Attempting to define two-spirit will cause a loss of context. Attempting to provide a context for the two-spirit will blur any simple and specific definition of the experience. This is not to say that any labels dealing with sexuality and gender are hopeless or self-defeating. As DeCecco and Elia suggest, "Such labels may have great utility in studies that treat them as loosely descriptive social constructs rather than as intrinsic traits that are predictive of the sum of an individual's erotic and affectional desires" (1993:45). Problems arise in the Godelesque attempt to describe what ultimately lies outside of one's ability to define.

Before I let the Dragonfly go free, I suggest that I have always found that Native American traditions provide a floor rather than a ceiling; one is provided a foundation of understanding rather than a limitation. Perhaps the truth of the two-spirit is best understood by Foster's definition: "A truth, they might say, that could be approached only along a ladder of parables and enigmas and silent little explosions of enlightenments" (1975:207).

Ana kush nai (it is finished).

NOTE

1. *M. Butterfly* is not to be confused with *Madame Butterfly*, Giacomo Puccini's operetta about the relationship between a Japanese woman and an American army lieutenant, later rewritten as *Miss Saigon*, the story of a Vietnamese woman and American serviceman.

REFERENCES CITED

Blumstein, Phillip, and Pepper Schwartz, 1977. *American Couples: Money, Work, Sex.* New York: Pocket Books.

DeCecco, John P., and John P. Elia, 1993. "A Critique and Synthesis of Biological Essentialism and Social Constructionist Views of Sexuality and Gender." In *If You Seduce a Straight Person, Can You Make Them Gay? Issues in Biological Essentialism vs. Social Constructionism in Gay and Lesbian Identities*, ed. John P.

DeCecco and John P. Elia. New York: Harrington Park Press.

Foster, M. A. 1975. *The Gameplayers of Zan.* New York: DAW Books.

Foucault, Michel. 1978. *The History of Sexuality. Volume I: An Introduction.* New York: Pantheon.

Freud, Sigmund. 1914. In *The Standard Edition of the Complete Psychological Works of Sigmund Freud,* Volume 2 (1953–74), ed. James Strachey. London: Hogarth Press.

Goldberg, Johnathan. 1992. *Sodometries: Renaissance Texts and Modern Sexualities.* Stanford, CA: Stanford University Press.

Hayles, Katherine. 1993. Quoted in Janet Stites. "Bordercrossings: A Conversation in Cyberspace." *OMNI* 16(2): 38–48, 105–13.

Hillerman, Tony. 1986. *The Boy Who Made Dragonfly: A Zuni Myth.* Albuquerque: University of Mexico Press.

Hwang, David Henry. 1989. *M. Butterfly.* New York: New American Library.

Irvine, Janice M. 1990. *Disorders of Desire: Sex and Gender in Modern American Sexology.* Philadelphia: Temple University Press.

Masters, William, and Virginia Johnson. 1979. *Homosexuality in Perspective.* Boston: Little, Brown.

Patton, Cindy. 1990. *Inventing AIDS.* New York: Routledge.

Paul, Jay P. 1993. "Childhood Cross-Gender Behavior and Adult Homosexuality: The Resurgence of Biological Models of Sexuality." In *If You Seduce a Straight Person, Can You Make Them Gay? Issues in Biological Essentialism vs. Social Constructionism in Gay and Lesbian Identities,* ed. John P. DeCecco and John P. Elia, 41–54. New York: Harrington Park Press.

Salmoral, Manuel Lucena. 1990. *America 1492: Portrait of a Continent Five Hundred Years Ago.* New York: Facts on File.

Sarris, Greg. 1993. *Keeping Slug Woman Alive: A Holistic Approach to American Indian Texts.* Berkeley: University of California Press.

Tannahill, Reay. 1980. *Sex in History.* New York: Stein and Day.

Weeks, Jeffrey. 1989. "Against Nature." In *Homosexuality, Which Homosexuality?* ed. Dennis Altman et al., 199–214. Amsterdam: Schorer Press.

Discussion Questions

1. What is the "gift wrap idea of language" and how does it apply to sexual identities?

2. Explain the Tafoya Principle of Uncertainty and its relevance to sexual identities, culture, and power. Do you agree or disagree with his analysis? Why or why not?

3. What do you see as the functions of identity labels? Do sexual identity labels reinforce the dominant power structure or empower nondominant groups? How so? How is Tafoya's take on sexual identity labels similar to and different from what Weeks says about how sexual identities function in society?

10

Migrancy and Homodesire

MYRON BEASLEY

REFLECTIONS OF A TRAVELER

Stuart Hall (2001) reminds us that it is always narrative that situates who we are and where we come from. In my narratives of international travels are constant reminders of where I come from geographically, politically, and sexually. In what follows, you will read how my body becomes the target of curiosity, vulnerability, and eroticism in different cultural spaces. Bell and Valentine (1995) locate sensual geographical experience as "fundamentally mediated by the body, it begins and ends with the body" (p. 34). The methods of autoethnograpy (Ellis & Bochner, 1996) and personal geography (Browning, 1996) encourage the researcher to be open, frank, and explicit about her or his life so that others will identify and empathize with the narrative. Through the performance of these stories, I make sense of who I am and how I negotiate my multiple identities (African American, Ethiopian, Jewish, academic, same-gender-loving man) in multiple locales. Throughout this essay, in discussing my sexual desires,

I explore borders as the conditions from which I turn as I move through questions of identity.

By telling my story, I create something new and alter and reconfigure my map of desire. I examine my map through the framework of my homodesires, for, as Audre Lorde (1984) said, "Silence equals death" and "silence will not protect you" (p. 107). I could have chosen not to mention my same-sex desires, but that would have denied who I am. I could have sought refuge in the terrain of silence, but that silence is deadly and not affirming.

In addition, when we tell our stories against cultural backdrops that nourish them, we transcend self-indulgence and contribute to a rewriting of the governing cultural narrative (Corey, 2002). In other words, narratives can disrupt heteronormativity. The body, which has been colonized by cultural law, is policed not only by border control, but also by the capacities of language. According to Corey:

> A story is then rooted in cultural norms, but through language, a storyteller is able to construct a form of identity, reshape

memory, sand a rough moment, curve a straight line, or build a bureau of clandestine drawers in which to hide things, things such as a place of birth, a line of flight, an undeveloped thought, or the pleasure of a name. (p. 93)

* * *

I love him so!

I landed in Holland chasing my partner of 5 years, Rhaan. We met in Cuba and later attended graduate school in Europe and worked together for the United Nations in several refugee camps in the Middle East. We both share a passion for international human rights issues, particularly among displaced peoples of the world; dedicated to grassroots organizations, we hoped in some part to observe the direct results of our labor in the field. Our zeal was fueled by our life histories: Rhaan is a man of Iraqi descent who, after spending time in a refugee camp, emigrated with his family to Holland during the Iran-Iraq war; he is a Dutch citizen and a practicing Muslim. I, on the other hand, am a child of Ethiopian émigrés who spent the formative years of my life in a refugee camp in Israel; I am a United States citizen and a practicing Jew. In 1996, we were separated briefly, he in Holland working for the World Court and I in the United States completing my doctoral work. Our relationship was bridged by (mostly) my traveling to Holland as often as possible, which acquainted me with the landscape and culture of the Netherlands.

The recent legislation concerning gay unions and adoptions, relaxed drug regulations, and the legalization of the sex industry have made Holland one of the most progressive countries in the European commonwealth. This is a point of contention among members of the European community, particularly in regard to the Dutch "tolerance" of drugs. Holland's progressive attitude is based in the origin of the Netherlands. According to William (1932), Holland was founded by immigrants who were rejected in their homelands or were searching for freedom, such as

Puritans from England, Huguenots from France, and Indonesians—peoples in search of places where they could freely believe, worship, and engage in other cultural practices without fear of persecution.

The Netherlands is the only country in Europe that has never officially outlawed same-sex practices (William, 1932). According to Dutch gay folklore, King Albert himself was a gay man. He was married to a woman only for the purpose of producing children to continue the royal lineage. Whether this is truth or fiction, Dutch gays and lesbians take pride in their history—a legacy that is an integral part of their country.

In 1992, the Dutch government officially legalized same-sex marriages, which made it the first country in the world that legalized such unions. Many of my Dutch friends have spoken of a related increase of gay and lesbian immigrants, particularly those in search of marital bliss, a privilege rarely extended in the United States or elsewhere. My two friends Kamoua and Fred are among the gay migrants who have descended upon this "gay-friendly" Mecca. Although their shared goals of meeting Dutch men were successful, their stories of inhabiting this space represent two different views of being immigrants to Holland. Let me begin with Fred and our trip to the margin.

I have known Fred for almost 11 years. He is a 38-year-old native of San Francisco who, in 2005, relocated to Holland to live with a Dutch man he met in San Diego the year before. He gave up his career as a successful stockbroker to be with a man, for when they met he claimed it "was love at first sight."

One evening, Fred and I cycled from the city center of Amsterdam, where I was staying, to what is known as the Belmer, where Fred and his partner lived. I was told that the Belmer and the city center, where I was residing during my stay in Holland, were the two recognizable "queer spaces." As we drew closer and closer to the Belmer, I noticed the difference, a change not only in the architecture, which changed from 12th- and 13th-century canal homes to modern matchbox living quarters (which look to me like low-income government housing found in the United States), but a change in the inhabitants. Fred, who is white, also observed the communities of Moroccans, Surinames, Indonesians (i.e., communities of color). What was ever present to me on this trip through that city was that perhaps the Dutch culture was indeed tolerant of some "others" but maybe not so accepting of people who might look a little different; for example, the people who lived or were positioned at the borders or margins of the city were noticeably the people of color. I was told that slang definitions of the word *belmer* in Dutch were "on the wayside," "outside," and "basement." Naming the space "the Belmer" denoted notions of placement, control, and no admittance to the mainstream.

Later that evening, we connected with Rhaan for dinner. While engaging over food, we discussed the possibilities of him moving back to the States. In the course of the conversations, two specific comments left me perplexed. First, Rhaan referred to himself as a *refugee*, a term I had not previously heard him use in reference to himself. The word triggered desperate moments in my own historical memory. Images arose of my time working in a refugee camp in Turkey a few summers before and unpleasant images of my childhood, when I lived in a refugee camp outside of Tel Aviv. I never refer to myself as a refugee, a word that communicates exile, foreigner, outcast. My body shudders, wanting to understand where exactly I locate my national identity. Am I authentic anything? Where do I belong? *Am* I a refugee still? The Dutch refer to *all* immigrants as refugees. Despite Rhaan's naturalization as a Dutch citizen, inscribed on his national identification card and driver's license is the term *refugee*. He is branded, reminded that he will never be an authentic, *real* Dutchman. In discourse that maps a geography of exclusion (Sibley, 1997), there is the allure of admittance and entry but not true inclusion.

I briefly reflected on some of the historical actions of the Dutch. It was the Dutch who constructed ships used in the great African slave trade, turned their backs on the Jews, and allowed Hitler's army to capture Anne Frank and her family. In addition, it was the Dutch who installed the system of apartheid in South Africa, a racist system of government privileging the white culture over the indigenous African communities. I wondered, what does it mean to be tolerant?

During the time spent in the margins of the city, I became acutely aware of the word *tolerance* and how it is sometimes mistaken for *freedom*. According to *Webster's New World Dictionary* (1997), tolerance is defined as "a tolerating or being tolerant, esp. of views, beliefs, practices of others that differ from one's own" (p. 1407). Could it be that Holland, this progressive country, tends to tolerate rather than embrace or confront difference?

Time spent with Kamou provided new insight into race and sexuality. Kamou is a 41-year-old African American who has been living in Amsterdam since November 1997. I met Kamou when I lived in Atlanta, where he was an associate pastor of one of the largest churches in the city. Kamou, like Fred, met his partner Lou (a Dutch man) while Lou was vacationing in the United States. My time with Kamou foregrounded the forbidden (at least for me) and highly contested terrain of interracial armours. I have gleaned from my life in the African American community that, at least in my circle of acquaintance, interracial romantic bonding continues to be problematic, particularly among women and gay men of African descent. The historical images of slavery are ever present, particularly in regard to how the black body (both male and female) was sexually used. In the United States, these performances are reproduced and repeated in mediated images every day.

In some gay communities in the United States, representations of the black male body are usually linked to sexual desire. Mercer

(1994) and hooks (1992) explain the concept of the white man's gaze as a process of presenting frozen images of the African American body as a sexual object that fulfills fantasies for white onlookers. According to Mercer (1994), this objectification of the body is "deadly," for it consciously situates the white man as in control (p. 174). Many gay men and women of African descent have grappled with the notion of interracial amours in the gay and lesbian community (Julien & MacCabe, 1991; Mercer, 1994; Riggs, 1991). I have long questioned such unions—I wonder if within the psyche of whiteness, the notion of sex with people of color is a demonstration of power or mere fulfillment of sexual desire or fantasy. In her autobiography *Wounds of Passion: A Writing Life* (1997), bell hooks shares that, at one moment in her life, she could never love a white person simply because their hands "are filled with blood" (p. 37)—blood that was and is spilt to make whites feel in control. How can I *not* think of oppressive racial discourse when my body is marked and defined by it daily? This is best illustrated by my sharing an event that occurred during my first evening in Amsterdam.

I was greeted at the airport by Eric, a Dutch man I have known for 5 years, and Rhaan, both eager to share a special trip with me. It was their idea to surprise me by taking me to a sauna party to be held on the outskirts of the city in a blue-collar town in the south of Amsterdam. On the way, I inquired about the sauna party, not knowing exactly what one was. Eric described the event as something that takes place in a gymlike facility frequented for sexual activities. Thoughts of the bathhouses that were prevalent in the pre-AIDS era in the United States came to mind. I felt moderately uncomfortable about attending such an event. I have struggled and continue to struggle with traditional familial alliances. It is not easy to rid my cognitive mapping of the orthodox religious ideology with which I was reared. I struggle daily to combat that oppressive way of thinking and believing, particularly as it pertains to sexuality. Fanon (1967) reminds me of the rhetoric of guilt and fear that religion and the colonizers use(d) to control and enslave the oppressed. The ghosts of such discourse are inscribed on the bodies of the colonized (who were and continue to be objectified, sexualized, othered), and many traditional knowledges were forever forbidden, their remnants destroyed and erased from indigenous memories.

Negative feelings about my physical body also surfaced as we moved toward the party. I had never walked around in a spa completely naked, and the thought made me uncomfortable. My ass becomes magnified, and my protruding stomach becomes more pronounced in my thoughts. Immediately, I compare myself to all of the other beautiful men who might be present, not considering myself one of them.

As children, my parents taught my brother, sister, and me about the importance of giving and gratitude. The one major characteristic that I love most about my parents is that they always gave from hearts filled with charity. For me, however, the act of giving was an act of self-denial. I was the pleaser of the family, always in need of approval, and I took to heart the admonition of the Scriptures to "give of ourselves and our possessions" and "deny" oneself. In the act of giving, I was subjecting myself to feelings of unworthiness. I really thought that my physical body was not deserving of any desires, and for this reason, I denied myself much, even my homodesires. This denial of self and guilt from religious ideology problematized my partaking in the ritual of the sauna party. (I include my thoughts on religious ideology not to use them as a scapegoat, but to address why I do not like my body. Through a retracing of my cultural map, I might discover a way out, a means of reconfiguring my map.)

In the car on the way to the party, Eric and Rhaan informed me of the rules of the party.

"Listen carefully," said Eric in his deep voice, with a touch of condescension in his tone, "if a man puts his hand on your leg, that means that he likes you." He smiled. "If you're not interested in him, just simply lift his hand off of your leg and he will leave you alone." He continued, "We're all respectful of each other here." I smiled. My curiosity was piqued. OK, I was a little excited!

After being briefed on the do's and don'ts, I entered the steam room of the "bathhouse" with Eric at my side. Immediately, several (four, to be exact) white men (Rhaan and I were the only men of color in the entire facility) rushed toward me and began touching me all over my body. I did exactly as I had been coached to do—I removed their hands from me. But they did not leave me alone; they kept touching me. I closed my eyes—I'm not sure exactly why; and attempted to push them away, but several were extremely forceful and adamant about touching and feeling and tasting my blackness. I became extremely uncomfortable and Eric, seeing my discomfort, said, "We can leave at any time" and helped me escape the mad crowd that hovered over my body in the steam room. As soon as we departed the room, Eric said to me, "You're popular, they really like you, man."

But did they like me, or was I an object of their sexual desire? As I sat in that room with the white men touching and tasting me, I felt nothing more than disgust at being in that space. In that moment, it was an illustration for me that I was nothing more than a slave. I was objectified.

Two days later, Eric and others took me to a locals' pub, which was nothing more than a small room with a bar and a couple of tables. Upon entering the space, I could not help but notice the nude pictures of black men on the walls. That evening I was the only man of color in the bar, and according to many in the pub, this particular spot was not very popular among people of color for reasons that were not explained to me. I questioned why

Mapplethorpe's images from the *Black Book* (1986) were prominently displayed on every wall of the pub.

As I continue to travel, perhaps my position on interracial amours will change. Maybe one day I might come to understand that love can be shared between people of different races and transcend oppressive racial discourses. Audre Lorde, Marlon Riggs, and James Baldwin have profoundly influenced my understanding of myself, as well as the politics of race and sexuality. After all, they were African Americans, gay, and, at significant times in their lives, had white partners whom they loved fiercely.

NATIONALISM OVER DINNER

As one travels, one becomes aware of the new terrains one visits or inhabits, as well as becoming aware of one's own position in the world. I recall the 7½ years I spent in France as a student, during which time the bulk of my learning derived from discovering things about my personal life and demystifying "Americanisms." This trip was no exception. As I traveled in Holland, I had to confront several political issues that challenged my Western capitalistic ideology, my way of thinking, my culture, my map. My relationships and alliances with my fellow travelers were affirmed and maintained through our shared queer identities and discourse, the elements that created and sustained our sacred space. However, borders are often drawn and contested when one claims a national identity. Articulating borders, making them known when at moments they may seem subtle or hidden, can be dangerous. A dinner conversation provides insight to this claim.

On my second evening in Amsterdam at a Thai restaurant, I found myself adamantly defending the United States of America. Eric stated that he felt the United States thinks it is the police of the world. I chimed in, "Oh, it's not that we want to police the world, it's that we volunteer our services when asked to aid in world crises." I continued, "Personally, I think the U.S. should reconsider their membership with the UN." At this point, Lou, a little testy, probably due to my nonchalant attitude, which could have been interpreted as arrogance, stated, "Don't you think that the U.S. should pay their dues to the United Nations?" I replied again with a great deal of assurance, "No, did we not donate the land? Did we not build the building?" Eric, a little heated, shouted, "Why do you guys think that you're so rich?" I responded, again in a confident manner, "We are, aren't we the richest nation in the world?" Eric shouted even louder, "You have the largest national debt of any country, how can you be so rich?" I could not respond to Eric's remark. The United States does indeed have a very large national debt, and I was only repeating what I had always heard: that we are the richest country in the world. We who live in the United States consume more gas, electricity, and water than any other country in the world. Lou's comment lingers in my mind: "The United States consumes six times the amount of electricity the Dutch use. You guys are takers!" Is the United States the richest nation on earth? Are we greedy? The dinner became even more delectable.

"Did you know Americans can go anywhere around the world with little exception? However, other countries cannot exercise that right or privilege," said Eric, as we began eating our dessert. Lou pulled his AIDS test card out of his pocket, "I have to have this to enter the U.S." I was shocked to hear that the borders of the United States are closed to those who are HIV-positive. I was familiar with contemporary policies regarding entry into the United States and the difficulties faced particularly by those from "Third World" or developing or almost developed countries, but I did not realize that countries that I would not place in any of those categories (such as the European Commonwealth) must adhere to strict guidelines before gaining admittance. I

remembered the motto of the American Express commercials: "Membership has its privileges." The power of having a U.S. passport is immense, allowing access to many countries around the world without harassment, an ongoing set of loopholes, and endless questionnaires.

"Give me your tired, your poor. . . ." is the invitation inscribed on the Statue of Liberty, words that I personally hold dear as a child of immigrants but whose meanings ring hollow in light of the tragic events of 9/11 and their aftermath. Entry into the United States has become more rigorous and legalistic for internationals; a new conception of the word *freedom* is being formulated, contested, and challenged; and boundaries and maps are being redrawn.

MESMERIZING MOROCCAN MEN

I walk through the medina, the old town, in traditional Moroccan garb.

My eyes meet two men leaning against the tall thick gray walls of the tiny labyrinthlike maze of the medina.

I enjoy the security of the medina: the place of solace for Moroccans—the space of danger for the French.

I smell the fragrances of the fresh spices, fresh fish, and the natural vivid smell of bodies rubbing against each other in the narrow paths.

I look at the two men.
They gaze back at me.
I dote on the two men leaning against the wall.
They acknowledge my gaze.

I proceed through the medina, when I realize that the two men are walking alongside of me.

They introduce themselves in Arabic.
My Arabic is not very strong.

So I respond in French, hoping that they will respond accordingly.

Ali responds in French.
　He is tall and thin,
　Pale, dark hair
　A Berber.
But my eyes sway toward Mohsin
　Dark skin
　　Dark hair
　Beautiful infectious smile
5´11´´, athletic build—he claims to be
Arab—he says.

I wonder if they know that I'm American
I wonder if they know that I like men
I wonder what they are thinking of me
　The question comes, "Are you African?"
　I respond, "Je suis American."
Their eyes open wide.
　They become excited.
　　"Would you like to join us for mint
tea?" Ali asks in English.
　I then become astonished.
　I love Moroccan mint tea!
Mohsin only speaks Arabic, no French, no
English.

They take me to a café to have mint tea.
　We sip and then we chat
　Ali says "We love Black Americans."
He proceeds by mentioning Mohammad
Ali, Louis Farrakhan, and Michael Jackson.
　"We love black Americans," he says.
Mohsin sits silently.

I wonder if they know that I like men
I wonder what they are thinking of me

Ali asks if I've been to a hamam.
I respond by saying yes, but it was in Cassa.
He jumps up and says let's go . . . I want to
take you to a hamam.
　As we rush to the door, he says to me, "We
love black Americans."
　And he grabs my hand and we walk
through the medina hand in hand.
　I'm so excited. Realizing men holding
hands in this cultural context is so normal

I feel comforted, I feel secure. But I continue
to wonder if they know that I like men.
　We proceed down the narrow streets of the
Medina and find the hamam.
　Mohsin follows.

We enter the hamam.
　Ali orders the workers to take good care of me.
　I get undressed, enter the steam room
　And two, then three men begin to scrub,
clean my body,
　Wash my hair, massage my body . . . I
love it—I'm in ecstasy, three men working on
various parts of my body. . . .
　Ali is across the room with men working
on him.
　Mohsin remains outside waiting for us.

I feel so refreshed,
I feel so clean,
I feel really excited.

　Ali looks in my eyes. He asks, "So, do you
like my friend?"
　I say, "Yes, I do," trying hard not to insin-
uate too much.
　Mohsin, in Arabic, invites me over to his
home for mint tea.
　I eagerly reply with an anxious, "Sure, I'd
love to have mint tea with you at your home."

Ali hails a taxi for me and Mohsin.
　The taxi arrives, and as we enter the auto-
mobile, Ali pulls me aside and says,
　"Mohsin's fee is 200 American dollars."

REFERENCES

Bell, D., & Valentine, G. (Eds.). (1995). *Mapping desire: Geographies of sexualities*. New York: Routledge.
Browning, F. (1996). *A queer geography: Journeys toward a sexual self*. New York: Crown.
Corey, F. C. (2002). Crossing an Irish border. In J. N. Martin, T. K. Nakayama, & L. A. Flores (Eds.), *Readings in cultural contexts* (2nd ed., pp. 88–94). Mountain View, CA: Mayfield.

Denzin, N. (1997). *Interpretive ethnography: Ethnographic practices in the 21st century.* Thousand Oaks, CA: Sage.

Ellis, C., & Bochner, A. (Eds.). (1996). *Composing ethnography.* Thousand Oaks, CA: Sage.

Fanon, F. (1967). *White skin, white masks* (C. L. Markmann, Trans.). New York: Grove Press.

Hall, S. (2001). Negotiating Caribbean identities. In B. Meeks & F. Lindahl (Eds.), *New Caribbean thought: A reader* (pp. 24–39). Mona, Jamaica: University of the West Indies Press.

Hernandez, G. (1995). Multiple subjectivities and strategic positionality: Zora Neal Hurston's experimental ethnography. In R. Behar & D. Gordon (Eds.), *Women writing culture.* (pp. 148–165). Berkeley: University of California Press.

hooks, b. (1992). *Black looks: Race and representation.* Boston: South End Press.

hooks, b. (1997). *Wounds of passion: A writing life.* New York: Holdt.

Julien, I., & MacCabe, C. (Eds.). (1991). *Diary of a young soul rebel.* Bloomington: Indiana University Press.

Langellier, K. (1989). Personal narratives: Perspectives on theory and research. *Text and Performance Quarterly, 9,* 243–276.

Langellier, K. (1998). Voiceless bodies, bodiless voices: The future of personal narrative performance. In S. Dailey (Ed.), *The future of performance studies: Visions and revisions* (pp. 207–213). Annandale, VA: NCA.

Langellier, K. (1999). Personal narrative, performance, performativity: Two or three things I know for sure. *Text and Performance Quarterly, 19,* 125–144.

Lorde, A. (1984). *Sister outsider: Essays and speeches.* Freedom, CA: Crossing Press.

Mapplethorpe, R. (1986). *Black book.* New York: St. Martin's Press.

Mercer, K. (1994). *Welcome to the jungle: New positions in black cultural studies.* New York: Routledge.

Riggs, M. (1991). Tongues untied. In E. Hemphill (Ed.), *Brother to brother: New writings by black gay men* (pp. 77-79). Boston: Alyson.

Schechner, R. (1993) *The future of ritual.* New York: Routledge.

Schechner, R. (2002). *Performance studies: An introduction.* New York: Routledge.

Sibley, D. (1997). *Geographies of exclusion.* New York: Routledge.

Stern, C., & Henderson, B. (1993). *Performance: Text and context.* White Plains, NY: Longman.

Tattelman, I. (1999). Speaking to the gay bathhouse. In W. Leap (Ed.), *Public sex gay space.* New York: Columbia University Press.

Webster's New World dictionary. (1997). New York: Random House.

William, T. (1932). *Observations upon the united provinces of the Netherlands.* Cambridge, England: Cambridge University Press.

Discussion Questions

1. Beasley describes his approach in this essay as a form of storytelling in which he explores who he is in different cultural spaces. What do you see as the potential advantages and drawbacks of this approach to the study of sexual identity and communication?

2. Beasley shares his musings on the subject of whether interracial love relations based on equality are possible. What are your thoughts on this subject?

3. Beasley self-identifies as "African American, Ethiopian, Jewish, academic, same-gender-loving man" and U.S. citizen. Doubtless, he could add other identifiers. How do you identify yourself? How have your identifications been affected (challenged, informed, enriched, complicated, illuminated, etc.) by your travels?

11

Performing "I Do"

Weddings, Pornography, and Sex

ELIZABETH BELL

Several times a year, I am invited to weddings. When the invitations arrive in the mail, I am always genuinely touched. I like being included in the circle of family and friends drawn together on the guest list, and I always pore over the invitations. I trace the embossed lettering on the heavy paper; I sort the envelopes, the reply card, the onion-skin covers. I always RSVP promptly, knowing how difficult it is for caterers and couples to pin down the numbers. And my reply is always the same: "I regret that I will not be able to attend."

Weddings make me angry. I am angry at our culture's demands on the bride to expend inordinate amounts of time, energy, and money. The emotional costs of these expenditures are tremendously high, and I ache for the bride-to-be as she is consumed—for months—with orchestrating the event. I am angry at the fictional "ideals" of perfect weddings, whether produced by *Bride* Magazine, Britain's royal family, or *The Bold and the Beautiful*. Who could replicate such perfection? Most of all, I am angry that "the bride's big day" is her one moment in the spotlight. Why does our culture offer so few moments for women to shine? To be the center of attention? And why should *this* moment, as she is passed from father to husband, be valorized? Such fuming makes me a very bad guest at weddings, so I know better than to attend.

About as frequently as I receive wedding invitations, I watch pornographic videotapes. This is an admission, I realize, that places me—a white, heterosexual, middle-aged feminist—at precarious odds with antipornography feminists and the Christian right, as well as in the middle of debates about family values. As I watch porn, I experience the same

Author's Note: Much of this chapter is taken from my 1999 article "Weddings and Pornography: The Cultural Construction of Sex," originally published in *Text and Performance Quarterly, 19*(3), 173–195. I would like to thank the publisher for permission to recast portions of that article here.

anger prompted by weddings: What are the emotional costs of this? Who could replicate such perfection? And, again, most important: Why does our culture offer so few moments for women to shine? To be the center of attention? And why should *this* moment, as she is passed from partner to partner, be valorized?

Weddings and pornography are too often seen as opposites: Weddings traditionally represent, enact, and perform social order; pornography traditionally represents, enacts, and performs social chaos. From a performance perspective, however, weddings and pornography are surprisingly the same: They are both cultural performances; they both depend on the intent and consent of their participants; and they both arise from historical conventions determined by church and state. Most important, they both have sex at their center: A wedding ceremony must be consummated by sexual intercourse, and hard-core pornography must depict penetration and ejaculation.

Weddings and pornography, I propose, are not opposites. They are *mirror doubles of the cultural performance of sex*. To support this odd statement, I feature specific words in that sentence. As *cultural* performances of sex, weddings and pornography are socially and politically organized to serve culture: They create insiders and outsiders, rules for appropriate sexual behavior, and performance frames that fluctuate between play and belief. As cultural *performances* of sex, weddings and pornography both depend on the successful enactment of conventions and scripts, performance consciousness of the performers, and the imposition of frames of belief and play. As cultural performances of *sex,* they both hold consent and sexual intercourse as their *sine qua non*. As mirror doubles—not mirror opposites—they are complementary and mutually dependent: If there were no socially *sanctioned* coupling through weddings, there would be no socially *demonized* coupling through pornography.

This construction of weddings and pornography as complementary cultural performances shifts the emphasis from *sex* as the operative term in the pornography debates to *performance*. In the rhetoric of pornography debates, various camps use the term *performance* to describe and to evaluate the content, performers, audiences, and discourses of pornography. Depending on their divergent political agendas, these camps conveniently condemn, embrace, erase, or displace the term *performance* to describe the sex in pornography.

This chapter is divided into two parts. The first half details how weddings and pornography are performances with similar ends and means at the service of culture. The second half examines the use of the term *performance* in the pornography debates. Together, weddings and pornography serve to control sex—how it is constructed, enacted, and policed in contemporary culture. When the bride and groom say "I do" and the porn actor climaxes on the breasts of his video partner, these performances create sex that is either approved or condemned, but always warranting culture's control.

WEDDINGS AND PORNOGRAPHY AS PERFORMANCES

With the metaphor of a centrifuge, Dwight Conquergood (1986) claims that all cultures have "a moral center," or core of organized social values. As cultures spin, they "throw off forms of themselves—literally, 'expressions'— that are publicly accessible" (p. 58). These "expressions" are performances—from events as varied as the off-key, but sincere, rendering of "Happy Birthday" at a family get-together, the carefully choreographed and polished Broadway musical, and the liturgy of the Catholic Mass. How to make sense of such a wide variety of forms and functions called performance?

In 1972, Milton Singer coined the term "cultural performance" to describe performance events unique to a particular culture. Common cultural performances in the United States include the Superbowl, Mardi Gras, the Miss America pageant, and the Democratic and Republican national conventions, to name just a few. Singer claims that all cultural performances have similar characteristics: a limited time span, an organized program of activity, a set of performers, audience, and place (p. 71). Cultural performances usually involve large numbers of participants and observers. As both public and ceremonial, "display and exhibition" are the purposes of the performers, and "the bodies of the performers are their instruments" (Stern & Henderson, 1993, pp. 26–27). Most important, cultural performances are "at the service of the culture, and the ceremony is designed principally to reinforce cultural values and to solidify social organization or stimulate political action, rather than principally to please and entertain" (Stern & Henderson, 1993, p. 27).

Weddings easily adhere to this definition of cultural performance—as ceremony, as display, as site of cultural values:

> Although there is no such thing as "the typical American wedding"—as many styles of weddings exist as the styles of citizens given them—every single one possesses the same ritualistic ingredients, the same replay of ancient custom and primeval symbolism, the same predictable plot and standard players. A wedding is, after all, a wedding. (Seligson, 1973, p. 4)

But pornography, too, is a cultural performance—as ceremony, as display, as site of cultural values. All cultures have expressions deemed pornographic, "but not every culture distinguishes the erotic from the pornographic, nor is pornography defined in the same way in every instance" (Findlen, 1993, p. 53). Sallie Tisdale (1994) maintains that "the sexual material of a culture reflects that culture's concerns," and she details differences:

In America, the adolescent rut—eternal erection and ready orgasm. In England, book after book about spanking, sex across class lines, and a detailed interest in underwear; in Germany, leather-clad blondes whipping swarthy men; in Italy, an interest in feminized men; in Japan, a preoccupation with icons of innocence (schoolgirls, nurses, brides), soiled innocence (widows), and maternal nurturing. In Japanese pornography active female pleasure is considered a turnoff. I've never seen an American film that didn't feature it. (p. 138)

Weddings and pornography are cultural performances that both reflect cultural concerns and offer an opportunity for us to be reflexive about those concerns. For Richard Bauman (1992), cultural performances mirror "some primary cultural realities such as values, patterns of action, structures of social relations, and the like" (p. 47). As opportunities for reflexivity, studying what might be available in the mirrored reflection, "performance may be seen as broadly metacultural, a cultural means of objectifying and laying open to scrutiny culture itself" (p. 47).

In both weddings and pornography, performance is the vehicle for intention and consent. The phrase "I do" is a performance that enacts a contract, and contracts must be consensual to be valid.[1] Moreover, for a marriage to be legal, it must be consummated through sexual intercourse. Likewise, the making of pornography is one of the few forms of "degrading labor" that must "emphasize that its conditions of paid employment are not just contractual . . . but that they are also entirely consensual" (Ross, 1993, p. 224). Both weddings and pornography are consensual contracts consummated in and through the performance of sex.

The "performative contract" is only one way to view performance of sex. Conquergood (1998) explains that performance has been theorized in three different ways: "faking," "making," and "breaking." "Faking" was the centerpiece for Erving Goffman's (1959) conception of performance—the deliberate roles constructed and embodied in the "presentation of self in everyday life." Good students "act" the part—paying attention in class and asking good questions—just as good scam artists convince us of the sincerity of their roles in a "con job." Victor Turner (1987) shifted the emphasis from faking to "making." Individual and collective performances make cultures through the embodied and participatory enactment of structured forms—such as "Happy Birthday" and the Catholic Mass. Postmodern and postcolonial theorists emphasize performances that "break" conventional roles, events, and structures. Drag performances, for example, break the conventions of gender, demonstrating that the performative rules for masculine and feminine can be put on, or taken off, at will.

Weddings and pornography involve all three kinds of performances. Both weddings and pornography can be faked, they make relationships, and they can break the cultural structures that form them. Most important, when weddings and pornography are examined as making, breaking, and faking sex, they reveal the political stakes in these cultural performances of sex.

Making, Breaking, and Faking Weddings

> Current marriage formalities still derive from the long-standing concern of Church and State to control who is and is not married, and is still based on verbal consent (followed by sexual intercourse, otherwise the marriage is voidable) made in an authorized place (church or register office) in front of an authorized person, and then recorded at the General Register Office. (Leonard, 1980, p. 12)

Wedding ceremonies are acts "made" through performance at the intersection of church and state. Whether the ceremony takes place in a sacred or a secular setting, all wedding ceremonies are "rites of passage." Anthropologist Arnold Van Gennep (1960) coined this phrase in 1908 to describe and to

classify ceremonies that move individuals from "one situation to another, or from one cosmic or social world or another" (p. 10). For Van Gennep, the wedding is a rite of incorporation, uniting two people. His description of wedding rituals and rites from cultures across the world is a fascinating one, especially when these rituals are compared to contemporary U.S. weddings.

> All ceremonies include some combination of giving or exchanging belts, bracelets, rings, or clothes which are worn; binding one to the other with a single cord; tying parts of each other's clothing together; touching each other reciprocally in some way; using objects belonging to the other; . . . offering the other something to eat or drink; eating together (communion, confarreation); being wrapped in a single piece of clothing or a veil; sitting on the same seat . . .; entering the new house; and so forth. These are essentially rites of union. (Van Gennep, 1960, p. 132)

Weddings also follow the three-fold structure of all rites of passage:

> a separation from the old phase, transition through a liminal period, and incorporation or aggregation into the new phase. The ritualized celebration (we might say "performance") of such a change signals the personal and communal significance of the event, providing a pattern of behavior for those involved that is simultaneously conventional and symbolic. (Rehm, 1994, p. 5)

The liminal period,[2] the wedding ceremony itself, is almost always fraught with the betwixt-and-between doubts of "What will happen next?" punctuated by the traditional question in many contemporary Christian ceremonies, "Is there anyone present who knows why these two should not be joined in marriage? Let him speak now or forever hold his peace." Long a stock phrase and dramatic moment in soap operas, melodramas, and romances, this moment in the ceremony is the crux of the wedding's liminality as a rite of passage. The kiss at the end is the promissory note for sex to come, as well as the demarcation of safe passage through the liminal space.

Weddings are more than rites of passage, however; weddings also "make" private sexual relationships a public and state concern. In ancient Greece, the purpose of marriage was to sanction "a relationship between a man and woman which had the primary goal of producing children and maintaining the identity of the *oikos* unit (the household) within the social and political community" (Patterson, 1991, p. 59). The Catholic Church in 13th-century Europe made marriage a sacrament—with its insistence on a priest officiating—as a way to consolidate its power over individual behavior, as well as to protect women and children "from easy abandonment" (Johnson, 1996, p. 45). First-wave feminism five centuries later was, in large part, a reaction against women as chattel, owned by their husbands, granted in the contractual agreement of marriage (Ettelbrick, 1992). Even today, marriage is seen as a way to curb the promiscuous sexual activity of men, as if "bachelorhood [is] equivalent to moral lassitude, where all sexual expression outside wedlock is morally tainted" (Johnson, 1996, p. 47). Indeed, the church and state join forces to create a sanctioned relationship that serves many "idealistic" purposes: procreation, economic stability, sexual regulation, and the maintenance of unequal gender roles.[3] Art critic Dave Hickey (1997) maintains that a community's *highest* interest is manifested in its construction and regulation of courtship and sexual relations; hence, each culture maintains elaborate cultural constraints against and rewards for coupling appropriately.

In the United States, state marriage laws are under constant revision—testifying to the cultural and political shifts in what is considered appropriate "coupling."[4] For the past 15 years, gay marriage has been high on the cultural radar and in the courts. In 1991, three

couples in Hawaii tested same-sex marriage as a politically and socially viable contract (Eskridge, 1996); in 1993, the Hawaii Supreme Court ruled that the denial of same-sex marriage was a violation of equal protection under the law. As proponents and opponents made arguments, the implicit norms of heterosexuality, procreation, and gender roles in the state's interests were made visible in legislatures across the nation, culminating in the passage of the "Defense of Marriage Act" by the U.S. Congress in 1996. This act guarantees federal privileges for different-sex marriages and maintains the states' rights in denying recognition of same-sex marriages performed in other states. In 2003, the Massachusetts Supreme Judicial Court ruled gay marriage constitutional. In November of 2004, 11 states held and passed referenda that banned gay marriage, to much media speculation about its impact on garnering votes in the presidential election.

As cultural performances reflective of social, political, and religious values, weddings serve several important functions: They *grant* political, social, and economic privileges to their sanctioned participants but, conversely, *create* outsiders to those entitlements; *instantiate* sexual norms; and *depend* on frames of belief for their efficacy. What is too often lost in the gay marriage debates is the long list of political and economic benefits that come with state-sanctioned marriage. Chrys Ingraham (1999) lists 10 federal entitlements that range from the convenient to the monumental and 24 state entitlements that run the gamut of life's activities.[5] Our culture carefully protects these privileges when policing and regulating their dispersal through marriage.

Although numerous churches and congregations are recognizing same-sex unions and performing church-sanctioned ceremonies, most are not labeled "weddings." They are called "bonding ceremonies," "celebrations of commitment," "blessings," "union ceremonies," or other euphemisms (Sherman, 1992). Despite the media's portrayal of same-sex marriages during the 2004 presidential election, even the gay community is divided on same-sex marriage: "It is both radical and conservative. . . . For some, gay marriage is unnatural or abominable. For others, it is an assimilative sellout" (Eskridge, 1996, pp. 4–5). In the discourse about same-sex marriage, the implicit assumptions of heterosexuality, procreation, sexual regulation, and asymmetrical gender roles are unveiled when church, state, and community are unable to reconcile religious doctrine with political policy. Performances of weddings that "break" the bonds among the sacred, performance, and the state, like gay marriage, expose the underlying assumptions of the institution of marriage, assumptions that have much more to do with contracts—heterosexual, fiduciary, and proprietary—than with relationships.

While gay couples are demanding equal access to these privileges, a second group of "outsiders" are those who will *lose* political and economic privileges *if married*. The Rev. Wallace Tervin offered his services through Ann Landers' (1998) syndicated newspaper column to "Florida Jill," an "80-year-old woman who had met her sweetheart at the senior center and wanted to marry him but didn't want to run the risk of losing her pension and health benefits from her previous marriage. Living together was out of the question" (p. 2D). Ann Landers "blessed" Rev. Tervin for his benevolent offer to "marry" the elders in a church-sanctioned, state-less wedding, but Rev. Tervin had certain stipulations: "I must first be convinced that a true commitment exists and the couple's belief in God is the motivating factor behind their request. Secondly, I must see that a legally binding wedding would cause undue hardship because of the resulting loss of pension or medical benefits by one or both parties" (p. 2D). Here the contract shifts its emphasis: Although the state may *deny* economic privileges to same-sex couples for violation of the heterosexual contract, the church ensures that the state does

not *withdraw* economic privileges from elderly, God-fearing heterosexuals.

These contractual obligations and privileges instantiate sexual norms. That is, they police who should and who should not have church- and state-sanctioned sex. Church and state are an elaborate check-and-balance system in regulating "coupling": Homosex/uality is dangerous, subversive, excessive, and should never be sanctioned by the state; heterosex/uality at 80 is harmless, laughable, doubtful, yet still deserving of sanction by the church. The respective lines drawn in the sand by church and state cross each other at the most normative—gender-, age-, and blood-appropriate—intersections. Always and already at the center of this diagram is sex. Organizing society around "sexually connected people is wrong," according to American University law professor Nancy Polikoff. "The more central units are dependents and their caretakers" (quoted in Johnson, 1996, p. 48). The truly radical approach to the gay marriage debate would be to withdraw *all* state and federal entitlements from marriage: no more insurance benefits, tax breaks or penalties,[6] inheritance rights, or any other automatic benefits for *anyone*. Then the debate would involve the *unearned privileges*—not the sex or gender of the people seeking recognition of their union—in the eyes of church or state.

If the state, performance, and the church "make" weddings, and "breaking" with these conventions reveals their underlying normative sexual structures, then weddings can also be "faked."[7] Here the performance frames created in and through the ritual guide the actions of the participants. Under the tutelage of Victor and Edie Turner, graduate students in the Anthropology Department at the University of Virginia staged a wedding. Their collective goal was to move anthropology out of the cognitive realm into the experiential and to gain "the actors' 'inside view,' engendered in and through performance, as a powerful critique of how ritual and ceremonial structures are cognitively presented" (Turner, 1987,

p. 140). As the Turners unpack conclusions about this performance of wedding, one stands out:

> Most participants told us that they understood the cultural structure and psychology of normative American marriage much better for having taken part in an event that combined flow with reflexivity. Some even said that the fabricated marriage was more "real" for them than marriages in the "real world" in which they had been involved. (p. 144)

For the Turners, the wedding was a smashing success—as educational play. The stakes for the performers, however, were elided. "Of course," write the Turners, "in a real marriage the couple's intentions are all-important. They must seriously 'intend wedlock'" (Turner, 1987, p. 142). Although Austin's performative utterance, "I do," is operative here as both intention and consent, the Turners' easy claim about a *real* marriage is much too simplistic—for gay couples in Massachusetts and for Florida Jill—and glosses over the state-performance-church matrix in the creation and maintenance of insiders-outsiders, appropriate sex, and performance frames.

Making, Breaking, and Faking Pornography

> "Pornography" names an argument, not a thing. We have always had obscenity, at least as long as we have had a scene of public, reportable life that requires a zone of darkness to lend sense to it by contrast. (W. M. Kendrick, 1987, p. 31)

Pornography, too, is a particularly interesting interplay of "faking," "making," and "breaking" sex, and, like weddings, pornography is "made" at the intersection of the church, public performance, and the state. In

The Invention of Pornography, Lynn Hunt (1993) argues that, indeed, pornography was invented: "pornography was not a given; it was defined over time and by the conflicts between writers, artists and engravers on the one side and spies, policemen, clergymen and state officials on the other" (p. 11). In 16th-century Europe, the availability and consumption of print pornography was made possible with the rise of the printing press, burgeoning markets of literate consumers, and the desire of both church and state to monitor and regulate behavior in rapidly shifting political and cultural times.

Most literary historians agree that pornography in Europe—written by and distributed among the elite classes of white men—was not considered a "problem" until the works of Pietro Aretino in 16th-century Italy. The "first modern pornographer," Aretino laid the groundwork for pornographic conventions in print that would last for centuries across Europe: "the explicit representation of sexual activity, the form of the dialogue between two women, the discussion of the behavior of prostitutes and the challenge to the moral conventions of the day" (Hunt, 1993, p. 26). Paula Findlen (1993) characterizes the sea change in pornography with the works of Aretino:

> Aretino was more dangerous than all the erotically inclined artists and humanist pornographers put together, not because of his frank portrayals of sexual behavior but because of his refusal to restrict his audience to men of virtue who were allowed to read the erotic classics due to their "eloquence and quality of style." (pp. 101–102)

The state and the church converged to produce lists of "banned" books and to criminalize their production, sale, and possession, thereby "making" pornography a distinct canon, a canon that even Rousseau evoked in Book One of the *Confessions* as "those dangerous books that a beautiful woman of the world finds bothersome because, as she says, one can only read them with one hand" (quoted in DeJean, 1993, p. 110).

The audience, canon, and conventions of print pornography in 16th-century Europe also created a distinct cast of literary performers in pornographic texts. By writing sexual exploits as if heard from the mouths of courtesans and courtiers, street prostitutes and learned noblemen, and by centering much of their descriptions on anal intercourse between men, pornography created a "third sex"— writers of pornography, sodomites, and whores. Contemporary same-sex marriages, elderly pensioners, and the "third sex" of pornography are "outsiders" created by the performance of heterosexuality, procreation, and normative sexual contracts:

> Neither [prostitutes nor homosexuals] had to answer for the procreative relations between men and women, but their omnipresence in pornography and everyday life threw into doubt the stability of the heterosexual regime. Their membership in the so-called third sex gave them a privileged view of the practices of others and, thus, empowered them to speak, quite literally to "authorize" a portrait of society. Their gaze, however, was not the pornographic one, though they existed to foster it. Instead, it was the critical gaze of the pornographer, who looked into the souls of men and told them what they least wanted to hear. (Findlen, 1993, p. 107)

Indeed, weddings and pornography, as and when "broken" performances, create and maintain "insider-outsider" roles through normative cultural assumptions about sex. In Robert Stoller's ethnographic interviews with pornography industry workers, he reiterates the claim of the 16th-century "third sex": "The primeval joy in pornmakers is 'fuck you,' not 'let's fuck'" (Stoller & Levine, 1993, p. 119).

The "making" of pornography experienced another sea change, however, with the invention of motion pictures. Pornography was no longer limited to still depictions of sexual acts

in engravings, paintings, and photographs, and the "performance of pornography" was no longer simply the "writing" of pornography. Indeed, with the invention of film, "performance of pornography" became the "performance of sex." As Steven Marcus (1974) claims, film was what the genre of pornography "was all along waiting for," as language in literary pornography had only been a "bothersome necessity" (p. 208).

The difference between "faking" sex and "making" sex has long been the line of demarcation between soft-core and hard-core pornography. Here the performance frame, like that of "belief" in the ritual of weddings, is implicated. The codes and conventions of hard-core porn depend on an ironic tension between "real" sexual acts within "faked" sexual contexts. In nesting boxes, the performance frame of hard-core pornography implies "faking." Still, the sex taking place within that "let's pretend" frame is very real; and the autoeroticism, if masturbation is the result of pornography's "singleness of intention" (Marcus, 1974), of viewers is also very real. Indeed, the tension in pornographic film between "faking" and "making" sex and the concomitant "breaking" of sexual norms creates its own opposite; that is, the "breaking" of sexual norms "makes" pornographic conventions, and the "faking" of sexual contexts "makes" sexual acts possible.

Mirror, Mirror on the Wall

Viewing weddings and pornography as complementary, not oppositional, cultural performances allows the mirror metaphor to reveal striking similarities: Both weddings and pornography depend on the state-performance-church matrix for their histories and current enactments, slipping among the making, breaking, and faking of sex. They both create insiders and outsiders to the rights and privileges granted by church and state. They both erect interchangeable frames of belief and play for their performances. Most important, they both hold sex as and at their center.

Indeed, it is not the presence or absence of sex that is problematic for weddings or pornography; rather, it is the word *performance*, as it slides across the field of social meanings in the service of political agendas, that mobilizes the discourses surrounding pornography.

THE USES OF PERFORMANCE IN THE PORNOGRAPHY DEBATES

Sex is at the center of both weddings and pornography—as both implicit and explicit assumptions. In the institution of marriage in the West, sex is the physical complement to the performative utterance "I do." Marriages must be *consummated* through sexual union. The centrality of sex to weddings is most apparent in its noncontroversial acceptance as a cultural practice—until, of course, outsiders question its exclusivity, norms, and privileges. Sex is also—inescapably and controversially—at the center of pornography, a proverbial battlefield with its multiple camps, strongholds, generals, foot soldiers, and defensive strategies. Indeed, the rhetoric of war pervades the pornography debates.

It is surprising, however, that a rhetoric of performance also pervades the same debates. If pornography is seen as a cultural performance at the service of society, then the camps aligned around pornography—pro, con, feminist, and postmodern—manipulate the term *performance* to serve their political ends, variously highlighting sex, erasing sex, or replacing sex in their use of the word *performance*. *Performance* as a term slips and slides around the pornography debates in four ways: performance is doing, acting, evaluated, or representation.

Performance No. 1: Doing Real Sex

Almost all theoretical treatments of hard-core pornography, despite their widely divergent agendas, begin with the declaration that the performers are engaged in real sexual activity. Stoller defines pornography as "adult men and women performing, not simulating, erotic acts" (Stoller & Levine, 1993, p. 3). Linda Williams, feminist film theorist, begins her definition with the distinction between "real" and "faked" sexual acts, landing on "performance" as doing.

> A first step will be to define film pornography minimally, and as neutrally as possible, as the visual (and sometimes aural) representation of living, moving bodies engaged in explicit, usually unfaked, sexual acts with a primary intent of arousing viewers. What distinguishes film and video pornography from written pornography—or even, to a lesser degree, from still photography—is the element of performance contained in the term *sexual act*. (Williams, 1989, pp. 29–30)

For antipornography feminist Susan Cole (1989), pornography "is a practice consisting of specific activities performed by real people" (p. 18). For Marxist philosopher Alan Soble (1986), such definitions of pornography are valuable only if they enable communication without the need for claims about truth or falsehood. Indeed, ground zero in the pornography debates rests on "performance" as the doing of sex.

For makers of heterosexual video pornography, the "doing" of sex is shaped by fairly limited depictions. Ira Levine, X-rated actor, assistant director, and screenwriter, distinguishes between hard- and soft-core pornography: "Hard-core is footage of people having intercourse, complete with genital close-ups. If you do not actually see the hydraulics—even if the players are really performing intercourse—it is soft-core" (Stoller & Levine, 1993, p. 16). Hard-core porn also has conventions of sexual activities—penetration, oral sex, and masturbation—and jargon to describe the performers—boy-girl, girl-girl, threesomes, and orgies. U.S. heterosexual pornography values "meat and heat" or "meat shots and money shots"—the graphic close-ups of genitalia, erections, and ejaculations.

In *The Film Maker's Guide to Pornography,* Stephen Ziplow claims: "There are those who believe that the come shot, or, as some refer to it, 'the money shot,' is the most important element in the movie and that everything else (if necessary) should be sacrificed at its expense. . . . If you don't have the come shots, you don't have a porno picture" (quoted in Williams, 1989, p. 93). The male orgasm is the organizing principle of U.S. heterosexual pornography: It punctuates, constitutes, and ends the performance as both the "visible proof of pleasure" (Williams, 1989) and the visible proof of the *reality* of the performance.

As performance, "Pornography in the making is nothing if not all-too-real" (Stoller & Levine, 1993, p. 234). This "reality" of *doing* sex in video pornography both undergirds and undermines the term "performance" in its subsequent uses.

Performance No. 2: Sex Workers Are Acting

Sex workers and filmmakers are quick to arrive at the word *performance* to describe what they do. Levine compares pornography to other aesthetic and athletic performances:

> That cassette you are watching documents a spontaneously created physical performance, more related to dance or gymnastics than to conventional film or theatre. Elements of drama or comedy may be used to stage this performance, as music structures ballet. . . . Porn actors are physical performers. They're more like athletes than actors. (Stoller & Levine, 1993, p. 178)

Elsewhere, he offers further comparisons: Pornography is like burlesque, documentary (akin to footage of animal copulation), performance art, even the circus; the physical comparison most often made, however, is to athletics.

Indeed, Randy Spears, praised by all the production staff and crew interviewed in *Coming Attractions,* is the consummate "professional" X-rated video actor. Spears describes his performance—to maintain an erection and to ejaculate both on cue and in the center of the frame—as a football game:

> You want to be able to deliver when somebody leans on you like that. It's like, okay, there's one minute left, you're on the twenty, the quarterback's down, get in there and throw the long one. When you throw a touchdown, everybody's happy. If you bungle it, then the game is suffering. (Stoller & Levine, 1993, p. 171)

Nina Hartley, veteran porn performer, comments on her own awareness of herself as a performer: "I'm always thinking: 'back arched, stomach in, tits out, make a pretty picture and enjoy as much of it as you can'" (Stoller & Levine, 1993, p. 148). Hartley's description echoes Michael Kirby's (1995) continuum of acting and nonacting: Actors are "aware of an audience—to be 'on stage'—and they react to this situation by energetically projecting ideas, emotions, and elements of their personality, underlining and theatricalizing it for the sake of the audience" (p. 47). "At what point does acting appear?" Kirby asks. "At the point at which the emotions are 'pushed' for the sake of the spectators" (p. 47). Hartley's description of her responses are, indeed, "pushed." "My responses are real," says Hartley. "I just turn the volume up. I magnify them because it is cinema" (Stoller & Levine, 1993, p. 153). Lisa Palac, founder of *Future Sex* and pornographic film maker, also lands on "acting" as characteristic of performance in pornography:

> I don't care if the actors are really fucking or really coming. I don't care as long as I believe they're coming. Everyone knows that the people who are shot and killed in *Lethal Weapon* don't really die. They *know* what acting is. Why can't they believe pornography is acting, too? (quoted in Tisdale, 1994, p. 137)

For sex workers, "performance" is acting. Performance, as a label, is a safehouse and borrows from the legitimacy of other staged-for-the-camera performances—dance, film, and sports. Sex workers, perhaps more than any other camp in the pornography battlefield, cannot escape the physical materiality of their work, but *performance,* as a term to describe it, rescues and legitimates the sex.

This rescue and legitimation, however, is always compromised by the *reality* of the sex. Female performers endure uncomfortable, if not dreadful, sexual positions in their performances of pleasure; male performers must display a markedly different performance competence. "Other men look at these pictures and say, 'Those lucky sons of bitches. They get to fuck all these great-looking girls. I wish I could be one of them,'" says Ira Levine. Behind the camera and on the set, Levine continues with his insider's viewpoint: "But when I watch [male performers] work, the impression is not of men having a good time. It is the impression of men doing a grim piece of work" (Stoller & Levine, 1993, p. 219).

The pornography industry values men's and women's performances differently. Women are valued, not just for their bodies and faces, but for their novelty—the "new girl" is replaceable when she is no longer new. Men are "valued primarily for their ability to perform on cue. Perhaps a dozen men consistently display that skill" (Schlosser, 1997, p. 48). Schlosser's use of "perform" is, of course, a euphemism for maintaining an erection and ejaculating on cue, but this sense of the word *performance* is the double bind for "actors" in pornography. Men in X-rated videos have little room for failure "to perform" in the industry's "search for wood"; after the third time it happens on a set, the man is no longer hired (Stoller & Levine, 1993, p. 93).

Acting, then, is very much a part of the discourse of performance of sex workers, but performance as "faked" is undermined by the "real" competence necessary to enact the conventions of the genre. Male actors perform in both senses of the word. Female actors, valued for a different performance competence, are not mined for their orgasm—always a dark

and mysterious interiority with no distinct visual "proof" of pleasure—instead, female pleasure is erased by both conventions and discourses of sex work. The "come shot" is the *sine qua non* of video pornography, but female orgasm is unrecordable, unspeakable, and—quite literally—unperformable. Tisdale (1994) interviewed numerous pornographic film stars, and Howie Gordon told her of his early days in porn and of his first scene with a woman he'd never met before: "We started, took about fifteen minutes, whoosh, everything was perfect. After we came—after *I* came—I said, 'Do *you* want to come?' And she said, 'Are you kidding? In front of all these *people?*'" (p. 271).

Performance No. 3: Real People Watching Sex

The third use of the term *performance* is an evaluative one, and performance competence, according to Richard Bauman (1977), is always measured by the audience. *Audience,* however, is a terribly problematic term for pornography, and the term is rarely used. Instead, we are "viewers," "consumers," occasionally "spectators," terminology that emphasizes the solitariness of watching and the explicit masturbatory effect of porn.[8] The intent to arouse, after "real" sex, is a second uncontested component of pornography. At the same time, audience "desires" are implicit in the conventions of porn; "raincoaters" and "lunchbuckets," the pejorative characterizations of the once-typical audience member, want "meat and heat." As the typical venue for pornography has moved from adult bookstores and theatres to the neighborhood X-rated video store, however, the *typical* audience member has changed, too. Even 15 years ago, women accounted for 40% of X-rated video rentals (Williams, 1989, p. 231). If women now "consume" pornography in the privacy of their homes, then "the socially shared meanings" of "what arouses members of the intended audience" (Soble, 1986, p. 110) is an ongoing reconstruction.

The relatively unproblematic "doing" of sex (no. 1) and the gendered problematics of the "acting" of sex (no. 2), now incorporate audience in this third use of the term *performance*. Here audience quickly splits into a number of factions, all attempting to capture and to evaluate performance competence—how well the performers fulfill their performance obligations.

Performance No. 3a: Watching Real People Acting Badly

This, for me, is the most interesting tension between audience and performer in its reversal of performance competence: Because the performers are such *bad* actors, they are not really *acting;* they are simply *doing* (back to Performance No. 1). For Al DiLauro and Gerald Rabkin, this tension is the hallmark of the early stag film: "Here were real people and real sexual activity made all the more real because their esthetic embodiment was so weak, the 'performers' so clearly not 'actors'" (quoted in Williams, 1989, p. 58).

The amateurism of the early stag film is returned to in the fastest growing component of the pornography market, "home porn." These are "short videos produced by 'real' people, with ordinary bodies, who then sell the tapes of their sexual encounters for public viewing" (McElroy, 1995, p. 28). Wendy McElroy wonders about this return to amateurism, but she also lands on home porn's audience appeal: "Buyers knew the action was real" (p. 29). Ordinary, aroused people—not actors, and by implication, not performing— hold a special attraction for audiences who value the "real." Homegrown Video, an amateur porn company in San Diego, is one clearinghouse among many for amateur hard-core videos, taped and sent in by "real people" and then collected and distributed by the company. Schlosser (1997, p. 48) maintains "these crude

but authentic sex tapes" now comprise approximately one fifth to one third of the pornographic video market. "Authenticity" for this camp is measured, interestingly enough, by performance *incompetence.*

Performance No. 3b: Watching Real People Not Acting Married

Although the audiences for (and against) pornography are divergent and multiple, it is surprising how many of these audiences cast the sexual performances in pornography over and against the performance of "married" sex. Indeed, in the 1986 report of the Attorney General's Commission on Pornography, Commissioner Park Elliott Dietz blames pornography, not for its explicit performance of sex, but for its lack of performance of "married" sex:

> A person who learned about human sexuality in the . . . pornography outlets of America would be a person who had never conceived of a man and woman marrying or falling in love before having intercourse . . . who had never conceived of vaginal intercourse with ejaculation during intromission, and who had never conceived of procreation as a purpose of sexual union. (p. 43)

This endorsement of love, marriage, monogamy, heterosexuality, procreation, and asymmetrical gender roles, at once made explicit and public by both church and state in the marriage contract yet performed implicitly and privately in the marriage bed, is thoroughly routed in pornography. This audience vilifies pornography not for the performance of sex, but for the performance of the wrong *kind* of sex.

A number of anticensorship feminists follow this line of argument, but instead of lamenting the lack of "married" sex, they celebrate it. Even if limited by the conventions of male-produced, male-oriented sexual scenarios, pornography is "one of the few areas of narrative where women are not punished or found guilty for acting on their sexual desires" (Williams, 1989, p. 260). Moreover, pornography presents women's sexual desires outside "zones protected and privileged in the culture: traditional marriage and the nuclear family" (Vance, 1984, p. 3). For McElroy (1995), both feminism and pornography

> rock the conventional view of sex. They snap the traditional ties between sex and marriage, sex and motherhood. They both threaten family values and flout the status quo. Because of this, when conservatives look at both feminists and women in porn, they see homewreckers, harlots, and sexual deviants. (p. 128)

Pat Califia (1988, p. 16), self-described sexual "pervert" and writer, maintains that "sex alone can't liberate us, but in the meantime it comforts us." She continues:

> Women want and need the freedom to be outrageous, out-of-doors, out-of-bounds, out after dark, without being silenced or punished by stigma, battery, forced reproduction or murder. We have a right to pleasure ourselves, and access to pornography is part of that. (p. 16)

So while the sex performed in these scenarios is not perfect, anticensorship feminists look to pornography for sex that celebrates female desire, is scripted outside marriage and procreation, and is one accessible site of pleasure. Ultimately, anticensorship feminists, like many sex workers, celebrate the breaking of taboos; again, the attitude is not "let's fuck," but "fuck you!"

Performance No. 3c: Watching Real Women Who Are Really Hated

If anticensorship feminists are watching female desire, antipornography feminists are watching female subordination, degradation, and exploitation. Here performance competence

takes an interesting turn. No longer is the performer "accountable to an audience for the way in which communication is carried out, " (Bauman, 1977, p. 11). Indeed, women performers are victims of, and unwitting perpetrators of, the sexist production, consumption, and depictions of pornography. Performance competence is erased and replaced with performance of consent. Antipornography feminists maintain the impossibility of consent and sexual pleasure in a patriarchal system in which the power imbalance always, already casts women as victims—in society and in pornography. In short, watching pornography is watching "concentration camp orgasm" (Williams, 1989, p. 21).

For antipornography feminists, pornography is not really about watching sex, but about watching the graphic, sexually explicit subordination of women. For Cole (1989), "pornography is not a picture, or words or ideas, but a practice of sexual subordination in which women's inferior status is eroticized and thus maintained" (p. 9). Ultimately, for Andrea Dworkin, sex is not really the performance of physical activities, but the dancing of attitudes: "sex is a medium to convey hostility and antagonism and ownership and control and outright hatred" (quoted in Stan, 1995, p. 60). Dworkin (1980) writes, "The woman's sex is appropriated, her body is possessed, she is used and she is despised: the pornography does it and the pornography proves it" (p. 223).

The discourse of audience for antipornography feminists is a discourse of "other." Industry jargon distances itself from audience as "raincoaters" and "lunchbuckets," but antipornography discourse creates a symbolic order of the phallus, linking male audience members with male performers:

> Pornography, like rape, is a male invention. . . . The staple of porn will always be the naked female body, breasts and genitals exposed, because as man devised it, her naked body is the female's "shame," her private parts the private property of man,

while his [genitals] are the ancient, holy, universal, patriarchal instrument of his power, his rule by force over *her*. (Brownmiller, 1975, p. 394)

Performance competence, measured by the audience, is a gendered construct here, too. For women performers and women audience members, no performance competence is possible in an a priori system of dominance and submission; for men performers and men audience members, performance competence is a given—as power, as violence, as will. Their performances are "picture perfect" posters for patriarchy.

Performance No. 4: There Is No Real, Really

For pornography, this fourth sense of the word *performance* places the emphasis not on sexual activity, performance consciousness, or on audience evaluation, but on representation. Here postmodern film theorists, cultural critics, and historians are interested in the tense relationship between the *real* and the *representational* created in the term *performance*. In Andrew Ross's (1993) astute summary of the history of intellectuals' debate about pornography, he notes that the focus has been on "the vexed relationship between sexual performances and real sexual conduct: often abstract questions about representation, its distance from the real, its place in and its effect upon the real, and its relation to fantasy and the construction of sexuality" (pp. 224–225). True to Ross's perspective, Williams (1989) arrives at the tension between reality and representation implicit in the performance of sex:

The genre of pornography . . . works very hard to convince us of its realism. . . . sex as spontaneous *event* enacted for its own sake stands in perpetual opposition to sex as an elaborately engineered and choreographed *show* enacted by professional performers for a camera. (p. 147)

This tension not only complicates pornography as a "realistic" genre but complicates all four senses of the term *performance*. Performance is a construction that falls in the middle of a continuum with language at one end and physical bodies at the other.

Still another move in this problematic definition of performance is the tendency to erase sex all together; here materiality of sex is elided, and discursive constructs envelope the entire continuum. Sallie Tisdale, Walter Kendrick, and Jean Baudrillard all claim that sex is not the subject matter of pornography at all. For Tisdale (1994), pornography is "a story we tell about ourselves—and maybe the only, or most revealing, way to tell certain secrets that are not necessarily sexual at all" (p. 140). Kendrick (1987) unpacks the rhetoric of metaphors in the discourses of pornography:

Metaphors are essential in this realm of discourse, because there seems, and always has seemed, to be no possibility of a literal statement. . . . [When Comstock] spoke of poisoned swords piercing tender flesh, or of diabolical parents giving their children scorpions to play with, he could count on arousing powerful emotions. The history of "pornography" is a political one [and its rhetorical metaphors] . . . sidestep the literal at every opportunity. (p. 218)

For Baudrillard (1997), "there is no longer any identifiable pornography," as pornographic images "have passed into things, into images, into all the techniques of the visual and the virtual." In advertising, "the comedy of the bared female body . . . is played out. Hence the error of feminist recriminations: if this perpetual striptease and sexual blackmail were real, that would be unacceptable" (p. 139). Phelan (1993) substitutes the "real" for "power" and makes a similar claim, "If representational visibility equals power, then almost-naked young white women should be running Western culture" (p. 10).

Postmodern theorists, disclaiming the *real* but claiming its performance, have written sex out of the pornographic picture. Sex workers, by comparison, cannot so conveniently erase sex or performance consciousness in their material practices. Language and bodies, for both anticensorship groups and antipornography groups, are defined conversely: as desire and agency on one hand and as coercion and victimization on the other. *Performance*, then, is the operative term for all camps in the pornography debates. The divergent, overlapping, and contradictory uses of the term unveil the politics not only of performance but of the cultural construction of sex.

LOOKING IN THE MIRROR AT SEX

The sexual center of weddings and pornography is a reminder that "this culture always treats sex with suspicion. It construes and judges any sexual practice in terms of its worst possible expression. Sex is presumed guilty until proven innocent" (Rubin, 1989, p. 278). Married sex, created in and through heterosexual, age-appropriate, blood-appropriate consensual weddings, is our culture's "proven innocent" sex; pornography is our culture's "worst possible expression." In both constructions, the relationship between culture and sex is an adversarial one: culture is a block to sexual drives, a means of redirecting and channeling sexual energies. This "hydraulic model" maintains that "sex is like a gushing stream whose force can be given full reign, or dammed, left to roam free or channeled into harmless byways" (Weeks, 1986, p. 8).

If cultural performances are always at the service of the culture, then what ends are created and served in the performance of sex? Weddings are expressions of, indeed, creations of, the need for order, control, stability. Every culture guards its coupling with implicit and explicit regulations, doles out rewards and punishments, and measures individuals by their enactments. Weddings are celebrations, ultimately, of individual complicity in societal conspiracy to control sex—the necessary channeling of the gushing stream.

What societal ends are created and served in the performance of sex in pornography? Here the gushing stream of sex takes two turns. Pornography is a destabilizing force: an unchecked, undammed, chaotic anarchy that undermines social orders of family, heterosexuality, and normative sexuality; for others, pornography is a stabilizing force in its perpetuation and valorization of women's oppression and men's power—just one more example of the status quo. Although the stream forks here, pornography is still a *force,* a rushing current of sex, and society conspires to control its performance.

There is no "pre-social" sex (Connell & Dowsett, 1992, p. 50). Sex cannot be attended to apart from the language, social systems, and material practices that create it. Pornography and weddings are not cultural opposites, but mirror doubles, complementary and necessary to each other for the construction of sex as always, already in need of control. There's the rub in the mirror that is both reflective and reflexive. The complementarity of weddings and pornography is necessary to *complete* sex as control. Complementarity demands a partner, just as "Thank you" demands "You're welcome" and "I'm sorry" demands "That's all right," to complete the communicative interaction and to reestablish balance in the relationship. Weddings and pornography thus demand each other to complete the construction of sex-as-control. If a culture's most important interest is the control of sex, then the performances that perpetuate that economy are its most dear and unexamined, and the performances that subvert that economy are its most despised and problematic. Indeed, when cultural performance is approached as a mirror held up to a culture, it not only *reflects* basic cultural values, it *deflects* attention from the backdrop of control against which these performances are enacted. In short, we are so busy watching performances of sex that we forget to pay attention to the scenery—until, of course, a performance occurs that transforms the scene.

I've been married for 20 years. Nine years ago, I took off my wedding ring and decided I would no longer participate in that particular symbolism—a visible sign of my wedded status—in the Western institution of marriage. In the first few days after I removed my ring, I was uncomfortably aware of its absence: My left hand felt awkward and incomplete as I rubbed the back of my third finger with my thumb and felt the seemingly new, smooth skin, protected all those years by gold. I studied my fingers for days, and I was quite sure that my third finger had atrophied in more than a decade of stricture. It did not look as strong, as well formed, as capable as the others. Chinese foot-binding came to mind.

Ever since then, I have made a point of paying attention to the hands around me. Married women, I have discovered, wear wedding rings: From thin, plain gold bands to elaborate clusters and mixtures of gems to knock-your-socks-off diamond solitaires. Married men show no such variety, but they do seem to make a more fundamental choice. In my informal poll, the chances are 50% that a married man will not be wearing a ring at all.

Why the gendered difference? Although married women *seem* to have many choices regarding the *kind* of ring they wear, the choice *not to be marked* as married does not appear to be an option. Indeed, even considering it, for many women I spoke with, seemed unthinkable. Although weddings and pornography are mirror doubles, the images of our hands in that mirror are evidence of control: choices that are not choices and a gendered grammar of deep structures for coupling. These familiar, unexamined, unquestioned performances of sex—like wearing a wedding ring, like participating in a traditional wedding, like viewing pornographic videotapes—always manifest what we hold dear and what we despise.

Today, as I put an X-rated videotape into the VCR, I look at my bare fingers. I'm comfortable now with their blankness, the clean slate, my unmarked status. But I wonder, as the scene on the tape comes into view, about my own complicity—my own loves and hates—in saying "I do."

NOTES

1. Philosopher J. L. Austin (1975) proposed the term *performative* to describe a class of utterances that do not state something ("This is a room") or describe something ("This room holds 50 people"); instead, the utterance is "the doing of an action." His examples include "*I do*" in the wedding ceremony, "*I name* this ship" in a christening, "*I give and bequeath* my watch to my brother" in an inheritance, and "*I bet* you sixpence it will rain tomorrow" (p. 5). In each instance, the performative creates an obligation, a promise, and a relationship between participants. Parker and Sedgwick (1995) offer another example of a performative: "I dare you."

2. *Limen* means "threshold," recalling the threshold of a doorway between two rooms. All rites of passage involve the experience of an uncertain and dangerous moment, or "liminality," in which the ritual participant is suspended between the two stages.

3. The inequality of gender roles and division of labor within the marriage contract have been elegantly argued elsewhere; two classics—Simone DeBeauvoir's *The Second Sex* and Germaine Greer's *The Female Eunuch*—come to mind.

4. In 1967, for example, the U.S. Supreme Court struck down laws in 16 states forbidding mixed-race marriages (Eskridge, 1996). According to Cornell Law School's Legal Information Institute (n.d.), age of consent varies across states, the lowest being 14 (Alabama). There are also differences in some states according to sex or gender: Girls in New Hampshire can marry (with parental consent) at 13, and boys at 14. Most states set the age of consent at 18 (without parental consent).

5. Federal benefits include "access to military stores, assumption of spouse's pension, bereavement leave, immigration, insurance breaks, medical decisions on behalf of partner, sick leave to care for partner, tax breaks, veteran's discounts, and hospital visitation rights; state benefits include assumption of spouse's pension, automatic inheritance, automatic housing lease transfer, bereavement leave, burial determination, child custody, crime victim's recovery benefits, divorce protections, domestic violence protection, exemption from property tax on partner's death, immunity from testifying against spouse, insurance breaks, joint adoption and foster care, joint automobile

insurance, joint bankruptcy, joint parenting (insurance coverage, school records), medical decisions on behalf of partner, medical insurance family coverage, certain property rights, reduced-rate memberships, sick leave to care for partner, visitation of partner's children, visitation of partner in hospital or prison, wrongful death benefits" (Ingraham, 1999, pp. 175–176).

6. Many people have claimed that the "marriage tax" punishes married couples. Ingraham (1999) argues that the joint income of most middle and upper class couples affords them benefits (e.g., health insurance) that offset that tax. For couples living at or below the poverty line, however "marriage disqualifies many for the benefits they need to survive. . . . As the 1997 census data indicate, an increasing number of couples are choosing to live together without "benefit" of marriage in order to avoid losing these programs [food stamps, school meals, and child care], Social Security income, and some tax breaks. Ultimately, then, marriage only privileges those who already have the earnings to stay out of poverty" (p. 32).

7. Just as the "speak now or forever hold your peace" is a stock moment, the mistakenly "faked" wedding is also a common device on television situation comedies. Lucy and Ricky Ricardo, Rob and Laura Petri, the Howells on *Gilligan's Island,* even Greg's parents on *Dharma and Greg,* all found themselves "not married" through some technical glitch in the state apparatus. The comedic results of long-married couples being suddenly "not really married" throws their personal habits, and their socially sanctioned relationship, into question.

8. This solitary viewing was not always the case. Al DiLauro and Gerald Rabkin's *Dirty Movies* (1976) points to the communal functions of the early stag film (1896–1911). They claim that "smokers" were a ritualized setting for male bonding. Peggy Reeves Sanday, in *Fraternity Gang Rape* (1990), makes a similar, but much less celebratory, case for the group "consumption" of pornographic films in contemporary college fraternity houses. In both situations, male bonding takes place through, and at the expense of, women's bodies in pornographic film.

REFERENCES

Attorney General's Commission on Pornography. (1986). *Final report.* Washington, DC: U.S. Government Printing Office.

Austin, J. L. (1975). *How to do things with words* (2nd ed.). Cambridge, MA: Harvard University Press.

Baudrillard, J. (1997). The "laying-off" of desire. In P. Lopate (Ed.), *The Anchor essay annual* (pp. 135–140). New York: Anchor.

Bauman, R. (1977). *Verbal art as performance.* Prospect Heights, IL: Waveland.

Bauman, R. (1992). Performance. In R. Bauman (Ed.), *Folklore, cultural performance and popular entertainment* (pp. 41–49). New York: Oxford University Press.

Brownmiller, S. (1975). *Against our will: Men, women and rape.* New York: Simon and Schuster.

Califia, P. (1988). *Macho sluts.* Boston: Alyson.

Cole, S. G. (1989). *Pornography and the sex crisis.* Toronto, ON: Amanita.

Connell, R. W., & Dowsett, G. W. (Eds.). (1992). *Rethinking sex: Social theory and sexuality research.* Philadelphia, PA: Temple University Press.

Conquergood, D. (1986). Performing cultures: Ethnography, epistemology, and ethics. In E. Slembeck (Ed.), *Miteinander sprechen und handeln: Festschrift fur Hellmut Geissner* [Communicate and act: Festschrift for Hellmut Geissner]. Frankfurt, Germany: Scriptor.

Conquergood, D. (1998). Beyond the text: Toward a performative cultural politics. In S. Dailey (Ed.), *The future of performance studies* (pp. 25–36). Blackburg, VA: NCA.

DeJean, J. (1993). The politics of pornography: L'Ecole des Filles. In L. Hunt (Ed.), *The invention of pornography* (pp. 109–124). New York: Zone.

DiLauro, A., & Rabkin, G. (1976). *Dirty movies: An illustrated history of the stag film, 1915–1970.* New York: Chelsea.

Dworkin, A. (1980). *Pornography: Men possessing women.* New York: Putnam.

Eskridge, W. N., Jr. (1996). *The case for same-sex marriage: From sexual liberty to civilized commitment.* New York: Free Press.

Ettelbrick, P. L. (1992). Since when is marriage a path to liberation? In S. Sherman (Ed.), *Lesbian and gay marriage* (pp. 20–28). Philadelphia, PA: Temple University Press.

Findlen, P. (1993). Humanism, politics, and pornography in Renaissance Italy. In L. Hunt (Ed.), *The invention of pornography* (pp. 49–108). New York: Zone.

Goffman, E. (1959). *The presentation of self in everyday life.* Garden City, NY: Doubleday Anchor.

Hickey, D. (1997). *Air guitar: Essays on art and democracy.* Los Angeles: Art Issues Press.

Hunt, L. (Ed.). (1993). *The invention of pornography: Obscenity and the origins of modernity, 1500-1800.* New York: Zone.

Ingraham, C. (1999). *White weddings: Romancing heterosexuality in popular culture*. New York: Routledge.

Johnson, F. (1996, November). Wedded to an illusion: Do gays and lesbians really want the right to marry? *Harper's Magazine*, 43–50.

Kendrick, W. M. (1987). *The secret museum: Pornography in modern culture*. New York: Viking.

Kirby, M. (1995). On acting and not-acting. In P. Zarelli (Ed.), *Acting (re)considered* (pp. 43–58). New York: Routledge.

Landers, A. (1998, February 16). Marriage ceremony a hit with elderly. *St. Petersburg Times*, p. 2D.

Legal Information Institute. (n.d.). Retrieved February 13, 2006, from the Cornell University Law School Web site: http://www.law.cornell.edu/topics/Table_Marriage.htm

Leonard, D. (1980). *Sex and generation: A study of courtship and weddings*. London: Tavistock.

Marcus, S. (1974). *The new Victorians*. New York: New American Library.

McElroy, W. (1995). *XXX: A woman's right to pornography*. New York: St. Martin's Press.

Parker, A., & Sedgwick, E. K. (1995). Introduction. In A. Parker & E. K. Sedgwick (Eds.), *Performativity and performance* (pp. 1–18). New York: Routledge.

Patterson, C. (1991). Marriage and the married woman in Athenian law. In S. Pomeroy (Ed.), *Women's history and ancient history* (pp. 48–72). Chapel Hill: University of North Carolina Press.

Phelan, P. (1993). *Unmarked: The politics of performance*. New York: Routledge.

Rehm, R. (1994). *Marriage to death: The conflation of wedding and funeral rituals in Greek tragedy*. Princeton, NJ: Princeton University Press.

Ross, A. (1993). The popularity of pornography. In S. During (Ed.), *The cultural studies reader* (pp. 222–242). London: Routledge.

Rubin, G. (1989). Thinking sex: Notes for a radical theory of the politics of sexuality. In C. Vance (Ed.), *Pleasure and danger* (pp. 267–319). London: Pandora.

Sanday, P. R. (1990). *Fraternity gang rape: Sex, brotherhood, and privilege on campus*. New York: New York University Press.

Schlosser, E. (1997, February 10). The business of pornography. *U.S. News and World Report*, pp. 43–52.

Seligson, M. (1973). *The eternal bliss machine: America's way of wedding*. New York: William Morrow.

Sherman, S. (Ed.). (1992). *Lesbian and gay marriage: Private commitments, public ceremonies*. Philadelphia, PA: Temple University Press.

Singer, M. (1972). *When a great tradition modernizes: An anthropological approach to Indian civilization*. New York: Praeger.

Soble, A. (1986). *Pornography: Marxism, feminism, and the future of sexuality*. New Haven, CT: Yale University Press.

Stan, A. M. (Ed.). (1995). *Debating sexual correctness: Pornography, sexual harassment, date rape, and the politics of sexual equality*. New York: Delta.

Stern, C. S., & Henderson, B. (1993). *Performance: Texts and contexts*. White Plains, NY: Longman.

Stoller, R. J., & Levine, I. S. (1993). *Coming attractions: The making of an X-rated video*. New Haven, CT: Yale University Press.

Tisdale, S. (1994). *Talk dirty to me: An intimate philosophy of sex*. New York: Doubleday.

Turner, V. (1987). *The anthropology of performance*. New York: PAJ.

Vance, C. (Ed.). (1984). *Pleasure and danger: Exploring female sexuality*. Boston: Routledge and Kegan Paul.

Van Gennep, A. (1960). *The rites of passage* (M. B. Vizedom & G. L. Caffee, Trans.). Chicago: University of Chicago Press.

Weeks, J. (1986). *Sexuality*. London: Tavistock.

Williams, L. (1989). *Hard core: Power, pleasure, and the "frenzy of the visible."* Berkeley: University of California Press.

Discussion Questions

1. According to Bell, what makes weddings and pornography complementary rather than oppositional performances?

2. Bell provides a listing of state and federal entitlements that come with marriage. Which do you think are of the greatest consequence? How would you feel about removing all these entitlements from marriage, as opposed to extending them to same-sex couples?

3. Discuss "making, breaking, and faking" sex in weddings and pornography.

4. What do weddings and pornography as cultural performances reveal about our primary cultural concerns?

12

A Critical Appraisal of Assimilationist and Radical Ideologies Underlying Same-Sex Marriage in LGBT Communities in the United States

GUST A. YEP, KAREN E. LOVAAS, AND JOHN P. ELIA

The centerpiece of [the] new [homosexual] politics . . . is equal access to civil marriage.
—Andrew Sullivan (1995, p. 178)

We must not fool ourselves into believing that marriage will make it acceptable to be gay or lesbian. We will be liberated only when we are respected and accepted for our differences and the diversity we provide to this society. Marriage is not a path to that liberation.

—Paula Ettelbrick (1997, p. 124)

Same-sex marriage has entered the center stage of contemporary U.S. politics. Indeed, some argue that same-sex marriage has been elevated "as the [gay] movement's leading goal" (Warner, 1999, p. 146) in recent years. At the national level, the topic has been debated on historical, philosophical, religious, moral, political, legal, personal and emotional grounds (see, e.g.: Baird & Rosenbaum, 1997; Eskridge, 2002; Kaplan, 1997; Smith & Windes, 2000; Sullivan, 1997; Wolfson, 1996). In lesbian, gay, bisexual, and transgender (LGBT) communities,[1] the issue has produced considerable disagreement. Some believe that same-sex marriage is a crucial issue of equality and acceptance into the center

SOURCE: This chapter was originally published as "A Critical Appraisal of Assimilationist and Radical Ideologies Underlying Same-Sex Marriage in LGBT Communities in the United States" in the *Journal of Homosexuality* (vol. 45, no. 1). Copyright © 2003 The Haworth Press, Inc. Reprinted by permission.

of U.S. American life as Sullivan (1995) states, "[same-sex marriage] is the highest public recognition of personal integrity" (p. 179). Others see it as potentially damaging to feminist and queer agendas:[2]

> Traditional marriage is integral to the corrupt authoritarian structures of society; it is a suspect institution embodying within itself the patriarchy . . . the most important issue for gay and lesbian couples is whether or not they should "sell out" to the enemy—the patriarchal culture—that seeks to oppress and eliminate them. (Baird & Rosenbaum, 1997, p. 11)

In the midst of these blistering exchanges, Evan Wolfson, director of the Marriage Project at the Lambda Legal Defense and Education Fund, put out a plea to LGBT communities to "end, or at least suspend, the intra-community debate whether to seek marriage. The ship has sailed" (cited in Warner, 1999, p. 83). Regardless of whether and how these debates continue in LGBT communities, one thing remains clear: There are fundamental conflicts over sexual ideologies in the debates. McKay (1998) points out that conflict between sexual ideologies "is a fight between combatants who are often competing on different conceptual playing fields. They are, in effect, attempting to play the same game but with different rules" (p. 36). The purpose of this chapter is to examine the sexual ideologies undergirding the same-sex marriage debate in LGBT communities in the U.S. More specifically, it attempts to identify and examine how these sexual ideologies in U.S. LGBT communities inform and influence relationship construction in general and same-sex marriage in particular. To accomplish this, we first discuss the nature of sexual ideologies. Next, we examine some of the fundamental features of current sexual ideologies in LGBT communities and their implications for relationship construction with a focus on same-sex marriage. We conclude with a discussion of what is potentially gained and lost by gay matrimonial

bonds if a specific sexual ideology within these communities becomes hegemonic, and explore some of the prospects of relationship construction within LGBT communities in the future.

THE NATURE OF SEXUAL IDEOLOGY

Ideology is a highly complex, elusive, and contested term with an extensive and controversial history (Cormack, 1992; Hawkes, 1996; Larrain, 1979; McLellan, 1995). As a subset of ideology, sexual ideology shares this complexity (McKay, 1998). In this section, we first offer a conceptualization of sexual ideology. Then we discuss some of its functions. Finally, we identify some of the current sexual ideologies in LGBT communities in the U.S.

Toward a Conceptualization of Sexual Ideology

Ideology focuses on the connection between social ideas and politics, power, and individual and collective practices and every person in a social system is implicated in ideology (McLellan, 1995). In spite of the pervasiveness of ideology in everyday life, researchers have conceptualized the term in diverse and competing ways (Cormack, 1992; Lannamann, 1991, 1994; McKay, 1998; McLellan, 1995). Lannamann (1991) notes that "the meaning of the term 'ideology' varies between theorists and is often polysemous even within a single theoretical treatment" (p. 180).

Adopting from conceptualizations of ideology proposed by Althusser (1984), Hall (1996), Lannamann (1991, 1994), McKay (1998), and Troiden and Platt (1987), we define sexual ideology as mental frameworks that different social and cultural groups use to define, assign meaning, and render intelligible the regulation and expression of sexuality in society within a particular historical period. Such mental frameworks are constantly produced, reproduced, and reconstituted in practice through the way people think, act, and talk about human sexual conduct. In our definition, sexual ideology is not simply located in the consciousness of individuals or groups but in the material practices of cultural members. In short, sexual ideology is discursively and materially realized through language, communication, and systems of representation.

Sexual ideology provides individuals and cultural members with ideas, guidelines, and answers to questions about the nature and purpose of human sexuality and its role in human relationships (McKay, 1998). At the same time, how individuals and groups enact and interpret their sexuality influences sexual ideology in a dynamic, productive, and imperfect circular process.

Ideologies reflect and reproduce relations of power in society (Lannamann, 1991). For example, ideas and perceptions about "normal" sexuality and "proper" sexual relationship are ideologically saturated. Likewise, conceptions of how to seek, pursue, develop, define, maintain, and represent loving sexual relationships invariably occur in an ideological context. In her examination of the dominant contemporary U.S. American sexual value system, Rubin (1993) notes, for example, that monogamous and committed sexual relationships are constructed as "good, normal, natural, and blessed" while promiscuous and casual relationships are deemed "bad, abnormal, unnatural, and damned" (p. 13). Although sexual relationships in LGBT communities are outside of Rubin's "charmed circle" (1993, p. 13) of heteronormative sex, a similar sex hierarchy clearly exists in such communities. Rubin (1993) points out that long-term and committed lesbian and gay relationships are more valued in U.S. LGBT communities than casual and "uncommitted" relationships. More simply put, sexual ideologies in LGBT communities drive and constrain relationship construction.

Functions of Sexual Ideology

Sexual ideology serves several functions both at the macrocultural and intra-community levels (Cormack, 1992; McKay, 1998). Macroculturally, sexual ideology functions to perpetuate the prevailing sexual system by reifying existing cultural practices (e.g., marriage) and legitimizing current social arrangements (e.g., heterosexuality as the norm, homosexuality and bisexuality as the margins). To uphold the system, sexual ideology "typically fixes meaning, naturalizing or eternalizing its prevailing forms by putting them beyond question, and thereby also effacing the contradictions and conflicts of the social domain" (Dollimore, 1991, p. 86). In this sense, sexual ideology frames the struggle over which meanings about sexuality and relationship construction are normalized and naturalized as common sense.

In LGBT communities, sexual ideology serves other functions. McKay (1998) identifies three functions: (1) it helps individuals organize their thoughts and beliefs about themselves and the social world, (2) it creates a sense of community for individuals who share it, and (3) it reduces uncertainty and defines reality for individuals or a social group.

First, sexual ideology helps LGBT community members to organize their thoughts and beliefs about themselves and society. It provides individuals with a cognitive structure and way of thinking around which they can organize their thoughts into a unified set of ideas and perceptions about the social world. In other words, it helps people make sense of the world through a seemingly coherent and consistent framework. For example, an individual might hold the belief that sexual autonomy and any form of human sexual expression between consenting adults is healthy and desirable (e.g., Rubin, 1993; Warner, 1999). Based on this ideology, the individual might act, talk, share, and defend sexual freedom and oppose various forms of regulation and social control.

Second, sexual ideology can create and sustain a sense of solidarity and community between individuals sharing similar perspectives and frameworks. For example, various members of the U.S. LGBT communities might unite and organize to implement an assimilationist or normalizing agenda (e.g., Rauch, 1997; Rotello, 1997; Sullivan, 1995) with messages like "We are really no different than heterosexuals" and "We just want the same rights and responsibilities that heterosexual citizens enjoy." In this situation, individuals might develop a feeling of community and collective action while overlooking or downplaying important social differences such as race, gender, social class, and national origin, among others.

Finally, sexual ideology can provide individuals with ways to define reality in the face of social contradictions and uncertainties. In this sense, sexual ideology creates and sustains an epistemological framework and knowledge system for addressing philosophical, moral, social, and intellectual questions regarding human sexual conduct. For example, U.S. LGBT communities were divided on the issue of closure of gay public sex environments such as bathhouses as a public health measure to stop the spread of HIV infection (Shilts, 1987). Although the debates ranged from philosophical and moral, to social, intellectual and personal, the underlying differences were usually ideological.

Current Sexual Ideologies in U.S. American LGBT Communities

Sexual ideologies are the foundation of many conflicts in U.S. society, including tensions in LGBT communities, as Seidman (1991) observes, "contemporary American culture constructs sex in highly ambiguous and contradictory ways that . . . are at the root of many sexual strains and conflicts" (p. 126). Sexuality has become a major site of social conflict since the post–World War II years (Seidman, 1992). Such conflicts have played out in a number of settings, including legal, medical, scientific, and religious institutions, popular culture and the media, urban streets and neighborhoods, and personal relationships. Seidman concludes:

"American society today exhibits a clash of sexual ideologies" (1991, p. 126).

Although a wide spectrum of sexual ideologies exists in U.S. LGBT communities, some fairly discernable "ideological types"[3] can be identified. Such types are somewhat artificial classifications and we are using them primarily for purposes of discussion and illustration. Although most individuals in U.S. LGBT communities might be able to identify with a specific ideological type, we do not imply that these individuals fit neatly and completely into the typology of sexual ideologies that we propose. Based on the writings by Weeks (1985, 1986), Seidman (1991, 1992, 1997), McKay (1998), Sullivan (1995, 1997), and Warner (1999), we propose that there are two prominent sexual "ideological types"—assimilationist[4] and radical[5]—in LGBT communities in the U.S. In our next section, we discuss these sexual ideologies in greater detail.

TWO COMPETING IDEOLOGIES

Within U.S. LGBT circles there is an ongoing debate about whether or not same-sex marriage should exist. The purpose of this section is to adumbrate the *assimilationist* and *radical positions* on same-sex marriage. The *assimilationist position* supports same-sex marriage based on the premise that it will lead to more acceptable, equitable, stable, and healthier lives for gays and lesbians. Next, we explore the *radical position,* which challenges same-sex marriage based on the notion that it subscribes to heteronormativity and is not a way of liberating individuals from oppressive attitudes and practices.

The Assimilationist Position on Same-Sex Marriage

The assimilationist view suggests that people of the same sex should have the right to get married, and indeed should get married, for a variety of reasons, which range from the idea that gays and lesbians will be fully recognized as equals of heterosexuals to the notion that same-sex marriage will allow gays and lesbians to settle down and enjoy a stable family life. The assimilationists have sought same-sex marital rights as the true and unmistakable sign that gays and lesbians have "arrived" in terms of being treated equitably. A number of authors who take the assimilationist position on same-sex marriage advance several arguments for why they believe their views are superior to the *radical view*.

One of the central themes of the assimilationist position is that sexual behavior has to be moderated, because unstructured sexual license leads to considerable social destabilization, which among other things, is destructive to the process of raising children (Rotello, 1997). Along the same lines, one cannot be free to mate with anyone one wishes, and at the same time have a stable family, which requires a long-term mate. Capturing these sentiments, Rotello concludes, "the core institution that encourages sexual restraint and monogamy is marriage" (1997, p. 250). Marriage would put pressure on gays and lesbians to stay sexually faithful to partners, as the benefits of family life—and the threat of a family breakup—has been a major incentive for married heterosexuals to try and remain faithful. He asserts that it comes down to sexual desire versus the social status of marriage. While the crux of his argument and plea is to stem the tide of HIV/AIDS, he adds that same-sex marriage would help prevent STD transmission in general.

Individual and social stability is advanced as a reason for same-sex marital unions. Specifically, same-sex marriage would serve as a stabilizing force in general, because men in particular are in deep need of being "civilized," "tamed," and "settled" (Rauch, 1997, p. 177). In this view men are mischievous and dangerous. To get men under control and keep them out of trouble, Rauch suggests marriage as a panacea. According to him, marriage

binds people together not only in their eyes but also in the eyes of society at large. He goes on to assert that marriage creates certain expectations within a couple, viz., that married partners will "spend nights together, go to parties together, take out mortgages together, buy furniture at Ikea together, and so on" (Rauch, 1997, p. 178). He warns readers about the depravity of men prowling about in parks and soliciting anonymous sex. For instance, when referring to the merits of marriage, he says, "surely it's a very good thing, especially compared to the closet-gay culture of furtive sex with innumerable partners in parks and bathhouses" (p. 178).

The idea of commitment at both personal and social levels is inextricably linked to marriage. It is said that "[t]hey [married people] make a deeper commitment to one another and to society; in exchange, society extends certain benefits to them. Marriage provides an anchor, if an arbitrary one, in the maelstrom of sex and relationships to which we are all prone" (Sullivan, 1995, p. 182). Sullivan urges LGBT communities to move in the direction of homogeneity and to become more mainstreamed. In his essay, "Here Comes the Groom: A (Conservative) Case for Gay Marriage," he declares that heterosexual marriage should not be questioned or in any way undermined. He urges the legalization of "old-style marriage for gays" (1996, p. 255). Sullivan claims that in years past it was important for gays to rebel, but now "gay marriage also places more responsibilities upon gays: it says for the first time that gay relationships are not better or worse than straight relationships and that the same is expected of them. And, it's clear and dignified" (1996, p. 255).

Sullivan (1996) goes on to declare that "Legalizing gay marriage would offer homosexuals the same deal society now offers heterosexuals" (p. 256). Besides the issue of equal status, he states that gays and lesbians would gain social approval, then adds that same-sex marriage would make it more difficult for those involved in such relationships to dissolve their unions. A related argument advanced by those who take the assimilationist position is that same-sex marriages—like the major function of heterosexual marriages—would allow for raising children in a stable, socially sanctioned, highly functional, and an economically viable setting.

The Radical Position on Same-Sex Marriage

The decision to place the right to marry at the front of efforts by gay and lesbian organizations is, from the perspective of Michael Warner and numerous other queer authors and activists, antithetical to the principles upon which queer thought and action have been based. These principles, as enunciated by Warner (1999), include recognition of the ways in which the institution of marriage has been idealized; affirmation of and respect for a variety of intimate relationships; and resistance to the application of the norms and standards associated with straight culture to the lives of queers.

In this section, three of the rationales offered in critique of the same-sex marriage movement are explored. These are: (1) That marriage is an inherently flawed, oppressive institution; (2) That should the pursuit of same-sex marriage succeed, the potential consequences are more negative than positive; and (3) That alternative relationship structures have significant advantages over marriage.

Michael Warner's interrogation of the notion of same-sex marriage in *The Trouble with Normal: Sex, Politics, and the Ethics of Queer Life* (1999) is perhaps the most extensive one to date. The work of several other lesbian and gay writers is also drawn from; however, this summary does not purport to be an exhaustive review of the literature.

Of course, arguments against the institution of marriage did not originate with the lesbian, gay, bisexual and transgender movements of the 1970s; the free love movement of the mid-19th century was a contemporary of

significant efforts to reform the legal and economic inequities of the marriage system. Women have had particular reasons to critique marriage. Echoing Gayle Rubin's landmark 1975 article, "The Traffic in Women: Notes on the 'Political Economy' of Sex," Catherine Saalfield writes: "Marriage is embedded within heterosexuality, property relations, dependence, monogamy, and traditional parenthood, all of which affect women in a particularly debilitating way" (1993, p. 191).

This is the same reasoning underlying the first argument against gays and lesbians struggling for access to marriage, i.e., that participation in such a historically patriarchal and heterosexist institution will do more to perpetuate a state governed system of unequal relations than to reform it from within (Walters, 2001). Individuals tend to view marriage as a private and separate relation, its form shaped by the will of the individuals involved and safe from the intrusive arm of the state. As Warner says, "The recognition drama of marriage also induces a sort of amnesia about the state and the normative dimensions of marriage" (1999, p. 133). Gays and lesbians working to legalize same-sex marriage may be buying into this viewpoint and ignoring the extent to which marriage invites the state to exercise a right to extend or withhold sanctions over the most intimate aspects of our lives. And marriage is no guarantor of a happy union. Regardless of its structure, label, and social status, one faces similar kinds of challenges in any intimate relationship: "In a dishonest or repressed relationship you're just as vulnerable on Sunday nights as someone in a nontraditional situation" (Saalfield, 1993, p. 189). Saalfield goes on to quote Emma Goldman's contention that "Marriage is the antithesis of love, and will necessarily destroy it" (p. 193).

The second rationale for rejecting same-sex marriage is that there would be significant negative consequences in the wake of the legalizing of same-sex marriage. Queer writers such as Paula Ettelbrick point to two primary harmful outcomes. First, the greater degree of assimilation resulting from same-sex marriage is less likely to advance queer interests than it is to reinforce dominant social norms, defang queer movements, and increase queer invisibility. As Carmen Vasquez warns, "We must stop pretending that our assimilation into this culture will tame the hate-filled hearts" (1999, p. 278). And would, could queers effectively push for recognition of diverse kinds of relationships? Second, it would create a new hierarchy within queer communities, with the highest tier reserved for those cushioned by the respectability of marriage and further marginalize those who have chosen alternative relationships (Butler, 2001a; Walters, 2001). Again quoting Ettelbrick, "we would be perpetuating the elevation of married relationships and of 'couples' in general, and further eclipsing other relationships of choice" (1997, p. 121). Would single queers suffer the same kind of condescension and condolences formerly reserved for unmarried dubbed "old maids"? Or worse:

> You tell mom that you're just like her, that you're married, that she doesn't have to accept lesbians or lesbianism, but if she can just see herself in your pseudo-heterosexual, familial scenario, everything will be all right. That leaves the rest of us dykes to be seen as difficult, unacceptable, disease-spreading, sex-crazed, pathological, unstable, adolescent, unfocused, unsuccessful, slutty perverts. (Saalfield, 1993, p. 194)

The third rationale for rejecting same-sex marriage celebrates the advantages of other relational networks. Fundamentally, in contrast with the bonds of marriage, queer relationships are, according to Jeffrey Weeks, "freely chosen by autonomous individuals" (1995, p. 35). While marriage, particularly in the post-industrialization eras, has been closely aligned with the nuclear family structure and predicated monogamous relationships, queers have, by necessity and by choice,

created a range of alternative social support networks. Frank Browning (1997) writes, "We gay folk tend to organize our lives more like extended families than nuclear ones. We may love our mates one at a time, but our 'primary families' are often our ex-lovers and our ex-lover's ex-lovers" (p. 133).

Michael Bronski might agree. In *The Pleasure Principle,* Bronski (1998) claims that a number of benefits accrue from being unencumbered by the norms of heterosexual society:

> These include less restrictive gender roles; nonmonogamous intimate relationships and more freedom for sexual experimentation; family units that are chosen, not biological; and new models for parenting. But most important, homosexuality offers a vision of sexual pleasure completely divorced from the burden of reproduction: sex for its own sake, a distillation of the pleasure principle. (p. 9)

A number of authors have argued similarly that to attempt to recreate the straight, ostensibly monogamous nuclear family is to lose what is valuable in less sexually constraining lifestyles. Warner suggests we remember the "important pleasures and intimacies in promiscuous sex"; enjoying nonmonogamous relationships need not be a means of "rejecting all of society—only a hostile and restrictive version of morality" (1999, p. 137). Saalfield proclaims, "I would rather feel exhilarated about the loves that constitute the fabric of my life than nostalgic for some tame ideal of what it means to be family" (1993, p. 195).

How, then, do the scales of queer opponents of the legalization of same-sex marriage measure the advantages of and disadvantages of this campaign? Are there sufficient benefits to outweigh the potential collective and individual costs? According to Vasquez, to opt for the social sanction that marriage may provide is not a worthwhile tradeoff for queer desires: "I will not exchange my sexuality for citizenship" (1999, p. 272).

IMPLICATIONS FOR RELATIONSHIP CONSTRUCTION

The Assimilationist Position

Before embarking on an exploration of the implications of the assimilationist position on relationship construction, we must first turn to the sexual attitudes that undergird it. The proponents of same-sex marriage treat sexuality—particularly nonheteronormative sexual expression—as dangerous and downright evil. Rotello (1997) proposes using marriage to abate HIV/AIDS and sexually transmitted diseases among gay men. Rauch (1997) urges gay men to rush to the altar to prevent shifty sexual encounters with other men, and at the same time marriage creates and maintains tamed, civilized men. Sullivan (1995, 1996) maintains that marriage provides an anchor for married gay men and a stabilizing force for society. One does not have to read too much between the lines to realize that an anti-sex theme runs throughout their arguments. There is also the theme of containment and social control. One is reminded of Gayle Rubin's (1993) notion of the *charmed circle* and the *outer limits*, mentioned earlier. The assimilationists want desperately to fit into the *charmed circle*, primarily because of the perceived social benefits and medical advantages. Even though gays are automatically excluded from the charmed circle, there is nevertheless a valiant attempt to adopt as many of the trappings of heterosexual life as possible in an effort to gain equality and social acceptability, not to mention "immunity" from unbridled sexual expression and HIV/AIDS and other sexually transmitted diseases.

The ideology that undergirds the assimilationist position has a distinct impact on the way relationships are constructed and maintained. As outlined previously, it is clear that those who support the idea of same-sex marriage wish to reproduce the heterosexual marital experience. The idea is that gays and lesbians are no different than heterosexuals.

While this sounds appealing at first, a closer analysis reveals that it is myopic. Aping traditional heterosexual marriage has implications for gays and lesbians. First, being that marriage has been afforded only to heterosexuals, it is reasonable to believe that same-sex marriage might reproduce conventional gender roles, thereby reinforcing the binary gender system. In many ways, same-sex marriage is contrary to the queer conception of relationship construction, which deeply challenges the taken-for-granted traditional notions of sex, sexuality, and gender. Second, such an arrangement reproduces the kind of containment and control that has been so much a part of heterosexuality (Rubin, 1993) along the lines of role conformity, monogamy, viewing partners as property, and other signifiers of traditional marriage. Accepting the notion that same-sex couples be permitted to share the same privileges as heterosexually married people means that many lifestyle options become *officially* foreclosed.

Another pitfall with same-sex marriage as proposed by the assimilationists is that it reproduces a custom that is not on *terra firma*. As we know from legal documents, the popular press, and Gallup polls, at least half of all marriages in the United States end in divorce. The lives of the children in these unions are often severely disrupted. The legal process of divorce takes up an enormous amount of time and is often destructive. These are just a few of the problems that often result. Why would same-sex marriage proponents want to imitate an institution that is often unworkable?

Same-sex marriage would perpetuate a brand of sexual and relationship hierarchy. According to some of the assimilationists—namely Rotello (1997) and Rauch (1997)—sexual expression, particularly among gay men, is dangerous, potentially "out of control," and often seedy. According to them, being married creates a sociomedical safe zone, which is respectable and socially appropriate. This, of course, reinforces the notion that sexuality—particularly homosexuality or queer sexuality—is dangerous and suspect, and that sexual appropriateness (defined and prescribed by hegemonic heteronormative folks) can only be attained within a marital union. The traditional relationship construction of marriage is never problematized by Sullivan, Rotello, Rauch, and others. Assimilationism—and not questioning or breaking free from social and sexual conventions—seems to be the road to equality, sexual bliss, and social acceptability for many proponents of same-sex marriage.

It is clear that many gays and lesbians are pushing for same-sex marriage in the hope of attaining legal rights, social acceptability, and equality. However, same-sex marriage may be a mirage in a cultural desert. It is assuredly not a panacea to cure sexual prejudice, gain social acceptance, and achieve widespread personal fulfillment. Perhaps, the road to greater freedom, social equality, and the acceptance of sexual pluralism, can be better achieved by taking seriously the work of queer theorists, and what they propose in terms of destabilizing gender and sexual categorization.

The Radical Position

Contemplating the implications of the radical position on same-sex marriage for relationship construction is an exciting speculative exercise. Like many important decisions in life, the choice to pursue or not to pursue same-sex marriage could be a high-stakes gamble. Here, we explore the possibility that abandoning same-sex marriage as a central organizing issue frees up human and material resources for advancing other projects with greater liberatory potential for a variety of relationships.

Rejecting the regime of marriage is a means of transcending the traditional church/state monopoly on relationship options. Separate advocacy efforts might then focus on reform or revolution within religious and spiritual

communities as well as on equal legal rights, responsibilities and social benefits for queer individuals and relationships. Choice of relational partners and commitments based on factors other than legal and economic necessity and social approbation becomes a more realistic option for all. In this context, the evolution of alternative relational structures and networks would likely continue apace, thus creating more opportunities for discovering new social arrangements that work in ways we have yet to conceive. Growing support for individuals and relationships outside of marriage with a concomitant lessening of stigmatization and shame can be, hopefully, hastened. And the rigid categories of gender and sexuality can be increasingly destabilized.

Dare we venture further? Picture an immense and truly *charmed circle* sporting signs of "welcome" rather than "do not enter." A profusion of sexual pleasures sans hierarchical ranking, sans confining expectations about linkages between sexual activities, relationships, and procreation. Imagine the emancipation of the sexual project.

WHAT IS GAINED WITH SAME-SEX MARRIAGE?

Some of the gains of being married include: feeling a sense of security and conformity, having financial comfort and stability, and feeling empowered to raise children due to the context of a marital union, primarily because of the respect afforded to married individuals by others. Additionally, married individuals have a sense of personal pride for having made this kind of commitment to their partner. This derives from the feeling of going through this long-standing rite of passage.

Besides the gains at the level of the individual, there are clearly collective benefits. Some of these include: gaining social approval and full recognition, being able to participate in an institution that offers rewards on the societal level (e.g., being able to have a "traditional family" configuration, being viewed as socially stable and accountable). Additionally, many proponents of same-sex marriage have claimed that there will be a cultural transmission/reproduction of monogamy, which leads to helping to reduce the incidence of sexually transmitted diseases, including HIV/AIDS. In many ways, the proponents of same-sex marriage (especially Rotello) feel that the public's health will be far better off as a result.

WHAT IS LOST WITH SAME-SEX MARRIAGE?

Should the drive to enact same-sex marriage succeed, unmarried queers face the prospect of greater social disapproval and discrimination from sources close and far. This places additional burdens on individuals and relational partners, reminiscent of the predicament confronting generations of single women past a certain age, as they become subject to the weight of inevitable pressures to marry. Such factors belie the notion of marriage as a freely entered into arrangement.

Alongside the impact on queer individuals are a number of collective losses. Marriage reinforces a hegemonic, heteronormative relationship style. Marriage continues to be linked to patriarchy (Ettelbrick, 1997; Walters, 2001) and, therefore, same-sex marriage might reproduce conventional gender roles, especially given how assimilationists usually portray these unions. The more lesbian, gay, bisexual, and transgender individuals marry, the more they and the queer challenge to sexism and heterosexism disappear.

As previously excluded partners join the married population, queer communal networks will weaken and a new hierarchy of socially acceptable and unacceptable relationships develop (Butler, 2001a; Walters, 2001). Though, as Browning has said, "Each of us, hetero or homo, has a stake in nurturing a diverse landscape of families" (1997, p. 134), more likely, the ability to strengthen and extend the range of diverse relationship styles that have emerged from creative responses to oppression would be debilitated.

CONCLUSION

In this chapter, we argue that sexual ideologies are the foundation of much of the debates about same-sex marriage in LGBT communities in the U.S. Such ideologies provide individuals and groups with ways to make sense of sexuality in the social world by organizing and structuring beliefs and thoughts, defining reality, and creating and sustaining a sense of community for people. These ideologies are located in individual and group consciousness (e.g., how people think) and in material practices (e.g., how people live).

We identified two prominent sexual ideological types—assimilationist and radical—underlying the ongoing same-sex marriage debates in U.S. LGBT communities. In this study we also note that the most vociferous widely published proponents of the assimilationist position were middle class, European American, gay-identified men. On the other hand, supporters of the radical position appear to come from more diverse social locations and identifications, including women, people of color, working class individuals, and middle class, queer-identified European American men. Although some scholars (e.g., Chambers, 2001; Duclos, 1991) have discussed the relationship between same-sex marriage and social class based on socioeconomic status, we believe that future research examining the interplay between sexual ideologies and the dynamic intersections of race, social class, gender, and sexuality would be fruitful.

While the debate over same-sex marriage proceeds and changes in U.S. LGBT communities and in the larger American political landscape, other mechanisms to secure legal recognition of gay and lesbian relationships, including domestic partnerships and civil unions, have emerged. For example, Vermont's civil union bill that was signed into law by Governor Howard Dean and subsequently went into effect on July 1, 2000, provides same-sex couples with every benefit and responsibility attached to marriage (Chambers, 2000). Other legislation, like domestic partnerships, has provided some recognition and limited benefits for gay and lesbian relationships. However, the differential treatment of these relationships continues legally, politically, socially, materially, and discursively as Wolfson (1996) reminds us, "Allowing lesbians and gay men access only to domestic partnerships, while reserving marriage for different-sex couples, is a form of second-class citizenship, and perpetuates discrimination" (p. 84). Arguing emphatically for the need to fight for marriage rights for lesbians and gay men, Wolfson (1996) concludes that "ultimately, domestic partnership alone is not enough" (p. 85).

The notion of same-sex troubles most U.S. Americans. Marriage, according to Chambers (2000), "is an enchanted term that each society reserves for its most highly valued sexual relationship" (p. 304), that is, the heterosexual union that has been taken "to represent the *principle of social union itself*" (Warner, 1993, p. xxi; our emphasis). For many LGBT people, marriage has become a fantasy to be accomplished, fuelled by the impulse to be recognized and validated. According to Butler (2001b), recognition renders these individuals and communities intelligible; lack of recognition is a site of suffering. Same-sex marriage, in this sense, might be an attempt of LGBT people to relieve themselves of their own objection (Butler, 2001b). The recognition of gay and lesbian relationships within the "magical title" (Chambers, 2000, p. 304) of marriage then becomes a symbolic yearning for acceptance and universality. The interplay between symbolic yearning and the material realities and consequences of the social organization of sexuality must be carefully considered.

Focusing on the material consequences of marriage, Warner (1999) writes:

> A principled political program would have to say that marriage is a desirable goal only insofar as we can also extend health care, tax reform, rights of intimate association extending to immigration, recognition for joint parenting, and other entitlements currently yoked to martial status. It would have to say that marriage is desirable only insofar as we can eliminate adultery laws and other status-discriminatory regulations for sexuality. It might well also involve making available other statuses, such as expanded domestic partnerships, concubinage, or something like PACS [abbreviated from the French phrase *pacte civil de solidarité*, which means a "civil solidarity pact" that bestows benefits on households of all types, including cohabiting siblings] for property-sharing households, all available to straight and gay people alike. Above all, a program for change should be accountable to the queer ethos, responsive to the lived arrangements of queer life, and articulated in queer publics. (p. 146)

To sum up, it is clear that the issue of same-sex marriage is hotly contested from a variety of perspectives. One of our aims in researching and writing this essay was to illustrate just how complicated an issue same-sex marriage is, and how it is inextricably linked to sexual ideologies. It is clear that a discussion about same-sex marriage must include an exploration of sexual ideologies and how they inform individuals' positions on this topic. Although we focused on two competing ideologies, viz., *assimilationist* and *radical* positions, it is likely that people have various ideas—even competing and conflicting ones—about same-sex marriage that are an amalgamation of these two polar-opposite positions. It is our hope that we shed some theoretical light on a topic that has an enormous impact on lived experience. We hope our analysis adds to the understanding of the complexities of individual wishes and collective struggles in a diverse landscape of sexual ideologies in LGBT communities in the United States.

NOTES

1. We deliberately use the term in the plural to highlight the tremendous diversity in these communities. This diversity is lived, manifested, and expressed in terms of race, class, gender, nationality, political ideology, religious affiliation, and sexual practices, among many others.

2. Although there are a number of similarities in feminist and queer struggles, we are neither implying that feminist and queer agendas are identical nor are we suggesting that there is a singular feminist or queer perspective. We recognize that there are multiple feminist, womanist, and queer viewpoints.

3. We argue that these sexual "ideological types" are fluid—that is, an individual's sexual ideology is constructed and reconstructed in everyday life. They are also located in a personal and historical context—in other words, an individual's sexual ideology is interconnected with his or her social location (e.g., race, class, gender, etc.) and social and historical circumstances. More simply stated, we suggest that these ideological types are not fixed and unchanging attributes of individuals or communities.

4. We use the term "assimilationist view" to refer to the position on same-sex marriage that reflects heteronormative standards upheld and reinforced in heterosexual marital unions. In the literature, this position is sometimes referred to as the "liberal" or "conservative" view.

5. Radical here does not mean "extreme" as it is often used dismissively in common parlance. Rather, it is used in reference to a politically conscious position that challenges/interrogates heteronormative notions and institutions and espouses alternative practices and structures understood as having greater liberatory potential.

REFERENCES

Althusser, L. (1984). *Essays on ideology*. London: Verso.

Baird, R. M., & Rosenbaum, S. E. (Eds.). (1997). *Same-sex marriage: The moral and legal debate*. Amherst, NY: Prometheus.

Bronski, M. (1998). *The pleasure principle: Sex, backlash, and the struggle for gay freedom*. New York: St. Martin's Press.

Browning, F. (1997). Why marry? In A. Sullivan (Ed.), *Same sex marriage: Pro and con* (pp. 132–134). New York: Vintage.

Butler, J. (2001a). "There is a person here": An interview with Judith Butler (compiled by M. S. Breen, W. J. Blumenfeld, with S. Baer, R. A. Brookey, L. Hall, V. Kirby, D. H. Miller, R. Shail, & N. Wilson). *International Journal of Sexuality and Gender Studies*, 6(1/2), 7–23.

Butler, J. (2001b, April 25). *Is kinship always already heterosexual?* Inaugural lecture presented to the Center for the Study of Sexual Culture, University of California, Berkeley.

Chambers, D. L. (2000). Couples: Marriage, civil union, and domestic partnership. In J. D'Emilio, W. B. Turner, & U. Vaid (Eds.), *Creating change: Sexuality, public policy, and civil rights* (pp. 281–304). New York: St. Martin's Press.

Chambers, D. L. (2001). What if? The legal consequences of marriage and the legal needs of lesbian and gay male couples. In M. Bernstein & R. Reinmann (Eds.), *Queer families, queer politics: Challenging culture and the state* (pp. 306–337). New York: Columbia University Press.

Cormack, M. (1992). *Ideology*. Ann Arbor, MI: University of Michigan Press.

Dollimore, J. (1991). *Sexual dissidence: Augustine to Wilde, Freud to Foucault*. Oxford, UK: Clarendon Press.

Duclos, N. (1991). Some complicating thoughts on same-sex marriage. *Law & Sexuality*, 1(Summer), 31–62.

Eskridge, W. N. (2002). *Equality practice: Civil unions and the future of gay rights*. New York: Routledge.

Ettelbrick, P. (1997). Since when is marriage a path to liberation? In A Sullivan (Ed.), *Same-sex marriage: Pro and con* (pp. 118–124). New York: Vintage.

Hall, S. (1996). The problem of ideology: Marxism without guaranties. In D. Morley & K. H. Chen (Eds.), *Stuart Hall: Critical dialogues in cultural studies* (pp. 25–46). London: Routledge.

Hawkes, D. (1996). *Ideology*. London: Routledge.

Kaplan, M. B. (1997). *Sexual justice: Democratic citizenship and the politics of desire*. New York: Routledge.

Lannamann, J. W. (1991). Interpersonal communication research as ideological practice. *Communication Theory*, 1(3), 179–203.

Lannamann, J. W. (1994). The problem with disempowering ideology. In S. A. Deetz (Ed.), *Communication yearbook 17* (pp. 136–147). Thousand Oaks, CA: Sage.

Larrain, J. (1979). *The concept of ideology*. London: Hutchinson.

McKay, A. (1998). *Sexual ideology and schooling: Toward a democratic sexuality education*. Ontario, Canada: The Althouse Press.

McLellan, D. (1995). *Ideology* (2nd ed.). Minneapolis, MN: University of Minnesota Press.

Rauch, J. (1997). For better or worse? In A. Sullivan (Ed.), *Same-sex marriage: Pro and con* (pp. 169–181). New York: Vintage.

Rotello, G. (1997). *Sexual ecology: AIDS and the destiny of gay men.* New York: Dutton.

Rubin, G. S. (1993). Thinking sex: Notes for a radical theory of the politics of sexuality. In H. Abelove, M. A. Barele, & D. M. Halperin (Eds.), *The lesbian and gay studies reader* (pp. 3–44). New York: Routledge.

Saalfield, C. (1993). Lesbian marriage . . . (k)not! In A. Stein (Ed.), *Sisters, sexperts, queers: Beyond the Lesbian Nation* (pp. 187–195). New York: Penguin.

Seidman, S. (1991). *Romantic longings: Love in America, 1830–1980.* New York: Routledge.

Seidman, S. (1992). *Embattled eros: Sexual politics and ethics in contemporary America.* New York: Routledge.

Seidman, S. (1997). *Difference troubles: Queering social theory and sexual politics.* Cambridge, UK: Cambridge University Press.

Shilts, R. (1987). *And the band played on: Politics, people, and the AIDS epidemic.* New York: Penguin.

Smith, R. R., & Windes, R. R. (2000). *Progay/antigay: The rhetorical war over sexuality.* Thousand Oaks, CA: Sage.

Sullivan, A. (1995). *Virtually normal: An argument about homosexuality.* New York: Alfred A. Knopf.

Sullivan, A. (1996). Here comes the groom: A (conservative) case for gay marriage. In B. Bawer (Ed.), *Beyond queer* (pp. 252–258). New York: The Free Press.

Sullivan, A. (Ed.). (1997). *Same-sex marriage: Pro and con.* New York: Vintage.

Troiden, R., & Platt, J. (1987). Does sexual ideology correlate with level of sexual experience? Assessing the construct validity of the SAS. *Journal of Sex Research, 23*(2), 256–260.

Vasquez, C. (1999). Citizen queer. In K. Kleindienst (Ed.), *This is what a lesbian looks like: Dyke activists take on the 21st century* (pp. 269–278). Ithaca, NY: Firebrand.

Walters, S. D. (2001). Take my domestic partner, please: Gays and marriage in the era of the visible. In M. Bernstein & R. Reinmann (Eds.), *Queer families, queer politics: Challenging culture and the state* (pp. 338–357). New York: Columbia University Press.

Warner, M. (1993). Introduction. In M. Warner (Ed.), *Fear of a queer planet: Queer politics and social theory* (pp. vii–xxxi). Minneapolis, MN: University of Minnesota Press.

Warner, M. (1999). *The trouble with normal: Sex, politics, and the ethics of queer life.* New York: Free Press.

Weeks, J. (1985). *Sexuality and its discontents: Meanings, myths, and modern sexualities.* London: Routledge.

Weeks, J. (1986). *Sexuality.* London: Routledge.

Weeks, J. (1995). *Invented moralities: Sexual values in an age of uncertainty.* New York: Columbia University Press.

Wolfson, E. (1996). Why we should fight for the freedom to marry: The challenges and opportunities that will follow a win in Hawaii. *Journal of Gay, Lesbian, and Bisexual Identity, 1,* 79–89.

Discussion Questions

1. How do the authors define what a sexual ideology is and does?

2. In their analysis of the competing ideologies regarding same-sex marriage, why do Yep, Lovaas, and Elia categorize positions on this issue as assimilationist versus radical?

3. To what extent, if at all, do you think that the arguments for and against same-sex marriage that are summarized here apply to heterosexual marriages?

4. What do you see as the most important points to consider in coming to an individual decision about the issue of marriage?

5. What are the current views on this subject in what you define as your community (peers, family, region, religious affiliation, political affiliation, etc.)?

6. Overall, are you in favor of or against same-sex marriage? What are your reasons?

PART III

Performing and Disciplining Sexualities in Public Discourses

13

Performing a Rhetoric of Science

Dr. Laura's Portrayal of Homosexuality

PAUL TURPIN

Laura Schlessinger, who is known as Dr. Laura and is the leading nationally syndicated female talk-radio host at the time of this writing (McDowell, 2000), became a center of controversy in the spring and summer of 2000 because of her description of homosexuality as a form of "deviance" and "biological error" in shows broadcast in 1999. A number of gay and lesbian organizations mobilized in opposition to Schlessinger's television debut on September 11, 2000, arranging picketing at television stations around the country and orchestrating a sizeable and effective threat of consumer boycott by asking sponsors to withdraw their advertising from her shows (both television and radio). By late August, the controversy had produced an extensive Web site (Aravosis, 2000) that publicized local gay organizers and protests around the country, commentary from Schlessinger on her radio show, responses from Schlessinger and her allies in the press, censure from the Canadian Broadcast Standards Council (CBSC Ontario Regional Council and Atlantic Regional Council, 2000), and commentary in the press at large.

Public controversy over sexuality produces what Ralph R. Smith and Russell R. Windes (1997) have called oppositional interaction, in which argumentative strategies are altered in response to challenges from opponents (p. 28). Smith and Windes situate their work in the view that ongoing social controversies amount to "an extended rhetorical engagement . . . bridging the personal and public spheres" (Olson & Goodnight, 1994, p. 249). The value of studying oppositional interactions can be fruitfully supplemented, I believe, by in-depth case studies of the various positions in conflict. In this chapter, I will give a brief overview of the two sides of the Dr. Laura controversy and will then concentrate on Schlessinger's position.

A major challenge in analyzing a case like the Dr. Laura controversy is to do justice to its performative aspects, in addition to the more usual tasks of the rhetorical critic in accounting for its use of language and its argumentative structures and presumptions. The spoken word ought to be preeminently an object of rhetorical analysis, but because it is ephemeral, its performative nature is more elusive, making assessment of it more difficult than textual analysis.[1] I propose to address this problem in looking at the Schlessinger controversy by reconsidering Aristotle's three modes of persuasion—ethos, pathos, and logos—under the headings of performance, trope, and argument. I take this approach in the spirit of what John Angus Campbell (1998) has called "the revival of neo-classical rhetorical principles," to go beyond the classificatory tendencies of neo-Aristotelianism and look for dynamic principles operating in rhetorical encounters (p. 291). The aim of such analysis is not merely to identify the parts of rhetoric, in a "here a trope, there a figure" fashion, but to demonstrate how intertwined rhetorical appeals support and advance (or hinder) an argument whose presumptions and implications are the critic's task to make plain and explicit. Ultimately, the task of rhetorical analysis should be not merely to identify persuasion at work but to identify what we are to be persuaded *of*.

A concern with the persuasive message implies that rhetorical analysts are not merely observers but are involved in evaluation by, at the very least, their position of critical observation. My own position is that I have listened to Schlessinger's radio show periodically since the late 1980s, when she had an evening show in Los Angeles, with some sympathy and a fair amount of disagreement for her social pronouncements. At the same time, I have supported the goals of gay liberation. When the controversy erupted, although opposed to her position, I became interested in investigating what Schlessinger's remarks meant within the context of her own framework.

Over the 10-plus years of listening to her radio shows, I had noticed Schlessinger becoming more and more outspoken about her social conservatism. This became especially pronounced

in the mid-1990s, when her show became nationally syndicated. At that point, the focus of her show, which had been that of a psychologist's call-in advice show, changed to one explicitly centered on moral issues. One of the most noticeable changes at that point was in Schlessinger's performance. To test my hypothesis that ethos, pathos, and logos can be discussed productively by examining performance, trope, and argument, I now turn to an assessment of Schlessinger's performative characteristics.

PERFORMANCE

The term *performance* indicates the embodiment *cum* enactment of a rhetorical performance— the live event, as it were, although I consider texts to be performative as well. I linked performance with ethos; that is, with the embodiment and enactment of credibility. My reading of ethos comes from Book II of Aristotle's *Rhetoric* (1954). According to Aristotle, ethos is made up of good sense, good moral character, and good will (p. 91). These three elements are qualities of the speaker, but they also reflect the modes of persuasion themselves—logos, ethos, and pathos. I take ethos to be those same persuasive qualities literally personified by the speaker, or, because Aristotle insists that more than reputation is involved in ethos, *performed* by the speaker.

Ethos is materially manifest, as well. It is a commonplace of basic public speaking classes that mumbling and looking down at your notes is an inadequate material performance that undermines credibility. In a radio show, the speaking voice is especially important.[2] Schlessinger's voice is mobile and expressive, and her range is wide enough to include hilarity, sympathy, gentle chastisement, forcefulness, and ranting. Above all, though, her vocal performance contributes to the impression that she is not acting—that the listener is hearing her as she is. She has the quality of seeming alive and present as herself (Shriver, 2000), which greatly enhances her ethos.

The strength of Schlessinger's early period, before national syndication, was her ability to deal with callers in a sympathetic and incisive way, in a short span of time. Calls would typically be only a few minutes in length. The most successful (i.e., interesting and compelling) calls involved Schlessinger eliciting some degree of self-insight from the caller. The tone of interactions with callers was typically dialogic. As her moral focus emerged, the tone became more monologic, with more frequent interactions in which callers would send Schlessinger into a monologue while still on the phone with a caller. The contrast between the two styles of dealing with callers was noticeable, and it sometimes appeared to be arbitrarily applied as well, leading some commentators to say that she bullied her callers (Shriver, 2000). The opening monologues became increasingly important in the show as well, and they often had a didactic and sometimes hectoring tone. Schlessinger herself has described her job as being a public nag about moral issues (McDowell, 2000).

Schlessinger's tone of sympathetic dialogue has never entirely disappeared, and it is the mainstay of her ethos. The shift in her focus between a call-in counseling format and a moral instruction format, however, has produced a shift in how her ethos emerges. In her earlier period, good will and good sense predominated, and they were apparent in her ability to deal sympathetically with emotionally distressed callers and lead them to insights. This is not to say that she did not also evince good character. In the later period, though, good character emerged as the most forceful impression she made on listeners, sometimes at the expense of the other aspects of ethos and, particularly, of good will toward her callers. This was especially noticeable in the year following national syndication, when she often just chewed callers out instead of leading them to lessons (Shriver, 2000). For some, however, the forcefulness of her emphasis on moral rectitude had a negative effect,

lowering her credibility rather than increasing it.[3] Schlessinger claims to believe what she says (McDowell, 2000), and in that respect she performs a strong ethos.

TROPE AND ARGUMENT

Just as I reconsidered *ethos* as the performative presentation of self, *trope* and *argument* are my terms for the choices of words and the lines of reasoning in a rhetorical artifact or exchange, and I linked them to pathos and logos, respectively. The link to pathos concerns why and how we should care about a subject, and the link to logos, how we should think about it.

If we begin with Aristotle, pathos involves putting the audience in the proper frame of mind, which Aristotle (1954) treats pragmatically in Book II (p. 90) as understanding how different emotions work, with an eye toward being able to generate them in an audience. I interpret "proper frame of mind" to mean why the audience should care about an issue, which would include what its attitude toward the issue ought to be. *Trope* means "to turn," and I see the choices of language, metaphor, and so on to be the bricks and mortar of the rhetor's broader effort to turn our emotional attention in a certain direction.

Turning attention is what Kenneth Burke (1966) discusses in his chapter "Terministic Screens," in which he describes the dramatistic approach to language as "attitudinal or hortatory" (p. 44). In this chapter, Burke is concerned with the way language choices necessarily screen, or filter, perceptions, setting up one line of implications as they deflect another. Referencing Jeremy Bentham's idea of "fictions," Burke notes that we must express many of our ideas about human nature and society "by the use of terms borrowed from the realm of the physical" (p. 46). The metaphorical nature of language necessarily affects our attitude toward the subject as well as our view of it.

The relationship between trope and argument can be a close one, supplying vivid imagery and emotional attitude to argumentative force. Before elaborating Schlessinger's position in terms of trope and argument, it is worth taking time to review the controversy interaction.

STRUCTURE OF THE CONTROVERSY: TROPE AND ENTELECHY

In the Schlessinger controversy, the situation is nearly a classic instance of what Ware and Linkugel (1973) called the "speech set" of *kategoria* (attack) and *apologia* (defense), with Schlessinger's gay critics calling her remarks "hate speech" and Schlessinger responding with accusations of a leftist-McCarthyite witch hunt. In particular, the controversy is characterized by highly charged moral stances on both sides, with language of praise and blame—especially blame—operating at often high voltage.

Smith and Windes (1997, 2000), with their concentration on oppositional interaction, stress the way in which rhetorical strategies shift to accommodate oppositional moves. I want to emphasize the tendency to entelechy in this controversy—the kind of logical extension that Kenneth Burke described as something taken to its logical extreme. Stan A. Lindsay (1998) describes Burke's concept of entelechy as an aspect of the human propensity to be "rotten with perfection" (Burke, 1966, p. 16), arguing that Burke adapted Aristotle's idea of *telos* (end, purpose) metaphorically from its basis as a biological analogy to a rhetorical tendency in both thought and language (Lindsay, 1998, p. 17).

In the Schlessinger controversy, similar entelechial-argumentative moves and countermoves can be seen on both sides: in kategoria, claiming that the other's actions and remarks must have a necessary meaning and consequence and, in apologia, denying charges by claiming that such an extension commits a

slippery slope fallacy. For Schlessinger's opponents, the entelechy was that her words about the biological error of homosexuality were harmful on a scale ranging at one end from being damaging to self-esteem in and of themselves to, on the other end, providing support (as in moral support and justification) for violent attacks on gays (Garry, 2001). Implicitly included within this scale of harms was opposition to legal equality for gays in a variety of civic issues, including the possibility of gay marriage. Schlessinger, on her part, denied that she ever meant to hurt anyone's feelings, apologized if any were hurt, and categorically denied giving any support to those who would use violence. Opposition to gay rights such as civil marriage, however, was very much at the center of her argument. To Schlessinger, her opponents committed the slippery slope fallacy of extending her arguments to areas to which she had not intended them to go and, she claimed, to which they did not go.

On her side, Schlessinger countercharged that the attacks on her constituted an attack on freedom of speech, and supporters have characterized the opposition to her as a form of left-McCarthyism. The entelechy of her apologia is that criticisms of her statements and positions have turned into an attempt to silence her by intimidating her sponsors. In particular, she singles out the opposition of radical "agendized groups"[4] (gays in this case, although feminists and others are sometimes included in that phrase) as being responsible for the attacks on her (Schlessinger, 2000a).

The charge of a left-McCarthyism is not without some resonance. Much of the damage of Senator Joseph McCarthy's campaign against "communists in the government" was collateral damage, so to speak, that happened not through official government action but through pressures to act privately so that one could be seen to be conforming to policy. Thus the Hollywood blacklists, for example, were not the result of government edict but a reaction by studio heads—private individuals, so to speak—anxious to be seen conforming to and supporting an anticommunist policy. In Schlessinger's case, the implied threat was an activist consumer boycott against sponsors of her radio and television shows, leading to a considerable drain of advertisers. The charge of left-McCarthyism fails, though, in the difference of the source of the threat: McCarthy's aim was to mobilize the power of the federal government; the activists opposing Schlessinger are conducting a social movement campaign in which they appeal to advertisers to withdraw their sponsorship—a consumerist rather than governmental approach, and one that the religious right has itself used on occasion (Confessore, 2000).

The sponsors who withdrew[5] also maintained a moral tone in their public pronouncements. Their most common theme was that they did not want to be identified with a divisive show, but there were also frequent mentions of supporting diversity.[6] Although most were temperate in describing Schlessinger's position, they nearly all mentioned that her views were not in line with their advertising strategies. The opposition strategies of picketing, letter writing, and telephoning television stations and sponsors also clearly became more effective over time, suggesting an inverse bandwagon effect. Advertisers who early on described their sponsorship in terms of supporting Schlessinger's freedom of speech later withdrew, with remarks about divisiveness or inappropriateness.

The charge of infringing on her freedom of speech that Schlessinger has leveled at her opponents is problematic in that freedom of speech usually is cast in terms of individual rights versus governmental control. Examples range from controversies over parade permits for neo-Nazis in Skokie, Illinois, to efforts to overturn prohibitions on prayer in public schools on the grounds both of freedom of speech and freedom of religion. There simply is no governmental agency involved in the Schlessinger case, which there would be if, for

example, Schlessinger's opponents were lobbying the Federal Communications Commission to stop the show instead of lobbying advertisers to withdraw their support.

Schlessinger's remarks did draw censure from the Canadian Broadcast Standards Council Ontario and Atlantic Regional Councils (2000) after complaints were filed. In answering the complaints, the CBSC found that "the host's unremittingly heavy-handed and unambiguously negative characterisation of those sexual practices is abusively discriminatory and in breach of the Code." The stations that broadcast the shows in question were required to broadcast statements that Schlessinger's remarks were in breach of the Canadian Association of Broadcasters Code of Ethics (CBSC Ontario Regional Council and Atlantic Regional Council, 2000).

Accusations of fascism have also been traded that are mainly hyperbolic. Schlessinger occasionally imputes totalitarian motives to her opponents, as in the McCarthyite comments, and she takes offence at being characterized as fascist herself. She relies on a table-turning tactic of claiming that those attacking her are the real fascists because of their intolerant political agenda.

The entelechial character of these tactics functions to ascribe a trajectory of thought to one's opponents. The question for the critic, and for the multiple audiences of the Schlessinger-gay controversy, is whether the logical extension—the entelechy—is actually warranted. In the main, the analogies offered as framing devices (free speech, McCarthyism, fascism) are figurative rather than literal and function mainly to evoke passions in support of the desired framing on both sides. Partisans on either side may well disagree with my analysis, and their disagreements would take the shape of explaining, for example, on one side, that Schlessinger functions as a fascist intellectual, giving justification to the actions of thugs and de facto brownshirts,[7] or, on the other, that radical gays are intolerant of conservative religious values and want to undermine traditional family structure. In each of those cases, however, there is a good deal of preaching to the choir.

In a social controversy, preaching to the choir can have the beneficial effect of bolstering morale and solidifying support, but there is also the need to enlarge one's audience and broaden support. The rhetorical competition for the uncommitted among the public is a strong factor driving strategizing oppositional interaction. In her search for common ground, Schlessinger mobilizes an argument based on science. I now turn from looking at the controversy as a whole to examining Schlessinger's rhetoric of science.

RHETORIC OF SCIENCE, FIRST LAYER: THE "DOCTOR" IS IN

The most obvious place to start in assessing Schlessinger's position in terms of a rhetoric of science is the "doctor" of her Dr. Laura persona. A central complaint in gay protests against Schlessinger has been that she misrepresents herself as a professional authority on psychological matters. Her doctorate is in physiology, on which she lectured briefly at the University of Southern California before changing careers. Her qualifications for her early talk show were a marriage, family, and child counselor degree and a counseling practice that she pursued after her doctorate and before she started her radio career.

For Schlessinger, the Dr. Laura name is virtually a trademark. The telephone number to call her show is 800-DRLAURA, which she announces repeatedly on the show. The preferred form of address or reference in on-air conversations with callers is "Dr. Laura." In all the time I have listened to the program, only rarely did I hear anyone calling her Laura or Dr. Schlessinger. Schlessinger's insistence on her title has drawn criticism for the air of clinical authority it claims (CBSC Ontario Regional Council and Atlantic Regional Council, 2000, Garry, 2001).

The "Dr." of Dr. Laura is an exemplary case of Burke's terministic screen; it is an authority term that orients our attention to Schlessinger in an attitude of deferential expectation, implying both care and expertise. This, of course, is its medical connotation, and it is this connotation to which Schlessinger's opponents object. The same words and arguments coming from "Mother Laura" instead of "Dr. Laura" would, arguably, carry different weight.

Although she features the Dr. Laura title and name prominently, Schlessinger tempers the formality and potentially forbidding aura of "Doctor." This happens in two ways: First, the informality of the title used with the first name instead of the surname (Dr. Laura rather than Dr. Schlessinger), and second, by the trademark introductions she gives at the beginning of each show (and sometimes at each hour). The introductions are of her staff: the person screening the calls, the engineer, the person selecting the music (if different from the engineer), the general staff person, and, finally, herself. The pattern is to say the person's name and then what they do on the show (engineer, etc.); Schlessinger's self-introduction invariably follows the pattern: ". . . and me, I am my kid's mom!" announced in a tone of high cheer. The effect is one of authority, but authority that is friendly and approachable. It is a remarkable case of having one's cake and eating it too: Schlessinger is *both* Dr. Laura and Mother Laura.

RHETORIC OF SCIENCE, SECOND LAYER: THE ENTELECHY OF LIFE

Schlessinger's remarks about "biological error" sparked a great deal of the controversy. In her subsequent defenses of her statements, she followed a pattern of claiming to discriminate between a condition (homosexuality) and persons (gays themselves), claiming that she never meant to attack or hurt anyone personally. This pattern is similar to the general precept used in the Roman Catholic church and other Christian religions to "love the sinner, hate the sin" (but with the important distinction that sin is not a condition, but an immoral behavior). Here are two statements from Schlessinger:

> I have never called homosexuals biological mistakes. I have said that the sexual orientation is clearly an error. With penises and vaginas we were meant for heterosexual sexual acting out in order to procreate the species. I mean that is just irrefutable. (CBSC, 2000, transcript of August 24, 1999)

> So, here's what I said; human beings, all creatures on the face of the Earth, reproduce in some way. Some just have cell division. That's it. One microbe divides into two: now you have two individuals. That's not how human beings do it. Human beings do it heterosexually, that's how we're geared. Egg, sperm. Penis, vagina. That's just how the biology of it goes. What I did say is that when an individual is not so drawn to a member of the opposite sex, in biology, that's some kind of error. Because it doesn't result in reproduction. That is so far—you have to understand, my original—all my original degrees were in biology. And physiology. So for me to speak from a clinical or—'cause I'm a marriage and family therapist—or a biological point, is normal for me, because I've taught this stuff. We are basically geared to reproduce heterosexually. So, when I said "biological error," I did not say a human being was a biological error. I never would call a human being a biological error, that is despicable. But, I need you folks to know the activists are lying to you. I never said that. (Schlessinger, 2000b)

Schlessinger's argument that homosexuality is a "biological error" is based on her view of the telos of human sexuality as the reproduction of the species through families. The Greek word *telos* is appropriate because it captures a sense of purpose and goal that is inherent in something's nature. Her view of this telos is partly scientific, insofar as she accepts a generalized notion of biological behavior that operates via sexual selection.[8] It is also partly religious, insofar as the only morally correct form of sexual selection for her is through heterosexual marriage. Finally, it is also social (and thence, political), insofar as the traditional norm of marriage has likewise been heterosexual, and she wants to keep it that way.

Schlessinger's reasoning from these grounds is commonsensical: If the purpose of life is to reproduce, then anyone who does not is by definition a "sport," in the genetic sense—a biological oddity. She makes an exception for those who remain celibate from religious convictions but otherwise considers bearing and raising children to be the natural—and therefore central—purpose of sex in particular and life in general. She has even said on occasion that heterosexual people who marry and elect not to have children may not be fully mature; that is, not fulfilling their telos.

In her judgment of homosexuality as biological error, Schlessinger exploits an ambiguity inherent in the definition of normativity that permits her to slide back and forth between claims about values and claims about facts, thereby (a) enabling her to define homosexuality such that it is a moral issue, and then (b) supplying her moral objections to homosexuality with a veneer of scientific objectivity—or more accurately, with a veneer of plausible reasoning, like that which Chaim Perelman and Lucile Olbrechts-Tyteca (1969) called "quasi-logical reasoning":

> In every quasi-logical argument it is necessary first of all to set forth the formal scheme on the model of which the argument is constructed and after that to display the operations of reduction which make it possible to insert the data into this scheme and which aim at making the data comparable, similar, homogenous. (p. 193)

For Schlessinger, the formal scheme is that of biological reproduction, supported by a scientific background. The reduction she performs (all human beings must reproduce) supports the purpose of eliding all ambiguities by holding that the world is a single whole, encompassing mundane life and the divine as well.

The ambiguity can be illustrated by considering the properties of the normal curve in statistical analysis. *Norm*, in this case, has a technical meaning that identifies the predominant characteristics of the sample; the norm identifies the majority of the cases and locates them in the middle of the curve. The tails of the curve are where the exceptions occur (with very low frequency). This sense of *norm* is that of a set of common characteristics arrayed around (and close to) a mean, but it has no moral implication. Consider Schlessinger's defense of using the word "deviant" to describe homosexuality:

> Because human beings are, by nature of their genitalia and reproductive systems, the scheme is male and female—and so behavior that is deviant from that or off that, I mean that's [a] clinical term, if a word choice is what has been damaging [to gays], it was never my intent. (Shriver, 2000)

Moral norms, on the other hand, are of two kinds: behavioral prescriptions from religious or philosophical beliefs, and behavioral expectations from social convention. What Burke (1966) calls the hortatory function of language is more explicit in the thou shalt–shalt nots of religion; both forms of moral judgment carry weight in their praise and in their censure. If one marries the scientific idea of the normal to the religious and social ideas of the norm, as I claim Schlessinger does, then there is a great temptation to view natural phenomena through moral lenses. The conjuncture of moral, social, and scientific norms poses a risk of majoritarian tyranny underwritten by a rhetoric of science.

Schlessinger's attempt to fuse these ways of looking at the world is neither new nor unique, of course. It is fairly typical of socially conservative religion, which helps explain why Schlessinger, who became an Orthodox Jew in the 1990s, has a strong following among conservative, nondenominational Christians. The effort to maintain such a view, however, is faced with sustaining not just a coherence but an indivisible unity among her religious, social, and scientific beliefs. How and why Schlessinger maintains this unity is the next issue to be addressed.

RHETORIC OF SCIENCE, THIRD LEVEL: CERTAINTY, AMBIGUITY, AND FEAR

Schlessinger's avowed mission is to protect children. The central touchstone for all her judgments is that children must come before everything else. Part of her definition of what is good for children is that they be in a heterosexual—"a mom and a dad"—family. Anything less than that, she has said, is a tragedy. Although she acknowledges that parents sometimes die, her argument against single-parent families, along with her resistance to divorce, is that to start out with less than, or to divide, what she defines as a full family is to willfully create what in other circumstances would be seen as a tragedy. Schlessinger defends her "a mom and a dad" heterosexual model of marriage as both psychologically preferable for children and socially normative (in the sense of being the common form of families), which is also supportive of children's interests.

Schlessinger draws a distinction between civil rights for gays on the one hand and social acceptance for homosexuality on the other (CBSC 2000, transcript of April 14, 1999). She defines civil rights as the right to employment, housing, and so on, without discrimination on the basis of sexual orientation. Her definition is negative, in the sense that such rights should not be denied; homosexuality should be tolerated. She is, however, opposed to efforts to have homosexuality openly accepted, something she calls the normalization of homosexuality (CBSC, 2000). Note the mix, again, of moral opprobrium and the hint of the margins of the normal curve. She is particularly opposed to any family status for gays, including adoption, lesbian couples bearing children, and, most of all, marriage rights; her opposition extends to any open display of homosexuality that seeks social approval. Gays should not be discriminated against, but neither should they make any show of their sexuality—"don't ask, don't tell" amended by "and don't mention it."

Schlessinger's reasoning stems from the centrality of children in her definition of family. According to her, acceptance of homosexuality would in general be a source of confusion to children, who depend on reliable heterosexual sex and gender models to develop properly, and that confusion would be aggravated by any notion of homosexuals as parents.[9] Reliable sex and gender models, in this context, would include marriage at a minimum and, ideally, common religious beliefs. Beyond the immediate impact on children, though, Schlessinger argues that normalizing homosexuality would seriously damage the family as a social institution. Already upset at single-parent families as corrosive of what she thinks families should be, Schlessinger considers anathema the thought of gay families with the same legal rights as heterosexual families. Schlessinger's reference to "agendized" gay groups refers specifically to gay efforts to have homosexuality accepted socially, not just tolerated.

Schlessinger's argument is a combination of conservative social values and black-and-white reasoning. The danger legitimate homosexual marriage would pose to traditional families is that it would stand as an alternative form of family, which would ipso facto destroy the traditional family's position as the sole moral means to sexual relations, reproduction, and raising children. Not just specific children would be at risk of becoming confused by gay adults; all children would be at risk due to being exposed to an altered and alternative status of the family itself.

Schlessinger's rationale for this line of reasoning is that children are easily misled and confused. If, in developing their own sexuality, they see that homosexuality is an option, they might mistakenly go in that direction. The job of adults as parents, in her view, is to eliminate any ambiguities of that sort so as to best direct the development of children. Similarly, if children grow up seeing alternatives for the family besides the mom-and-dad model, they might mistakenly think it is all right to choose a different one. The job of adults—and this view definitely has a political component—is to maintain the preeminence of the heterosexual, two-parent family.

Schlessinger's conception of the child, however, has a curious twist. She rarely talks about adolescence as a stage of development. She does talk about—and to—teenagers frequently on her show, but she consistently refers to them as children, and says this to them when they call in. Their duty, as children, is to follow their parents' guidance in questions of behavior. Schlessinger acknowledges adolescence as the period of life in which teenagers want to start controlling their own lives, but for her that must be done in compliance with parental direction. For Schlessinger, the ambiguities and uncertainties of adolescence are problems to be solved by fiat of good parenting, because their causes are nothing more than the unformed judgments of a teenager.

The disappearance of adolescence in a universe of moral certainty is a reflection of Schlessinger's dislike of ambiguity and ambivalence. It is extremely rare for her to talk about being of two minds about something, and even rarer for her to permit a caller to remain so. Ambivalence and ambiguity alike are problems to be solved. The root of most ambivalence to her is feeling one way while thinking another; this invariably emerges when Schlessinger tells a caller, "I didn't ask what you *feel*, I asked what you *think*." Emotion is an untrustworthy guide to Schlessinger and should yield to reason (CBSC, 2000, transcript of July 1, 1999).

The reason that she employs, however, is very often a reductive, black-and-white type of rationality. A typical line of argument that she employs is that anyone who does not oppose something—single parenthood, for example—promotes or endorses it. Her reasoning is very often of an "either you're with me or against me" sort, going immediately to the end of the entelechial line, a vivid illustration of Burke's (1966) definition of humans as "rotten with perfection" (p. 16).

Her own story of why she changed her attitude towards gays illustrates this point. In describing her conversion to Orthodox Judaism, Schlessinger said she

> had to struggle with many things . . . one in specific, and that's homosexuality. So, until about last year and a half or so, I would say—and get hundreds and hundreds of letters from religious Christians and Jews just condemning me—I would say that I couldn't, in my conscience, tell two people—even of the same gender—that they had to be alone, that they couldn't have a companion, that they couldn't have love. That I couldn't go there, because my compassion—I couldn't go there. (Schlessinger, 2000b)

Schlessinger goes on to describe a letter that she received from a minister, that she read on the air, that "was the first thing that made sense and that my compassion was misplaced."

> I don't know if he said misplaced or misdirected or—it was an error. He said for the following reason, if you're moving in the direction of accepting that we are not the highest power—that there is God; that there is God—then you have to be concerned with souls. And you are morally obligated—I'm paraphrasing 'cause I couldn't find the letter last night—I am, that you are morally, we each are morally obligated not to undermine each other's journey toward God and toward growing our souls in a positive way. And that when I said that out of my compassion, I could not say to somebody, homosexual or lesbian, that quote "They

> had to be alone," unquote that I was hurting people. (Schlessinger, 2000b)

Students of rhetoric will recognize the reasoning that resonates from Plato's *Phaedrus* (1956) through Christianity, thanks in large part to the affinities between Platonism and Christianity seen by Paul of Tarsus (St. Paul), who is responsible for a considerable part of the Christian church's teaching on sexuality of all sorts, and the influence of Augustine of Hippo (St. Augustine), whose *Confessions* (1992) detailed his own grateful conversion to celibacy from a tormenting addiction to sex: Sex is bad for the soul. Western culture is well known to have powerful aversions to sexuality in general, and homosexuality in particular, that have ever been in contest with the ongoing emergence of human desire.

Schlessinger's "conversion" story, which I have just related, hinges on reasoning from first principles as a trump over the emotional inclination of her earlier, emotionally tinged compassion. Religious and scientific reason join hands and help reveal the rationale for her holding so tightly to her unified view of scientific, social, and religious principles. The great value of religious faith is the escape from uncertainty, and the value of a literalist interpretation of scripture is liberation from ambiguity. She has said numerous times on her show that she gained a great peace when she began her Orthodox practice and that peace came from the certainty of a divine warrant for moral judgment and a feeling of purpose in God's plan for the world. She has likewise said on the air that she does not see that morality has any valid justification outside of a religious framework; that is, without an authorizing divine warrant. She has also talked about the near despair she felt earlier in her life, recognized mainly in hindsight, at being unsure whether there was any purpose to life.

These are very human reactions to the troubles and uncertainties of life, of course, and Schlessinger is hardly the first to cling to a straitened reason in the face of uncertainty. Her effort to hold together all three of her worldviews—scientific, social, and religious—leads to some problematic statements, though, as we have seen in her description of homosexuality as a biological error. The same kind of problem develops in her argument that homosexuality is a psychological malfunction that can be corrected in some cases, an argument that leads her to promote what is called reparative therapy.

Although it offers itself as a solution to a problem, the argumentative work reparative therapy does is to recast homosexuality in a moral light. One of the central successes of the gay movement over the last two decades has been to get a wide, although not yet universal, acceptance of homosexuality as a natural condition. As a natural condition, it is not something that one wills and therefore is not properly subject to moral judgment.[10] One of Schlessinger's central defenses of her statement that homosexuality is a biological error is that she meant the condition of being homosexual was a mistake of nature, not of gays themselves as people. Being able to separate the condition from the person makes it possible to view homosexual behavior as either a psychological condition akin to neurosis, which might be amenable to psychotherapy, or as willful bad behavior, in which case it becomes the proper object of moral censure. Gays, in refusing to accept the condition as separate from themselves, ironically risk being evaluated as *both* neurotic and immoral—neurotic because they are erotically drawn to their own sex, and immoral because they indulge those feelings instead of "curing" them.

CONCLUSION

My effort in this essay has been to map Laura Schlessinger's rhetorical effort of performance, trope, and argument in the controversy over her remarks about homosexuality from 1999 through 2000. I have tried to resist psychologizing her but, rather, have attempted to follow

her logic and language and uncover the presumptions and implications of her statements and expressed beliefs. I have been sympathetic toward some of Schlessinger's actions as a talk-show host, particularly when she is able to be a sympathetic interlocutor, but I have been less sympathetic since her shift to a focus on moral education. I am opposed to nearly all her expressed political positions, especially with regard to gay rights.

My intention, similarly, has not been to dismiss her conservative beliefs but, rather, to examine them as closely as I could. I find many admirable concerns in conservative philosophy, but I find them intermixed with unacceptable constraints on other people. I am hopeful that this analysis helps reveal the very real and major clash of belief in our culture about the nature of human development, both in terms of what it means for children and what it means for understanding human sexuality. The value of rhetorical analysis in this clash is to make clear the presumptions and assumptions in which lie the values that are under dispute.

My own experience as audience to the controversy leads me to conclude that Schlessinger's gay opponents fare better than she does in recognizing and caring about the worries, ambiguities, and fragility of adolescence. In her desire to protect children under the banner of traditional moral normalcy, Schlessinger, inadvertently or not, places gay adolescents in the worst possible position: of being the bizarre outcasts they might be afraid they are. That is too high a price to pay, and it is underscored by the recurring tragedies of suicide by those who despair that their desire is not normal.

In a way, Schlessinger is a Socratic figure; to this rhetorician, that is, at best, a left-handed compliment. Like Socrates, she is intensely passionate about moral issues and can generate a strong ethos and appeal. Also like Socrates, however, she demands that she control the conversation and set its terms, on the grounds that she knows best. As a rhetorician, I find that attitude a challenge that is impossible to let pass.

NOTES

1. Not least is the difficulty of obtaining a material record of the artifact on which to base scholarly references. Transcripts are often difficult or impossible to obtain; usually the only route open to the scholar analyzing live television or radio events is to find research money to build a library of representative material. This strategy is difficult to follow in the case of a breaking event such as Schlessinger's remarks on gays.

2. In addition to the problem of capturing the artifact, a second problem is adequately conveying the artifact in its original medium. A text can be quoted, but a visual or aural effect must be transcribed or described in text. The technological advances in computer-mediated communication in recent years might one day mean that scholarly multimedia journals could become possible.

The scholarly problem with transcription is that the richness of the oral performance is lost, and the textuality of what was originally an extemporaneous oral performance can exaggerate the stylistic differences between speaking and writing. To me, this problem is noticeable in the transcriptions of Schlessinger's monologues, which flatten her performative ethos and make her sound ill-spoken because of the fidelity of transcription to oral hitches and repetitions that the ear in the moment forgives more easily than the eye on the page.

3. Hence the Internet publication of nude photographs of her by a former mentor and lover who became disgusted by her moral posturing. Her detractors claimed the photographs proved her hypocrisy, but that charge was ineffective with her supporters. Schlessinger had already talked, although not in detail, about how she had taken wrong paths when she was younger. The nude photographs were easily incorporated into that theme.

4. *Agendized* might be a coinage of Schlessinger's; I have not yet encountered the term in other places.

5. StopDrLaura.com lists 22 corporate sponsors who withdrew.

6. A sample posted on StopDrLaura.com: "Albertson's is committed to embracing diversity in its many forms. . . . Once we learned that we were inadvertently advertising on the Dr. Laura show, we directed the media buying service to pull our advertising from this program."

7. For a performance that is clearly an attack on Schlessinger's ethos, see the photo depicting her at http://www.stopdrlaura.com/

8. Her acceptance of a biological model of evolution is not necessarily also Darwinian, if Darwinian is to be interpreted as random rather than divinely influenced propagation of the species. See Ronald L. Numbers' (1998) *Darwinism Comes to America* for a discussion of the varieties of religious interpretations of evolution.

9. Schlessinger gives no credence to studies showing that children of gays develop no differently from those of heterosexual couples; she considers them to be politically motivated junk science.

10. Smith and Windes (2000), in *Progay/Antigay*, note the tension within the gay community between (a) an essentialist position that characterizes homosexuality as a natural condition and argues a civil-rights style social equality argument and (b) a radical critique of all essentialized sexual roles, heterosexual included, that argues for the liberatory value of difference.

REFERENCES

Aravosis, J. (2000). *Stop Dr. Laura: A coalition against hate*. Retrieved February 16, 2006, from http://StopDrLaura.com/home.htm

Aristotle. (1954). *Rhetoric* (W. Rhys Roberts, Trans.). New York: Modern Library.

Augustine. (1992). *Confessions* (H. Chadwick, Trans.). Oxford, England: Oxford University Press.

Burke, K. (1966). *Language as symbolic action: Essays on life, literature, and method*. Berkeley: University of California Press.

Campbell, J. A. (1998, Summer). Rhetorical theory in the twenty-first century: A neo-classical perspective. *Southern Communication Journal, 63*(4), 291–308.

Canadian Broadcast Standards Council. (2000, February 9 & 15). *Appendix B to CFYI-AM and CJCH-AM re the Dr. Laura Schlessinger Show*. Retrieved March 20, 2006, from http://www.cbsc.ca/english/decisions/decisions/2000/000510bappendix.htm

Canadian Broadcast Standards Council Ontario Regional Council and Atlantic Regional Council. (2000). *CFYI-AM re the Dr. Laura Schlessinger Show (CBSC Decision 99/00-0005) and CJCH-AM re the Dr. Laura*

Schlessinger Show (CBSC Decisions 98/99-0808, 1003, and 1137). Retrieved February 16, 2006, from http://www.cbsc.ca/english/decisions/decisions/2000/000510.htm

Confessore, N. (2000). Boycotts will be boycotts. *American Prospect, 11*. Retrieved from the *American Prospect Online Edition* Web site: http://www.prospect.org/web/page.ww?section=root&name=ViewPrint&articleId=4246

Garry, J. M. (2001, July 9). *Letter: A gay and lesbian organization responds to Dr. Laura.* Retrieved from the TIME.com Web site: http://www.time.com/time/nation/printout/0,8816,49395,00.htm

Lindsay, S. A. (1998). *Implicit rhetoric: Kenneth Burke's extension of Aristotle's concept of entelechy.* Lanham, MD: University Press of America.

McDowell, J. (2000, July 3). Preacher, teacher, nag: Dr. Laura speaks her mind. *Time, 156*, 59–60.

Numbers, R. L. (1998). *Darwinism comes to America.* Cambridge, MA: Harvard University Press.

Olson, K. M., & Goodnight, G. T. (1994). Entanglements of consumption, cruelty, privacy, and fashion: The social controversy over fur. *Quarterly Journal of Speech, 80*, 249–276.

Perelman, C., & Olbrechts-Tyteca, L. (1969). *The new rhetoric: A treatise on argumentation* (J. Wilkinson & P. Weaver, Trans.). London: University of Notre Dame Press.

Plato. (1956). *Phaedrus* (W. C. Hembold & W. G. Rabinowitz, Trans.). Upper Saddle River, NJ: Prentice Hall.

Schlessinger, L. (2000a, May 3). Dr. Laura discusses her views on child rearing (Interview). *Larry King Live*. Retrieved March 20, 2006, from the CNN Web site: http://transcripts.cnn.com/TRANSCRIPTS/0005/03/lkl.00.html

Schlessinger, L. (2000b, August 15). *Laura Schlessinger on . . . defending her anti-gay comments*. Retrieved February 16, 2006, from the Gay and Lesbian Alliance Against Defamation, Inc., Web site: http://www.glaad.org/publications/resource_doc_detail.php?id=2822&

Shriver, M. (2000). *Which way for Dr. Laura?* Retrieved March 18, 2006, from the Topica.com Web site: http://lists.topica.com/lists/drlaura/read/message.html?sort=a&mid=801163825

Smith, R. R., & Windes, R. R. (1997). The progay and antigay issue culture: Interpretation, influence, and dissent. *Quarterly Journal of Speech, 83*(1), 28–48.

Smith, R. R., & Windes, R. R. (2000). *Progay/antigay: The rhetorical war over sexuality.* Thousand Oaks, CA: Sage.

Ware, B. L., & Linkugel, W. A. (1973). They spoke in defense of themselves: On the generic criticism of *apologia. Quarterly Journal of Speech, 59*, 273–283.

Discussion Questions

1. Evaluate Turpin's rhetorical analysis of Dr. Laura's argumentative strategies in defense of her remarks about homosexuality.

   • Identify key aspects of his analysis and evaluate the evidence he uses to support his claims.

   • In the light of previous chapters, are there other ways of analyzing this controversy that would offer additional insight? Identify and discuss.

2. Schlessinger argues that anyone who does not oppose something endorses it. What examples does she give to support this? Do you agree with this argument? Why or why not?

14

Disciplining the Transgendered

Brandon Teena, Public Representation, and Normativity

JOHN M. SLOOP

How can we have a discussion of how much sex and gender diversity actually exists in society, when all the mechanisms of legal and extralegal repression render our lives invisible?

—Leslie Feinberg (1996, 102)

Re-envisioning rhetoric as a constructor of gender rather than as constructed by gender is an essential step toward . . . liberation.

—Celeste M. Condit (1997, 110)

The core of the story of Brandon Teena is fascinating enough, and emotional enough, that most people remember its outline with very little prompting. This story was retold repeatedly and widely, in local newspapers, as well as in *The Village Voice* and *Playboy*. It has been the subject of a true crime book, multiple web sites, a play, a documentary

SOURCE: Versions of this chapter were presented at the Second Biennial Feminism(s) and Rhetoric(s) Conference in Minneapolis (October 1999) and at the Southern States Communication Association Conference in New Orleans (April 2000), and it was published in the *Western Journal of Communication* (vol. 64, no. 2). Copyright © 2000 Western States Communication Association. Reprinted by permission.

Author's Note: The author would like to thank David Henry, the anonymous reviewers, Carole Blair, Bonnie Dow, and, most notably, Sarah Projansky. This chapter is dedicated to Brandon Teena.

film (*The Brandon Teena Story*), a feature film (*Boys Don't Cry*), and the first on-line Guggenheim art project.[1] The bare bones of the story, *as recounted through mass mediated outlets,* go something like this: Brandon Teena (born Teena Brandon)[2] was a 21 year old woman who moved from Lincoln, Nebraska, where she had been "living as a man," to the smaller town of Falls City, Nebraska in late 1993.[3] While Brandon's move was prompted by a number of brushes with the law based on his tendency to forge checks and use credit cards without permission, it was also a move that allowed Brandon a fresh start with a male identity in a community where he had no history as a woman. In little time, Brandon found a circle of friends and, as he had done in Lincoln, began dating several of the women in that circle, with many of them reporting later that Brandon was the "ideal man." His financial problems continued, however, and Brandon was once again arrested for check cashing fraud. During a court appearance on that charge, Brandon was served with another warrant for a check fraud case in Lincoln. This time, though, the warrant was issued using Brandon Teena's birth (female) name, and he was jailed as a female. It was with this arrest that the Falls City community, including Brandon's friends, became aware that Brandon was "really" a woman.

Confusion about Brandon's gender in Falls City continued, however, if only because there were so many stories circulating about what Brandon "really was," in part because of Brandon's own use of multiple narratives and in part because so many women claimed intimate knowledge of his "maleness." Perhaps, some argued, Brandon was a hermaphrodite, perhaps he had an accident as a child, or perhaps he was at some stage in the process of a female to male transition. Whatever the case, given Brandon's success with the local women, his "true" gender was a matter of great concern to his friends, especially the men. Regardless of what theory people held about Brandon, his presence provided a clear case of gender trouble in the local community, although none of those involved had much interest in celebrating gender or sexual fluidity.

Events took a much uglier turn while Brandon was attending a party on Christmas Eve. While most of those at the party celebrated the holidays, two of Brandon's male friends—Tom Nissen and John Lotter—decided to clear up any ambiguity by forcing Brandon to reveal his genitals. Discovering that Brandon had a vagina, clearly marking him as a woman in Nissen and Lotter's eyes, the two forced Brandon to leave the party with them and proceeded to drive to a desolate area of town where each in turn raped him. Nissen and Lotter then returned to the party with Brandon, threatening to kill him if he reported the rapes. While acting as if he was washing up in the bathroom, Brandon locked the door and escaped through a window, making his way to the local police department to report the crime. A week later, with the rape "under investigation" by local authorities (who were skeptical of Brandon), Nissen and Lotter drove to the farmhouse where Brandon was staying with friends, and fatally shot him and two others living in the house. Nissen and Lotter were quickly arrested and, after a media saturated trial, Lotter was given a death sentence and Nissen life imprisonment (in exchange for testifying against Lotter).

The trial was covered widely in the local and national press both because of its unusual nature and because a large number of transgender activists made appearances in and outside of the courthouse. As a result, the story of Brandon Teena's life and death provides a large body of discourse that reflects public discussions of sex, gender, sexuality, and transgenderism.[4] It is a story that begs cultural reflection on gender, sexuality, and the possibilities of public performance. Given the topic and the rather large body of discourse the case produced, it is an ideal case through which one can investigate, as Lauren Berlant would suggest, one area of ideological tension over identities within the American landscape (1, 4).

Historically, cases of gender ambiguity brought on by public disclosure of transgenderism or hermaphroditism have marked ongoing transitions in the meaning of gender within a given cultural context (see, e.g., Garber 11, Holden, Dreger 6). Indeed, Alice Dreger notes that the entire "history of hermaphroditism is largely the history of struggles over the 'realities' of sex—the nature of 'true' sex, the proper roles of the sexes, the question of what sex can, should, or must mean" (15). While the Brandon Teena case is not about hermaphroditism[5] (although hermaphroditism does get invoked), the quantity of discourse that surrounds the case can be read as a site through which we can see public understandings of the "true" meaning of sex, a location at which we might learn something about the struggle over gender as it takes place in a contemporary, and mass mediated, cultural context. Before I provide a reading of the discourse surrounding this case and illustrate the case's articulation through a particular gender/sex ideology, I will lay out my assumptions regarding gender, rhetoric, and cultural/critical politics.

PERFORMATIVITY, GENDER DIVERSITY, AND CRITICAL RHETORIC

As has become commonplace in many contemporary discussions of gender and sexuality, at least since the publication of Judith Butler's *Gender Trouble*, gender and sexuality are assumed in this chapter to be potentially fluid, held into check by each individual's interpellation into a cultural ideology that maintains male-female differences. That is, gender is taken here to be performative, at least within the "the forced reiteration of norms" (*Gender* 94–5). While Butler's work focuses on both the ways in which gender normativity is tightly bound by cultural logics and the ways that subversion of these logics may take place, a

great deal of critical work that takes a performative position on gender has focused on cases of gender transgression (e.g., transgenderism, drag) to understand how gender might be destabilized. Marjorie Garber, for example, sees transsexualism as a confirmation of the constructedness of gender, and as a result, as tied to the deconstruction of the male-female sexual binarism and of heterosexual normativity (110), and, in a recent special issue of *GLQ* devoted to transgenderism, editor Susan Stryker notes that "transgender phenomena emerge from and bear witness to the epistemological rift between gender signifiers and their signifieds" (147). In noting that transgenderism can be aligned with queer politics, Stryker acknowledges that transgendered bodies and logics can work to deconstruct those binaries (149).[6] Further, in the introduction to their early '90s volume, Julia Epstein and Kristina Straub note that ambiguous gender identities "offer a point at which social pressure might be applied to effect a reevaluation of binary thinking" (4). In such works we are rightly pointed to the ways transgendered phenomena and queered ideologies could *potentially* work to loosen, to make fluid, gender binaries and heteronormativity.

While this move to celebrate or highlight potential disruptions of the gender binary system is indeed a vital project, it can come at the cost of focusing on ways that the dominant rhetoric/discourse of gender continues to ideologically constrain. As a rhetorical and cultural critic interested in the politics of *doxa*, I am more interested in the disciplinary side of the coin—the ways in which, using the words of Ronald Greene, public arguments are based on logics of articulation that work materially to make possible "the ability to judge and plan reality"(21).[7] Hence, while cases of gender ambiguity obviously have the potential to cause "gender trouble" and disrupt bigender normativity, in terms of the "dominant" discussions that surround such cases, critics would also be well served by thinking through the ways that the "loosening of gender binarisms" is a potential that often goes unrealized for many audiences.[8] Hence, even if we hold Butler's position that gender is performative, that sex is always already gendered, we must still pay careful attention to the fact that, in public discourse (*doxa*), a major assumption still stands that individuals are, at base, "sexed." Public discourses concerning cases such as the Brandon Teena narrative—indeed, the reactions of the young men responsible for Brandon's death—are due in part to the fact that so many institutions and individuals work to stabilize sex, to reiterate sexual norms, rather than to encourage/explore gender fluidity.

As a result, in Butler's words, the discourse surrounding the Brandon Teena story should be read as a public iteration of sexual norms, as "a ritualized production, a ritual reiterated under and through constraint, under and through the force of prohibition and taboo, with the threat of ostracism and even death controlling and compelling the shape of the production" of gender and sexuality (*Bodies* 95). Hence, while not to deny the *potential* of the case to "loosen" cultural rules concerning gender, sex, and sexuality, I am approaching the Brandon Teena case as a site of the public stabilization of what Sabrina Ramet refers to as gender culture: "A society's understanding of what is possible, proper, and perverse in gender-linked behavior, and more specifically, that set of values, mores, and assumptions which establishes which behaviors are to be seen as gender-linked" (2). In this study, I am building a "critical rhetoric" narrative, a "gathering of fragments," concerning a case where gender trouble seemingly begs to lead to a transgression of gender barriers and heteronormativity.[9] While pointing out how gender is renormalized and reessentialized, I am borrowing the assumptions of the critical project of gender diversity outlined by Celeste Condit, a project that critiques gender dichotomy feminism for failing to see how gender is produced through discourse and for failing to see gender

and identity as mobile ("In Praise" 91). Ultimately, aligned with the performative turn in gender studies, Condit's project asks us to view rhetoric as a constructor of gender rather than as constructed by gender and to critique the ways public rhetorics meld gendered positions. Here, I take Condit's perspective on rhetoric and gender to the task of building a critical rhetoric narrative concerning the Brandon Teena case in order to critique a specific historical construction of gender.

Further, rather than attempt to comment about "transgendered" subjectivities or the experience of transgenderism, I discuss the case as it was represented in a variety of news outlets, placing my primary focus on discourses available on common library research databases (e.g., Lexis-Nexis) as well as Aphrodite Jones' *All She Wanted* (the true crime account of the case).[10] My focus is on "dominant" or commercial discourses rather than marginal or individual discourses for at least two reasons: As argued above, mainstream discourses illustrate the rhetorically material ways that those who do challenge dominant ideology are ideologically disciplined, the ways gender normativity is upheld. As Kate Bornstein notes, caricatures of transgendered people are "creeping into the arts and media" (59). These are the very caricatures I analyze in this chapter in asking, "How do nontransgendered people (who are not concerned with transgendered issues) configure transgenderism through mass mediated representations?"

Secondly, I keep my claims curtailed to mainstream rearticulations of gender norms because I want to be careful not to suggest that such a study explores transgenderism as a subjectivity. Hence, while I am sympathetic with Susan Stryker's claim that "It is no longer sufficient . . . to approach the topic as Marjorie Garber did in *Vested Interests*, where she proceeded solely by looking at transsexuals and transvestites and the cultural gaze that both constructs and regards them, with absolutely no concern for transgender subjectivity" (148), I take Stryker's claim to concern the critical community as a whole. That is, I assume that some readings of the case will be interested in the politics of transgendered subjectivity while others, such as this one, should focus on the constraints of the public rhetoric *about* transgenderism. In short, I utilize the public discussion surrounding this case to understand one dimension of gender ideology in contemporary culture and not the position of transgendered people in contemporary culture.[11]

In the following sections of the chapter, I provide a critical reading of mainstream discourses and argue that this is a case of ideological discipline in which Brandon Teena's gender is tied back into "sex." Again, regardless of a theoretical assumption that sees sex as always gendered or "discoursed," in mainstream public discourses, a transgendered person becomes a foil in which the presuppositions of the gender and sexual norms of contemporary culture are reiterated and reaffirmed, in which ritual and taboo operate to assure this. This reaffirmation of norms takes place in a number of ways. First, by telling the story through a narrative concentrating on *deception*, most news stories represent Brandon as a "real" woman who was intentionally posing as a man in order to fool others. Second, news reports and public narratives reify the physicality of Brandon Teena's body (including what Brandon does with the body) as following traditional male-female heterosexual activities. While Brandon's body is clearly marked as female, Brandon's use of the body is marked as a successful performance of masculinity. Third, popular cultural discussions of the causes of Brandon's transgenderism explain the body/psyche of Brandon Teena as a caused abnormality that could have been prevented had Brandon been given proper physical and emotional care as a child. Finally, discussions of Brandon's body as either hermaphroditic or as in preparation for a surgical female-to-male transition reveal a cultural

impulse to work the body into a traditionally sexed position and to align genitalia (sex) with "true gender."

Each of these themes works by positing Brandon's body and behavior as simultaneously familiar and alien, and, in this way, the overall representation reifies heteronormativity. That is, because Brandon's behaviors and appearance are illustrated as strikingly and familiarly masculine, the behavior of the women attracted to him can be configured as a "normal" expression of healthy heterosexuality. Simultaneously, because Brandon's "alien" desires and gender deception are ultimately revealed, we learn that in the end no one can fool the gender binary system. Each of the themes discussed below highlights the ideology of gender and sexuality in contemporary culture, laying bare the ways that transgenderism and gender fluidity continue to be disciplined back into binary norms.

DECEPTION IN THE HEARTLAND

Consistently, reports tell the story of Brandon Teena as, at base, the story of "deception in the heartland," a story of how a young woman deceived others about her gender in the pursuit of her own desires. A cursory glance at the titles and subtitles of accounts of the case alone starkly makes this point. The subtitle of Aphrodite Jones' account is "A True Story of Sexual Deception and Murder in America's Heartland." The movie poster for the film, *The Brandon Teena Story*, called the film "A true story of love, hate, and revenge in the Heartland of America" ("Zeitgeist"). A lengthy report in the *Omaha World Herald* was entitled "Romance, Deceit and Rage" (Burbach and Cordes) while another in *The Des Moines Register* was "Charade Revealed Prior to Killings" (Fruhling 1). *The Advocate* used the title "Heartland Homicide: Smalltown Nebraska life was fine for a 21 year old man—until everyone discovered he was actually a woman" for its first major article on the case

(Ricks) and entitled its shorter follow-up "Deception on the Prairie" ("Deception"). A one act play that dealt with the case was named "Murder in the Heartland" (Delmont) and, finally, *Playboy* entitled its essay "Death of a Deceiver" (Konigsberg).

When told that one is about to hear a story of "deception," one expects a story with something sinister afoot, a story of a predator who successfully preys on others by keeping them from the truth. Indeed, deception implies the intent to make truth out of appearance. In this case, deception is a term that logically favors fixed notions of sex/gender over an ideology of gender fluidity. While there are multiple ways one could logically tell this story such that Brandon's gender would not be seen as deceptive (e.g., one could argue that gender or masculinity is performative, hence making Brandon male because he performed masculinity), the reports of this case, both those sympathetic and those unsympathetic to Brandon's position, clearly portray the story as one of deception. Given the prominence of the deception narrative, other potential ways of thinking about gender and gender identity are closed off. To say that Brandon was "deceiving others" (and was caught in the act of deception) is to say that Brandon knew he was a woman but wanted others to really think of him as a man. The deception narrative implies that Brandon actively lied to others, hiding what she knew to be her "true" sex, and acts within a traditional iteration of gender norms and desires that ultimately serves to protect and reaffirm the normative heterosexist ways of making sense of gender and of disciplining gender trouble.[12]

Obviously, a case involving a transgendered person like Brandon Teena, who was attractive to self-identified heterosexual women as a sexual partner and to heterosexual men as a friend, is interesting as a potential case of gender trouble and confusion. However, it is on the grounds of familiarity (i.e., she appeared male) and alienation (i.e., we were deceived by

her) that the story is told, hence reifying rather than troubling gender norms. In short, as the examples below illustrate, rather than make sex and gender identity "messy," the story as told configures Brandon as a woman based on genitalia alone.[13] Aphrodite Jones, for example, quotes Michelle Lotter, sister of one of Brandon's murderers, as saying that she believed Brandon's "deceptive" behavior indicated that she was lesbian and that the two men murdered her because both were "angry after learning about Brandon's deception" (245).[14] Jones further notes that on the *Maury Povitch Show*, Brandon was described as a woman who "posed as a man" (258). A press release for the film *The Brandon Teena Story* noted that "the catalyst for the murders was the sexual persona of Brandon Teena ... that Brandon was *actually* female, passing as a male and dating local women" ("Zeitgeist," emphasis mine). Chris Burbach and Henry Cordes describe Brandon Teena in the *Omaha World Herald* as "charmingly playing the role of a young man" (1A) and Burbach notes that Brandon's mother testified that Brandon "started portraying somebody that she wasn't"—a male (Burbach "Prosecutor Sees"). In a single article in the *Des Moines Register*, Larry Fruhling notes that "Brandon's *charade* ended in the bathroom of the small house with her trousers pulled down to her knees," "Brandon's *pretense* began unraveling," and "Brandon's *true* identity came to light" (emphases mine).

Eric Konigsberg observes in *Playboy* that "posing as a man gave Teena Brandon what she couldn't get as a woman—adoring girlfriends and a fiance. It also got her killed" (94). Not only does Konigsberg utilize the "female" birth name "Teena Brandon" throughout the article as Brandon's "real name," but he does so in the context of an article that makes it clear that Brandon was "posing" as male, again emphasizing gender as physically tied to genitalia (sex).[15] Konigsberg's explicitness about Brandon's "deception" is highlighted throughout the essay; Konigsberg notes, for example, that "Teena didn't seem to have trouble finding new people to *con*, new women to woo—women who desperately wanted to be charmed by a man who understood their needs. Her relationships were with girls whose ideal of a man had never been realized until they met Teena" (194).[16] Further, Konigsberg includes portions of an interview with murderer Tom Nissen in which Nissen said raping Brandon was an "ego thing. I felt like I'd been fucked. Me and Brandon had a long conversation that evening, and Brandon started to feed me another line." While clearly not offering an apology for the murderers, Konigsberg makes clear that the logic of deception was at work.[17]

The second half of this articulation—the Heartland in which the deception occurs—works metaphorically and semiotically to heighten the impact of the deception.[18] The coupling of *deception* with *heartland* encourages us to think of Brandon's transgressions as the corruption of innocence and normality. In that "the heartland" is understood as the "normal," "average," and most purely American segment of the nation, Brandon's deception of numerous young "midwestern" women is represented as particularly vile. Transgendered deception is more than the deception and corruption of individuals here; it is the deception and corruption of the heartland of America.

TEENA'S FEMALE BODY, BRANDON'S MASCULINE PERFORMANCE

Body, Play, and Clothing

Kate Bornstein argues that while there could potentially be "as many types of gender as could be imagined," Western society has culturally taken on "sex" (as in genitalia) as a sign of gender, and hence enables us to utilize visible cultural markers to make judgments about each other's sex and proper public behavior (30). Alice Dreger similarly observes

in her history of hermaphroditism that a "one body, one sex" logic has ensued over the last several centuries, with the presence or absence of gonads being determinate of gender/sex in the medical arena and the assumed presence or absence of gonads being the grounds on which proper gender behavior is judged publicly (109).[19] Indeed, rhetorically, gender still works along a male-female binarism in mediated accounts, and the discourse surrounding the Brandon Teena case illustrates that gender is tightly articulated with genitalia *on a rhetorical and ideological level*.[20] Discussions of Brandon's body continue to employ a sex-gender split with multiple reports pointing to the body of Brandon (i.e., the genitalia) as proof positive of Brandon's "femaleness" while simultaneously observing that Brandon's physical appearance and behavior were marked by masculine signifiers. Whether Brandon is represented as particularly adept at understanding how to act like a "natural man" or his masculine behavior is explained as a psychic or physical defect, Brandon is posited as "physically" a woman who learns (or is compelled by defects) to perform behaviors that are naturally those of men. By pointing out the genitalia that made Brandon "really" a woman and the activities that made Brandon "appear" to be a man, the signifiers of masculinity and femininity are reified, the binarisms held intact.

Here, then, I pay particular attention to those behaviors and physical features employed as evidence of Brandon's "masculinity" or Teena's "femaleness." I should emphasize that I am not questioning the veracity of the claims and observations being made (nor, of course, am I verifying them). Rhetorically, what is significant is that particular behaviors and signifiers are consistently reported and reified, whether they occurred or not, indicating the importance of these behaviors as elements of the iteration of gender norms within contemporary U.S. culture. In turn, I discuss the discourse that outlines Brandon's gender and genitalia, Brandon's behavior and aesthetic as a child and as an adult, his physical appearance as an adult, and, finally, his (heterosexual) physical activities.

First, then, examples of the coupling of Brandon Teena's "real" gender with Brandon Teena's genitalia are ubiquitous and work hand in hand with the deception metaphors discussed above. For example, when Aphrodite Jones opens her account of the case, she notes that Brandon had told a friend that "he was really a female, that he had female parts" (105). One of the most striking examples of the equation of gender with genitalia occurs when Jones reports that on the night when Brandon was eventually raped, Lotter and Nissen had become increasingly dissatisfied with Brandon's explanation as to his gender and "after awhile, . . . the guys decided they needed someone to see this guy's cock or else" (208). Elsewhere, *The Advocate* report on the case notes that Brandon was "actually a woman" (Ricks 28).[21] In each example, Brandon Teena is posited as having a "true" gender which could be evidenced by genitalia (in effect, the lack of a "cock") and a deceptive one (insolar as one cannot be male without a penis).

In terms of male/female activities, Brandon's behavior is often examined through references to his/her behavior/dress as a child. In general, when the story of Brandon's youth (as Teena Brandon) is recounted, it is a narrative that suggests that while Brandon was physically a girl and should have developed "feminine behaviors," he developed masculine behaviors as a result of an aberration (as I will discuss below). When Jones focuses on the story of Brandon's childhood and that of his sister, Tammy, she sets up a pattern of descriptions that persistently emphasizes the differences between Tammy's femininity and Brandon's masculinity. First, femininity and masculinity manifest in the clothes each liked to wear and in how each liked to play. While feminine Tammy decorated her room with stuffed animals and dolls, "Teena collected things—stop signs, beer signs, whatever" (32).

While Tammy wasn't especially fond of insects, one of Teena's favorite activities was to "place snakes in a lunch box and throw the snakes and a collection of bugs at Tammy" (32). While Tammy played with dolls, Teena "mostly played with sturdy things like Tinkertoys and Lincoln Logs. She liked to construct and destroy" (32). Tammy enjoyed wearing "frilly little flowered dresses and lace ankle socks; Teena was always in T-shirts, jogging shorts, and unsightly boy's tube socks, the kind trimmed with red and blue stripes" (33). Tammy wore makeup while Teena refused (33). While Teena was forced to wear dresses for pictures, she tried to tear them off (33–4). The *Omaha World Herald* observes that, as a child, Brandon "preferred playing with a garter snake to playing with a doll. She preferred taking an old radio apart to doing her hair. Rather than dress up, she would just as soon play basketball" (Burbach and Cordes).[22] Similarly, *Playboy's* Eric Konigsberg notes that Teena, "awkward and impish," rebelled against her school's dress code by "wearing pants and a tie. She kept her hair short and told people she was allergic to makeup. She was into weight lifting" (94). In *The New Yorker*, John Gregory Dunne repeats the snake stories told by others and adds that Brandon had a "secret desire" to become her school's quarterback (50). In each description, the details work to emphasize the signs of masculinity and femininity. It is not just that Tammy wanted to wear dresses, she wanted to wear "frilly, little flowered" dresses with lace ankle socks. Brandon did not simply want to wear shorts and T-shirts but jogging shorts and those "unsightly" tube socks with stripes. The masculinity here is one of spiders and snakes, beer and cars, and unsightly athleticism versus a femininity of frilly flowers and lacy ankles, domestic dolls and stuffed animals. Regardless of the "essential" or cultural assumption about gender being made by those describing it, the descriptions ultimately provide a reifying crystallization of cultural expectations of gender normativity.

Descriptions of Brandon as an adult also focus on specific clothing choices and body movements as signifying masculinity. For example, in terms of Brandon's style choices, Minkowitz observes that Brandon was buried in "men's clothing, wearing her favorite cowboy shirt and black cowboy hat" (24). Ingrid Ricks similarly notes that Brandon "dressed in men's clothing, often Western wear, and wore her dark brown hair close-cropped" (29). Dunne observes in the *New Yorker* that Brandon died dressed as a man, in "black Jockey-style underwear, sweat shorts, a sweatshirt, a T-shirt and sweat socks" (46). Whether rugged cowboy or jock, Brandon's clothing is consistently used to signify his masculinity.

In addition to his clothing, Brandon's physical appearance is articulated onto specific icons of American promiscuous masculinity. For example, Minkowitz notes that after Brandon arrived in Falls City, every young woman in town was "after this pool player with the jawline of a Kennedy" who gave gifts with "Elvis-esque extravagance" (24) and goes on to observe that in one photograph Brandon looked "like JFK, at once serious and mischievously conscious of his good looks" (26). Aphrodite Jones makes a similar observation when noting that when a young woman named Heather had her first kiss with Brandon, she did so because "she was bowled over by his slick crew cut and Kennedy jaw line" (58).[23]

Again, these descriptions of clothing and dress, coupled with the overall assumption of Brandon as deceiver, pick at a cultural concern with being "fooled" about "true gender." Rather than allowing for gender ambiguity or for a configuration in which Brandon was male because he identified as male, we are led to understand that Brandon was able to deceive because "she" so clearly utilized hypermasculine signifiers. As a whole, the discourse draws out the signifiers of masculinity to explain the gender confusion experienced by those who encountered Brandon Teena. As Marjorie Garber might note of this discourse,

It is as though the hegemonic cultural imaginary is saying to itself: if there is a difference, we want to be able to see it, and if we see a difference (e.g., man in women's clothes), we want to be able to interpret it. In both cases, the conflation is fueled by a desire to tell the difference, to guard against a difference that might otherwise put the identity of one's own position in question. (130)

Urination and Heterosexuality

This same ideological work to restabilize gender signifiers is evident in questions about Brandon's physical and sexual behaviors. In brief, physically, the signifiers of Brandon's masculinity as crystallized in public recountings of the case range from the way he urinated (standing, of course) to his heterosexual behavior with women. While Brandon is configured as a lesbian in some accounts of the case ("Fierce" 27), what is important here, and what I illustrate below, is that most discussion about the case provides a lens through which to see the expected "iteration" of masculinity and femininity within heterosexual expectations. Because the discourse explains how women were "deceived" by Brandon, it also implicitly reassures us that our readings of masculinity and femininity are generally correct.

Questions about the movements and appearance of Brandon's body are generally centered on questions of how those who were intimate with him were "deceived." Aphrodite Jones attempts to explain how Lana Tisdel, one of Brandon's last girlfriends, could have possibly thought that Brandon was "really" male; Jones notes that Tisdel claimed in conversations with others that she had indeed felt a penis when she had engaged in sexual relations with Brandon, and "she had sworn she'd seen Brandon stand up and pee . . . Even Tom (Nissen) had seen Brandon stand up and piss at one of the urinals at the Oasis [a local bar], so . . . that part of the story seemed real" (209). In the *New Yorker*, Dunne makes a similar observation: "Brandon moved from

Humboldt into Linda Gutierrez's house, and Lana Tisdel's bed. The sex was good, Lana reported, and Brandon stood up to pee" (54). Moreover, Donna Minkowitz notes that women told each other that Brandon had a penis because they had "seen him pee!" (28). What is important here is the impulse for those writing about the case to explain how the "difference" between male and femaleness was missed. As Lacan notes about "urinary segregation," despite all the differences that males have with each other, and despite all the differences that females have with each other, we culturally take the act of urination to signify that in this act, all men are equal, as are all women (cited in Garber 13–17). That Brandon's "standing up to pee" is so often raised in the discourse of the case works simultaneously both to destabilize urination as a marker of the essentiality of gender and to reaffirm its status as one way such difference is publicly signified. That is, the evidence is raised to explain how women were fooled, hence destabilizing the sign, but simultaneously reaffirms that it is one way to keep gender straight and binary. Moreover, while Brandon may have been able to use this signifier to "deceive" his peers for a time, in the end, the story reveals, the truth of gender wins out.

Somewhat similar observations can be made of the coverage of Brandon's sexual relations and the way his physical relations with women troubled heterosexual norms. Regarding contemporary observations that heterosexuality has "made a comeback" in popular culture, Lauren Berlant notes that "Nowhere in the United States has heterosexuality gone into a decline or 'left' in a way that makes the idea of a comeback even remotely possible" (16). The discourse surrounding this case highlights the ways the assumption of heterosexuality continues as a dominant theme in popular culture. In particular, this is so not because Brandon's sexuality is denigrated (or even the primary focus) but more because one of the primary implied themes of the discussion is the protection of the sexual identity and *sexuality* identity of those "fooled" by Brandon. In protecting the "deceived," the discourse protects cultural norms as a whole, assuring all of us that the iteration of compulsory heterosexuality remains stable regardless of the misidentifications in this particular case. Rather than Brandon and his partners being positioned as engaged in queer or transgendered sexuality, the public discussion persistently confirms that those who were engaged in sexual relations with Brandon were themselves practicing what they thought to be normal heterosexuality. Again, referring to Marjorie Garber's claim that the desire to see and know gender differences is an impulse fueled by a desire "to guard against a difference that might otherwise put the identity of one's own position in question" (130), this public discussion upholds normalized iterations of heterosexuality. While I do not want to discount the possibility that for particular individuals the case destabilizes gender identity and sexual desire by recognizing that heterosexual masculinity is performative, I do want to suggest that the case works discursively to protect heterosexuality both by allowing Brandon's "girlfriends" to remain heterosexual and by emphasizing that Brandon's "lack" ultimately undermines the heterosexual masculine performance. Brandon's temporarily successful performance of heterosexual masculinity does not destabilize gender binarism or heterosexuality because it ultimately does not trouble masculinity or femininity.

Marjorie Garber notes that in public discussions of the case that inspired M. *Butterfly*, the one question that was raised repeatedly, almost obsessively, in the public sphere concerned sexual relations between the two men: "What did they do in bed?" (236). This same fascination predictably follows Brandon and his paramours: not only "what did they do in bed," but "how were the women persuaded to get into bed with Brandon in the first place?"

This question is most generally answered in narrative form, a story beginning with a discussion of Brandon's dating behavior. Repeatedly, Brandon is referred to as the perfect gentleman, the ideal man, with this ideal masculinity being drawn within heterosexual romance narratives. Aphrodite Jones quotes Heather, Brandon's first girlfriend, as observing that Brandon would be any woman's dream guy: "He knew how a woman wanted to be treated. . . . He took you out to dinner, bought flowers, roses, just everything" (61). Jones also observes that Brandon's one time finacé asserted that Brandon was the "perfect gentleman," always taking her out to eat, opening doors for her, and never allowing her to pay for anything (100). The *Denver Post* observes that numerous people described Brandon as "a dream suitor. She [*sic*] showered them with gifts, showed them respect and swept them off their feet" (Will).[24] The *San Francisco Chronicle* begins a story by observing that "There wasn't much that Brandon Teena didn't know about pleasing a woman. His girlfriends praised his courtliness, his sweetness, his generosity" (Guthman). Even Brandon's "less gentlemanly moments" are consistently described by those women quoted as behaviors that made him "a normal guy." Jones quotes one of his girlfriends as saying Brandon "was a pervert, just a regular guy, always making jokes" (126). In *The Advocate*, Brandon's final girlfriend (Lana Tisdel) notes that Brandon "was like a normal guy. He talked like one; he acted like one" (Ricks 29). In each case, we learn that Brandon was successfully able to seduce women because he was able to so successfully perform heterosexual masculinity.

Furthermore, because so many women reported having sex with Brandon, the performance of the act itself is a matter of obvious conflict throughout the discourse. Once again, Brandon is posited both as the perfect man (i.e., the familiar—his attention was on the women without pressure) and as simultaneously

not a man (i.e., the lack of a penis). Jones notes that one young woman claimed to have received her first orgasm from Brandon during oral sex and quotes others remarking on Brandon's stamina during intercourse (269–270). Konigsberg notes that Brandon provided many of the women with their first impression of "What all the fuss was about," that sex was not simply something to be done for their boyfriends (194). Konigsberg quotes one woman as observing that, after her first time with Brandon, "'I don't think there was a time with him when I didn't come,' the girl said, 'orally, going all the way, even dry humping.'" (194). Further, Dunne relays stories from women who claimed to have to go on the pill because of sex with Brandon (51) and Minkowitz observes that "every former girlfriend . . . said Brandon was "'the best lover' they ever had" (24).

This consistently repeated evidence of Brandon's sexual prowess and success could obviously complicate normative understandings of gender and sexuality. However, the irony that the ideal man had female genitalia, an irony that could destabilize gendered meanings, ultimately works instead to reify them. Rather than stress gender trouble, the body of discourse consistently suggests that heterosexual women were fooled because Brandon performed masculinity so well. It is significant, then, that many of Brandon's girlfriends are quoted as noting that Brandon was able to deceive them sexually either because he used a dildo or because he performed oral sex without reciprocation. For example, Dunne observes that Brandon's early girlfriends thought he was an expert kisser and that they could have sex with him and think he was a male because he either "stuffed socks into his shorts" or would "wear a dildo" (50). The problem again is one of maintaining strict boundaries between male and female while leaving heterosexuality untroubled. While Brandon's sexual success cannot help but somewhat trouble gender normativity, public discussion of the case maintains that the women are fooled and hence were, in their own minds, performing heterosexuality, and that Brandon's deception would ultimately be discovered.

We find a number of examples of ways the women who had sex with Brandon are allowed to "confess" their heterosexuality after the fact, redeeming themselves rather than rethinking sexuality and gender as performative. Because the deception metaphors discussed earlier work to protect heteronormativity for those who were "fooled" by Brandon, they should also logically indicate potential lesbianism on Brandon's part (i.e., Brandon fooled others into thinking he was a man when he was actually a woman having sex with other women). However, not only is Brandon's voice recuperated to ward off lesbianism, but so are those of the women who slept with him. In the clearest example of this configuration, Lana Tisdel is quoted in Minkowitz' article as repeating two mantras to help her understand the experience: "1. When I kissed Brandon, I wasn't kissing a woman, I was kissing a man; 2. Brandon didn't love the way a woman loves a woman, he loved me the way a man loves a woman" (27). Minkowitz skeptically notes that while Tisdel cannot explain what difference such a mantra meant, she adamantly wanted to be considered heterosexual (27). Minkowitz also observes that Brandon's former fiancé, Gina Bartu, "freaked out" when she was in a gay bar with Brandon and had the sense that people might think she and Brandon were a lesbian couple (26). The only sexual configuration allowed in such discourse is a heterosexual one; there is no fluidity in these descriptions. In a sense, as has been illustrated throughout this section, the only two options that appear to be allowed are based on gender binarism rather than on, for example, Kate Bornstein's description of stylistic differences which would configure Brandon and his girlfriends as something other than either homosexual or heterosexual (32).

While Brandon's girlfriends are protected from the lesbian label because of the deception narrative, Brandon's desires could easily be coded as lesbian ones. However, Brandon's fear of, and disgust with, lesbianism is reported repeatedly, reaffirming his own investment in gender binarisms. Jones reports that Brandon once had a confrontation with her mother over her sexual identity, and Brandon insisted that lesbians were "disgusting" (68–69).[25] Burbach and Cordes note in the *Omaha World Herald* that Brandon's mother observed that Brandon "told me she wasn't a lesbian and was very adamant about that. She didn't want to be with a female in that way." Konigsberg notes that Brandon did not attend "gay parties" if many lesbians would be attending because Brandon found them disgusting (193). Minkowitz pursues this theme strongly, noting both that Brandon had told a high school classmate that she was "disgusted by lesbians" and that she was going to "love women like a man" (28). While it is certainly the case that the idea rarely arises, as Hale observes, "that the words female bodied and woman might not be coextensive with regard to some people's self-identifications" ("Consuming" 315), here all the evidence brought to bear is situated to work firmly within gender binaries and heteronormativity. Given a paucity of ways to think, the potentially transgressive and blurry configuration of Brandon's gender/sexuality is ultimately tied down in binarisms as is his sexuality (i.e., Brandon is homosexual if we take the body as gender and heterosexual if we take into account her self-identity). There is no public blurring of sexuality and identity; it is clearly one or the other for both Brandon and Brandon's partners in the configuration allowed by public discourse. What we have seen to be the case with play, clothing, and style, then, is true of sexuality as well—the discourse around Brandon Teena's sexual activities and desires reactivates heterosexual norms.

BRANDON'S BODY: ATTITUDE
OF A HERMAPHRODITE[26]

Marjorie Garber notes that it is paradoxically the case that transsexuals and transvestites are more concerned with maleness and femaleness than persons who are neither transvestite nor transsexual (110). While I have illustrated this to be the case in the discourse alleged to have been spoken by Brandon Teena and the public discourse about Brandon Teena's activities and appearance, another interesting aspect of this case concerns the way Brandon's troubled body is talked about—both by Brandon (reported) and by others. In the multiple narratives of the case, stories consistently recount times when someone "discovered" that Brandon did not have a typical male body, placing Brandon in a position of having to explain what "he was." Either because Brandon actually thought in these terms or because the pressure of his audience forced him to speak in these terms (or because those reporting the case could only work within certain dynamics), Brandon is reported to have consistently discussed his body in such a way that he clearly saw the penis as the marker of "maleness" or manhood. Brandon's two responses—to posit himself as an hermaphrodite or as a preoperative transsexual—focus on the penis and its importance to being a man. I should point out that while Brandon's words as quoted seem to have more of a transgressive tone to them, at times indicating his own ability to see a disjuncture between body and identity, the reports about the case generally push back in a direction in which body and identity are articulated together.

Given a lack of vocabulary to describe oneself as "transgendered," Brandon reportedly described himself on more than one occasion as a hermaphrodite awaiting surgery (Dunne reports that Brandon got the idea from an episode of *Montel Williams*) (50). Jones notes that Brandon told Heather, his first girlfriend, that "he was a hermaphrodite, born with both

sexes, that he was raised as a female" and was planning on having an operation to make himself completely male (63; see also Ricks 29). *The Omaha World Herald* observes that "When questioned about her sexuality, Miss Brandon told people she was a hermaphrodite, a person with both male and female sex organs" (Burbach and Cordes; see also Wheelwright).[27] Further, Dunne notes that this was the same story Brandon told his earliest girlfriends (50; see also Minkowitz 25) and that each time, he made it clear that he would someday become completely male. Alice Dreger notes that modern medicine has developed an attitude about hermaphroditism that forces hermaphroditic bodies into one of the two "natural" sex categories based on particular aspects of what the person has (the "one body–one sex" rule).[28] Evidently, in the case of Brandon Teena, this understanding translated into his own need to confine his body to one sex rather than to understanding gender itself as fluid or as not related directly to the body. If that body was hermaphroditic rather than female, Brandon could take the attitude with others that the body was genuinely male, that it came equipped with a "real" penis.

The second explanation offered about Brandon Teena's gender is that he was a preoperative transsexual. Jones, for instance, notes that when his *mother* told his first girlfriend that he was neither a male nor a hermaphrodite, Brandon confessed he felt like a man inside and wanted to have a full sex change operation (81). Perhaps more telling culturally, many news articles began their discussion of the case with a biography of Brandon Teena that states this preoperative narrative as fact. For example, one story begins, "Brandon Teena, whose birth name was Teena Brandon, was originally from Lincoln, Nebraska, and moved to nearby Humboldt in 1993, shortly after beginning to live full-time as a man in preparation for eventual sex-change surgery" (despite the fact that Brandon is never reported to have had solid plans to have surgery) ("Brandon Teena Murderer"). Burbach and Cordes note that Brandon told people "She was a transsexual in the process of getting a sex change." Further, Ed Will observes in the *Denver Post* that Brandon told others that she was either "considering or had had sex-change surgery" while Konigsberg notes that Brandon called himself a preoperative transsexual and claimed he was having trouble raising the funds to complete the operation (see also Minkowitz 26). Jay Carr of the *Boston Globe* takes the claim that Brandon was in the process of a sex change as factual, noting that Brandon had "begun a series of sex-change operations by the time she moved from Lincoln" (see also "Best").

In short, both the hermaphrodite and preoperative discourses put heavy focus on the penis as a natural sign of masculinity and malehood, reinscribing the gender-as-sex ideology. Whether positing himself as a hermaphrodite or as a preoperative transsexual, Brandon Teena, and reports about Brandon Teena, work within the same gender constraints that we all are faced with. To be male demands the presence of a penis, and Brandon was metaphorically adding one with either rhetorical strategy.

THE CAUSES OF ABERRATION

In her history of hermaphroditism, Alice Dreger notes that while hermaphrodites' mothers have traditionally been considered by medical personnel to be "poor witnesses with regard to the 'sex' behavior of their 'doubtful' children, they were frequently expected to account for the deformity in their offspring," to explain the cause of the unnatural body (71). What is significant, as transgender activists continually point out, is that hermaphroditism is *natural* in the sense that it is the "natural body" a person is born with.[29] Hence, surgical changes to a body to make it more closely resemble a male or female body could logically be seen as acts of deformation.

In similar fashion, one could argue that Brandon Teena's identity and desire are as "natural" as anyone else's. Nonetheless, in the case of Brandon Teena, multiple threads work to configure Brandon's transgendered body as an aberration, a mistake that could have been prevented. In general, bodies are forced into male/female categories; once in these categories, they either need to properly perform (i.e., perform according to gender norms) or the search is on for the causes of their "malfunction." This is precisely what occurs in discussions of Brandon's body. While few of the essays and articles surrounding the case make an explicit claim to understand the "cause" of Brandon's sexual identity, it is an underlying theme throughout. While one would never expect to find attempts to explain the cause of a person's heterosexuality, the "cause" of Brandon's gender and sexuality ambiguity is discussed as a matter of routine.

In the most general terms, Brandon's "transgenderism" is posited as resulting from either a chemical/physical imbalance (e.g., "extra hormone shots during pregnancy") or from psychosexual abuse at an early age. In both cases, Brandon's mother is at least partially implicated as part of the problem that led to Brandon's "condition." In terms of a chemical imbalance, Aphrodite Jones at several points suggests that problems during Brandon's gestation may have been the cause of his nontraditional desires. Jones quotes Brandon's mother JoAnn as saying that during the early portion of her pregnancy with Teena, the uterus was not growing at a sufficient rate and had not "tipped" as it was supposed to, so her doctor "gave me hormone shots or something, and they were so thick, a thick serum. . . . I went through this for two weeks, and then she started to grow" (27). As this telling of the story unfolds, it becomes obvious that one way of reading the story, of understanding Brandon's aberrant condition, is to see it as resulting as a mistake in the hormone process. If Brandon had been able to grow as the body intended, this condition would not have occurred.

Secondly, there are a number of intimations of Brandon's having been sexually abused as a child with this abuse linked to her transgenderism. Jones claims that Brandon disclosed this sexual abuse to his first girlfriend (63) and that, during a therapy session after a suicide attempt, told the counselors about "hours of sexual abuse in her childhood and adolescence, saying that she felt intimidated by certain men, that she always felt sexually orientated toward women" (83). Minkowitz quotes Brandon's sister Tammy as asserting that Brandon was unhappy as a woman because "we were both molested by a male relative when we were little" (29). JoAnn, Brandon's mother, upon hearing about the sexual abuse during the counseling sessions, is reported by Jones as observing that the abusive relative had "destroyed Teena, and that was why Teena wasn't interested in men" (86). Konigsberg also situates the story of Brandon's having been raped and abused at the center of her transgenderism (193). Dunne, in perhaps the clearest example of this form of causal reasoning, makes note of Brandon's sexual molestation and observes that somewhere in all this, "there might be an early clue, a *first cause*, a reason that would make Teena's subsequent ventures across the gender divide easier to accommodate" (italics mine, 50).

Whether chemical or psychological, rather than taking Brandon's identity as "natural," we see here a search for the cause of the anomaly that encouraged Brandon to act outside the realm of normal behavior. While no cause would have been searched for if Brandon had not been transgendered, here the search for a cause seems vital. If gender operates on iterated norms, cases of transgression must be explained. More, and this is significant in terms of parental roles—particularly those of the mother—in both cases, the mother is partially implicated as responsible for the problem either because of hormones taken during

pregnancy or for not having done enough to circumvent the physical and sexual abuse.

CONCLUSIONS

The public iteration of the Brandon Teena story provides us with a number of observations about *doxastic* understandings of gender/sexuality. I will begin with observations drawn directly from this case and then provide observations on the direction/purpose of criticism from a gender diversity perspective. First, I want to be clear that the discourse studied here is part of a cultural ideology that affects all of us; it is a discourse that is defining, disciplinary, even while we negotiate within its boundaries. As Leslie Feinberg notes, everyone is constrained by the same body of public argument; hence, critical readings of the disciplinary discourses about transsexualism, transgenderism, or intersexualism are simultaneously critiques that help everyone understand their own interpellation within gender and sexual discourses (92).[30] Hence, those discourses that shape the ways Brandon Teena was understood are the same discourses that shape each of us, the same discourses that reiterate gender norms and their influence. While I assume that these discourses could be read transgressively or "against the grain," they are the discourses with which all of us must negotiate and hence should be everyone's shared critical responsibility.

Second, when a subjectivity is either not represented (symbolically annihilated) or represented negatively, those people, including adolescents, who are developing a similar subjectivity are more likely to do so relatively alone, without the idea that a supportive community might exist. While this can have tragic implications in cases of adolescent homosexuality, as Kielwasser and Wolf have pointed out, it is surely more of a problem with transgendered individuals, as Leslie Feinberg poignantly observes in the opening of *Transgender Warriors*. Maturing in a world that either does not acknowledge one's existence, or degrades the subject position one wishes to "take on," would certainly make one's path difficult.[31] Obviously, critical work that underscores the "naturalness" of transgenderism and highlights the complexity of desire would be in service of those whose desires and identities are outside of cultural norms.

Third, despite the fact that numerous contemporary theoretical voices posit an already existing blurring of gender categories, the Brandon Teena case is one site where the meaning of gender in dominant culture remains fairly constraining. Not only do we find it in the signifiers of masculinity and femininity that lace this discourse and in the metaphors of "deception," but it also exists significantly in the idea that transgenderism is an abnormality. As the opening epigram indicates, there cannot be a blurring of gender/sexual categories when that blurring makes sense of a large array of subjectivities by understanding them as a form of deformation or when so many discourses continue to discipline transgenderism into a system of bigender heteronormativity. Hence, it is not only that the experience of transgenderism is negatively represented, but that gender and sex are "talked about" in ways that are radically limited. Hence, when Brandon Teena is situated discursively, he becomes "really" a woman, "really" Teena, because of his "female body." The way that body is allowed to desire works along the same axis of male-female body types (rather than, for example, as Bornstein suggests, style) and along the lines of homosexual and heterosexual desire.

Finally, I am not trying to suggest that "male" or "female" and heterosexual are not categories under which some individuals want to constitute themselves. However, it is the case that the discourses surrounding this case, a case very open to numerous possibilities to refigure gender and sexuality, instead fold it back into a traditional iteration of heterosexual normativity. As C. Jacob Hale notes in his brilliant essay on the Brandon Teena case, we would be wise to recognize that borders and categories are necessary as starting points. In short, while Hale sees the need for categories on which to base identity, he argues that these borders must be refigured as creatively contingent (338).[32] As I argued earlier, the first step in making this move, and a step that this chapter adds to, is to reenvision rhetoric as a constructor of gender rather than as constructed by gender (Condit "In Praise" 110) and to pursue criticism that builds upon this understanding of the relationship of gender and rhetoric. In criticizing the logic of heteronormativity in particular cases, we open the door for the possibility of a variety of ways to "talk about" gender and sexuality.

NOTES

1. I will cite the news sources as they are utilized in the essay. The Guggenheim art project, entitled "Brandon" can be found at http://brandon/guggenheim.org. The film is *The Brandon Teena Story*, directed by Susan Muska and Greta Olafsdotir, distributed by Zeitgeist Films. For discussions of proposed films and plays, see Minge; Moton "Documentary;" Moton "Story;" Moton "Film;" Burbach "3 Judges;" "Murder;" Delmont.

2. Throughout the chapter, I will refer primarily to "Brandon Teena" and hence will often be using the masculine pronoun. There will be times in the chapter, however, when I will either be quoting others who talk about Brandon as a woman or when I am discussing her as female (e.g., when working through stories of her childhood). At such times, the feminine pronoun will be employed. I mark such moves as clearly as possible.

3. I am retelling the story as I would in a face to face interaction rather than by looking back at any given essay or book. One could look at any of the sources I cite in this chapter to get a similar telling of the story. Aphrodite Jones' true crime book is the fullest treatment.

4. Of course, as Leslie Feinberg has pointed out in *Transgender Warriors*, transgender activism has a long and varied history under a number of different names. However, the Brandon Teena case and the activism surrounding it did take transgender activism to a much broader public

level, especially given the vocal presence of activities at the trial. A good web resource that allows one to follow in narrative form some of the activism that took place around the trial is the FTM International Website (http://www.ftm-intl .org/).

5. The more contemporary term *for hermaphrodites* is "intersexed." To a large degree, I am using the term hermaphrodites in this paper because it is the term commonly used in public arguments, and it is the impact and implications of public arguments that I am investigating.

6. If one can point to a celebratory period in Judith Butler's work, it would be in *Gender Trouble* when she notes the ways in which examples "that fail to comply with the categories that naturalize and stabilize that field of bodies for us within the terms of cultural conventions" significantly upset the meanings that are said to inhere within sexed bodies (110). Another clearly celebratory reader, at least at times, is Kate Bornstein in *Gender Outlaw*. However, even here, while Bornstein might celebrate the position of the gender outlaw (those who are neither man nor woman but can be fluid between positions) in a fashion that makes sexual binarism appear as if it is easily waved away, she is well aware that multiple cultural and ideological pressures (and people enacting these pressures—gender defenders) work to keep our gender binary house in order (71–2). One could also see Judith Halberstam's *Female Masculinity* in which her interest is in maintaining some of the "spaces in which gender difference simply does not work right now," to "hasten the proliferations of alternate gender regimes in other locations" (41).

7. While I will not draw upon them by name heavily throughout this essay, my theoretical assumptions about rhetorical materialism are heavily influenced by recent works by Ronald Greene and Celeste Condit (1994). I am also influenced by Lauren Berlant's *The Queen of America Goes to Washington City* in which she notes that she is studying mainstream documents and discourses because they should not be seen as white noise but as powerful language, not mere fiction but discourse with material effects, often violent material effects (13).

8. If I were to put my project in conversation with Elliot and Roen's discussion of the need for both a psychoanalytic take on the "role of the unconscious in the formation of subjectivity," and a historian's approach to the social regulation of subjects, I am clearly pursuing the social regulation of subjects.

9. While the "critical rhetoric" umbrella of refinements is now wide reaching, I would note that I see my project as one of drawing together news "fragments" in order to create a critical narrative that can act within the larger body of discourses about this case and about gender in general. The founding essays of "critical rhetoric" are those by McKerrow and McGee.

10. I searched using Pro*Quest Direct to get access to major publications and resources. I also used Lexis-Nexis to uncover over 100 newspaper articles dealing with the case, both locally and nationality. To a large extent, I am allowing the combination of Pro*Quest and Lexis-Nexis to determine what are "dominant" discourses about the case. I assume that there is some space for argument over these sources, but I also assume that my overall reading of this discourse is fairly consistent across all of the material with which I worked. While I also took a look at web resources, I'm a bit more selective in my use of them, as I am trying to get at discourses available in the public sphere through "commercial" outlets. While I will discuss some of the discourse of advertisements for, and reviews of, *The Brandon Teena Story* from the web, I will not discuss the narratives of those transgender activists who attended the trial of John Lotter or Tom Nissen. That discourse, as well as much popular discourse, has been analyzed in a brilliant essay by C. Jacob Hale, "Consuming the Living, Dis(re)membering the Dead."

11. In large part, I am taking my cues on how to proceed with this analysis by observing a particularly pointed set of "rules" about writing in this area: C. Jacob Hale's "Suggested Rules for Non-Transsexuals Writing about Transsexuals, Transsexuality, Transsexualism, or Trans—" (http://www.actlab.utexas.edu/-sandy/hale.rules. htm). One of the points most pertinent to my analysis is Hale's claim that such writing should not attempt to tell transgendered people about transgendered subjectivity but should instead work to note what the discourse tells about non-transgendered people, about dominant understandings of transgenderism and the way that gender ideology works in part to constrain all of us, regardless of our gender identities or sexual desires.

12. This is not the case in many of the online reports authored by transgender activists who attended the funeral. While they may have had an interest in "essentializing" Brandon as male, as Hale observes, they clearly did not posit what was occurring as a case of deception.

13. I should point out that every news report found through my Lexis-Nexis search referred to Brandon as "Ms. Brandon."

14. For other examples of discussions of people's claims about anger due to "lies and deceptions," see Fruhling; Keenan; Strawbridge; Gabrenya; Ebert.

15. For other examples of this "posing" or "masquerade" metaphors, see Burbach and Cordes; Burbach "Officer: Sheriff;" Burbach "Jury Told;" Burbach "Tight;" Burbach "Mothers;" Burbach "Jury Convicts;" Burbach "Jury Chosen;" Burbach "Ex-Girlfriend;" Powell; "Prison;" "Second;" Moton "Story;" Moton "Film;" Burbach "3 Judges;" Will; Wheelwright; Wade; Boellstorff; "Murder;" "New Trial;" Hartl; Gabrenya; Hammel; Dunne; "Woman;" "Crossing."

16. Konigsberg also quotes one of Brandon's former girlfriends as saying "I just couldn't understand why a girl would trick you into that if she knew you liked the opposite sex," again implying that Brandon was the same sex as the girlfriend (194).

17. Michelle Lotter, one of the murderers's sisters, makes a similar claim in an article in *The Advocate* (Ricks 30). For usage of the phrase "true sex" to refer to Brandon Teena as a female, see also Burbach and Cordes; "Dateline."

18. In addition to the headlines using "heartland" cited above, see Will.

19. While Dregor is discussing the historical treatment of hermaphrodites, Suzanne Kessler (1990) has cogently argued that this same logic operates today in that those physicians who treat intersexed children often begin with the assumption that these children should be surgically transformed into males or females. There is no space for ambiguity. Furthermore, Dreger begins her history in a period that would follow Thomas Lacquer's period of the "one sex" model and hence the logic of her history fits well with his.

20. The actual terms "sex" and "gender" may not be employed although the notions that they generally represent are certainly put into action.

21. Similar observations are made in the *Los Angeles Times'* review of *The Brandon Teena Story* (Thomas F16). See also Brucker-Cohen; Minkowitz.

22. Burbach and Cordes go on to note "Miss Brandon's hair usually was cropped short in front and long in the back. She liked to wear sweaters, turtlenecks, button-down shirts and casual slacks." Other examples of this clothing/make up articulation can be found in Wheelwright.

23. For other examples of this masculine icon articulation, see Will; "A Brief."

24. For other examples of "dream guy" discourse, see Wheelwright; Bernard; Carr; Taubin; Ebert; Atherton; Boone.

25. What is significant is not that Brandon Teena made this statement but that the statement gets worked into every account of the case.

26. I am playing off of "Hermaphrodites with Attitude," the activist group headed up by Cheryl Chase. For a discussion of the group, see Chase's recent essay in *GLQ*.

27. For more articulations of Brandon as a hermaphrodite, see Konigsberg 194; Elliott; Atherton; Boone.

28. Again, for a full account of such thinking amongst physicians today, I would highly recommend Suzanne Kessler's *Lessons from the Intersexed*.

29. One should see Chase (1998) and Kessler (1998) on this point.

30. Similarly, Kate Bornstein tells the story of a heterosexual man who noted after one of Bornstein's book readings that while he had no idea what it felt like to feel transgendered, her presentation forced him to think about the pressures that constrained him as a man. The point being that critiques of any public representations of cases concerning gender/sexuality are useful to everyone, regardless of their gender and sexuality.

31. As Feinberg puts it, "Every single child today—no matter how their sex or gender is developing—needs to know about these militant battles and the names of those who led them" (81).

32. Such a call for the production of new identities, to encourage the production of new taxonomies that would intervene in the hegemonic practice of naming and defining, has been argued by Judith Halberstam, drawing from Eve Sedgwick (8, 46–7). As Halberstam goes on to note, "The sexual discourse we have settled for is woefully inadequate when it comes to accounting for the myriad practices that fall beyond the purview of homo and heteronormativity. The development of a new sexual vocabulary and a radical sexual discourse is happening already in transgender communities, in sexual subcultures, in clubs" (139). Similar calls for an enlarged public vocabulary can be found in Feinberg (102), Stone (297), and Condit (110).

WORKS CITED

Atherton, Tony, "A Poignant Story of Brutal Intolerance." *Ottawa Citizen* 1 May 1999: E5.

Berlant, Lauren, *The Queen of America Goes to Washington City: Essays on Sex and Citizenship*, Durham, NC: Duke UP, 1997.

Bernard, Jami, "Tragic Death of a Girl Who Lived as a Guy." *Daily News* 23 September 1998: 48.

"Best Bets." *Detroit News* 8 February 1999: C4.

Boellstorff, Leslie, "Nissen's Lawyer Says Juror Misconduct Tainted Trial." *Omaha World Herald* 3 December 1996: 13SF.

Boone, Mike, "A Chilling Tale of Rural Ignorance." *The Gazette* (Montreal) 1 May 1999: C9.

Bornstein, Kate, *Gender Outlaw: On Men, Women, and the Rest of Us*, New York: Routledge, 1994.

"Brandon Teena Murderer Sentenced." http://data.cc.emu-edu/~julie/teenarage.html

Brandon Teena Story. Dir. By Susan Muska and Greta Olafsdottir, Zeitgeist Films 1998.

"A Brief Reminder of Hate." *Toronto Star* 30 April 1999.

Brucker-Cohen, Jonah, "Brandon." *ID* Sept/Oct. 1998: 86.

Burbach, Chris, "3 Judges to Decide Lotter's Fate." *Omaha World Herald* 19 November 1995: 1B.

Burbach, Chris, "Ex-Girlfriend Testifies Lotter Threatened One Victim Earlier." *Omaha World Herald* 19 May 195: 13SF.

Burbach, Chris, "Jury Chosen for Lotter Murder Trial." *Omaha World Herald* 11 May 1995: 15SF.

Burbach, Chris, "Jury Convicts Nissen in Slayings of 3 at Humboldt Farmhouse." *Omaha World Herald* 4 March 1995: 1.

Burbach, Chris, "Jury Told How Bodies Found Triple Slaying Trial Begins." *Omaha World Herald* 21 February 1995: 11SF.

Burbach, Chris, "Mothers of 3 Victims First to Testify in Slaying Trial." *Omaha World Herald* 22 February 1995: 15SF.

Burbach, Chris, "Officer: Sheriff Delayed Falls City Suspects' Arrest." *Omaha World Herald* 27 October 1994: 17SF.

Burbach, Chris, "Prosecutor Sees 'Intent' in 3 Killings." *Omaha World Herald* 16 May 1995: 1.

Burbach, Chris, "Tight Security Planned for Triple-Murder Trial." *Omaha World Herald* 21 February 1995: 1.

Burbach, Chris and Henry J. Cordes, "Romance, Deceit and Rage." *Omaha World Herald* 9 January 1994: 1A.

Butler, Judith, *Bodies that Matter: On the Discursive Limits of "Sex."* New York: Routledge, 1993.

Butler, Judith, *Gender Trouble: Feminism and the Subversion of Identity*. New York: Routledge, 1990.

Carr, Jay, "Denial and Death in Falls City." *Boston Globe* 15 January 1999: D7.

Chase, Cheryl, "Hermaphrodites with Attitude: Mapping the Emergence of Intersex Political Action." *GLQ* 4 (1998): 189–212.

Condit, Celeste M., "Hegemony in a Mass-mediated Society: Concordance about Reproductive Technologies." *Critical Studies in Mass Communication* 11 (1994): 205–230.

Condit, Celeste M., "In Praise of Eloquent Diversity: Gender and Rhetoric as Public Persuasion." *Women's Studies in Communication* 20 (1997): 91–116.

"Crossing Over." 20/20. ABC News 1 Aug. 1997.

"Dateline Iowa," *Des Moines Register* 8 May 1998: 7.

"Deception on the Prairie." *Advocate* 8 Feb. 1994: 16–17.

Delmont, Jim, "'Murder' Vividly Portrays Shocking Triple Killings." *Omaha World Herald* 24 May 1997: 61SF.

Dreger, Alice Domurat, *Hermaphrodites and the Medical Invention of Sex*. Cambridge: Harvard UP, 1998.

Dunne, John Gregory, "The Humboldt Murders." *New Yorker* 13 Jan. 1997: 45–62.

Ebert, Roger, "Ignorance Spawns Murder in 'Teena' Documentary." *Chicago Sun Times*, 5 March 1999: 31 (Weekend Plus).

Elliot, Patricia and Katrina Roen, "Transgenderism and the Question of Embodiment: Promising Queer Politics?" *GLQ* 4 (1998): 231–262.

Elliott, David, "A Tortured Soul Sinks into the Bleak Landscape of 'Brandon Teena Story.'" *San Diego Union Tribune* 26 March 1999: E10.

Epstein, Julia and Kristina Straub, "Introduction: The Guarded Body." *Body Guards: The Cultural Politics of Gender Ambiguity*. Ed. Julia Epstein and Kristina Straub. New York: Routledge, 1991. 1–28.

Feinberg, Leslie, *Transgender Warriors: Making History from Joan of Arc to Dennis Rodman*. Boston: Beacon, 1996.

"Fierce Flicks." *Ms.* Sept/Oct. 1998: 85.

Fruhling, Larry, "Charade Revealed Prior to Killings." *The Des Moines Register* 9 January 1994: 1.

Gabrenya, Frank, "Tale of Masquerade, Murder Should Spark Conversation." *Columbus Dispatch* 7 January 1999: 4.

Garber, Marjorie, *Vested Interests: Cross-Dressing and Cultural Anxiety*. Routledge: New York, 1992.

Greene, Ronald Walter, "Another Materialist Rhetoric." *Critical Studies in Mass Communication* 15 (1998): 21–40.

Guthman, Edward, "'Brandon' Makes Simple Plea for Compassion." *San Francisco Chronicle* 19 February 1999: D3.

Halberstam, Judith, *Female Masculinity*. Durham: Duke University Press, 1998.

Hale, C. Jacob, "Consuming the Living, Dis(re)-membering the Dead in the Butch/Ftm Borderlands." *GLQ* 4 (1998): 311–348.

Hale, C. Jacob, "Suggested Rules for Non-Transsexuals Writing About Transsexuals, Transsexuality, or Trans—," http://www.actlab.utexas.ude/~/sandy/hale.rules.html.rules.html

Hammel, Paul, "Relatives Say Victim Was Threatened by Two Men." *Omaha World Herald* 3 January 1994: 9FS.

Hartl, John, "Seattle International Film Festival." *Seattle Times* 7 June 1998: M1.

Holden, Stephen, "A Rape and Beating, Later 3 Murders and Then the Twist." *New York Times* 23 Sept. 1998: 5.

Jones, Aphrodite, *All She Wanted: A True Story of Sexual Deception and Murder in America's Heartland*. New York: Pocket Books, 1996.

Keenan, John, "'Brandon Teena' a Chilling Documentary." *Omaha World Herald* 21 October 1998: 45.

Kessler, Suzanne J., *Lessons from the Intersexed*. New Brunswick, NJ: Rutgers University Press, 1998.

Kessler, Suzanne J., "The Medical Construction of Gender: Case Management of Intersexed Infants." *Signs: Journal of Women in Culture and Society* 16 (1990): 3–26.

Kielwasser, Alfred P. and Michelle Wolf, "Mainstream Television, Adolescent Homo-sexuality, and Significant Silence." *Critical Studies in Mass Communication* 9 (1992): 350–373.

Konigsberg, Eric, "Death of a Deceiver," *Playboy* Jan. 1995:92–94, 193–199.

McKerrow, Raymie E., "Critical Rhetoric: Theory and Praxis." *Communication Monographs* 56 (1989): 91–111.

McGee, Michael Calvin, "Text, Context, and the Fragmentation of Contemporary Culture." *Western Journal of Speech Communication* 54 (1990): 274–289.

Minge, Jim, "Film to Depict Triple Murder." *Omaha World Herald* 21 October 1995: 61SF.

Minkowitz, Donna, "Love Hurts." *Village Voice* 19 April 1994: 24–30.

Moton, Tony, "Documentary Only the First." *Omaha World Herald* 22 October 1998: 41.

Moton, Tony, "Film Tracks Murder Case." *Omaha World Herald* 13 October 1996: 1E.

Moton, Tony, "Story Inspires Filmmakers." *Omaha World Herald* 5 November 1995: 1E.

"Murder Case Inspires New Play." *Omaha World Herald* 18 May 1997: 11.

"New Trial Sought in Triple Killing." *Des Moines Register* 8 May 1998.

Powell, Joy, "Lawsuit Against Former Sheriff Dismissed in Humboldt Case." *Omaha World Herald* 11 August 1995: 18.

"Prison Term in Death of Cross-Dresser." *Des Moines Register* 1 September 1995: 7.

Ramet, Sabrina Petra, "Gender Reversals and Gender Cultures: An Introduction." *Gender Reversals and Gender Cultures: Anthropological and Historical Perspectives*. Ed. Sabrina Petra Ramet. New York: Routledge, 1996. 1–21.

Ricks, Ingrid, "Heartland Homicide." *The Advocate* 8 March 1994: 28–30.

"Second Trial in Killing of 3 Begins Today." *Des Moines Register* 15 May 1995: 2.

Stone, Sandy, "The Empire Strikes Back: A Posttranssexual Manifesto." *Body Guards: The Cultural Politics of Gender Ambiguity*. Ed. Julia Epstein and Kristina Straub. New York: Routledge, 1991. 280–304.

Strawbridge, Patrick, "Judge Dismisses Federal Suit in Slaying of Teena Brandon." *Omaha World Herald* 10 November 1998: 21.

Stryker, Susan, "The Transgender Issue: An Introduction." *GLQ* 4 (1998): 145–158.

Taubin, Amy, "Splitting Image." *Village Voice* 29 Sept. 1998: 128.

Thomas, Kevin, "Outfest '98 Saves Its Best for Last." *Los Angeles Times* 18 Sept. 1998: F16.

Wade, Gerald, "Author Hopes Crime Books Can Make a Difference." *Omaha World Herald* 27 May 1996: 33SF.

Wheelwright, Julie, "The Boyfriend," *The Guardian* 30 February 1996: T6.

Will, Ed, "Murder in a Small Town." *Denver Post* 6 March 1994: 10.

"Woman Who Posed as a Man Is Found Slain with 2 Others," *New York Times* 4 Jan. 1994: A11.

"Zeitgeist Films: The Brandon Teena Story: The Crime." http://www.zeitgeist.com/current/brandonteena/brandoncrime.html.

Discussion Questions

1. Briefly summarize the key points in Sloop's argument and how he supports them.

2. In his conclusion, Sloop says the public "discourses that shape the ways Brandon Teena was understood are the same discourses that shape each of us . . . they are the discourse with which all of us must negotiate and hence should be everyone's shared critical responsibility."

   • Do you agree? Why or why not?

   • If you agree, what public discourses on gender and sexuality have played the greatest role in shaping your gender and sexual identities?

   • What are some of the specific ways that we can exercise our "shared critical responsibility" for the public discourses on gender and sexuality?

15

"Ah, Yes, I Remember It Well"

Memory and Queer Culture in Will and Grace

CHRISTOPHER CASTIGLIA AND CHRISTOPHER REED

MEMORY, GAY IDENTITY, AND THE TELEVISION SITCOM

Cultural identities depend crucially on memory, collective as well as personal. The cultural critic Stuart Hall goes so far as to define "identities" as "the names we give to the different ways we are positioned by, and position ourselves in, the narratives of the past."[1] Hall's formulation stresses the mutable, reciprocal nature of identity as a constant negotiation of memory closer to what some theorists call "identifications" than to notions of identity as essentialized and static.[2] Assaults on memory— on particular memories and on the value of memory itself—therefore threaten not only our knowledge of the past, but our ability to imagine, reshape, and make claims for identifications in the present and future as well.

Assaults on gay memory in particular have been virulent in recent years, abetting the forces that would render us sexually anxious, isolated in dynamics of shame and guilt. Such assaults are often overtly homophobic: initiatives to prevent affirmative acknowledgment of homosexuality in history classes, campaigns to obscure the same-sex attractions of historical figures in museum exhibitions, objections to the designation of gay neighborhoods, and so forth.[3] But antipathy to gay memory runs deeper than these examples. The mainstream press plays up arguments over the locutions of

SOURCE: This chapter is a slightly reduced version of "'Ah, Yes, I Remember It Well': Memory and Queer Culture in *Will and Grace*," which first appeared in *Cultural Critique* (vol. 56, Winter 2004). Copyright © 2004 University of Minnesota Press. Reprinted with permission.

Authors' Note: Funding for the research and writing of this paper was provided by the Gay and Lesbian Alliance Against Defamation Center for the Study of Media and Society. Additional research funding was provided by the Richter Scholar Program of Lake Forest College. For their support and contributions to this essay, we would like to thank Ron Gregg and our research assistants, Ryan Inton and Becca Shrier.

"gay" versus "queer," emphasizing genera-
tional differences in conceptions of sexual self-
definition in ways that frustrate efforts to
strengthen bonds among people—old and
young, male and female, straight and gay—
outside conventional sex/gender norms.[4] Even
the not-overtly-homophobic media rehearse
versions of gay history as victims' tales, in
which sexual and political self-assertion leads
to violent assault. While the murders of
Harvey Milk and Matthew Shepard are
important to gay history, we lose something
when these become the primary paradigms of
the gay past, of cultural memory. The mainstream's focus on gay martyrs, moreover, follows two decades of stories featuring the
doomed homosexual victimized by an immature culture that in the 1970s promoted the
"promiscuity" that led to AIDS. In this view,
the solution to the "problem" of memory is a
willed amnesia, in which gay men forget our
past in order to assimilate to purportedly
healthier mainstream norms.

This campaign for amnesia has been abet-
ted by both nominal allies and media-
appointed spokesmen for the gay community
who urge us to renounce forms of gay culture
generated by sexual dissidents in earlier
decades. *New York Newsday* columnist
Gabriel Rotello, for instance, played a central
role in a National Public Radio feature, calling
on gay men to make "a complete break with
the past" in order to "totally rethink the way
they conceive their sexual behavior." This is
typical of calls on gay men to reject the legacy
of the immediate post-Stonewall generation
and to reinvent ourselves along supposedly
cleaner, healthier lines that end up looking just
like the borders of "normalcy" defined by a
coupledom conceived as monogamous and (at
least in Vermont) state-sanctioned, and by
property rights, including the production of
progeny.[5]

Please pause a beat here for comic timing.
Then repeat with Jack McFarland's sarcastic
hesitancy: "I'm not really getting the theme of
this party." Jack's reaction when he finds his
"man-tan reunion" has become a play-date for
gay couples with children encapsulates his
blissful obliviousness to what we've just
described as a range of sex-negative, club-
negative, camp-negative impulses at work in
and on gay culture. In contrast, Jack's happily
wholehearted identification, through his memory of past parties, with the clichés of gay
culture—disco, musicals, fashion trends—
constitutes a principle pleasure of *Will and
Grace*, helping to make it, according to one
study, the most-watched television show for
gay audiences.[6] If the chat rooms devoted to
the show are any indication, not "Just Jack"
individually, but the way *Will and Grace* as a
whole revels in the rich resources of gay memory arouses strong identification with the
forms of subculture it models from a wide
range of viewers manifesting the various forms
of antagonism to heteronormativity yoked by
the term "queer."[7]

It might seem unlikely that a sitcom should
recoup such powerful assaults on subcultural
memory. Our claims, it should be clear, are
not assertions of fact, but the outcome of a
strategy of interpretation that, like Jack, finds
pleasure and subcultural identification in areas
overlooked or dismissed by a more authoritative gaze.[8] *Will and Grace* has been criticized
by mainstream media critics for characters
they perceive as superficial and self-involved,
while a major study of "gay visibility" in mass
culture gave up all pretense of analysis of the
show it said was

> a puzzle. Dabbling in double standards yet
> indubitably gay. Apolitical yet surreptitiously
> aware. Familial yet hedonistic. Gay male cen-
> tered yet with two of the strongest female
> characters on TV. Devoid of larger commu-
> nity yet assuredly not tokenized. . . . And,
> through it all, very funny.[9]

But television entertainment—and sitcoms
in particular—have often gone where news
and drama feared to tread. In the 1970s,

Norman Lear's hit series, including *All in the Family, Maude,* and *The Jeffersons,* famously troubled dominant attitudes toward race, gender, class, and the political ruptures of the Vietnam era.[10] Even before these overtly political sitcoms, the alibi of humor allowed shows like *My Three Sons* and *Green Acres* to visualize certain queer potentials. The three sons of Fred MacMurray demonstrated more about male intimacy, with the help of gruff Uncle Charlie, than almost any show on television, while Hooterville was inhabited by a fashion-crazy drag-wannabe, a female carpenter who always wore her tool belt loaded, several elderly gentlemen who lived alone, and a man in love with a pig.

More broadly, sitcoms, by presenting sympathetic, recurring characters whose eccentric misreadings of their environments constitute the primary pleasure of the genre (Eva Gabor's Lisa Douglas in *Green Acres,* Uncle Martin on *My Favorite Martian,* and all the characters except—tellingly—the Professor on *Gilligan's Island*), validated strategies of non-normative interpretation that are a hallmark of subculture. A T-shirt seen in gay-identified neighborhoods lists three names—Buffy, Jody, Sissy—with a red check next to the last name, a joke that presumes not only common memories of *Family Affair* but also shared strategies of pleasureful misreading.

In addition to the plots and characters of television sitcoms, phenomenologies of the medium and genre have unique importance in the construction of minority sexual identity. Television, George Lipsitz argues, powerfully "addresses the inner life," not only because its "dramatic and social locus is the home," but because the formal logic of productions for the small screen—zoom shots, tight framing, quick cuts, and so on—"focus attention inward." In "maximizing the private and personal aspects of existence," as Lipsitz puts it, television permits an especially intense bond between individual experience (the affective pleasures of viewing) and collective formations (the shareable

set of references, or memory-narratives, made available by the diegesis) that transcend kin.[11] At the same time, the seriality of the sitcom format, flexible and prone to revision, subordinates presumptions of identity as unchanging historical fact to more playfully malleable and self-willed models of identification. For Lipsitz, the way "television colonizes intimate areas of human sexuality and personality" is part of its invidious undermining of political identities organized around race, ethnicity, class, and family.[12] But what about sexual identity, which is almost invariably formed outside—and in opposition to—racial, ethnic, and class bonds nurtured in families, and requires an ability to revise the personal memory narratives (revaluing that same-sex crush in the first grade, for instance, while downplaying heteronormative participation in a high school prom)? Accommodating such nonfamilial identifications, television sitcoms' fascination with non-normative or chosen families from *I Dream of Jeannie* and *The Courtship of Eddie's Father* through *The Brady Bunch* to *Cheers* and *Friends* sutures the privatized affect of domestic viewership to increasingly self-motivated, collectively maintained forms of affiliation.

This analysis suggests links between the histories of television entertainment and of sexual identity overlooked by studies focused on plotline and character (though encapsulated in the playwright Neil Bartlett's claim, "The history of mainstream entertainment is the history of gay culture").[13] The sitcom's roots lie in the nineteenth-century forms of "commercialized leisure" that, Lipsitz argues, replaced traditional rituals of communal memory with theaters where "role playing . . . suggested identities could be changed," where "theatrical 'time' presented an alternative to work time," encouraging "audiences to pursue personal desires and passions," and where "theatergoers . . . shared these intimate and personal cultural moments with strangers." The same historical forces that replaced community rituals with commercial theater—increasing social and geographic mobility, rapid urbanization, and higher levels of disposable incomes—helped generate modern gay culture.[14] Although Lipsitz ignores sexual community, his descriptions of the characteristics of mediated memory suggest its ties with emergent gay culture, which often took shape in the commercial spaces of popular entertainment and shared its constitutive features. Particularly relevant is mass media's yoking of collective memory and anonymity, in marked contrast with more conventional forms of remembering that assume unmediated memory (of family, of village) as the basis of identity. Mass media allow audiences to share intimacy without familiarity and to create new memories—and hence identities—from seemingly impersonal and specularized encounters. Lipsitz's description of the dynamics of popular theater—"The unfamiliarity of the crowd with each other provided a kind of protective cover—a 'privacy in public' whereby personal feelings and emotions could be aired without explanation or apology"—echoes recent historical analysis of the sexual counterpublics that allowed simultaneous anonymity and community formation, secrecy and collective code-making, defying stereotypes of both the exclusively heterosexual "public" and the isolated gloom of the "closet."[15] These parallels between the viewing logic of televised entertainment and gay identity suggest that sitcoms in general—and, with its unprecedented gay focus, *Will and Grace* in particular—should be a rich site for explorations of the dynamics of gay memory as they play out in constructions of subcultural sexual identity today.

THE PLAYERS

Like other classic sitcoms (*All in the Family* is an obvious model), *Will and Grace*'s weekly episodes focus on the interaction of characters who are less coherent, believable people than embodiments of competing attitudes or social positions.[16] Two pairs of characters—Will and Grace on one hand, Jack and Karen on the other—represent (among other things) different attitudes toward memory and, because of that, toward sexuality, self-worth, and community.

Jack is the "gayest" character. That is, he most exemplifies gay cultural codes, many of which he enacts through rehearsals of gay memory to create sexual and social bonds with other gay men. In one paradigmatic scene, when Jack and another man, after eying each other in a store, start to speak, they perform an updated version of the lyrics from the 1958 movie musical *Gigi,* adapted to express a series of sexual memories ("We met in Soho. / It was the Village. / Gay Pride? / Wigstock. / Ah, yes, I remember it well. / In a cage. / On a box. / Vodka neat? / On the rocks. / Ah, yes, I remember it well").[17] Here memory (both of gay cruising habits and of midcentury movie musicals) allows Jack to connect with another gay man and to affirm his sexuality in a way that merges gay eroticism with camp knowledge of movies like *Gigi,* cultural geography, and community events (Gay Pride, Wigstock). This scene is paradigmatic in the way it presents memory neither as just individual nor particular to these two men, but as the basis of gay identity. With Jack on-screen, *Will and Grace* offers television audiences the unprecedented spectacle of gay subcultural interaction depicted as a practice of shared pleasure for those involved and deployed to include viewers who take their own pleasure in recognizing (which is to say remembering) the sexual scenario and camp allusions.[18] In contrast to the long history of films and television shows that deployed gay codes in ways that isolated or pathologized particular characters, expanding that effect to viewers who wondered, "Do others see what I see? Does that make me sick?" *Will and Grace* affirms gay memory as a viable basis for identity.

In contrast to Jack, Will has a more ambivalent relationship to memory and consequently to gay cultural codes. Except when under Jack's influence, he lacks Jack's enthusiasm for the memories attached to camp or cruising, and his own memory-narratives regularly rehearse experiences of humiliation and shame: breakups, missed opportunities, childhood embarrassments. Will's is typically the conservative voice, criticizing Jack for his campy deployments of gay codes and for his unembarrassed enjoyment of his sexuality. As a result, unlike Jack, who often mentions friends in what seems an extended gay network, Will seems oddly and unhappily isolated, locked into a heterosexual-seeming relationship with Grace (in the show's first episode, they pretend to be newlyweds).

When Will does use memory to make a "love connection," the results don't pay off for him as they do for Jack. This is clear in the episode titled "Love plus One," in which Jack, working as a Banana Republic salesman, is smitten with a handsome shopper.[19] Sensing that Matthew is a "smarty," Jack convinces Will to hide in a dressing room, feeding him dialogue through a headset. Will proffers references that are both straight (John Updike's *Rabbit Run,* for example, which Jack turns, John Waters-like, into *Rabid Nun)* and "high cultural" (shopping for art at the Spielman Gallery). The elite and non-gay quality of their memories grounds Will and Matthew's relationship in the dominant cultural values that quickly become its undoing: A few episodes later they break up when Matthew refuses to challenge his boss's homophobia and acknowledge Will as his lover (by comparison, Jack's carefree display of affection with his latest boyfriend unwittingly "outs" the boss's son to his dad).[20]

Although Jack is the gayest character, Will is not not-gay: One of the greatest attractions of *Will and Grace* is its recognition of a range of positions within gay identity. Will often stands up for "gay pride" against straight and potentially homophobic audiences: He organizes a sensitivity training for police officers, insists that his closeted lover acknowledge his

sexuality, and is himself vocally "out" in the workplace. Significantly, Will's memory-narrative of his sexual identity, staged in the flashback-heavy Thanksgiving 2000 special, credits Jack with pulling him out of the closet. Camp and cruising, represented by Jack, are thus acknowledged as a deep history that enables and remains allied with the more mainstream gay politics represented by Will.

In the original conception of *Will and Grace,* Will's friendship with Jack was balanced by Grace's relationship with her socialite secretary, Karen. Will and Grace, the more normative title characters, share, among other things, a difficult relationship to memory, marked by embarrassment and shame (an episode in which guilt motivates Grace's return to Schenectady to apologize to a grade school classmate whose malicious nickname she initiated, only to be called a "bitch" in front of a funeral parlor full of strangers, is typical).[22] Even the bond between Will and Grace is founded on a shared memory of humiliation occasioned by their failure to achieve heterosexual fulfillment. This is the theme of the hour-long 2000 Thanksgiving special, which rehearses their dysfunction in twinned plots— "the story I like to call 'When Mary Met Sally,'" quips Jack—set simultaneously in the past and present (this structural assertion of the formative relevance of memory is reinforced by the plot, in which these memories are recalled in order to explain to a woman they meet in a bar why her relationship with her boyfriend is failing). Not coincidentally, Grace is, like Will, socially awkward and sexually anxious (Karen calls her "Prudence McPrude, Mayoress of Prudie Town").[23] Nevertheless, Grace, like Will, is capable of fierce loyalty to her gay friends and of an imaginative relation to her own sexuality. If Will's pride relies on his memory of Jack's campy influence, so Grace's relies on her memory of Will's steadfast friendship: Memory thus fosters bonds, not only across differences within the gay community, but across supposed divides of gay and straight, male and female, as well.

This passing of memory across boundaries of gender and sexuality is clearest in the character of Karen, nominally a straight woman, who matches Jack's pleasure in eroticism and his repertoire of camp references. Karen's cheerful failure to sustain any conventional social role associated with subordinate femininity—caring wife, nurturing mother, helpful secretary—is linked to Jack's status as the happy homosexual in her response when he asks why she never makes coffee in the office: "For the same reason you don't have a wife and three kids: that's the way god wants it."[24] While Grace is getting called a bitch in Schenectady, Karen tells Jack fondly, "You're simple, you're shallow, and you're a common whore: that's why we're soul-mates." And when they argue, Karen is equally equipped from the arsenal of camp knowledge, suddenly quoting *Gypsy*, for instance, as she spits at Jack: "You ain't gettin' 88 cents from me, Rose!"[25] (In a riposte several episodes later into their quarrel, Jack invokes *The Wizard of Oz* to instruct Karen, "Now be gone before someone drops a house on you!")[26] Despite her always offstage husband and children, Karen's participation in gay cultural memory "queers" her in ways that become occasionally explicit: When Jack first hears about the man-tan reunion, he tells Grace she can't come because it's "gay guys only," then murmurs to Will, "Remind me to invite Karen."[27] This remark recognizes Karen's character as a hilariously exaggerated projection onto an urban matron of stereotypes of gayness as a self-centered combination of ruthless materialism and devastating wit.

In a television genre that claimed documentary veracity, this attribution of gay stereotypes to middle-aged femininity might seem just one more tediously offensive reminder of the links between homophobia and misogyny; the humiliation of actress Sharon Gless as the pro-gay mom in Showtime's *Queer as Folk*

comes to mind as an example.[28] In the stylized structure of the sitcom, however, the over-the-top projection of Karen as a best friend for Jack can be enjoyed as a campy inversion of a genre of mainstream films (the 1997 blockbuster *My Best Friend's Wedding* and the derivative *The Next Best Thing*), which projected gay characters (played in both cases by Rupert Everett) solely as handsome and attentive best friends for straight women, but with no lives—certainly no gay plots—of their own. This tried-and-true dynamic was the original premise of *Will and Grace* and remains, presumably, some part of its audience appeal. In the early episodes, Karen and Jack appeared separately and only as sidekicks for Grace and Will.[29] With *Will and Grace*'s success, however, came its confidence to engage directly the common, but little discussed, phenomenon of heterosexual women who share enthusiastically in queer cultural codes, as—in a related development—the Jack/Karen relationship grew at least as important as the Will/Grace duo.[30] These shifts coincided, in *Will and Grace*'s second season, with several jabs at the movie precedent: jokes on Grace's insistence that she looks like Julia Roberts, the star of *My Best Friend's Wedding* (Karen responds, "The only thing you two have in common is horse teeth and bad taste in men"),[31] an episode titled "My Best Friend's Tush," and, most noticeably, the ongoing plot in which Karen arranges Jack's marriage of convenience to her maid, mocking the heterosexual romantic conventions of the films from which the show derived.

For our purposes, what is significant in these characters is that their abilities to revise stereotypes and to make community across identities often conceived as antagonistic are enabled by memory: personal memories of the characters' shared histories and, more important, cultural memories shared by a community of viewers. Insisting that gay cultural memory can create community across differences of sexual politics, gender identity, or class position, *Will and Grace* embodies the ways memory can not only cohere, but also transform ("queer") contemporary notions of identity.

"JACK HAS ORIGINALITY": MEMORY AND COLLECTIVE REFERENCE

The pleasure we take in *Will and Grace* derives in part from the scarcity of popular representations of subcultural memory. The hunger for such representations is often belittled in mainstream television commentary, but one sign of the dominant culture's privilege is its failure to recognize its own rehearsals of collective memory for what they are. People invested in normative identities (whiteness, maleness, heterosexuality) that are continually reinforced by mainstream media as the makings of unique individuality can afford to ignore the collective aspect of those memories. To be a privileged citizen is to imagine oneself an autonomous individual, though that "individuality" looks much like everyone else's.

For those outside mainstream culture, however, memories on which to ground alternative social identities must be more self-consciously recognized, cultivated, and shared. This self-consciousness, performed in relation to mass culture, is the basic component of "camp," the colloquial term for the pleasurable misreading that transforms mass-cultural phenomena into subcultural memories that help to cohere and strengthen gay identity in ways that challenge dominant cultural beliefs, including the belief in autonomous individuality. As a disruptive mode of interpretation that inverts authoritative claims to meaning and hierarchies of value, "camp" is notoriously hard to define, except by example.[32] We'll take our example of camp's power from the *Will and Grace* episode "I Never Promised You an Olive Garden" (itself a campy memory reference to Lynn Anderson's 1970 hit, "I Never Promised You a Rose Garden"). In this episode, Karen goads Jack into overcoming his traumatic

memories of grade school bullies so that he will accompany her to a principal's conference at her stepchildren's posh academy. Once there, Jack encounters John, who is being bullied into heteronormativity just as Jack was. Identifying with John, Jack thwarts the bullies first by camping it up (he grabs Karen's purse and condemns physical aggression from a fashion standpoint: "This macho bully schoolyard crap is *so* 1983 I could vomit. Now scram!"), then by sharing gay cultural codes with John (showing him how to perform "Just John" with Jack's signature "jazz hands"). Here the camp frivolity of fashion, femininity, and song-and-dance trumps the thudding viciousness of the normative hands down—or, rather, up. In the most explicit demonstration of the power of memory to form collective identity, Jack teaches John how to be himself, a self that is both Jack and John. Here queer memories are rescued from the trauma of isolated individualism (being alone, being beaten up) and transformed into a shared identity that empowers and delights both participants. "Thanks for your help," John says. "Same here," Jack replies.[33]

As a strategy for the useful misreading of popular culture, camp, at least in some measure, reciprocates the mass media's corrosive effects on gay subculture, cultivating an actively ironic viewership in place of the gullible passivity presumed of audiences by the mass media's harsher critics.

Will and Grace's depiction of camp strategies circulating within an explicitly gay context opens a new commercialized venue for the cultivation of gay memory. Though this is a shift more in scope than in kind from earlier commercial circulations of camp, the new scope does, significantly, widen the interpretive community for gay memory that is synergistically presumed and created by any performance of camp. Undoubtedly, some of the intensity and subversiveness of gay subcultural identification is traded for wider relevance—a move that echoes the broader cultural shift from relatively separatist and small "gay" and "lesbian" communities to the broader but vaguer "queer" identity. Jack's performances of camp deploy a repertoire of codes available to anyone—male or female, gay or straight—with access to the same forms of mass media. *Will and Grace* allows the straight women characters to pick up on Jack's strategy of using media references to disrupt conventional logics of conversation and plot. Karen's cultural references are perfectly in sync with Jack's, but even the more normative Grace has her moments: In a scene where Will tries to distance Grace by hissing bitterly, "You might as well be my wife," Grace deflects the insult by pretending to mishear him, responding incredulously, "Marcus Welby is my wife?" To camp on mass culture may make one less "original," less possessed of the unique individualism signaled by one's embodiment of a stable, autonomous "identity." But to dismiss mass entertainment for "selling out" gay culture misses the complex interactions between commercial co-optation and resistant interpretation, autonomous identity and cross-cultural identifications, individualism and the imagined community of viewers. The practices of camp viewing that *Will and Grace* depicts, however, show that queers co-opt mass culture—not only the other way around—allowing through such acts of reappropriative interpretation the possibilities for *collective originality* to emerge.

"I Guess Weddings Just Bring Out the Worst in Me"

The challenge that the recycling of queer cultural memory poses to the oxymoron of conventional individuality extends to that corollary of individualism: the perfect couple. What most distinguishes Will and Grace from Jack and Karen may be their differing relationship to the ideal of the all-consuming self-sufficiency of the couple. Will and Grace seem happiest, as evidenced in the failed experiment with Grace moving across the hall, when they

are in the same apartment, uninterrupted by visits—usually presented as "intrusions"—by Jack and Karen. What the title characters reinforce, then, is an overdetermined image of the conventional nuclear family: Mom and Dad happily ensconced in a privately owned home, with two unruly interlopers (boy and girl child) who must be affectionately indulged, though not treated as equals. This depiction has troubling consequences: It desexualizes Grace and Will (especially Will, whose homosexuality is repeatedly blamed for their failure to find complete fulfillment in each other); it presents queers as developmentally immature (emotional "children" who will grow into a "mature" recognition of the values represented by Will and Grace); and, above all, it validates a way of life cut off from the pleasures brought by more communal social formations.

Jack and Karen, in contrast, circulate promiscuously. While we typically see Will and Grace only at home or at work unless brought to another space by Jack and Karen, the latter are often in stores, restaurants, gyms, hotels, schools: all spaces that enable interaction with people—often queer people—who float in and out of the plot, often without names or fully developed characters.[38] These spaces and interactions allow Jack and Karen more fluid and expansive definitions of relationships, community, and identity. Despite—or maybe because of—their outrageous narcissism, which grandly assumes that everyone they encounter shares their sensibility, there is an element of generosity in Jack and Karen's relationship to the broader social world that is lacking in Will and Grace's tightly controlled, hermetic environment. Jack and Karen's disruption of the couple-centric dynamic is a crucial part of the appeal of *Will and Grace,* allowing the show to take its place with *Friends* (another hit sitcom that—to judge from chat room discussions and network marketing strategies—shares a significant component of its audience of young adults with *Will and Grace*) as a forum in which the contradictory dynamics of couple and community are negotiated for viewers at the stage in life when mainstream norms demand the prioritization of coupledom and marriage over friendship networks created in school.

These issues may be most explicitly at play in the episode titled "Coffee and Commitment," which involves the four regulars in the commitment ceremony of Joe and Larry (the former fast-life gay couple turned suburban dads already mentioned in connection with the failed man-tan reunion). "I love weddings" is Grace's immediate couple-centric response. "Well, it's not strictly a wedding; it's a same-sex civil union, which affords many of the same rights as a marriage," responds Will, articulating his legalistic grasp on the limitations of the dominant culture's acceptance of gay coupledom. Will and Grace's reflections on the usual range of liberal debate on this issue are interrupted by Jack, who bursts in, in a caffeine-induced delirium, announcing, "Did you see that? I almost did the half nelson. I almost bruised my delicates, my delicates, my domo arigato Mr. Tomatoes. Huge news! I have met—Are you ready for this? Mr. Right. Well, Mr. Right-Now, anyway. Ba-da-bum. Good night, folks, I'm here all week. Jack 2000!" Conventional coupledom doesn't stand a chance in the face of this promiscuous collapse of boundaries, not only between couples, but between languages, between denotation and euphemism, between authentic expressions of individual emotions and cultural clichés, between personal conversation and public performance.

The episode goes on to contrast the mock-hetero gay couple with the addictions of Jack (to caffeine) and Karen (to booze and pills), with Will and Grace angrily debating their own emotional and financial commitment to one another. This pairing of plots functions as a metaphor for the situation of sexual minorities today, caught between stereotyped ideals of coupledom indistinguishable from heterosexuality and equally stereotyped diagnoses of gay culture as a morass of disease and addiction.

The sly yoking of "commitment" and "addiction" suggests that one can end up addicted to the conventional rituals of the exclusive couple (in the final scene, Grace says of the wedding cake she is addictively gobbling, "It's got nine layers of chocolate and a Snickers bar in the middle. I may move into it"). This addiction, the episode suggests, has particularly bad effects on gay men, who end up "picking up the bill" (Will is angry throughout the episode because of Grace's assumption that he will pay for all their joint ventures). More figuratively, gay men pick up the bill for conventional coupledom by submitting themselves to conventional gender roles (Larry and Bob wonder which one of them is the bride), social isolation (no more man-tan parties in the Hamptons for this happy couple; in a later episode, Larry and Bob cancel a trip to Morocco with Will, unwilling to leave their daughter Hannah behind), and a sense of shame about alternative erotic or romantic arrangements. As Will tells Grace, "I guess weddings just bring out the worst in me."

Representing an alternative—and today often vilified—gay legacy, Jack and Karen, the more explicitly "addicted" characters, end up supplying each other with a form of companionship and support that is both harder to ritualize and hence to name (they decide to get over the D.T.'s by "touching each other inappropriately"), but no less trustworthy for that. And *their* addictions—to pleasure in its myriad forms—lead again, not to exclusion and shame, but to inclusion (Jack flirts with a man who offers him a cigarette, while Karen finds booze by seeking out the inevitable "sad sister," shamed by her single status at the marriage of her gay brother). If addiction to coupledom brings out the worst in Will and Grace, addictions to pleasure—reinforced through the expansive communities built through shared memory and circulated cultural codes—bring out the best in Jack and Karen. This episode suggests that the collective identities built through gay memory model at least one alternative to gay (or even, in the case of Will and Grace, queer) marriage and the exclusive couple at its center.

THE HISTORY OF
THE QUEER FUTURE

Out of our memories comes our future. Not only what we remember, but *how* we remember—with pleasure or pain, generosity or anxiety—shapes the futures we will enjoy (or endure) as communities or as individuals. This is the theme of the episode "There but for the Grace of Grace," in which Will and Grace make a pilgrimage to visit a beloved college professor, Joseph Dudley. They find him disillusioned and embittered, locked in a battle of resentments with his longtime companion, Sharon. Watching the two snipe at one another, Will and Grace recognize aspects of their own relationship. Grace exclaims to Will, "Them. They're us," adding, "when he put down the bottle of Correctol by her lamb chop, she said 'Ew.' I say 'Ew.' Will, she is exactly who I'm going to be." Ironically, this return to the past gives Grace a vision of her future, a vision she uses to change the course of her history. When Grace tells Sharon that she terminated an engagement after Will disapproved of the man, Sharon confronts Grace with "Because god forbid there should be any other man in your life besides Will." Sharon recognizes that coupledom has prevented her and Joseph from exploring the potential range of their pleasures, locking them into a life of frustrated resentment. Will and Grace seem to learn their lesson from this trip down memory lane: Several episodes later, Will encourages Grace to pursue a relationship with her new romantic interest, Nathan, and in the process meets a man he has admired bashfully from afar. Will and Grace use the past, strategically, to avoid the exclusive interdependence of the conventional couple that has doomed Joseph and Sharon.

Of course, Grace's immediate history always held a potentially "queer" future. Her own mother, Bobbi (played by Debbie Reynolds), is never depicted with her husband; instead, we see her with her effeminate accompanist, with whom she performs a camp repertoire of show tunes and disco hits. Although Grace asserts her difference from her mother, they both share a love of gay men and the culture they produce (Bobbi asks Grace, "What do the boys make out to these days? Is it still Judy?").[39] Unlike Grace's often fraught relation with gay men, Bobbi takes self-affirming pleasure in that relation, seeing it as compatible with more conventional connections (Bobbi has a husband and children). Grace's past, rightly remembered, thus offers her another means of escape from Sharon's frustrations into the pleasures and possibilities of a queer future.

Grace, in a later episode, offers Will a similar view into his queer future, giving him a visit to a clairvoyant, Psychic Sue, as a birthday gift. Sue predicts that Will will be contacted by a "strawberry blonde" with whom he once had a relationship and to whom he never got a chance to say goodbye. When she identifies this blonde as a "she," Will dismisses Sue's predictions as heterosexist smoke and mirrors, only to return home to find a package from his mother containing the collar of his beloved childhood pet, a strawberry blonde dog who died while Will was away at college. Sue has plunged Will back into his past, and his memory, like virtually all his memories, is at best bittersweet, associating affection with loss and disappointment. It is Grace who queers Will's memory: When he takes out the dog collar and announces it belonged to "Ginger," Grace asks, "That drag queen you and Jack hung out with last summer?" Will's memory takes him to his nuclear family, always for him a site of pain. Grace's comment, however, suggests a competing history: not of pain but of pleasure, not of heterosexuality but of queer gender-bending, not of childhood innocence but of adult sexual play. Above all, the memory Grace evokes is collective, involving not just Jack but also someone with at best a contingent relation to Will's life (someone he "hung out with" for a summer) who has nevertheless functioned as a source of queer pleasure, and the pleasure of this memory—for the laughing audience if not for Will—defuses the heavy sentimentality of Will's maudlin family memory.

As textual critics like to say, this scene is foreshadowing, for when, convinced now of Sue's psychic acumen, Will returns for a second visit, he wants to know what, sexually, awaits him in his future. Slowly, Sue reveals to him that he will spend the rest of his life with someone named . . . Jack. Will is traumatized by this revelation, and much of the episode's humor centers on his hysterical distaste for the idea of sexual union with Jack. Two narratives run side by side here. In one, Will seeks pleasure in a memory rooted in a past dominated by the heterosexual nuclear family (a memory that, we can see even if he doesn't, brings him pain). This familial memory, projected into the future, conjures a kind of mirror image: another man exactly like Will to play the missing half of his ideal couple. In contrast, the *queer* memory—of the drag queen who might have worn a dog collar—takes Will to another future, shared with Jack. That future will be very different from Will's normative ideal: When Jack learns of Sue's prediction, he insists that, in his "marriage" to Will, each must have his own apartment and his own boyfriends. The future with Jack—a future predicated by a "memory" of a summer spent "hanging out" (as opposed to Will's usual mode, "staying in")—busts the conventional couple wide open, suggesting a future founded in pleasure, gender-nonconformity, sexual play, and, above all, expansive community, not in the sentimental innocence of the exclusive couple.[40]

In all these episodes, *Will and Grace* suggests that memories can function not as signposts toward a future for which we are inevitably fated (or doomed), but as the materials from which we can construct new

relationships with ourselves and our communities. Using memory to create new futures takes several steps, as these episodes demonstrate. First, queers must learn to identify not according to biological "sameness" (sons must follow their fathers), but across cultural differences of sexuality, gender, and lifestyle. While these queered identifications may disrupt the nuclear family (Will's relationship to his own childhood) and the conventional couple (Will and Grace's sense of themselves as almost-married), they open up possibilities for new and expansive communities, which may include biological relations (like Bobbi) or conventional couples (like Larry and Bob) but are not restricted to them. Our memories take us, then, to places and people who, in our past, gave us pleasure (sexual pleasure, perhaps, but also the pleasure of good conversation, new experiences, fresh perspectives). These people and places are often erased by conventional sources of memory (albums featuring photos only of weddings, babies, or family gatherings), but their memories are carried by the traces of mass culture that allowed us to meet them in the first place and that gave us a shared vocabulary of remembrance. These cultural sources carry the memories of collective pleasure, whether in Bobbi's rendition of the disco hit "Gloria," in Karen's citations of *Gypsy,* or Grace's reference to drag, any one—or all—of which recall a history of gender nonconformity and campy defiance. Out of these memories, *Will and Grace* forms a new community and invites us, if we're willing to let the memories be ours as well, to share its pleasures.

CONCLUSIONS: THANKS FOR THE MEMORIES

Debates over gay history and identity can make us feel that we must choose sides. What'll it be: memory or amnesia, community or coupledom, subculture or assimilation? One of the pleasures of *Will and Grace* is its use of humor to stage an optimistic hope for a resolution of debilitating debates within the gay community between the positions Michael Warner describes as "the dignified homosexual" and the "queer who flaunts his sex and his faggotry, making the dignified homosexual's stigma all the more justifiable in the eyes of straights."[41] In place of this antagonistic scenario, *Will and Grace* repeatedly shows Jack pulling Will from his isolation, encouraging him into rehearsals of gay memory. Together they recall sexual exploits and perform apparently spontaneous yet carefully choreographed campy duets that suggest Will's unacknowledged store of gay memory. In return, Will protects Jack, providing him the emotional and financial support that allow him to pursue his more transgressive behaviors. This rapprochement between forms of gay identity that are often presented as antagonistic is crucial to the show's appeal, defusing a disabling sense of incoherence not only among different kinds of gay men, but within individuals defining their own sexual identity. "I am totally like Will, but I have a flouncing Jack inside of me waiting to come out and meet people," reads one posting in the show's chat room.[42]

Another aspect of *Will and Grace*'s appeal is its delight in exploring the bonds between certain forms of gay male and straight female identity and, by extension, the validation it offers for relationships between gay men and straight women, reversing the pejorative view of both parties implied in the common epithet "faghag."[43] The affirmation *Will and Grace* offers a queer community of gay men and their straight women friends does not depend primarily on plot, however. Other television shows have presented supposedly gay characters in friendship plots without gaining the powerful allegiance of gay viewers (the short-lived *Normal, Ohio,* which ran during *Will and Grace*'s third season, for example). What *Will and Grace* offers beyond demographic representation is a range of relationships to gay memory and identity, and, most important,

the continual, delighted, and delightful engagement of the audience in the dynamics of queer identity formation through memory. As references to the gay past and contemporary queer mores whiz past, we recognize, we recall, we repeat these remarks in ways that value not only the specific allusions to elements of gay history, but the related strategies of campy interpretation and performance that lie at the heart of gay identity.

NOTES

1. Stuart Hall, quoted in Andreas Huyssen, *Twilight Memories: Making Time in a Culture of Amnesia* (New York: Routledge, 1995), 1.

2. Diana Fuss, *Essentially Speaking: Feminism, Nature, and Difference* (New York: Routledge, 1989), 1–21, 97–112; *Identification Papers* (New York: Routledge, 1995), 1–19.

3. Specific recent examples include a referendum in Oregon to preclude affirmative mention of homosexuality in public schools, which was only narrowly defeated; the opposition whipped up by the *Washington Post* to the curatorial acknowledgment of Romaine Brooks's lesbianism in the exhibition on display at the National Museum of Women in the Arts over the summer of 2000 (see July 9 review, and on August 9 a letter, and an article about the letter, under the headline "Lesbianism may be all the rage, but what does it have to do with an artist's work?"), and the subsequent whitewashing of same-sex eroticism in major exhibitions on Thomas Eakins and Andy Warhol (Holland Carter, "Everything about Warhol but the Sex," *New York Times*, July 14, 2002, at www.nytimes.com). On controversies over the designation of a gay neighborhood in Chicago, see Christopher Reed, "We're from Oz: Marking Ethnic and Sexual Identity in Chicago," *Environment and Planning D: Society and Space* 21, no. 4 (August 2003): 425–40.

4. This chapter, therefore, uses "gay" and "queer" as overlapping terms, with the latter intended to stress continuities among those at odds with conventional heteropatriarchy.

5. This argument is made in more detail in Christopher Castiglia, "Sex Panics, Sex Publics, Sex Memories," *boundary 2* 27, no. 2 (summer 2000): 149–75.

6. Better World Advertising reported *Will and Grace*'s lead among television audiences of gay

and bisexual men in the San Francisco Bay area, among whom it earned a 36 percent share as opposed to its 6.3 percent rating in this area's population as a whole ("Surprise, Surprise," *Chicago Free Press*, November 29, 2000, 2).

7. Unless otherwise specified, chat room references are to the *Will and Grace* discussion group on the NBC site at http://nbc-tvclubs.nbci.com/willandgrace/forums.

8. Neither of us is trained in—though both teach courses in—media studies. Our interest in our students' and our own pleasures in (some) television motivates our purposeful divergence from academic approaches to mass media that seem to equate negativity with critical rigor. This tendency in film studies is demonstrated by the overwhelming influence of Laura Mulvey's "Visual Pleasure and Narrative Cinema," with its stated aim of destroying pleasure by analyzing it, over the same author's other writings analyzing her own viewing pleasures (most notably "Afterthoughts on 'Visual Pleasure and Narrative Cinema' Inspired by King Vidor's *Duel in the Sun*," both in her *Visual and Other Pleasures* [Bloomington: Indiana University Press, 1989], 14–38). The roots of this bias against pleasure are too numerous and complex to go into here, though they have been analyzed by some of the most provocative and lively writers in the humanities and social sciences. See, for instance, Pierre Bourdieu on intellectuals' need to claim an "ethical superiority" associated with "cultural capital"—an impulse intensified by the confluence of popular taste and intimidating economic capital in mass entertainment (*Distinction: A Social Critique of the Judgment of Taste*, trans. Richard Nice [Cambridge: Harvard University Press, 1984]), or Jane Gallop's analysis of the psychic drama of criticism as an act of aggression in which the critic triumphs by debasing his or her objects of study ("Psychoanalytic Criticism: Some Intimate Questions," *Art in America* 72 [November 1984]: 9–15).

9. Suzanna Danuta Walters, *All the Rage: The Story of Gay Visibility in America* (Chicago: University of Chicago Press, 2001), 111.

10. On *All in the Family*'s gay plots, and the ire they aroused in the Nixon White House, see Larry Gross, *Up from Visibility: Lesbians, Gay Men, and the Media in America* (New York: Columbia University Press, 2001), 81.

11. George Lipsitz, *Time Passages: Collective Memory and American Popular Culture* (Minneapolis: University of Minnesota Press, 1990), 19.

12. Ibid., 18.

13. Quoted in Paul Burston, "Just a Gigolo?" in *A Queer Romance: Lesbians, Gay Men, and Popular Culture*, ed. Paul Burston and Colin Richardson (London: Routledge, 1995), 120.

14. For an influential articulation of this argument, see John D'Emilio, "Capitalism and Gay Identity," in *Powers of Desire: The Politics of Sexuality*, ed. Ann Snitow, Christine Stansell, and Sharon Thompson (New York: Monthly Review Press, 1983), 100–113.

15. Lipsitz, *Time Passages*, 7–8, 16. For comparison, see, for example, George Chauncey, *Gay New York: Gender, Urban Culture, and the Making of the Gay Male World, 1890-1940* (New York: Basic, 1994).

16. The origins of this tradition—long before early sitcom characters or their precedents in the stock characters of nineteenth-century vaudeville and light opera—in Molière's plays and the "masks," as the characters were called, of the commedia dell'arte of the Renaissance, suggests a longer history of the social effects of popular entertainment than that sketched by Lipsitz.

17. "Whose Mom Is It, Anyway?" (season 2, episode 5). All scripts quoted from www.durfee.net/will/scripts.

18. One possible—but brief—precedent for such deployment of gay memory was the "coming out" season in the sitcom *Ellen*, but Ellen's obliviousness to—and outright denial of—subcultural allusions during the protracted buildup to the coming out (as described by Gross, *Up from Visibility*, 157–58, and Walters, *All the Rage*, 83) left little time for their development before the show's cancellation. What Walters describes as the "snatches of gay life" in the last shows of the season (88–90) did manifest many of the dynamics we find in *Will and Grace*, however.

19. Season 3, episode 6.

20. "Brothers, a Love Story" (season 3, episode 13).

21. . . .

22. "Alice Doesn't Live Here Anymore" (season 3, episode 20).

23. "Love plus One" (season 3, episode 6).

24. "Coffee and Commitment" (season 3, episode 10).

25. "Ben? Her?" (season 2, episode 23). That straight women characters prove as adept at camp as gay men is not surprising, given the history of camp, which often arose from figures—Bette Davis or Mae West, for example—who appealed to female and gay male viewers because of similar traits of endurance, self-assertion, and erotic inventiveness.

26. "Fear and Clothing" (season 3, episode 2).

27. Season 3, episode 6. Gay novelist Andrew Holleran, characterizing Karen as a "cross between Leona Helmsley, Lorena Bobbitt, Jacqueline Susann, Mother Goddam, and Margo Channing," claims her as "let's face it—the only really gay character on the whole sitcom: the straight woman." For Holleran, gay identification with Karen is a function of a nostalgic and collective yearning arising from strong cultural memory: "We miss Paul Lynde. We miss Wayland Flowers and Madame. We miss Bette Davis. We even miss the Golden Girls" ("The Alpha Queen," *Gay and Lesbian Review* 7, no. 3 [summer 2000]: 65–66). The perceived gayness of Karen's character seems also reflected in the Los Angeles Gay and Lesbian Center's selection of actress Megan Mullally (who declines to discuss her own sexuality) for its 2001 Creative Integrity Award, and in her starring role in Old Navy commercials, spoofing old-fashioned showgirl musical numbers.

28. Howard Buford, president of the advertising agency behind the campaign to market *Queer as Folk*, described his premise: "It's relevant to a broader audience if you convince them the show is an authentic slice of gay and lesbian life" (in Stuart Elliot, "Advertising," *New York Times*, November 28, 2000). Mainstream TV critics bought this claim, rehearsing clichés of the "hard-hitting" *Queer as Folk* as praiseworthy for the realistic "fullness of the characters" in contrast to the "role-model material" of shows like *Will and Grace,* and quoting *Queer as Folk*'s executive producer on the need "to be honest" (Steve Johnson, "On Television: On the Gaydar," *Chicago Tribune*, November 30, 2000).

29. In yet another rehearsal of memory, NBC reran the premier of *Will and Grace* during prime time on April 12, 2001.

30. The NBC chat room devoted to the show reveals that Jack and Karen's relationship at least equals—and threatens to overwhelm—the draw of the show's original couple. Discussion threads "Will & Grace or Jack & Karen?" and "Who's funnier Will and Grace or Jack and Karen" elicited only responses favoring Jack and Karen (typical among them, "I have been calling it [the show] Jack & Karen for a long time now"), with the exception of two participants who tactfully urged that the two pairs were equally funny. See also the discussion thread "Who loved that episode?"

31. "To Serve and Disinfect" (season 2, episode 7).

32. The pioneering attempt at definition, Susan Sontag's 1964 "Notes on Camp" (reprinted in *A Susan Sontag Reader* [New York: Vintage, 1983], 105–19) is largely a list of examples. Sontag's pre-Stonewall assumption that camp was apolitical has been supplanted by numerous scholars; see especially Andrew Ross, "Uses of Camp," in *No Respect: Intellectuals and Popular Culture* (New York: Routledge, 1989), 135–70; and three anthologies: Fabio Cleto, ed., *Camp: Queer Aesthetics and the Performing Self—A Reader* (Edinburgh: Edinburgh University Press, 1999); Moe Meyer, ed., *The Politics and Poetics of Camp* (New York: Routledge, 1994); and David Bergman, ed., *Camp Grounds: Style and Homosexuality* (Amherst: University of Massachusetts Press, 1993).

33. "I Never Promised You an Olive Garden" (season 2, episode 3). The power of this image of camp mentorship is registered in such chat room postings as "My favorite episode was when Jack came to the rescue of the young boy in the school hallway. We all could have used a Jack when we were that age!" (http://htmlgear.lycos.com).

34. . . .

35. . . .

36. . . .

37. . . .

38. A partial catalog might include the African-American girl Jack competes with on e-Bay, a trick named Mipanko and his unnamed father, a delivery boy, a temperance-oriented soccer mom, an INS officer, a crowd of "recovering" gays and lesbians, Martina Navratilova, a crew of ballet-dancing cater-waiters, a gay-acting heterosexual named Scott, a weeping woman in a bar, and a porn director.

39. "Whose Mom Is It, Anyway?" (season 2, episode 5).

40. "Gypsies, Tramps, and Weed" (season 3, episode 7).

41. Michael Warner, *The Trouble with Normal: Sex, Politics, and the Ethics of Queer Life* (Cambridge: Harvard University Press, 1999), 32.

42. Thread: "Which character do you relate to the best? Why?"

43. This validation has been a long time coming, as television lags behind social trends registered in well-known sociological studies since the 1970s; see Rebecca Nahas and Myra Turley, *The New Couple: Women and Gay Men* (New York: Seaview, 1979); and Catherine Whitney, *Uncommon Lives: Gay Men and Straight Women* (New York: Plume, 1990).

Discussion Questions

1. According to Castiglia and Reed, "sexual identity, which is almost invariably formed outside—and in opposition to—racial, ethnic, and class bonds nurtured in families . . . requires an ability to revise the personal memory narratives" (page 219). Support or challenge this claim.

2. "People invested in normative identities (whiteness, maleness, heterosexuality) that are continually reinforced by mainstream media as the makings of unique individuality can afford to ignore the collective aspect of those memories" (page 223). To what extent do you find your identities reinforced by mainstream media? Which aspects of your identity are rarely or never represented by mainstream media?

3. In what ways, according to Castiglia and Reed, does *Will and Grace* show "that memories can function not as signposts toward a future for which we are inevitably fated (or doomed), but as the materials from which we can construct new relationships with ourselves and our communities" (page 227)? Offer a couple of specific examples. Reflect on whether and, if so, how you find this to be true in your own life.

16

Living in the Middle

Performances Bi-Men

JOHN T. WARREN AND NICHOLAS A. ZOFFEL

The two of us enter this conversation from varied, yet strikingly similar, points of view. One of us is a bisexual man currently in a relationship with a woman—a relationship begun when they were 17. They have now spent more than 13 years together, 8 of them married. The other, a bi-curious man currently planning his wedding, is in a partnership that is now 4 years old. One of us was born and raised in the Midwest, where sexuality and difference persist through fogs of hate and innuendo. The other, a California boy who negotiates various levels of recognition and acceptance, is yet marked by his own ethnic and religious specificities. Both of us are interested in tracing the lines of our own position—our own location within competing desires, competing grand narratives, competing markings across our bodies.

The middle is an interesting cultural and social space. Victor Turner (1982) describes the middle as the liminal—the space betwixt and between, neither there nor here. The liminal is often characterized as a space of transition—a threshold from one point to another. In *From Ritual to Theatre*, Turner notes that the liminal can be thought of as a phase in ritual where subjects "pass through a period and area of ambiguity, a sort of social limbo which has few . . . of the attributes of either the proceeding or subsequent profane social statuses or cultural states" (p. 24). Think of the metaphor of a door frame—an actual threshold, locating the liminal as the transition from one point or social space to another. In this sense, the middle is nowhere really, not a place one would choose to stay within if one had the choice.

Turner (1982) argues that liminality is a space where things "seem to have been turned upside down," a space where "people 'play' with the elements of the familiar and defamiliarize them" (p. 27). He continues, "Novelty

SOURCE: A longer version of this chapter was originally performed at the 2004 Annual Convention of the National Communication Association (Chicago).

emerges from unprecedented combinations of familiar elements" (p. 27). Turner centrally locates the liminal as a space of transition—a temporary space such as a university (4 years at school) or a bridge (suspended between two more permanent shores)—but one can also see the liminal as a space of tension, a space of flux in the middle.

More recently, Jennifer DeVere Brody (1995) described the middle as a hyphen: "all those who think critically about this punctuation mark agree that the hyphen *performs*—it is never neutral or natural. Indeed, by performing the mid-point between often conflicting categories, hyphens occupy 'impossible' positions" (p. 149). Although Brody argues that no one ever really "escapes hyphenation" (p. 156), the metaphor of the hyphen—that impossible space located within and between often contradictory images or locations—captures the uneasy space of the middle, the focal point where competing desires play out their magic (Menchaca, 1995).

This chapter is about middles, about hyphens, about living in the liminal. It is a "dialogic performance," an engagement that itself is "more like a hyphen than a period" (Conquergood, 1985, p. 9). It is an aesthetic essay that, as Alexander and Warren (2002) say, balances voices and experiences, examining how meaning can get made through auto- or ethnographic exploration of lived experience. Like Pelias (1999), we offer the poetic because we believe it "offers a more nuanced account in keeping with the spirit of the performative event itself" (p. xi). We turn to the poetic because the questions we have center on our performances of self—selves that dwell in the impossibility of the middle, the tensions between binaries so carefully and powerfully woven into our consciousness that we constantly feel the flux and pull of our locations. Thomas Laqueur's (1990) analysis of sexual socialization engages the very language of performance, of difference, in relationship to the sexual identity that has not come to rest. Our questions should be answered in the poetic, in the "textual construction of, and thoughtful reflection about, the *lived experiences of [those selves]*" (Goodall, 2000, p. 191). In short, we write to "get at the *truth* of *our* experiences" (Goodall, 2000, p. 191). In this essay, we also embrace Della Pollock's (1998) reminder that "to write performance is not in and of itself to betray it" (p. 79). Given the nature of discourse surrounding issues of sexuality, race, citizenship, and identity, we concur: "the betrayal consists of not writing it" (p. 79).

Thus, here we write our performances—our narratives of ourselves, our bi-tales, our lived experiences as dwellers of the middle, the liminal, the hyphen. These stories are often sad, often representing pressure, denial, and loss. These stories also stem from hurt, containing anger and pain. These stories are about not belonging, not getting one's due, not being able to claim one's space at the table. However, these stories add up to a collage of experience that, when taken together, begin to sketch out a performance of the bisexual, the figure often torn between the poles of sexuality, not exactly gay and not exactly straight. The performance of which we write is simply often never enough, never legitimate, never real. In effect, because of the way we do sex, do the body, and do gender, we create for some only the liminal, only the doorway, only the transition between more permanent grounds. As the reader may see, the mark of that tension lives in our bodies, in our everyday performances of self, and in our stories.

CAUGHT

I've talked about this moment before (Warren & Fassett, 2002).

Are you gay too?

I've talked about the student who enters my office and asks me about my identity, about the student who calls me out, about the student who knows, somehow knows, that I'm not quite right, not quite.

He is a young man, probably a sophomore student in my large basic communication course. I think he attends the Thursday lecture, but perhaps it's the Wednesday—hard to remember as the days and faces blur, as the numbers increase and decrease depending on the proximity of the exam. He is thin and carries with him a powerful aroma of smoke blended with cologne. He is carefully groomed always, but groomed in such a way as to appear unkempt, to appear loose and at ease. It is a contrived look, but he wears it well.

When he enters my office that day, he is out of breath. He moans about climbing the three flights of stairs: *I have to quit smoking.* I agree and offer him a chair. Earlier that week I had promised him some lecture notes and our meeting was simply to turn over the notes, although I am confused about his presence as I had e-mailed him the notes already—to save him the trip up those flights of stairs. *I got your email . . . thanks.* He stands, refusing the chair, still panting. I wait for him to tell why he is here, panting in my office, when he already has the notes, our task already completed. We exist in awkward silence for a moment, neither of us talking. *Well, just wanted to say thanks for the notes,* he finally offers. OK, I say, not sure of what he is waiting for. Then, abruptly, he leaves.

His return is marked by more panting, more cursing about the stairs and his habit, his addiction. He has *one more question* before he takes the exam. *What is Communication Apprehension? I can't find it in my notes.* I look at him. He is removing a tablet and pen from his bag. Well, I begin, it is when you are apprehensive about speaking in public . . . or any other generalized fear of communication. He writes, I watch. *Great . . . whoa, I am so tired. I was up all night talking with an ex-boyfriend.* I smile: One of those calls, huh? *Yeah.* After a few more awkward silences, he leaves again.

His next return is more of the same—one last question, one more. As he puts his tablet away for the third time, he looks at me very carefully. *Can I ask a question?* Suddenly the room feels thicker, as if time has either moved into slow motion or we are now walking and talking through Jell-O. It is almost like deja vu, but not. Kind of like I have been here before, but not. Kind of like I know where this is going, but I don't. Slowly a yes falls from my lips. He rises and closes my door—moves the wooden door prop from the crack under the door and allows the door to close. He approaches me, his thin body leaning across my desk, his weight supported by his right hand on the left corner of my desk, the smell of smoke drifting across my desk filling my nose with his aroma of nicotine.

Are you gay too?

He stares at me, twisting a bit at the hips as he waits for my response. I feel caught in this moment, caught in the complexities of the question, caught in the space between the fluidity of desire and the fear of authenticity the question begs. Caught. I feel caught. Well, I begin, trying to ascertain his needs in this moment. Does he need to know, a burning desire to have easy answers, clean divisions? Does he need an ally, a queer friend on the faculty, a trusted someone to go to when he desires communion or safety? Does he need a pedagogical moment, a learning moment, a moment to discuss the intersection of pedagogy and identity, the meeting of our bodies, our desires, and the act of teaching? Does he desire more—is this a line, a spoken yearning across the commonality of our bodies, across academic ranks, across the many gulfs represented by the desk that separates us, seeking something important, seeking companionship, seeking love? Does he fear me, fear the sexual ambiguity that sustains my performance in class, that generates the possibility of the question, the question of who I am? Does this question stem from curiosity or stem from something more, something deeper? Does he understand the complexity of my own location; do I understand the difficulty of his position, his question, his risk?

Are you gay too?

Well . . . not exactly, I reply.

Oh, no offense, it's just that we thought we, my friends and I, thought we heard you slip up.

I opt for the truth, telling him I identify as bi, but that I am currently partnered with a woman. I tell him the ambiguity of my performance is strategic, that the question, the desire to know (and the reflection on that desire) is important pedagogical work. I tell him that sexuality is often more complex than a simple yes or no, an either-or, a this and not that. I tell him that the slippage he is worried about is exactly the point, exactly the place for reflection, exactly the moment of paradox that tells us of the power of these identities, these categories. I tell him these things and watch his face, searching for how my response finds resonance or dissonance within his own body.

He immediately does repair work: *I won't tell anyone, I was just curious, I won't tell anyone.* I try to tell him that I am not keeping secrets, not worried about who knows.

He leaves, this time for good. I will see him in class, he will stop by again, but never mention, never say anything more about me, about this talk. His friends in class watch me very closely in class, listening for the slippages, the moments of rupture that are inevitable, that are always present, that are strategic.

Are you gay too?

I do not tell many people that I am bi. It makes me uncomfortable. It makes me uncomfortable because I feel like I am assuming a risky identity which requires no risks—I get the privilege of "really" being married, of "really" being with a woman in public, of "really" appearing in every context, in every moment, as straight, as not-queer.

I have often thought about writing a piece on the closet—a kind of defense of the closet as a political choice that, in some circumstances, benefits gay, lesbian, and bi politics. I question whether it is politically sound for me to remain silent, to not voice my own queer location. It seems like saying I'm queer, I'm not-straight, is to bank on the exoticness, an almost chicness of the identity, without having to walk that line. I worry that my own privilege only strengthens heteronormativity, only

renders down my own identity as a tool for those who insist that "homosexual thoughts are normal, but acting on them is the sin." I worry that who I am hurts a cause I have a stake in more than it helps.

Are you gay too?

I've talked about this before. I've been here before in this liminal space of contradiction, a liminal space of fluidity.

COMING OUT WHILE STAYING IN

The fantasy:

It is 8:00 p.m. and I am standing at an ATM in front of a movie theater. I find a mantra-like comfort in the hum of my earned money being given back to me from the mouth of the machine. As I turn around and I see a lone young woman walking past me. She smiles, I collect my money, and then walk toward her, whistling the Benny Hill theme song. I catch up to her as she pauses to buy her ticket. I do the same. The woman looks at me suspiciously for a moment and then, seeing my smile, smiles back. The rest is a quite typical het-tale.

The fantasy:

It is 8:00 p.m. and I am standing at an ATM in front of a movie theater. I find a mantra-like comfort in the hum of my earned money being given back to me from the mouth of the machine. As I turn around and I see a lone young man walking past me. He smiles, I collect my money, and then walk toward him, whistling "Strange" by Depeche Mode. I catch up to him as he pauses to buy his ticket. I do the same. The man looks at me suspiciously for a moment and then, seeing my smile, smiles back. The rest is a quite typical queer tale.

My junior year in college was the first time that my armor of hetero–self-deception began to crack. One day, my friends and I were watching a soft-core porn video in a dorm room and I was horrified to realize that although these beautiful women had unqualified sexual appeal to me, the men equally captured my interest. As the semester went on, I increasingly became aware that I was interested in both the men and the women in my classes. Although the reasons differed, I found I could not get either sex out of my mind, which plagued me with guilt and caused my self-imposed hetero-world to fall apart.

Not knowing how to cope, I took a long walk through the university campus. I circled my final destination several times, as though I was trying to maneuver through a maze. I hoped when I emerged from around the next turn, I would know where I was; I would be in the clear. The reality was that I was trying to psych myself up to admit that I had no idea where I was. I fancied myself as someone who always knew how to mediate his world, his identity, his culture, and his ethnicity—I believed my sexuality was no different. Mustering up the courage, I looked for support, someone to validate my feelings and help me plan what to do. With stereotypes guiding me, I walked to the counseling center with all the gusto of how I imagined a man would be but vexed at my desires to cry like the woman I felt I had become. I suspected the giant talking head sitting across from me was searching for warnings that I might be crazy, signs that I might act out violently—but alas, I disappointed. I could see the dissatisfaction in her eyes that I was going to be another disappointment. I could read her disinterest in my stories, my exploits, my questions, my . . . self. All emotion in her face drained, creating a blank look that kept checking the clock, ignoring my search for answers and my need to hear her advice.

Then I said: "I might be gay, but I am still attracted to women." I hoped she would tell me that these dualistic feelings were okay. Instead, in the most soulless of voices, she told me that there was nothing I could do to change my experiences and feelings, that I would have to make a choice, that I needed to make a decision. She told me that no matter

what I chose to do, she could introduce me to the appropriate groups, the appropriate solution, gesturing to her wall of pamphlets and flyers lining the wall of her office. Horrified that I would *have* to choose, I ran away.

As my doubts of being gay grew more intense, I threw myself into my heterosexuality. In talking to a good friend who identifies as bisexual, I got a response that allowed me some peace. I retold my tales, almost verbatim, regarding my feelings, fears, frustrations, and the responses to my feelings, to my dual attractions. She began with a hug, then a gentle kiss. She asked me if I had ever played with scales when I was younger. She asked me to think of sexuality as weights placed on opposite ends of the scale. She asked me to imagine that there were times of flux as the conditions change. She asked me to think of bisexuality as living in that fluid space of competing weights. She asked me to not maximize or minimize my feelings toward either sex. She asked me to keep reflecting on my feelings and use that to help me grow as a more balanced person.

After these words, I actively pursued the development of relationships that would surround me with people who openly admitted that they were trying to achieve an experiential balance similar to mine. I sought people with whom I could discuss these issues, people who complicated issues. In many ways this made things more rewarding, but it also made things more difficult. Although I had long struggled with these issues, they had previously not been in the forefront of my mind. If anything, my newly found ability to be frank with my own closet, my own tensions, created a fear of being silenced. My struggle is constant and sharp, but I do not seek tolerance. In fact, I want my struggle to be in the face of others—I do not look for escape. Escape may bring temporary catharsis, but I fear that being quiet may just reseal my own closet door and I will be left hiding, again.

It is 8:00 p.m. and I am standing at an ATM in front of a movie theater. I find a mantralike comfort in the hum of my earned money being given back to me from the mouth of the machine. I collect my money.

The rest is just possibility.

QUESTION OF THE DAY

A ritual in my upper level undergraduate courses is the "question of the day." It is basically a roll-call question process, helping me keep attendance. I do it for several reasons—for instance, I'm terrible with names and, although I believe in the importance of knowing my students in meaningful ways, names escape me. This has never been more true than this fall—just this semester I have 10 white women students whose names resemble some shade of "Christina" (that is, Kristens, Krises, Christines, Carolines, and Katies). Names, especially in this context, escape me, and the question of the day is my attempt to get to know folks, connecting names to faces. I also do it because it makes folks talk in class. I feel the need to make sure everyone speaks: Everyone must break his or her own silences, everyone must do it even if just once, even if it is a silly opening-of-class exercise. This ritual starts the day with a light tone—I can ask for their favorite sitcom of all time and, together, we can joke and play before we get to the core of the day's agenda. I like the question of the day because it sets a tone and gives folks something to look forward to—and they do.

This summer, I had a good class—I was teaching a senior level seminar I created called "Communication, Race, and Power," in which I asked students to think about race and power as communicative constructs. I like this course mostly because it is the basis of my book—race as an ongoing communicative or performative process (Warren, 2003). It was week 5 in the 6-week intensive summer session. Thus far, my questions of the day were fairly innocuous: Best pizza in town? Favorite soda? They were safe questions, not really causing too much of a stir. In week 5, I had

planned on a guest facilitator—one of our graduate students, a woman who was writing her dissertation on interracial and intercultural communication, would come in to lead the discussion of Ruth Frankenberg's (1993) *White Women, Race Matters*. In the 4 days of her visit, I gave her the class, my class—including my question of the day.

On her first day, she approached me right before class and asked if I had heard about New York's first gay high school. I had: the Harvey Milk School, when it opened in the fall, would create a "safe space" for GLBTQ youth to go to school. I had read some stories on it. I felt strongly about it, remembering my own high school experiences, remembering how I felt, remembering that no amount of girlfriends could save me from critique. I felt strongly about it.

So I nodded. This graduate student knew me—knew that I identify as bisexual, knew that I struggle with how, in northwest Ohio, to create a persona, a space that allows me to exist under the weight of binary logic, under homophobia, under the consistent denial of my own experiences. We had had these conversations, and she had told me how I was perceived by many of our undergrads as the gay interpersonal communication professor. These are misreadings (?) of me that I welcome: I have created a performance of self that is ambiguous, and I want students to ask more questions about me than they find answers. I believe in the performative power of the question. I believe that when students have to ask, *is he?* that it disrupts the heteronormativity of my classrooms. For as soon as my relationship—my marriage to a woman—arises, I know that students often will rest, placing me easily into the binary that already denies the very possibility of my own complicated subjectivity. Thus I have chosen, for better or worse, to subvert from a distance, but it is a troubling location.

"I want to ask them their opinions for the question of the day." It was a statement, not a question—and that was what it should be. I nodded again.

Five minutes later, we were in class. I introduced her, noting that she would be leading class for the next few days. She immediately began with the question of the day: "In New York, they are opening the first gay public high school. What do you think?" My stomach turned. I realize that while I trusted the performative politics of questioning (e.g., inquiry, my ambiguous performances, our collective relationships, etc.), I did not trust these students. This was a scary conclusion, not only because it said something about my perceptions of these undergrads, but because it also reflected my own comfort with my sexuality. It begged the question I had not really asked: The politics of ambiguity are powerful—they do cause students, I believe, to question the heteronormativity of the classroom space—but how does that politic set up conditions for heterosexism? That is, does my silence (my ambiguous persona, as opposed to a more out persona) create the opportunity, the room, for violence to arise? Inside the "possibly straight" professor, is enough room generated for cruelty to breed?

The first student began, "So is this school going to teach gay math? This is stupid." As the responses came, I was reminded of the weaknesses of my own politics, my own politics of silence—this room had become violent for me, violent for any other GLBTQ bodies in it. Would my own early outing in this room have changed the tenor of this conversation? Would I have been able to stop this before it started? I was not sure, but I was sure that I wanted to leave. The ninth or tenth student, a favorite of mine in this class, is going to speak. I do not want him to—if he says something that hurts, it will really bother me. In this wish, I realize again the kind of pressure my silence has caused him—he now must risk his status with me as his instructor with his reply to this question of the day, and he does not even know this is a test. "Well, I think high school can suck for lots of people. As a black

man, there were times I wish I could have been in a space where I didn't have to deal with racism—why shouldn't we, until we create a less violent society, create a more safe space for homosexuals?" I sighed. He passed. I shuddered at what I was doing.

Eventually, the question came to me. My turn. Should I out myself, creating a space for these students to question the heteronormativity of this space? Or should I remain protected? Was I protected at all here? Why was protection my impulse? Should I choose to keep the heteroassumptions of my own performance or offer another kind of text? In either case, would such a reading be misunderstood? Did I have time for effective politics in the question of the day, especially when it was not even my own? My response:

> Let me begin by noting the communicative choices here—almost everyone has chosen to use constructs like "those people" or has felt it necessary to note their heterosexuality prior to answering the question. These kinds of maneuvers are interesting—a distancing of the self from the issue. I would note that, as some of you argue vigorously for the stupidity of this school, to remember that there are GLBTQ folks in this room. Statistically, there are several. Let us watch our tones and remember that GLBTQ students in high school have some of the highest suicide rates among today's youth. Let us remember the terror some students face in the midst of their math class. Let us remember that gay, lesbian, bisexual, transgender, and queer students are still beaten up in high school, left tied to fence posts to die. Let us remember that school is not a politically free space—that education, for many GLBTQ students, is always already about social judgment, physical, mental, and emotional violence. Let us remember why such a school is perceived to be needed before we dismiss it outright. And let us continue to discuss this in a way that doesn't create more violence for those of us here that might not identify as straight.

It was a good response, fit for an episode of *The West Wing*, but one that still allowed me a shadow of invisibility. The class blurred by, as the graduate student moved to the reading for the day. My hands eventually stopped shaking, stopped sweating. What remained was the constant question of costs to myself, costs to other GLBTQ students, and costs to the political struggle that I think of myself as fighting—at what costs? To whom? To what end?

ERASURE IN THE MIDDLE

In *The History of Sexuality,* Foucault (1978) argues that subjects that seem natural are really contingent on sociohistorical constructs of power and domination. Noting that knowledge and systems of power are not mutually exclusive, he claims that power is "a multiple and mobile field of force relations where far-reaching, but never completely stable effects of domination are produced" (p. 102). Rather, power is plural, fragmentary, differentiated, as well as historically and spatially specific, often taking the shape of reified binaries. Power, then, operates through the cultural logics of norms, political technologies, and the shaping of the citizen through repetitive discursive patterns.

Adapted to our aim, bisexuals find their sexuality an impossible identity—a repressive situatedness within a binary that denies their (our) subjectivity. Given the binary of hetero-homo, our placement as a liminal identity becomes an affirmation of nonexistence, an admission that such subjects have failed to correctly identify. However, what Foucault (1978) gives us is the knowledge that sexuality is an invented identification that, although reproduced and sedimented through discourse, simply works to marginalize and privilege. Our struggle is this: How do we critique the power of this binary logic upon our bodies in ways that do not simply locate us as victims? Certainly we acknowledge the loneliness of our own subjectivity, and we understand that in the end, we have the privilege of appearing in most situations as straight. But in the binary we are—a binary that was constructed at the expense of queer bodies (as the latest charge against gay marriage attests).

We concede that for many the bisexual represents a danger for sexual politics. If we claim a bi-identity (our queer identity) and yet remain in monogamous relationships with the women in our lives, how do we represent the inevitable choice that "The Right" wishes we would make? That is, desiring men is not the problem; acting upon those desires is. As men who desire men and women, our choice (to be with a woman, regardless of the circumstances) makes us the conservative dream—we chose correctly. Still, such constructions do more damage than simply deny us a certain sexual citizenship—do more than simply deny us membership in the queer communities that we may desire. Such constructions, by reproducing the binary logic sexuality is often bound within, reproduce modern notions of sexuality as an either-or, a stable and natural division between people. As Foucault (1978) and others are quick to remind us, binaries are powerful because they imply both hierarchy and mutual exclusivity; this is to say, hierarchies (men-women, white-black, good-bad, straight-queer) depend on clean divisions between situated categories favoring one over the other. Such constructions (and the concomitant reproduction of such constructions) not only hurt those (of us) who identify in the middle but those who occupy the secondary position in the binary. Bi identity, as Garber (1995) helps us to see, undoes the very hierarchy, calling into question the naturalizing (and confining) nature of our sexual imaginations:

> There is, in short, no "really" about it. The question of whether someone was "really" straight or "really" gay misrecognizes the nature of sexuality, which is fluid, not fixed, a narrative that changes over time rather than a fixed identity, however complex. The erotic discovery of bisexuality is the fact that it reveals sexuality to be a process of growth, transformation, and surprise, not a stable and knowable state of being. (p. 66)

Like Foucault, we seek a model of power based not on hierarchy, but on broader notions of political power—to replace static understandings with concepts of efficacy, the privileges of sovereignty with more democratic notions of "multiple and mobile field[s] of force relations, wherein far-reaching, but never completely stable, effects of domination are produced" (Foucault, 1978, p. 102). We seek to disrupt the normalized bonds that continue to produce power through a zero-sum relation. We think such conceptions of power create the possibility for multiple sexual identities beyond the expected binaries.

Our concern is that unless we reconceptualize sexuality, removing it from the sedimented binaries that have been so normalized over time, we create identities that are not only excluded but more and more invisible. During these conflictual times of the Federal Marriage Amendment, the middle has never been so obscured, so erased. The bisexual may blend into gay or straight communities, fearing questions or accusations of authenticity; efforts to come out may be abandoned as the slings and arrows of structured logic continue to deny space for their (our) own voices. Even if one wants "to tell the truth," our culture's hold on these binary logics results not only in the difficult task of claiming a queer identity but in one's defense of the right to exist in the first place.

A THRESHOLD

The middle *is* an interesting cultural and social space. When Victor Turner (1982) described the middle as the liminal, that space betwixt and between, he did talk about it as a space of possibility—it is the moment of transition. In this way, the liminal is a threshold from one point to another, a way to rethink and question the strictures of our own dualistic point of view. We do not see this chapter solving anything; the moment of transformation is embodied flux—it is a performance directed toward, but without a clear vision of, what lies beyond. As one stands on a long bridge (an apt metaphor for liminality), what is it one sees, looking toward the horizon? We see hope—and we hope that through voicing the locatedness of our own desiring and socially constricted bodies, we have identified a performance of sexuality, of self, that requires more examination.

WORKS CITED

Alexander, B. K., & Warren, J. T. (2002). The materiality of bodies: Critical reflections on pedagogy, politics, and positionality. *Communication Quarterly, 50,* 328–343.

Brody, J. D. (1995). Hyphen-nation. In S. E. Case, P. Brett, & S. L. Foster (Eds.), *Cruising the performative: Interventions into the representation of ethnicity, nationality, and sexuality* (pp. 149–162). Bloomington IN: Indiana University Press.

Conquergood, D. (1985). Performing as a moral act: Ethical dimensions of the ethnography of performance. *Literature in Performance, 5*(2), 1–13.

Frankenberg, R. (1993). *White women, race matters: The social construction of whiteness.* Minneapolis: University of Minnesota Press.

Foucault, M. (1978). *The history of sexuality: An introduction.* New York: Vintage.

Garber, M. (1995). *Bisexuality and the eroticism of everyday life.* New York: Routledge.

Goodall, H. L. (2000). *Writing the new ethnography.* Walnut Creek, CA: AltaMira.

Laqueur, T. (1990). *Making sex: Body and gender from the Greeks to Freud.* Cambridge, MA: Harvard University Press.

Menchaca, D. A. (1995). Fragments of memory: Shadowboxing the hyphen in border territory. In L. Lengel & J. T. Warren (Eds.), *Casting gender: Women and performance in intercultural contexts.* New York: Peter Lang.

Pelias, R. J. (1999). *Writing performance: Poeticizing the researcher's body.* Carbondale: Southern Illinois University Press.

Pollock, D. (1998). Performative writing. In P. Phalen & J. Lane (Eds.), *The ends of performance* (pp. 73–103). New York: New York University Press.

Turner, V. (1982). *From ritual to theatre: The human seriousness of play.* New York: PAJ.

Warren, J. T. (2003). *Performing purity: Whiteness, pedagogy, and the reconstitution of power.* New York: Peter Lang.

Warren, J. T., & Fassett, D. L. (2002). (Re)constituting ethnographic identities. *Qualitative Inquiry, 8,* 575–590.

Discussion Questions

1. Warren and Zoffel describe themselves as bisexual men in relationships with women. How do they narrate their experiences of being "in the middle"? What can we learn from this position? How do you relate to it?

2. Do you think being ambiguous about your sexual identity is a valid stance in the classroom for faculty and students? Why or why not? What are the advantages and disadvantages of this position?

3. What kind of persona do you create in the classroom, and how does it serve you? (Do you feel authentic or in the closet about some aspects of self? Open or closed? Trusting or mistrusting of how others might respond to you?)

4. In what ways do you see bisexuality as an "impossible" identity, and in what ways do you see it as offering new possibilities?

17

"Holly Kowalski"

Sex Across the Curriculum

JENNIFER TUDER

"*Holly Kowalski*" *is a monologue from the full-length performance* Sex Across the Curriculum. *Holly is one of the guest speakers in Mrs. Glasscock's "Sex Across the Curriculum 101," a remedial sex education course. Mrs. G, as Holly calls her, has just introduced Holly, then retired to the audiovisual room offstage for her customary smoke. Holly is 17 years old, dressed in a bubblegum pink velour track jacket and sporting pigtails. Holly takes her place in front of the class with adolescent disdain. Throwing her weight onto one hip, she begins reading from her notecards in a contemptuous monotone:*

Hello, my name is Holly Kowalski and I am here tonight to talk with you about being kind to people with different sexualities.

    I. Introduction
        A. Have you ever felt like you had a deep, dark, shameful secret that you couldn't share with anyone else? Well, that is how gays feel all the time. (And bi's.)
        B. I want to persuade you to accept and support gay, lesbian, bisexual, and transgender people in our school. And bisexual people.
        C. So today I will speak about:

1. What sexual orientation is and many of the different sexual orientations people can have. Like bisexuality.

2. What you can do to make gays and lesbians and bi's feel supported and safe—

Fuck this. (*Holly throws the cards down.*) Mrs. G can't hear me 'cause she's out having a smoke, just like she has the last seven times I've given this fucking speech. Believe me, I'm as tired of giving it as she is of hearing it. It's part of my in-school suspension, okay? And I guess you all think you know why I'm here

SOURCE: This chapter is a transcription of part of *Sex Across the Curriculum*, a solo performance first presented June 15, 2006, at Patrick's Cabaret in Minneapolis, Minnesota. Copyright © 2006 Sage Publications. Reprinted by permission.

since that little bitch Stacy Lindner has been spreading that rumor all over. So let's just talk about what you really want to know: Yes, I wrote DYKE across Tara Engelmeyer's locker. But it was not a hate crime. I did not vandalize Tara's locker because I hate lesbians, okay?

(*Holly takes a deep breath. Her brow furrows as she recalls the tragedy that led to her crime.*)

I did it because Tara Engelmeyer was my girlfriend and she broke up with me and I don't understand why. There. Now you know it's not like Stacy has been saying—I could care less who fucks Tommy Miller now, okay? I am so over beer-guzzling, ass-groping jocks it's not even funny. And apparently I'm really over them. Like so over them that I decided to make out with Tara one night while I was over at her house.

(*Holly turns to a classmate on her right*) And if you think I'm going to give you a play-by-play, *Brad,* think again.

So since Mrs. G won't be back for a good 10 minutes or so, and since you've pretty much got to listen to me for like the next 7 minutes, let me tell you the whole fucking thing and you tell me if it makes any sense to you:

Okay, so Tara's over at my house, and we're talking about stuff. Like we always did. We told each other everything, you know? So Tara says that she can't believe I ever had sex with boys, like how gross that would be. And I said, actually I like having sex with boys. And she gets all pissy about it, like Why would I even say that to her and calling me a fence-sitter and shit.

Like, hello, what the fuck are you talking about? And she goes, "Uh!" (*demonstrating exasperation*) and I go, "Uh?" (*demonstrating confusion*)

So then she gets *really* pissed and starts screaming about how she had to hold my hand and teach me everything and how much she hates fucking baby dykes. I don't even know what that's about. And then it's all about how

I won't come out and be honest about who I am and our relationship. And then it's all I'm just a waste of her time and I need to make a choice here. And I said, hello, I have made a choice—I'm with you! But she just ripped off my ring and most of the friendship bracelets I made her and ran out of my house.

And, *of course,* my mom heard everything. So she came in and you know what she said? Well, those people aren't ever very happy anyway, honey. Thanks, Mom. And then she says, You want to have a family, don't you? Um, excuse me, I'm 17 and if I got pregnant, she'd throw a shit fit. God. So after all that comfort, I was up all night crying and writing in my journal.

So I went to school really early the next day to get away from my mom, and I made the stupid decision to get out a Sharpie and write DYKE on her locker. So there. It's not a big, huge Hate Crime. It's just a crime I committed against my ex. But not because I hate her.

See. (*Holly takes out a folded piece of notebook paper and opens it.*) This is something I wrote that night and if you see Tara, tell her about it, okay? It's called "For Tara":

> Oh my darling Tara,
> Were you aware-ah?
> Of my love so true
> Of my heart so blue.
>
> Tara with your eyes of brown
> Tara who should never frown
> Won't you come back to me?
> It's only bisexuality.
>
> I'll love you 'til the day I die.
> Why, I ask myself, why oh why
> Come back, my love, and be mine.
> Baby hit me one more time.

(*Holly's face crumples. She's genuinely upset. Then she spots a classmate giving her "attitude" on her left and addresses her with vehement reproach:*)

Oh whatever Andrea! Like no one saw you all over Jenna Robbins at Tommy's Homecoming party. And that "Oh! I was so drunk, I didn't know what I was doing" crap doesn't fly, okay? You and Jenna mash every time you get a chance, so don't give me that look, like you don't like girls too.

(*Looking over whole crowd*) Don't any of you look at me like that. I've spent my whole life in this town with you assholes telling me that you think I am a queer and a dyke and a lesbo. So now I've actually done what you all seem to think I'm doing anyway and I'm honest about it and you have the nerve to act like you're surprised and disgusted and shit? Whatever. Do me a favor and do what you do best: Spread this all over the school. Maybe that way Tara will hear about it and come talk to me or something. Now if you'll excuse me, my 7 minutes are up. I hope you feel better informed.

Discussion Questions

1. Do you recall specific incidents from school in which students were labeled in an accusatory fashion according to what was perceived as their sexual identity? At what grade levels did these events occur? How did references to students' sexuality contrast or compare in elementary, middle school, and high school contexts?

2. At one point in this piece, Holly addresses a male student, Brad, indicating that she doesn't intend to provide a "play-by-play" rendition of making out with her girlfriend. What assumptions may be behind her statement to Brad?

3. Why, in this society, are women more likely to be seen as bisexual than men?

4. Tuder is clearly parodying her "remedial sex education course." What ideas do you have about how students can effectively learn to better understand and respect their own and others' sexual identities? What role, if any, should the education system play in this?

18

Queering the (Sacred) Body Politic

*Considering the Performative Cultural
Politics of the Sisters of Perpetual Indulgence*

CATHY B. GLENN

*Some people would say that we need a ground from which to act. We need a shared
collective ground for collective action. I think we need to pursue the moments of
degrounding, when we're standing in two different places at once; or we don't know
exactly where we're standing; or when we've produced an aesthetic practice that
shakes the ground.*

—Judith Butler (1994, question 6, ¶ 4)

While living in San Francisco, I took them for granted. For me, they were fixtures in SF's cultural milieu, a "natural" element in and of the sociopolitical landscape. I attended their Halloween-in-the-Castro celebrations; I saw them at AIDS Dance-a-thon and Walk-a-thon benefits; they greeted me at the Castro and Folsom Street Fairs; and they

SOURCE: An earlier version of this manuscript was presented as a top paper to the Gay/Lesbian/Bisexual/ Transgender Division at the 2002 National Communication Association annual meeting in New Orleans, Louisiana.

Author's Note: A version of this chapter appears in *Theory & Event* (vol. 7, 2003), and it was also presented as a top paper to the Gay/Lesbian/Bisexual/Transgender division at the 2002 National Communication Association annual meeting in New Orleans, Louisiana. I extend my warm thanks to Ronald J. Pelias, Jonathan M. Gray, Craig Gingrich-Philbrook, Sister Kitty, and Sister Camille for their valuable insights and suggestions on earlier drafts of this study. I also offer my appreciation to editors Karen Lovaas and Lee Jenkins for their helpful recommendations for this version, and to Philip C. Ho for the conversations that underlie parts of this chapter.

247

were always in the foreground at lesbian, gay, bisexual, and transgender Pride Day celebrations. If the Sisters of Perpetual Indulgence were absent from a major GLBT-supported benefit or critical action, somehow the event seemed to be missing something. The Sisters' presence signaled, at once, a deadly serious political critique *and* an opportunity to celebrate the wicked camp of the Sisters, tricked out in (among other things) nuns' habits, lace, high heels, rubber, and mascara.

Formally established in 1979, The Sisters of Perpetual Indulgence, Inc. (SPI), is a San Francisco–based not-for-profit organization[1] dedicated to social service and political activism, primarily focused on human rights concerns, HIV/AIDS prevention, and protection of freedom of expression. Although originally an organization of gay men, the SPI currently includes members who self-identify as gay, lesbian, bisexual, transgender, androgynous, and straight men and women. The Sisters are also self-identified performance artists. Donning nuns' habits and accessorizing with buttons, jewelry, hats, and make-up, they identify themselves as "holy sacred clowns" as well as "21st Century nuns" (Day, 1997, ¶ 26). According to their mission statement, SPI members vow to assist with "the *spiritual enlightenment* and *spirits lightenment* of the community" by "promulgating universal joy and expiating stigmatic guilt" and "help[ing] others through humor and hard work" (The Sisters of Perpetual Indulgence, Inc., 2001, p. 1).

The Sisters, because of their high profile presence in SF cultural politics, have attracted considerable media attention. Some supporters, defending against the critique of the Sisters' ostensible heresy, have described them simply as "drag artists" who merely "put on a show" as they raise money and awareness about important "gay issues" (Carroll, 1999, p. E8). SPI's public performances have been variously characterized as innocuous entertainment, satirical street theater, carnivalesque camp, and political parody (Carroll, 1999;

Garcia, 1999; Lattin, 1999). These descriptions, although they sketch an outline of the lighthearted aesthetic (or discursive and celebratory) aspects of SPI, tend to do so by foregrounding the campy characteristics evident at events and only parenthetically mentioning the Sisters' significant everyday (material) commitment to action in the communities they serve through political activism and critique.

When I became acquainted with them in 1994, I was not aware of other important facets of SPI's public persona: their solemn commitment to community service and their habitual participation in political activism. The Sisters' performances as glammed-out nuns are driven by a deeply held desire to materially contribute an affirming, nurturing, and joyful presence to, and affect positive change within, queer communities through a modality of queer performance art as activism. As such, SPI offers an intriguing and important example of the power of cultural politics, of the material political force of ludic discursivity, and of the playful ways that a wicked wit can work in political activism.

My objective in this study is to explore aspects of SPI's cultural politics that trouble what Judith Butler (1998) points out is a trend in reading and gauging the political efficacy of particular social groups:

> The untimely resurgence of the culture/material distinction is in the service of a tactic . . . that seeks to identify some social movements with the merely cultural and then the cultural with the derivative and the secondary, and what tends to happen then is that an anachronistic materialism becomes the banner for a new Left orthodoxy. (¶ 8)

I take Butler to mean, here, that those movements identified as "merely cultural" are understood as superfluous (derivative, secondary)—that is, the cultural constitutes little "real" material impact in the body politic. SPI's playfully discursive mode of cultural politics, from this perspective, can easily be dismissed as ineffectual in creating material change. The either-or characterization of the "merely" cultural and the "real" material (what I refer to in this chapter as a discursive-material or ideal-material binary) can have serious consequences for those groups who engage in cultural politics. At least one penalty imposed on groups identified as employing ludic (playful), discursive tactics is the dismissal of their efforts as useless, navel-gazing capriciousness, at best, and as being hostile toward collective political efforts, at worst. The "Left orthodoxy" to which Butler refers is reflected in Donald Morton's (1996) comment that "queer idealism is rendered more clearly as allied with the self-interested individualistic idealism of the bourgeois subject" (p. 15) than it is with making actual, material collective contributions to change. Such a charge, I argue, misses its target with respect to the Sisters' queer activism.

SPI embodies the very material political change and collective spirit for which Morton and other materialists call—precisely through the uniquely situated performative actualization of their ideals in the real constructs of the body politic. In other words, SPI's celebratory discursive idealism (the Sisters' playful, campy, aesthetic modality) does not neglect but, in fact, recognizes, embodies, and strengthens *the powerful materiality inherent in the discursive*. In what follows, I offer a fleshier reading of the Sisters (than has been offered by mainstream media representations) to examine the non-normative performative appropriation of "nun" by the queer bodies of SPI and how their cultural politics demonstrate the materiality of discursive ideals and the discursiveness of the material.

I recognize that the sense of taken-for-grantedness with respect to the Sisters I mentioned at the outset is bound up in the unique cultural strands that constitute San Francisco's diverse sociopolitical quilt; in many other contexts, the Sisters would probably stretch, even rip, that fabric. From its unique

beginnings, San Francisco has been recognized as a brawling, contentious, volcanic, "raw democracy" (Roff, 1996, p. 42), alive with fractured and fracturing cultural and community identities and diverse political factions. Various scholars have attended to this "politics of hyperpluralism" (Wirt, 1971, p. 101), and San Francisco's unique cultural personality has been considered in terms of its cosmopolitan character and tolerant, libertine ways of life (Asbury, 1933; Findlay, 1986; Matthews, 1997) and its bohemian counter-culture histories (Ashbolt, 1989; Cavan, 1972; Perry, 1984; Smith, 1995). More specifically, some scholars have focused on San Francisco's gay, lesbian, bisexual, and transgender communities with respect to social space (Castells & Murphy, 1982), queer culture and tourism (Howe, 2001; Stryker & Van Buskirk, 1996), and San Francisco's sometimes explosive political climate (Shilts, 1982; Weiss, 1982).

Scholars, however, could devote more attention to this distinctive cultural community and the myriad of intersecting queer identities, performances, and activist organizations. Several researchers make mention of San Francisco's queer culture and political critique in studies concerned with rhetorical strategies (Darsey, 1991; Slagle, 1995; Smith & Windes, 1997), and this study adds to that body of work by examining a specific example of San Francisco's queer activism. This is an effort to contribute to the ongoing conversation one noteworthy example (perhaps, exemplar) of a queer activist organization that demonstrates how the discursive power of performative and subversive appropriation of oppressive symbols of authority can instantiate material change.

In the first section, I suggest several theoretical points of orientation with respect to "queer" and "camp" and briefly outline the process through which a potential Sister advances to full-fledged Sisterhood. Described in the second section are the Sisters' aesthetic practices and activism. In the third and fourth sections, I analyze the performative nature of

SPI's artistic activism and situate it within a sociopolitical context. In the final section, I offer tentative implications for further analyses of the Sisters' activism in particular and locally situated camp activist performance in general.

CAMP AND VOWS: QUEERING THE (SACRED) BODY

> Queer is a symptom, not a movement, a symptom of a desire for radical change. (Alcorn, quoted in Smith, 1996, p. 277)

Queer is a contested term, one that incites much debate and discussion in the literature theoretically treating subjectivity as it relates to gender and sexual orientation. For opponents of queer theory and practice such as David Horowitz (1996), the "Queer revolution" represents "the ultimate subversive project" (p. 328). It is "a war against civilization and nature" (p. 336) that, ultimately, renders meaningless concepts such as God and Nature in an effort to break down the "natural" distinctions between sexes and empty those categories of any gender-related value or norm and that thereby moves toward creating "a gender free world" (p. 328). Others, like Cherry Smith (1996), take a less strident approach in describing "queer."

In her chapter "What Is This Thing Called Queer?" Smith (1996) reads the term through the politics of groups such as Queer Nation, OutRage, and Perverts Undermining State Scrutiny (PUSSY):

> [Queer] defines a strategy, an attitude, a reference to other identities and a new self-understanding. . . . Both in culture and politics, queer articulates a radical questioning of social and cultural norms, notions of gender, reproductive sexuality and the family. [It is a term that underlines] how much of our history and ideologies operate on a homo-hetero opposition, constantly privileging the hetero perspective as normative, positioning the homo perspective as

bad and annihilating the spectrum of sexualities that exists. (p. 280)

Rather than moving toward a "gender free world," as Horowitz (1996) would have us believe, queer projects open up the possibility of recognizing and honoring a vast array of genders and sexualities, according to Smith (1996). Although Horowitz understands the objective of queer politics as a "radical enterprise" seeking an "impossible ideal" (p. 336), Smith suggests that this "ideal" is present in the actual, in the material sociopolitical bodies of gendered and sexed subjects. Through their performative art and political activism, queer subjects actualize change by reinterpreting oppressively gendered or sexed "signs of the moment" (Smith, 1996, p. 285), thereby creating the conditions for the possibility of acknowledging, respecting, and celebrating a vast array of gendered and sexed subjects.

The Sisters of Perpetual Indulgence embrace a plurality of gendered and sexed subjectivities. In their mission statement, SPI describe how "queer" informs their organization:

> We are a queer family. "Queer" means the freedom to be an individual in a close knit family of individuals: diversity and unity. The sisterhood, priesthood or any subset of the Sisters of Perpetual Indulgence (SPI) membership is open to women and men, young and old, rich and poor, gay and lesbian, straight, bisexual and transgender; our organization includes masculine and feminine identified as well as androgynous personas. (The Sisters of Perpetual Indulgence, Inc., 2001, p. 2)

This description echoes Queercore's appropriation of the term. Dennis Cooper (1996) describes Queercore as "a place where 'queer' defines not a specific sexuality, but the freedom to personalize anything you see or hear then shoot it back into the stupid world more distorted and amazing than it was before" (p. 295). For SPI, that "anything" is the persona of "nun." The Sisters appropriate—through a subversive, discursive aesthetic—and embody the sign "nun," bending it, twisting it, distorting it, and, ultimately, making it amazingly their own.

Like *queer*, *camp* is also a contested term. For some, camp is simply pretense; it is a "certain mode of aestheticism . . . one way of seeing the world as an aesthetic phenomenon . . . not in terms of beauty, but in terms of degree of artifice" (Sontag, in Case, 1989, p. 287). Sontag, as Case points out, understands camp within a context of heterosexual aestheticization, a context that fixes the notion of camp against heteronormative standards of authenticity. Case suggests that the assimilationist tendency in such a move prompted a response in gay camp discourse to retain its "constantly changing, mobile quality" (p. 287).

Camp, then, like *queer*, is a fluid term and an embodied, ever-shifting performative practice: As Smith (1996) puts it, "Queer seems as chameleon as camp" (p. 285). Thus, rather than imposing a definition of camp onto the Sisters' practice, it makes more sense to read how SPI embodies and practices its own sense of camp. With respect to that queer embodiment and those camp practices, it is important to acknowledge the rigor of the demanding process through which a potential Sister embodies full-fledged Sisterhood.

It is not easy to become a Sister. Those interested in joining the order are warned that if they are not willing to make a lifelong commitment to the order and to the community, they should probably reconsider joining. Put simply, a habit and makeup do not make a Sister. Those who aspire to be Sisters actualize that commitment through a performative process of pledging to a seemingly simple vow and actualizing the ideal immanent in that vow through everyday material practices. Sister Mish, in a 1998 interview with *Gaywave* magazine, reads and explains the vow:

"While I remain a Sister of Perpetual Indulgence, I will ever strive to fulfill our

mission of promulgating universal joy and expiating stigmatic guilt. I pledge my support to my fellow Sisters toward our personal and collective enlightenment." And that is about as much as what we could agree upon [when SPI was established], but it's, I think, quite a lot. (Day, 1997, ¶ 33)

These "common vows," although seemingly vague and abstract tenets, require a specific, significant, and rigorous commitment on the part of aspiring and current Sisters. Also, these vows performatively merge the Sisters' embodied aesthetic with the materiality of the body politic.

There are three stages through which one must move to reach the "Black Veil" status and become a full-fledged Sister: (a) Aspirant, (b) Postulant, and (c) Novice. During the first stage, Aspirants are involved in meetings and activities but refrain from wearing a habit or speaking on behalf of SPI. After a minimum of 2 months, Aspirants can request the move to Postulancy, which requires them to develop a sponsorship relationship with a fully professed Sister. At this stage, Postulants learn the history of SPI by working in the archives, and they must attend at least four official events. Postulancy requires at least 4 months and, when completed, the Postulant's sponsorship relationship with SPI moves into mentorship as the Postulant becomes a Novice. Novices are mentored by a full-fledged Sister and spend at least 6 months rehearsing their own full membership. This involves consistently participating in community work and events, spending hours working in the archives, and wearing the nun's habit with whiteface and a white veil. At this point, Novices are always accompanied by their mentor ("Mother") and cannot speak on behalf of SPI. Finally, Novices can move into the "Black Veil" stage and become a fully professed Sister. It takes approximately a year to reach this stage, and three quarters of the fully professed Sisters must approve the move from Novice to Black Veil, which endows the new Sister with all the

SPI responsibilities, rights, and privileges (see "What it takes," 2006).

This is unmistakably a painstaking, time-consuming process, one that demands of aspiring members an embodiment of not only the camp but also the everyday sociopolitical commitment inherent in the spirit of SPI. This commitment to service and activism, over the more than 25-year span of SPI, performatively merges the Sisters' campy aesthetic performance with embodied queer politics and practice.

ARTISTRY AND ACTIVISM: REMAPPING AND RECLAIMING THE (SACRED) BODY

> We are artists as well as social activists, and our faces and bodies are our canvases. (The Sisters of Perpetual Indulgence, Inc., 2001, p. 1)

It is difficult to do justice to the array of practices that the Sisters use to appropriate and transform traditional "nun" personae. Because it is, in large part, an aesthetic mode of performance, the language I might employ to describe it can neither fully apprehend nor represent how that performance manifests in lived bodies. I offer the following descriptions as examples of the SPI aesthetic.

When I found myself, for the first time, in the presence of several Sisters, I read their performance aesthetic in primarily ludic terms. Even among all the other outrageously costumed revelers at the 1994 Halloween-in-the-Castro celebration, the Sisters stood out: Grouped together, offering a glance or a nod or a brief greeting to those brave (or inebriated) enough to approach such conspicuous celebrities, they were like a live, hot cluster of brightly colored neon lights. I was astounded by their artistic inventiveness: Each Sister was a highly individualized and stylized incarnation of his own imaginative vision. I remember one Sister in particular who wore a habit of hot pink satin and cool white lace adorned with luminous beads and brilliant bangles in every color of the rainbow. Strings of

shiny faux pearls and glittering crystals hung like garlands from his neck; shimmering white satin gloves offset by sparkling, oversized rings; thigh-high black stockings, and white mile-high heels peeked out from between the generous slits in his habit. And the makeup: blue, green, and pink eye shadow, impossibly arched black eyebrows, eyelashes that seemed to go on forever, and lush raspberry frost lipstick on a stark whiteface canvas. Like glamorous, grownup, consecrated cartoon characters, the Sisters were, for me, vibrantly embodied installations of artistic play, vivid imagination, and impertinent absurdity.

Put simply, when appearing at public events, the SF Sisters dress in traditional nun habits and accessorize with whatever accoutrements they desire; their camp is manifest, in part, through "nun drag."[2] As Sister Missionary P. Delight puts it,

> Each house has a traditional habit. . . . the only traditional part [in the SF order] is our wimples, our ear [brassieres]. But, we do have our long black flowing robes, and scapula, bibs, and what have you. We are also allowed to show our own individuality and our artistry as we see fit. . . . The [traditional] nuns are discarding this fabulous drag, and far be it from us to let fabulous drag molder in the closet, so we resurrected that drag and indeed [did it] in honor of all their [traditional nuns'] work. (Day, 1997, ¶ 31)

More than this, the Sisters' chosen names reflect the creative wit inherently a part of the SPI persona (e.g., Sister Homo Celestial, Sister Krishna Kosher, Sister Mysteria of the Holy Order of the Broken Hymen, etc.). The emphasis here, in both embodying and naming the nun persona is on creative human artistry, rather than on an effort to appropriate gender.

Sister Mish points out that although some interpret the Sisters as "just drag queens making fun of nuns" (Day, 1997, ¶ 24), Sister Phyllis Stein the Fragrant Mistress of Sistory suggests that

There's a vast difference between the Sisters and the drag community, while there is a lot of overlap. . . . Drag queens are about reclaiming your own gender identity, and female imper-sonation, and flexing those boundaries. The Sisters are not about drag. "Drag" is an acronym for "dressed as a girl." We're not dressed as girls, we're dressed as nuns. . . . We definitely minister to the spiritual needs of our community, while drag queens sort of focus on camp and fun within our communi-ties. . . . A lot of people refer to us as drag queens, but we say we're in nun drag. We are nuns. (McClelland, 1997, ¶ 16)

This distinction in focus and objective—between drag as campy gender appropriation and nun drag as appropriating the nun persona—is important in understanding how camp serves SPI's materially transformative manifestation of nun practice. Whereas the drag community focuses exclusively on "camp and fun," according to Sister Stein, the Sisters use—without abandoning the fun—this aes-thetic to further their sociopolitical commit-ments to the community.

Although it may be easy to read SPI as *only* playful entertainment, as a fabulous example of a ludic queer cultural phenomenon, they *are* that *and more*. The Sisters also devote them-selves to extensive sociopolitical activism and work: They lend their presence to various fundraising events; some perform wedding, blessing, and funeral ceremonies.[3] Often, with-out makeup or hoopla, the Sisters volunteer in various capacities for numerous not-for-profit organizations that lend assistance to needy populations. Moreover, through the Sisters' grant and scholarship programs, SPI has raised and donated more than half a million dollars to

> progressive projects that promote wellness, identity, tolerance and diversity within our communities. We have a vision that encom-passes diverse communities and groups that have a common interest in human rights, people of every gender, gender identity, race, class, age and sexual orientation. ("Grants," 2006, ¶ 3)

Given this focus, SPI's queer politics and community commitment extend not only to those individuals and communities that face the "realist [and material] terror mounted by heterosexist forces" (Case, 1989, p. 288), but to individuals in general who are marginalized by dominant discourses. In other words, artistry and activism merge, for SPI, to ironize, critique, and transform oppressive conditions.

PERFORMATIVITY AND *HABITUS*: ENTERING THE (SACRED) BODY POLITIC

> One kneels in prayer, and only later acquires the belief. (Butler, 1997a, p. 155)

In this section, I move to show how the Sisters' campy discursive performance of iden-tity also acts as a performative vehicle, through which ontological change (change of being) is fostered in the sociopolitical field. In other words, this section explores how "Perfor-mativity is the discursive mode by which onto-logical effects are installed" (Butler, 1997b, 134). I make this move to demonstrate how reading SPI offers a way to orient scholarship and polit-ical practice in between the either-or–ness of choosing to engage—in scholarship or not—at *either* a materialist *or* a discursive level to ana-lyze or create the possibility for change. Instead, the performativity of SPI helps us to understand that scholarly and political projects (certainly not mutually exclusive) find room for transformation *within the relational processes* of materiality and discursivity, the actual and ideal.

SPI's aesthetic performances do (and do more than) imitate nuns in a parody meant to satirize that normed identity, and those organized religious doctrines traditionally espoused and embodied. By adopting roles that find their grounding in the conventions of sacred individuals generally, the Sisters embody a mimetic identification that consti-tutes their lived experience as nuns and, in the process, transforms the sociopolitical field. Put simply, by imitating and embodying an idea(l) of traditional nuns, the Sisters *are* nuns. At the same time, by practicing an expanded array of nun subjectivities, the Sisters materially bring into being what they discursively embody in the sociopolitical field. To help make sense of this play between SPI's variety of performance art and the sociopolitical field, Butler's (1994, 1997a, 1997b) elucidation of performativity—or the constitutive aspect of discursive practices that has the power to produce what it names—is helpful. Moreover, the notion of *habitus* is instructive in making sense of the performative instantiation of the Sisters' identity as nuns in the actuality of the social field.

For Butler (1994), "performativity . . . contests the very notion of the subject" (¶ 3), and a subject, in these terms, is fixed: Subjects are autonomous entities whose identities are essentially unchanging and from whom all meaning originates. The constitutive aspect of performativity challenges this notion of the subject because it demonstrates how subjectivity is fluid and how meaning is created in the discursive processes between subjects and the sociopolitical field. In the Sisters' case, they do not perform "nun," presuming there is a *fixed* subject "nun"; rather, they challenge the commonsense idea that "nun" *is* a fixed subjectivity. By performatively appropriating—via vows and related practices—the sign or idea(l) of "nun" *as* subject and embodying "nun" in uniquely queer modalities, the Sisters expand both the practice and meaning of "nun." Moreover, it is because there actually (materially) exists a normed subjectivity of "nun" in the sociopolitical field that it is possible for the Sisters to ideally (discursively) appropriate it. At the same time, because of the power of performativity, the Sisters are not limited to (but are always, in part, limited *by*) "traditional" modalities of embodying and performing "nun."

The everyday lived commitment that the vow of the order demands of Sisters also contributes to the performative nature of their

cultural politics. The Sisters *live* their roles as nuns; they do not simply put on a drag "costume." They *embody* the roles of nuns in the way they live and take action in their everyday lives. For example, Sister Phyllis Stein explains:

> A lot of the work I do is done out of habit but people still know me as Sister Phyllis. I also do a lot of grant writing for smaller organizations, organizations such as the Tenderloin AIDS Resource Center. A grant proposal came across my desk and I thought "Hey, this proposal fits perfectly for this organization," and I called them up and told them that I wanted to write this grant application for them. I got them 5000 dollars, and I also got a donation of 10 Mac computers, and a laser printer with fax capability. It's also about being at the right place at the right time. People know that you're a nun and they say "I've got this thing, I've got something, I've got this venue, and I see that it could really help somewhere, where can you put it?" (McClelland, 1997, ¶ 34)

Because of his public persona as Sister Phyllis, people recognize the role he can play in his everyday life to contribute in material ways to social organizations that might be in need of assistance. Also, because he keeps an eye directed toward ways that his everyday professional persona connects to SPI's mission through his vows, Sister Phyllis is able to blend the everyday with what the public performance makes possible: access to material resources that can be of benefit to community service organizations. This is only one example, but it is one that is repeated over and over, in uniquely situated ways, by other SPI members.

It is in this performance of everyday life and its creation of the *habitus* that the constitutive nature of the Sisters' performative finds its power. Examining Pierre Bourdieu's notion of the *habitus*, Butler (1997a) clarifies her reading of the concept: "The *habitus* refers to those embodied rituals of everydayness by which a given culture produces and sustains belief in its own 'obviousness'" (p. 152). For a performative to produce what it names, it must be situated in and adopt, to some extent, the conventions of the social field. In the Sisters' case, by adopting and living their vows—by enacting "nun" through the conventions set forth in their vows and preceded by those legitimated by various organized religions—they set into motion a mimetic identification with their own adaptation of "nun." By constructing and practicing their vows over, through, and with the vows that constitute the legitimated social field of other religious organizations, the Sisters effectively create their own *habitus* and, through it, situate their obviousness in the *habitus* of the larger social field.

Further, by adopting these conventions and embodying them in everyday lived experience, the Sisters enact a process that "performatively produces a shift in the terms of legitimacy as an effect of the utterance itself" (Butler, 1997a, p. 147). Put differently, the Sisters, by appropriating "nun," put into effect an iterative process (more precisely a *reiteration*) and, in doing so, demonstrate how "an invocation that has no prior legitimacy can have the effect of challenging existing forms of legitimacy, breaking open the possibility of future forms" (Butler, 1997a, p. 147). The Sisters take on the legitimated persona of "nun," expanding what that subjectivity means, repeating over and over again practices that continually modify it, and, in the process, create the possibility of diversely legitimated ways of understanding and practicing "nun."

As a consequence of the possibilities created by the Sisters' performatively powerful discursive practices, a process of *resignification* is underway. Resignification means that power or discourse is not a stable entity, possessed only by some; rather, power is an unstable and fluid process, and the engagement of power is discursively available to anyone through reiteration. In the Sisters' case, they recognize that the power to call oneself a "nun" and, thus, to *be* a "nun" is not limited to those who are ensconced in centralized religious organizations.

Rather, that power is discursively available to them through their repeated and diverse performative appropriation of that identity. More than this, the sociopolitical power (discourse) process is modified by the Sisters' resistance of the commonsense acceptance that only certain individuals possess the power to legitimately call themselves "nuns" and to practice as "nuns." When the Sisters discursively perform *as if* their identities as "nuns" were legitimate (that is, they perform subjunctively), they actualize (bring into being) a reconstructed aspect of the material sociopolitical field. This reconstruction calls into question the idea that there is an essential, fixed material reality (or an essential, fixed subjectivity) that can only be imitated and from which all else is derivative. The Sisters' discursive cultural practices do not elide an actuality, nor are they simply derivative of an actuality; rather, the Sisters embody and, thus, constitute a *reconstructed* actuality.

The Sisters' performative embodiment of "nun" constitutes and reconstitutes the *habitus*. By performing and embodying their vows, the "simultaneity of the production and delivery of the expression" (Butler, 1997a, p. 152) merges what is thought and spoken with the realm of livable, living, and lived political reality. This formative notion of *habitus* means, in SPI's case, that the performativity of the Sisters' subversive, repetitive reiteration of identity alters the social field's reality constructs in such a way as to generate an inclination on the part of other subjects in that field to interact with and embody the actual changes instantiated by the Sisters' performances. In other words, the expectations for what constitutes a "real nun" in the social field are expanded by SPI's performances as queer, 21st-century nuns.

The "nun" subjectivity, considered by many to be "sacred" and unchanging, is productively destabilized and opened up to variation by the Sisters. However, the modality through which this destabilization occurs—the Sisters' political parody—has prompted resistance from those who consider the Sisters' performances blasphemous acts. The political consequences, then, of this challenge to the boundaries of the "sacred" raise an important question: How does one judge whether a parody is too bold to have a positive political impact?

POLITICAL PARODY: DISTURBING AND ALTERING THE SACRED BODY POLITIC

> The Sisters drag sexual politics onto the streets, and the streets are all the brighter and safer for it. (Chumbawamba, 1994)

I remove *sacred* from the parenthetical position it has occupied in this study thus far in order to examine, more closely, notions of the sacred as they relate to "the body" and "the body politic." *Sacred* is a term much like *queer* and *camp* in that each of these terms is contextually defined. According to *Strong's Hebrew and Greek Dictionary*, the Hebrew word for *sacred* (or *holy*) is *qadosh*. Its etymology traces to the verb *qadish*, meaning *to set apart*—in particular, setting apart *outside the temple*. The sacred, then, is set apart from the mundane in honor of a (or "the") divinity. In other words, when we deem something sacred (or sanctify it), we take what was outside the temple, in the mundane realm, and bring it inside, into the divine realm. (In contrast, the word *profane* simply means "before the temple" or "outside the temple" ["King James Bible," 2001].) SPI's political parody challenges the boundaries of what is sacred by sanctifying and bringing into the temple the queer bodies of the Sisters and, at the same time, explicitly situating the temple (in this case, organized religion and associated doctrines) in the mundane arena of the body politic. As such, through political parody, what constitutes a "sacred body" is open to contestation, critique, and, consequently, variation.

The critique inherent in the Sisters' appropriation and alteration of "nun" and SPI's unique mode of political activism provokes fierce reactions among some, and a number of SPI's critical actions have prompted harsh responses from SF's Catholic communities. For instance, in 1987 during the Pope's visit to SF, the Sisters performed an "exorcism" of the Holy Father in the middle of Union Square—while he passed by in the motorcade—to protest the Church's condemnation of queer lifestyles. This action ultimately landed the organization on the official Papal "List of Heretics" ("A sistory blow," 2006, ¶ 11). More recently, in 1999, the SPI 20th anniversary celebration in the Castro—which, coincidentally, coincided with Easter Sunday that year—prompted representatives of the Catholic Church to denounce the Sisters as "an anti-Catholic group" whose blasphemous, even fascist, exhibition on the holy day served to "mock nuns, mock the Mass, and mock the Pope" (Ostler, 1999, p. A3).

Along those same lines, according to the *Catholic League's 1999 Report on Anti-Catholicism*, the Sisters' appropriation of "nun" is "so vicious that it goes well beyond the bounds of parody," and the report goes on to compare the Sisters' whiteface makeup to blackface bigotry:

> If there were an Al Jolson society of white boys with black faces who mocked African Americans, no one would defend them because they give a few bucks to AIDS research. None of [the Sisters' actions] falls within the bounds of good humor. More properly, it is called hate speech. (¶ 2)

A similarly condemning accusation was lodged by Professor Hitchcock (1999), writing in the magazine *Catholic Dossier*. He argued that the Sisters represent "frenzied blasphemy" of the most dangerous sort:

> The frenzied symbolic assaults on religion [by SPI] are numerous and frightening, revealing as they do the barely suppressed violence which its enemies harbor and which, it is fair to judge, they would eagerly act out in life if given the opportunity.... Frenzied

blasphemy—the mocking of sacred symbols, the association of those symbols with the sickest kind of pornography—reveals the depth of the violent hatred because it represents an assault in some ways worse than the desire to do bodily harm. It aims to annihilate the sacred core of the believer's very being. It is a mentality in which the actual killing of individuals would be almost an anti-climax. (¶ 1)

To be sure, this is an overreaction on Professor Hitchcock's part. At the same time, charges of hate speech, the "defamation" of sacred symbols, and ostensible ontological assault and annihilation deserve some response, particularly if the Sisters' activism is to be understood as a useful political contribution in a context broader than that of San Francisco.

With respect to the hate speech charge, the interpretation of SPI's actions points to a significant misunderstanding of that doctrine. Butler (2000a) points out that hate speech is understood as "used by a person or group who occupies a dominant position in society against those who occupy subordinate positions, and that the speech act itself is a further act of subordination" (¶ 3). Clearly, then, those who charge the Sisters with hate speech misconstrue the power dynamic and political contingencies involved when a group of queer activist performance artists appropriate dominant (and often oppressive) symbols of massive religious organizations to reconceive them in the service of liberatory, joyful, and guilt-expiating discursive performances.

Professor Hitchcock's remarks (and those like his) are more difficult to answer. One response to this sort of reaction points to the contingency of context. That is, in San Francisco (or other urban settings where SPI orders are established), the freedom to express dissent or critique by diverse means may be more abundant, and, as such, tolerance levels may be higher. Even so, the move to bring the mundane into the temple, to sanctify the queer bodies and politics of SPI, constitutes profanity

for some and raises the issue of political efficacy.

Part of SPI's political usefulness may be located in their embrace of the idea(l) "nun." Even though various actions are explicitly meant to parody and critique some status quo religious doctrines (e.g., condemnation of same-sex partnerships, guilt as an instrument of discipline and control, etc.), the Sisters do not ridicule or disparage the idea(l) of "nun":

> We are not making fun of nuns, WE ARE NUNS. . . . We are an Order of 21st century nuns dedicated to the promulgation of universal joy and the expiation of stigmatic guilt. . . . We are very dedicated to our calling and our vows reflect our commitment to our community. We care for the sick and the disadvantaged, just like other orders do. We raise funds for the needy just as other orders do. We educate the masses on important and even life threatening topics just like other orders do. We strive to promote worldwide love and understanding just as (some) other orders do. . . . This is what it is to be a nun, what it is to support the community, and what it is to serve the human race. (The Sisters of Perpetual Indulgence, Inc., 2001, p. 3)

For SPI, "nun" is not an idea(l), a persona, a way of being, or a modality of activism limited only to persons who belong to traditional religious organizations. Rather, the Sisters' appropriation and embodiment of "nun" allows them, as an organization, to adopt general ethical conceptions (ideals) and commitments of community service that are understood as inherent in the normed role of "nun." That is, when "nun" is "queered" by SPI, it opens up a vast range of ethical subjectivities that can be associated with "nun." With respect to the question of political efficacy, then, at least in the case of the Sisters, perhaps they have been able to maintain an effective organization—even in the face of those who suggest they go beyond the bounds of propriety—because their practices sustain a close relationship with the ideal ("nun") they attempt to approximate. In other words, the Sisters' campy aesthetic may offend some, but it is difficult to argue with the community service ethic materially manifest and embodied in that camp—the material and ideal are effectively braided for SPI.

Moreover, the SPI may help us to understand how it is possible, more generally, to use identity politically without the traps of identity politics. Identity politics have a general tendency to limit and fix both the political ground on which groups stand and the subjectivities presupposed by the identities claimed in the name of political action (see Butler, 2000b, for an excellent general discussion of identity and identity politics along these lines). The Sisters use identity in their politics precisely by *unfixing,* from the norms established in various sociopolitical contexts, both the subjectivities they embody and the political ground they occupy. Put differently, rather than limit the possibilities for politics and the political subject, SPI queers both and creates the conditions for the possibility of a multitude of political subjectivities and modalities.

At the same time, attempting to measure political efficacy is a tricky business. Is there a scale by which we can tote up the costs and benefits of this type of performative activism? Butler's point (in the introduction) with respect to the "culture/material" distinction can be interpreted as questioning this notion of gauging political efficacy by standards primarily associated with materialist politics. From an orthodox materialist perspective, if the Sisters, through their camp aesthetic, enable some change in the sociopolitical field, it is far too easy to attribute that change primarily to their community service and to relegate to the derivative their discursive (camp aesthetic) mode of being. However, each mode finds its power in the other. This is not to say that it is unimportant to try and understand how political activism like that of the Sisters can work both for and against positive change. Rather, it is simply an acknowledgment that there is no

guarantee of change that accompanies any political activism. All political activism takes a risk in offending someone and "going too far." However, it may be that in going "too far"— in disturbing the actual—political activism of this sort helps us begin to understand and perhaps move toward what is possible.

SOME CLOSING THOUGHTS

> There can be no pure opposition to power, only a recrafting of its terms from resources invariably impure. (Butler, 1994, ¶ 2)

The performative nature of the Sisters' embodiment of differently gendered nun identities finds its power in the social field of conventions, and at the same time, it critiques and exceeds those conventions by producing a reconfigured *habitus.* Power, in this sense, is fluid and unstable, and the power and discourse process always already includes the potential for resistance. Further, the subversive, repetitive reiteration of identity suggests that SPI's performances have material effects in and through the discursive, thereby demonstrating the relational processes that braid these aspects together.

Of course, mine is only one reading, and by their very nature, the Sisters are not easy to define, nor are their discursive performances easy to read in connection with the sociopolitical field. However, it is precisely this difficulty that may enable effective responses to social recuperation:

> Subversive practices have to overwhelm the capacity to read, challenge conventions of reading, and demand new possibilities of reading. . . . [The performatives] that challenge our practices of reading, that make us uncertain about how to read, or make us think that we have to renegotiate the way in which we read public signs, these seem really politically important to me. (Butler, 1997b, p. 138)

Scholarship that attempts to read other locally situated queer performance art activism like SPI could demonstrate the constitutive—rather than derivative or secondary—power of discursive, celebratory cultural performances. Finally, continuing this line of analysis helps to recognize and acknowledge "the reproduction of persons and the social regulation of sexuality *as part of* the very process of production, and hence part of the materialist conception of political economy" (Butler, 1998, ¶ 11, my emphasis). My hope is that this study makes a contribution to that recognition and acknowledgment.

NOTES

1. The SF order "is often referred to as the 'Mother House'" ("World orders," 2006), but each order sets its own guidelines for Sisterhood, develops its own organizational structures, and personalizes its appropriation of the nun habit. There are U.S. SPI organizations (e.g., Seattle, Tennessee, Chicago, Iowa, Philadelphia, and Los Angeles) and international orders (e.g., Australia, France, Germany, and the United Kingdom).

2. The Sisters explain that "nun drag" does not mean "Catholic nun drag." Rather, "nun," for SPI, is a generic term for individuals who vow to dedicate their lives to serving their communities in a variety of different ways. Thanks to Sister Kitty for clarifying this for me.

3. Three of the Sisters—Sister Betty Does, LNM, Sister Camille Leon, and Sister MaryMae Himm—are legally ordained ministers or clergy who can provide services that any other clergyperson might perform.

REFERENCES

Asbury, H. (1933). *The Barbary Coast: An informal history of the San Francisco underworld.* New York: Alfred Knopf.

Ashbolt, A. (1989). *Tear down the walls: Sixties radicalism and the politics of space in the San Francisco Bay Area.* Unpublished doctoral dissertation, Australian National University, Canberrra.

Butler, J. (1994). *Gender as performance: An interview with Judith Butler* (P. Osborne & L. Segal, Interviewers). Retrieved February 21, 2006, from http://www.theory.org.uk/but-int1.htm

Butler, J. (1997a). *Excitable speech.* New York: Routledge.

Butler, J. (1997b). On transsexuality: Excitable speech (K. More, Interviewer). *Radical Deviance: A Journal of Transgendered Politics, 2,* 134–143.

Butler, J. (1998). Left conservatism, II. *Theory & Event, 2*(2). Retrieved September 7, 2001, from http://muse.jhu.edu/journals/theory_and_event /v002/2.2butler.html

Butler, J. (2000a). The value of being disturbed. *Theory & Event, 4*(1). Retrieved September 7, 2001, from http://muse.jhu.edu/cgibin/access .cgi?uri=/journals/theory_and_event/v004/4. 1butler.html

Butler, J. (2000b). Politics, power and ethics: A discussion between Judith Butler and William Connolly. *Theory & Event, 4*(2). Retrieved September 7, 2001, from http://muse.jhu.edu/ cgi-bin/access.cgi?uri=/journals/theory_and_ event/v004/4.2butler.html

Carroll, J. (1999, March 29). Sisters of perpetual controversy. *San Francisco Chronicle,* p. E8.

Case, S. E. (1989). Toward a butch-femme aesthetic. In L. Hart (Ed.), *Making a spectacle: Feminist essays on contemporary women's theatre* (pp. 282–299). Ann Arbor: University of Michigan Press.

Castells, M., & Murphy, K. (1982). Cultural identity and urban structure: The spatial organization of San Francisco's gay community. *Urban Affairs Review, 22,* 237–259.

Catholic League's 1999 report on anti-Catholicism. (1999). *Executive summary.* Retrieved February 21, 2006, from the Catholic League Web site: http://www.catholicleague.org/ 1999report/summary1999.html

Cavan, S. (1972). *Hippies of the Haight.* St. Louis, MO: New Critics Press.

Chumbawamba. (1994) Anarchy! (Album sleeve). London: One Little Indian Records.

Cooper, D. (1996). Queercore. In D. Morton (Ed.), *The material queer* (pp. 292–296). Boulder, CO: Westward Press.

Darsey, J. (1991). From "gay is good" to the scourge of AIDS: The evolution of gay liberation rhetoric, 1977–1990. *Communication Studies, 42,* 43–66.

Day, G. (1997). The sisters of perpetual indulgence: Part I. *Gaywave: An Online Magazine.* Retrieved April 28, 2006, from http:// online.sfsu.edu/~cglenn/

Findlay, J. (1986). *People of chance: Gambling in American Society from Jamestown to Las Vegas.* New York: Oxford University Press.

Garcia, K. (1999, March 25). If you think this is weird—just wait. District elections return next year. *San Francisco Chronicle,* p. A17.

Grants. (2006). Retrieved February 21, 2006, from the Sisters of Perpetual Indulgence Web site: http://www.thesisters.org/grants.html

Hitchcock, J. (1999, May/June). Are Christians prepared for persecution? *Catholic Dossier:Issues in the Round, 5*. Retrieved February 21, 2006, from http://www.catholic.net/rcc/Periodicals/Dossier/MAYJUN99/persecution.html

Horowitz, D. (1996). Queer revolution: The last stage of radicalism. In D. Morton (Ed.), *The material queer* (pp. 328–336). Boulder, CO: Westward Press.

Howe, A. C. (2001). Queer pilgrimage: The San Francisco homeland and identity tourism. *Cultural Anthropology, 16*, 35–62.

King James Bible: Strong's Hebrew and Greek dictionary index. (2001). Retrieved February 21, 2006, from http://www.sacrednamebible.com/kjvstrongs/STRINDEX.htm

Lattin, D. (1999, March 20). Catholic group threatens S.F. boycott. Outrage over OK to close block of Castro for "nuns" on Easter. *San Francisco Chronicle*, p. A16.

Matthews, G. (1997). Forging a cosmopolitan civic culture: The regional consciousness of San Francisco and northern California. In M. Steiner & D. Wrobel (Eds.), *Many Wests: Essays in regional consciousness*. Lawrence: University of Kansas Press.

McClelland, D. (1997). The sisters of perpetual indulgence: Part II. *Gaywave: An Online Magazine*. Retrieved April 28, 2006, from http://online.sfsu.edu/~cglenn/

Morton, D. (1996). Changing the terms: (Virtual) desire and (actual) reality. In D. Morton (Ed.), *The material queer* (pp. 1–33). Boulder, CO: Westward Press.

Ostler, S. (1999, March 31). San Francisco wages another holy war. *San Francisco Chronicle*, p. A3.

Perry, C. (1984). *The Haight-Ashbury: A history*. New York: Random House.

Roff, H. R. (1996). Reflections: San Francisco politics: Perspective of 40 years. *San Francisco Urban Institute Quarterly, 1*, 38–47.

Shilts, R. (1982). *The mayor of Castro Street: The life and times of Harvey Milk*. New York: St. Martin's Press.

The Sisters of Perpetual Indulgence, Inc. (2001). *The Sisters of Perpetual Indulgence, Inc., San Francisco order: Policies and procedures manual*. San Francisco: Author.

A sistory blow by blow. (2006). Retrieved February 21, 2006, from the Sisters of Perpetual Indulgence Web site: http://www.thesisters.org/sistory.html

Slagle, R. A. (1995). In defense of Queer Nation: From identity politics to a politics of difference. *Western Journal of Communication, 59*, 85–102.

Smith, C. (1996). What is this thing called queer? In D. Morton (Ed.), *The material queer* (pp. 277–285). Boulder, CO: Westward Press.

Smith, R.C. (1995). *Utopia and dissent: Art, poetry, and politics in California*. Berkeley: University of California Press.

Smith, R. R., & Windes, R. R. (1997). The pro-gay and anti-gay issue culture: Interpretation, influence, and dissent. *Quarterly Journal of Speech, 83*, 28–48.

Stryker, S., & Van Buskirk, J. (1996). *Gay by the bay: A history of queer culture in the San Francisco Bay Area*. San Francisco: Chronicle Books.

Weiss, M. (1982). *Double play: The San Francisco city hall killings*. Reading, MA: Addison-Wesley.

What it takes to be a Sister of Perpetual Indulgence. (2006). Retrieved February 21, 2006, from the Sisters of Perpetual Indulgence Web site: http://www.thesisters.org/meet_becominga-nun.html

Wirt, F. M. (1971). The politics of hyperpluralism. In H. S. Becker (Ed.), *Culture and civility in San Francisco* (pp. 101–124). London: Aldine.

World orders. (2006). Retrieved March 22, 2006, from the Sisters of Perpetual Indulgence Web site: http://www.thesisters.org/world_orders.html

Discussion Questions

1. Glenn makes several claims in regard to the Sisters of Perpetual Indulgence and the work that they do. Identify and summarize them.

2. How does Glenn define *camp*, and how is camp relevant to the Sisters? Can a performance be camp as well as politically significant? Offer a justification for your answer.

3. How have the Sisters of Perpetual Indulgence challenged conventional sexual identity images to advocate their platform of political activism?

4. How can we measure or evaluate the political efficacy of a performance?

PART IV

Transforming Sexualities and Communication

Visions and Praxis

19

The Spirituality of Sex and the Sexuality of the Spirit

BDSM Erotic Play as Soulwork and Social Critique

ROBERT G. WESTERFELHAUS

Few forms of sexual expression are as misrepresented and misunderstood as sadomasochism (BDSM).[1] For those outside the BDSM community,[2] terms such as *sadomasochism* conjure up images of leather and whips and chains—when they conjure up any images at all. BDSM, however, is a complex social phenomenon that involves far more than the sexual practices (e.g., abrasion, bondage, piercing, spanking, and whipping) and props (e.g., chains, handcuffs, leather jackets, riding crops, and whips) with which it has been associated traditionally by practitioners and nonpractitioners alike. Indeed, many within the BDSM community express the view that the practice of BDSM is a spiritual experience as well as a form of sexual expression. In this paper, I argue that this emergent understanding of the spiritual dimension of BDSM is part of a broader reevaluation of what Gergen (1991) calls the grand narrative of modernism.

Since the time of Augustine of Hippo (354–430 CE), the use of sexuality as a means of approaching and developing the spiritual has dropped out of the Western cultural repertoire, a lacuna that persists to this day. Indeed, in discussing the contemporary American view regarding the spiritual dimensions of sex, Mark Thompson (1991b) comments, "The idea that radical sexuality has spiritual value is a difficult one for most people to grasp" (p. xix). However, although Thompson acknowledges that there are those within the leather (i.e., BDSM) community who discount the notion that BDSM has a spiritual dimension, he questions whether any who practice BDSM would

deny the transcendent moments they've experienced through intense sexual ritual. For leather play [i.e., BDSM] is also about permitting ecstasy to enter our lives. The enhanced physical, visual, and aural sensations of radical sex allow for the transportation of self, or awareness of self, beyond normal everyday reference. Leatherfolk [an indigenous term for those who engage in BDSM practices] often speak about vivid out-of-mind-and-body experiences. (p. xix)

In this chapter, I suggest that BDSM can be conceived of as a form of erotic play that is both soulwork and social critique. For those who lack familiarity with BDSM or the scholarly literature regarding it, I provide a short account of the way BDSM has been viewed by the human sciences. This account is followed by an abbreviated history of the development of the contemporary American BDSM community. I then cite accounts by indigenous writers (i.e., members of the BDSM community) who describe their practices and perceptions regarding the spiritual side of the BDSM experience. I conclude by suggesting that the emergence of an appreciation of BDSM spirituality by BDSM practitioners is part of a broader reevaluation of the Western world's grand narrative of modernism.

SURVEY OF SCHOLARLY LITERATURE REGARDING BDSM

Sadomasochism is "a type of sexual behavior where the interaction between partners is concentrated on inflicting or receiving pain, or on ritualized submission and dominance" (Spengler, 1983, p. 57). As Weinberg, Williams, and Moser (1984) observe, depictions of this use of pain and exercise of power within an erotic context are found throughout the histories and literatures of both Eastern and Western civilizations. Although the literary depiction of sadomasochistic practices has a long history,[3] the scholarly study of BDSM does not. According to Weinberg (1987), this inquiry began with the publication in 1886 of Richard von Krafft-Ebing's *Psychopathia Sexualis,* in which Krafft-Ebing (1965) recognized sadism and masochism as distinct forms of human sexual behavior and assigned these

behaviors the names by which they are known today. The term *sadism* refers to the desire to inflict pain and the erotic pleasure derived from doing so; the term *masochism* refers to the desire to receive pain and the erotic pleasure derived from doing so. As Bullough, Dixon, and Dixon (1994) explain, "Krafft-Ebing borrowed the term 'sadism' from the attitudes expressed in the novels of the Marquis de Sade (Luis-Donatien-Alphonse de Sade 1740–1814)" (p. 47); the term *masochism* was borrowed by Krafft-Ebing from the name of another author, Leopold von Sacher-Masoch (1836–1895), an Austrian novelist whose best known work, *Venus in Furs* (1989), depicts the erotically charged relationship between a man who desires physical punishment and psychological abuse at the hands of his beloved, the woman who satisfies these desires.

In commenting on the social climate in which Krafft-Ebing and his immediate followers developed their understandings of the newly defined behaviors of sadism and masochism, Thompson (1991b) states:

The notion of sadomasochism arose in an identical time and manner as the concept of homosexuality. Both words were constructed out of medical discourse as a method of social control. Each word was meant to characterize, and thus pathologize, aspects of human sexual experience that had been eternally known. (p. xiv)

Or, as Weinberg et al. (1984) put it, "To recognize the historical roots of this classification is to understand that the 'sadomasochist' is a socially constructed category" (p. 380). In discussing this social construction, Bullough and Bullough (1977) observe, "Sadomasochism is a good example of the way a pathological condition is established by the medical community, for until it became a diagnosis it received little attention and was not even classified as a sin" (p. 210).

For more than a century after the appearance of Krafft-Ebing's groundbreaking work, there was little advance in the scholarly understanding of BDSM. Weinberg (1987) argues that this is because BDSM was studied primarily by psychologists (e.g., Ellis, 1942; Freud, 1938; Stekel, 1965) who followed Krafft-Ebing's lead and viewed BDSM as an individual pathology but ignored it as a form of social behavior. According to Weinberg (1987):

> Sadomasochism was treated in the earlier literature solely as an individual phenomenon, and the interactions between and among people with these desires were not examined. The person with sadistic or masochistic interests was generally treated as if he or she were living in a social vacuum. (p. 50)

This perspective was challenged by Paul Gebhard (1969), an anthropologist, who had worked with Alfred Kinsey and who later went on to head the Institute for Sex Research at Indiana University. Gebhard suggested that BDSM is best understood as a highly symbolic, interactive form of social behavior. In response to Gebhard's recognition of the social dimension of BDSM, sociologists began to study BDSM and came to view it in new ways. This research led to a growing appreciation on the part of sociologists of BDSM as ritualistic behavior or scripted performance (Kamel, 1983b; Lee, 1983; Moser, Lee, & Christensen, 1993; Moser & Levitt, 1987; Weinberg, 1983; Weinberg et al., 1984; Weinberg & Kamel, 1983). In addition, sociological inquiry has also fostered some understanding of the social dynamics between, among, and within the various BDSM communities—bisexual, heterosexual, homosexual, and lesbian (Houlberg, 1991; Kamel, 1983a; Kamel & Weinberg, 1983; Moser & Levitt, 1987; Weinberg, 1995; Weinberg et al., 1984)—and between these BDSM cultures and the broader Western culture in which they exist (Falk & Weinberg, 1983; Simon, 1996).

THE DEVELOPMENT OF THE CONTEMPORARY AMERICAN BDSM CULTURE

According to Guy Baldwin (1993), the contemporary BDSM culture of the United States emerged in the wake of World War II. As Baldwin explains, gay veterans returned home from that war profoundly influenced by their military experiences. These experiences included rigid discipline, strict regimentation, an acknowledged hierarchy, an easy camaraderie among buddies, an almost exclusively male environment, and, for some men, their first homosexual experience. Upon returning home, many of these gay veterans sought to recreate in civilian life those aspects of military life they had enjoyed in the service. Some of these men found what they were looking for in gay motorcycle clubs (notably in Chicago, Los Angeles, and New York; see Rubin, 1991). Just as the military had its rules, its rituals, and its insignia, so too did the motorcycle clubs.

According to Baldwin (1993), "The creation of the butch subculture by veterans began to allow people to specialize their sexual interests in a way that had been impossible before" (p. 109). It was within the gay biker culture of the 1950s that many of the customs and practices of the gay BDSM community became codified. This was the time, for example, when black leather became the standard uniform of men involved in BDSM. Like most uniforms, rigid rules governed how and when leather was worn. The highly codified style of sexual expression these men adopted, notes Baldwin, "makes sense given the erotic influences that shaped the inner lives of the men who were coming to age sexually at that time" (p. 114). The strictness of these codes did not make sense to a later generation of leathermen, however. Indeed, in common with other cultures, that of gay male BDSM has evolved over time. This evolution is, in part, a response to the historical circumstances in which the members of the culture find themselves. Just as gay leathermen of the 1950s were influenced by their experiences in World War II, leathermen of the 1990s are influenced by the images of the popular culture in which they are immersed.

The culture created by gay leathermen is the most organized, most visible, and most influential of those that comprise the broader BDSM community. As a result, this culture has exerted a profound influence over the cultural development of the heterosexual and lesbian leather cultures. Perhaps no period of time is of greater importance in the development of organized heterosexual and lesbian BDSM cultures than the 1970s. It was during that decade, according to Rubin (1991), that

> new kinds of leather and S/M social structures emerged. . . . The first political S/M organizations were formed in the seventies, as were the first publicly accessible groups for heterosexually oriented S/M and leather women and men. The Eulenspiegel Society held its first meetings in New York in 1971, and the Society of Janus began in San Francisco in 1974. Networking among S/M lesbians began in the seventies. Samois, the first successful lesbian S/M organization, was founded in 1978. (p. 120)

These organizations, and others like them, provided BDSM heterosexuals and lesbians with a social infrastructure within which to meet like-minded individuals and exchange information regarding sexual practices and other issues of interest. In describing the social functions of the nascent heterosexual clubs, Gagnon (1977) wrote:

> The formalization of the sadomasochistic aspects of the gay community has been paralleled by the creation of "clubs" for the heterosexual masochists and sadists. . . . Where once the problems of meeting were solved through word of mouth and through advertisements of various sorts, there is now a more public "velvet underground" in various cities which offers an opportunity for more interaction, and the creation of a local sadomasochistic culture. (p. 151)

Currently, the BDSM organizations that arose within the heterosexual and lesbian communities during the 1970s continue to provide their members with places to meet and invaluable conduits through which information of interest to the community can be circulated. This exchange of information facilitates the spread of BDSM culture and helps enculturate those who desire to participate within it. Within the past decade, the gay, heterosexual, and lesbian organizations just described have been joined by pansexual groups, organizations whose membership include men and women who have a variety of gender preferences.

THE EXPERIENCE OF BDSM SPIRITUALITY

> To extend into spirituality, a man may go head first as the yogis do, body first as fakirs do, heart first as monks do, or he may attempt the perilous task of going sexuality first as in certain tantric paths. . . . The spirituality of the bondage dungeon is moving within all [these] energy centers at once. It engages mind, heart, and body; focusing them by way of sexuality. (Bean, 1991b, p. 260)

Alex Comfort (1978) likens the rituals of BDSM, as well as those of other forms of sexual expression (e.g., transvestism), to religious and magical rites. Comfort bases this assertion on observations he made of nondysfunctional couples who practice BDSM. Gosselin and Wilson (1984) sum up Comfort's conclusions regarding his observations of the practice of BDSM by these couples in this way:

> [they] suggested to Comfort that these people were either engaged in what was ethologically play, or something very like yoga—a ritualized body-image manipulation for the purpose of heightening experience. The relationship of the manipulator to the manipulated, [Comfort] argues, is not that of master to slave but that of "facilitator of psychopomp, who uses control to evoke, to push into transcendent experience." . . . Comfort argues that psychiatry has too often sought to describe magical and religious behaviors as sadomasochistic guilt expiation when much more understanding

would be gained by considering sexual rituals as a kind of magical expansion of consciousness. (p. 107)

Mark Thompson (1991b), writing from the perspective of a practitioner, also sees participation in BDSM as a kind of magical experience; indeed, he notes that many who practice BDSM suggest that the letters S and M stand for sexual magic, not sadomasochism. Thompson describes his own experience of BDSM as "a journey into the 'other world' of personal and collective myth. It is that secret inner place where . . . healing occurs" (p. xviii). In explaining the nature of this experience, Thompson states:

> Dream images of strange drama and torture are not uncommon. The inner world is a place of blood and fire, tears and mud. It is the soul's nature to be in organic upheaval, a perpetual state of death and rebirth, just like the world around it. We cannot put a lid on our soul business and its disquieting work. (p. xviii)

This coupling of "strange drama and torture" with the sexual impulse is not as strange as it might seem at first blush. In *The Tears of Eros,* French philosopher Georges Bataille (1989) states that humans are erotic as well as sexual animals. Eroticism is unique to the human species, Bataille argues, because humans alone have the capacity to couple the simple act of sex with the "diabolical," which Bataille defines as the "haunting fear of death" (p. 23). In Bataille's view, pain, whether seen or experienced, serves as an intermediary between life and death. Understood in this way, viewing or participating in spectacles of pain serves the same function as a religious ritual; indeed, Bataille suggests, there exists "a fundamental connection between religious ecstasy and eroticism—and in particular sadism" (p. 206).

Some practitioners of BDSM speak of their experience as a profoundly spiritual one. Geoff Mains (1984) helped pioneer this perspective. In his now classic *Urban Aboriginals,* Mains draws parallels between BDSM rituals

and the rituals of aboriginal peoples, as well as those of certain marginalized cultures in Europe, Asia, and the Americas. Mains argues that BDSM has much in common with, and thus can be understood with respect to, these ritual practices. Mains draws parallels between BDSM sexual performances and the rituals of aboriginal peoples as well as those of certain marginalized cultures inEurope,Asia, and theAmericas, Mains argues. He argues that BDSM has much in common with, and thus can be understood with respect to, such non-Western ritual practices as immersion in samahdi tanks, the dancing of Dervishes, and the carrying of a Kavadi by the Penang. In common with such rituals, Mains argues, BDSM sexuality employs an admixture of pain and pleasure, sensory overload and sensory deprivation, denial and indulgence. Mains goes on to point out that the ritual practices of BDSM and aboriginal cultures, such as those of the Kavadi of Penang, involve intense pain-pleasure experiences that lead to an experience that is "cathartic, ecstatic and spiritual" (p. 21); at times, these practices also produce a profound sense of transcendence. Mains explains that the ecstatic states reported by BDSM practitioners are brought about, in part, by the physiological release of opioids, which chemically produce a shift of consciousness. This shift of consciousness, Mains suggests, is something that BDSM has in common with many spiritual practices, and, he continues, BDSM achieves this shift in much the same way that more ostensibly religious rituals achieve it: through an emphasis on the specialness of place, through ritualistic interaction, and through the focusing of interest.

In common with many religious rites, BDSM is often practiced in a special place that has been set aside; for many, the ideal setting for BDSM is dark and isolated. This darkness and isolation work to exclude the distractions of the outside world. As a result, the focus is on the individuals involved in the scene, and not upon the decorative details of the room in which the BDSM scene unfolds. BDSM also has in common with certain religious practices an emphasis on the use of costume and ritual. Many of the costumes and rituals employed in BDSM are designed to disrupt ordinary consciousness, such as hooding, bondage, and suspension, which promote sensory deprivation; these, coupled with or followed by activities producing sensory overload, such as paddling, whipping, and humiliation, are capable of bringing about an altered state of consciousness. As Mains (1984) explains, such practices tend to focus the mind in ways that exclude the world outside the "scene" (i.e., episode of BDSM erotic play). Many of these practices, such as paddling and whipping, are measured and repetitive. Mains claims that, like other ritual rhythmic practices (e.g., chanting or the beating of a drum), their repetitive nature is capable of inducing trance states. In addition, the pain produced by these and other BDSM practices (e.g., the use of nipple clamps, abrasion, piercing, ice, hot wax, etc.) is itself a useful tool in creating shifts in consciousness. According to Mains, these techniques "applied alone, alternatively or together . . . can induce non-hurtful pain and physical stress. All these have been linked with shifts in consciousness" (p. 101).

Within the context of BDSM, the practices discussed here serve other spiritual functions. One such function is the definition of personal boundaries and personal limits—both mental and physical. As Mains (1984) puts it, "Territory is recognized through infringement. Definition of self and of community comes from interaction with other individuals. A step toward or across an established boundary generates perspectives on both territory and its implications" (p. 136). Whipping, bondage, piercing, and other BDSM practices violate personal territory and test personal limits. Through such violation and testing, personal territory is more sharply defined, personal limits more broadly expanded.

Mains is not the only indigenous writer to point out and discuss the spiritual dimension of BDSM. Ganymede (1991), for example, states:

S/M practices involving bondage, domination, intense sensation, erotic pain, taboo breaking, and so on, are tantric explorations. . . . These forms of sexual play draw upon deep wells within the human psyche. Undertaken as rituals, they become powerful tools for spiritual and psychological growth. (p. 301)

Norman (1991), too, acknowledges the spiritual dimension of BDSM and likens BDSM practices, with their ability to affect certain states of consciousness, to the sacred sexual rituals of the Eastern tantric religious traditions. As he explains, "The use of ritual, rites of passage, initiatory practices—the ordeals of shamanistic training and those of S/M are similar. . . . Through the meditation of a long, slow whipping, for instance, a profound experience is achieved" (p. 279). Adds Norman, "Only in some Eastern traditions, such as tantra, has the concept of sex as a way of knowledge—as a tool on the spiritual path—been recognized" (p. 281). Indeed, Norman maintains that bondage in particular has much in common with other Eastern meditative religious practices, such as yoga: Like yoga, bondage often keeps a person immobile for extended periods of time; like yoga, bondage often distorts the body it confines; and, like yoga, adds Mains (1984), the result of this extended immobility and physical distortion on the mind is a "sense of well being . . . [and a] mental euphoria at the edge of physical limits" (p. 110).

The final result of a good BDSM session, according to Mains, is the predominance of Alpha brainwaves and an almost complete shutdown of the "thinking and memory-saturated hemispheres of the brain on the part of a *bottom* [i.e., masochist] at the hands of an experienced *top* [i.e., sadist]" (p. 106). In an interview with journalist Bill Moyers, Joseph Campbell explains that the difference between ecstasy of this kind and everyday experience is:

Campbell: . . . the difference between [being] outside and inside the garden. You go past fear and desire, past the pair of opposites. . . .

Moyers: Into harmony?

Campbell: Into transcendence. This is the essential experience of any mystic realization. (Campbell & Moyers, 1988, p. 107)

Some suggest that this is the essential experience of BDSM as well.

Among the pieces included in the influential anthology *Leatherfolk* is an interview conducted by Mark Thompson (1991a) with Purusha Androgyne Larkin (born Peter Allison Larkin). For 10 years, Purusha (as he prefers to be called) lived as a Roman Catholic religious and monastic. Later, reports Thompson, Purusha "began to seriously explore various forms of tantric sexuality" (p. 285). Eventually, Purusha went on to incorporate BDSM practices such as fisting into his sexual repertoire. In discussing these practices, he tells Thompson:

> The extreme sensations of pleasure *or* pain, or especially the combination of both . . . concentrates the mind. It *unifies* the consciousness in a way that leads in the direction of what is called the mystical state, or ecstatic states of consciousness. There are many names for it in many traditions. *Satori* in Zen or *samadhi* in tantric Indian traditions. There are many names. "Peak experiences," the psychologist Abraham Maslow called them. (p. 289)

Some cultures value such peak experiences; other cultures, however, are hostile to them. In *The Birth of Tragedy,* Nietzsche (1995) draws a distinction between what he calls the Dionysian and Apollonian approaches to life. Ruth Benedict (1959), recognizing the value of this distinction, imported it into the social sciences as a useful means of discussing differences between cultures. As Benedict explains, Dionysian and Apollonian are

two diametrically opposed ways of arriving at the values of existence. The Dionysian pursues them through "the annihilation of the ordinary bounds and limits of existence"; he seeks to attain in his most valued moments escape from the boundaries imposed upon him by his five senses, to break through into another order of existence. The desire of the Dionysian, in personal experience or in ritual, is to press through it toward a certain psychological state, to achieve excess. (pp. 78–79)

In contrast, Benedict (1959) continues, "The Apollonian distrusts all this, and has very little idea of the nature of such experiences. . . . He keeps the middle of the road, stays within the known map, does not meddle with disruptive psychological states" (p. 79).

The Dionysian attitude to life is named after the Greek god of wine, in whose honor festivals were held that were marked by frenzied abandon (and for whom the plays of classical Greece were written and performed; see, e.g., Hamilton, 1942). In describing these festivals, Nietzsche (1995) states that they were centered on "extravagant sexual licentiousness . . . the most savage natural instincts were unleashed, including that horrible mixture of sensuality and cruelty" (p. 6). According to Nietzsche, "the Dionysian revelers remind us . . . of the phenomenon that pain begets joy, that ecstacy may wring sounds of agony from us" (p. 6). Within those cultures that embrace the Dionysian, Mains (1984) asserts, "altered forms of consciousness, and the heavy and often turbulent experiences that bring such transcendence, are not only valued but institutionalized" (p. 114). On the other hand, Mains continues:

> an Apollonian culture is distrustful of excess and [seeks to] restrain life within what [it] regards as rational existence. . . . Often these societies do everything within their power to outlaw any tendency toward Dionysian experience. Apollonian cultures tend to be highly focused power structures, whether or not these are democratic. (p. 115)

Examples of cultures that approach life from an Apollonian perspective include those of Western Europe, North America (those of the United States and Canada), and some Far Eastern cultures (in particular, the Japanese). It is somewhat surprising that the cultures just identified as Apollonian are also the very cultures in which BDSM flourishes. Indeed, as Gebhard (1983) notes, "explicitly sexual sadomasochism, like fetishism, seems the monopoly of well-developed civilizations," and, he adds, in so-called primitive societies, "sadomasochism as a lifestyle is conspicuous by its absence" (pp. 38–39).

On the surface, it would seem unlikely that BDSM—which, in the Dionysian tradition, values sensuality and cruelty, pain and joy, turbulence and transcendence—would find its home in cultures that are antithetical to such Dionysian experiences. Norman (1991) offers a possible explanation for this seeming contradiction. Norman claims that BDSM is an Apollonian means of reaching the Dionysian. "In other words," he explains, BDSM "is a controlled, skillful, and thought-out process for reaching the intuitive/ecstatic state . . . a left-brain approach for triggering right-brain experiences" (p. 276). Mains (1984) echoes this sentiment:

> Individual shamans and sorcerers, warriors on their vigils, fasting pilgrims on arduous missions, Kavadi dancers and whirling Dervishes, all may find transcendence in their experience. This stepping outside themselves seems likely to touch at the same universal powers that leather does. . . . this transcendence could have social implications: these individuals [the shamans, sorcerers, etc.] may well come to see their world and their actions quite differently. But their cultures have, over time, adapted to the presence of these expectations. While the culture provides the necessary frameworks and freedom for Dionysian experience and expression, it remains for the most part socially rigid.
>
> Leather, in contrast, exists as a bridge between two worlds. Its adherents grew up

in and were indoctrinated by life in Apollonian culture. . . . They have been educated with the rationalist philosophy of that culture and are adept in applying it. (p. 162)

Mains (1984) adds, however, that although sadomasochists are

> enmeshed within this matrix, [they] have adopted rituals that put their lives into new perspectives and are based on a very different value system. They share mental and physical experiences with Dionysian cultures. . . . Leather [BDSM] is a countercultural experience—a Dionysian thrust in the midst of an Apollonian parry. (pp. 162–163, 169)

In other words, BDSM as practiced in the West is both a product of and challenge to the culture of which it is a part.

A DIONYSIAN THRUST IN THE MIDST OF AN APOLLONIAN PARRY: THE CHALLENGE OF BDSM SPIRITUALITY

I live in two worlds: mundane and magical. (Norman, 1991, p. 276)

For much of Western history, there was no label attached to individuals who engaged in BDSM behaviors or to the behaviors themselves. People who enjoyed the mixing of pain and pleasure within an erotic context did so largely in isolation from one another and certainly outside the context of the kind of organized community that emerged in the United States after World War II. With the development of such a community came attempts on the part of its members to make sense of their shared experience. Included in this effort was the conscious attempt to work out and articulate views regarding the spiritual dimension of BDSM. I suggest that this attempt is, in part, a component of a broader reassessment of modernism.

At the beginning of the 21st century, many Westerners have begun to question what social psychologist Kenneth Gergen (1991) calls the "*grand narrative* of modernism" (p. 30). As

Gergen explains it, this narrative "is a story told by Western culture to itself about its journey through time. . . . The grand narrative is one of continuous upward movement—improvement, conquest, achievement—toward some goal" (p. 30). The narrative's defining feature, then, is its promise of perpetual progress. This promise provides the West with a means of understanding its past as well as a roadmap for its future. Neither we humans nor the world in which we live are perfect, so the narrative goes, but both have the potential to be improved.

Beginning with the Enlightenment, many of the West's most influential thinkers came to view reason as *the* way of improving ourselves and the social and physical worlds in which we dwell. Throughout most of this century, a particular application of reason, that of modern science, has been touted as the means through which the grand narrative's promised improvements, conquests, and achievements would be realized. For a time, it seemed as though science was fulfilling the promises made on its behalf. Inventions made life easier, diseases were conquered, humans landed on the moon. Gradually, however, the West's optimism regarding scientific progress became tempered by a growing recognition that the benefits of science come with a cost. The products and processes that science makes possible take a toll on the environment and on the humans whose interests science ostensibly serves (Carson, 1962; Gaarder, 1994; Gergen, 1991; Ritzer, 1996).

Disillusioned by science's betrayal of its promise of unlimited progress and dissatisfied with the world science helped create, many Westerners have turned to nonscientific belief systems as a means of making sense of and coping with their lives and the world in which they live. Some have turned to such things as astrology, clairvoyance, faith healing, past lives, and psychokinesis (Humphrey, 1996). Others have explored prescientific and non-Western spiritual traditions. The exploration of the spiritual side of BDSM is a part of this same search for spiritual meaning. This increased interest in nonscientific ways of approaching experience does not necessarily imply an outright rejection of science. What such interest does suggest, however, is that there are human needs that science can neither fulfill nor understand. As Norman (1991) puts it, "Spiritual knowledge isn't learned from books. It's experiential. Personal, subjective gut feelings—those aspects discounted by our culture and which cannot be proved or validated by science" (p. 277).

For some of its practitioners, BDSM provides experiential spiritual knowledge. Unlike the knowledge generated by the scientific method, the knowledge that comes from BDSM experiences is unique to an individual and thus cannot be independently confirmed or replicated. Often, such knowledge can only be expressed in nonrational terms, if indeed it can be expressed at all. BDSM spirituality acknowledges the uniqueness of each person's experience. As Baldwin (1993) notes, the emphasis of BDSM spirituality is on the creation of such experience, not the imposition of dogma. Because BDSM spirituality emphasizes individual experience and not collective belief, many practitioners see BDSM as a contemporary Western form of shamanism. Shamanism, as explained by Norman (1991),

> uses ritual in learning, teaching, and practice. But the shaman's way isn't tied to ritual other than as a useful tool. Dogma and doctrine are traps. . . . Therefore, a shaman can only hold beliefs lightly and must be capable of changing them when presented with new facts or perceptions. Certain beliefs can be barriers to new ways of vision, too. Flexibility and openness are the shamanic way. . . . The shaman accepts life as the known, the unknown, and the unknowable. Life is a mystery to be joyously lived rather than fully understood. (p. 278)

The shamanic way of knowing, then, differs from the scientific. Some mysteries are to be embraced, not solved. Within the context of BDSM play, understood as a form of shamanism, some mysteries are to be encountered, not explained.

To expand the range of possible experiences and the potential mysteries encountered through those experiences, some American sadomasochists have borrowed from the ritual repertoire of non-Western cultures. Perhaps no one has done so with more enthusiasm than the man who calls himself Fakir Musafar. In an interview with Bean (1991a), the Fakir discusses how his participation in rituals such as the Native American Sun Dance (in which one is suspended from hooks that pierce the chest) produces an

> altered state, and once you're in this altered state, you have a choice of many doors to go through. And some people will go through this door, and some will go through that door. And the experience is going to be a little different depending which door you go through. (p. 311)

The Fakir goes on to suggest that the BDSM "top" (to use the indigenous term for the person who, for example, does the tying or beating in a "scene," which is an episode of BDSM play) serves as a shamanic guide for the BDSM "bottom" (another indigenous term, used for the person who, for example, is tied and beaten). As the Fakir tells Bean, "a top in a normal S/M scene is very experienced at sending people on trips, but generally doesn't go along" (p. 315). In other words, a top creates an experience through which a bottom is able to explore those dark spaces that are far removed from ordinary existence.

In the quote with which this section opens, Norman (1991) states that he lives in two worlds, one mundane, the other magical (p. 276). The world of the mundane is the everyday physical and social world in which we all live. This world is open to scientific investigation. The world of magic, on the other hand, is a private one. To use the Fakir's analogy,

there are as many such worlds as there are doors through which to enter them. These worlds are beyond the scrutiny of science. The turn to nonscientific ways of approaching the world, such as BDSM spirituality, is a response to deep-rooted Dionysian needs that have not been satisfied in the Western world's predominantly Apollonian culture.

The current reassessment of modernism is not a wholesale rejection of science; rather, this reassessment reflects, in part, an acknowledgment that science is limited in its ability to satisfy every human need. In this new millennium, there is room for both scientific and nonscientific ways of knowing. After all, Mains (1984), as a biochemist, uses his scientific knowledge as a means of understanding his BDSM experience. Such understanding enhances, rather than detracts, from those experiences. Although science can shed some light on the process through which sadomasochists travel to the dark spaces they explore, science cannot take them to those places. Still, it is through the exploration of such places, through chanting, meditation, tantric practices, yoga, or BDSM, that some realize their full human potential.

NOTES

1. To avoid confusion, it is useful to note that the various authors cited in this paper use different abbreviations to refer to the noun *sadomasochism* and the adjective *sadomasochistic* (e.g., SM, S&M, and S/M). These abbreviations are roughly synonymous. Throughout this chapter, I prefer to use *BDSM* because it is the term currently favored by many within the culture. The acronym can be interpreted thus: BD = bondage and discipline, DS = dominance and submission, and SM = sadism and masochism (the two middle letters do double duty).

Incidentally, the use of the abbreviation SM can be traced back to Alfred Kinsey, who, according to Steward (1991),

> invented the term S/M. . . . He and his staff had created a "little language" of initial letters so that they could discuss hair-raising

(and fascinating) sexual topics at lunch and not cause the waitress to collapse with cardiac arrest because of what she overheard. (p. 82)

2. For those unfamiliar with the BDSM community, I emphasize that the BDSM practices I discuss in this paper involve consensual behavior between two or more people who share an interest in the mixing of pain and pleasure within an erotic context. Indeed, a mantra constantly chanted within the BDSM community is "safe, sane, and consensual."

3. For early examples of literary depictions, Weinberg, Williams, and Moser (1984) point to *The Koka Shastra* (Kokkoka, 1965; the original was written circa 1150), *The Perfumed Garden* (Nefzawi, 1964; original circa 1400), and *The Kama Sutra* (Vatsyayana, 1962; original circa 450). A contemporary example of literature written in the same erotic vein is that of the popular (within certain circles) Beauty Trilogy, written by Anne Rice—famous for her popular vampire series—under the pseudonym A. N. Roquelaure (1983, 1984, 1985).

REFERENCES

Baldwin, G. (1993). *Ties that bind*. Los Angeles: Daedelus.

Bataille, G. (1989). *The tears of eros*. San Francisco: City Lights Books.

Bean, J. W. (1991a). Magical masochist: A conversation with Fakir Musafar. In M. Thompson (Ed.), *Leatherfolk: Radical sex, people, politics, and practice* (pp. 303–319). Boston: Alyson.

Bean, J. W. (1991b). The spiritual dimensions of bondage. In M. Thompson (Ed.), *Leatherfolk: Radical sex, people, politics, and practice* (pp. 257–266). Boston: Alyson.

Benedict, R. (1959). *Patterns of culture*. Boston: Houghton Mifflin.

Bullough, V., & Bullough, B. (1977). *Sin, sickness, and sanity: A history of sexual attitudes*. New York: New American Library.

Bullough, V., Dixon, D., & Dixon, J. (1994). Sadism, masochism, and history, or when is behavior sado-masochistic? In R. Porter & M. Teich (Eds.), *Sexual knowledge, sexual science: The history of attitudes to sexuality* (pp. 47–62). Cambridge, England: Cambridge University Press.

Campbell, J., & Moyers, B. (1988). *The power of myth*. New York: Doubleday.

Carson, R. (1962). *Silent spring*. Boston: Houghton Mifflin.

Comfort, A. (1978). Sexual idiosyncracies: Deviation or magic? *Journal of Psychiatry, 9*, 11–16.

Ellis, H. (1942). *Studies in the psychology of sex* (Vol. 1, Part 2). New York: Random House.

Falk, G., & Weinberg, T. S. (1983). Sadomasochism and popular Western culture. In T. S. Weinberg & G.W.L. Kamel (Eds.), *S&M: Studies in sadomasochism* (pp. 137–144). Amherst, NY: Prometheus.

Freud, S. (1938). *The basic writings of Sigmund Freud* (A. A. Brill, Trans.). New York: Modern Library.

Gaarder, J. (1994). *Sophie's world: A novel about the history of philosophy*. New York: Farrar, Straus and Giroux.

Gagnon, J. (1977). *Human sexualities*. Glenview, IL: Scott, Foresman.

Ganymede. (1991). Sacred passages and radical sex magic. In M. Thompson (Ed.), *Leatherfolk: Radical sex, people, politics, and practice* (pp. 294–302). Boston: Alyson.

Gebhard, P. (1969). Fetishism and sadomasochism. In J. H. Masserman (Ed.), *Dynamics of deviant sexuality* (pp. 71–80). New York: Grune and Stratton.

Gebhard, P. (1983). Sadomasochism. In T. S. Weinberg & G.W.L. Kamel (Eds.), *S&M: Studies in sadomasochism* (pp. 36–39). Amherst, NY: Prometheus.

Gergen, K. J. (1991). *The saturated self: Dilemmas of identity in contemporary life*. New York: Basic Books.

Gosselin, C., & Wilson, G. (1984). Fetishism, sadomasochism and related behaviors. In K. Howells (Ed.), *The psychology of sexual diversity* (pp. 89–110). New York: Basil Blackwell.

Hamilton, E. (1942). *Mythology: Timeless tales of gods and heroes*. New York: Mentor.

Houlberg, R. (1991). The magazine of a sadomasochism club: The tie that binds. *Journal of Homosexuality, 21*, 167–183.

Humphrey, N. (1996). *Leaps of faith: Science, miracles, and the search for supernatural consolation*. New York: Basic Books.

Kamel, G.W.L. (1983a). The leather career: On becoming a sadomasochist. In T. S. Weinberg & G.W.L. Kamel (Eds.), *S&M: Studies in sadomasochism* (pp. 73–79). Amherst, NY: Prometheus.

Kamel, G.W.L. (1983b). Leathersex: Meaningful aspects of gay sadomasochism. In T. S. Weinberg & G.W.L. Kamel (Eds.), *S&M: Studies in sadomasochism* (pp. 162–174). Amherst, NY: Prometheus.

Kamel, G.W.L., & Weinberg, T. (1983). Diversity in sadomasochism: Four S&M careers. In T. S. Weinberg & G.W.L. Kamel (Eds.), *S&M: Studies in sadomasochism* (pp. 113–128). Amherst, NY: Prometheus.

Kokkoka. (1965). *The koka shastra* (A. Comfort, Trans.). New York: Stein and Day. (Original work published ca. 1150)

Krafft-Ebing, R. von. (1965). *Psychopathia sexualis* (F. S. Klaf, Trans.). New York: Stein and Day.

Lee, J. L. (1983). The social organization of sexual risk. In T. S. Weinberg & G.W.L. Kamel (Eds.), *S&M: Studies in sadomasochism* (pp. 175–193). Amherst, NY: Prometheus.

Mains, G. (1984). *Urban aboriginals: A celebration of leather sexuality.* San Francisco: Gay Sunshine Press.

Moser, C., Lee, J., & Christensen, P. (1993). Nipple-piercing: An exploratory-descriptive study. *Journal of Psychology and Human Sexuality, 6,* 51–61.

Moser, C., & Levitt, E. E. (1987). An exploratory-descriptive study of a sadomasochistically oriented sample. *Journal of Sex Research, 23,* 322–337.

Nefzawi, S. (1964). *The perfumed garden* (R. Burton, Trans.). New York: Putnam. (Original work published ca. 1400)

Nietzsche, F. (1995). *The birth of tragedy.* (C. P. Fadiman, Trans.). Mineola, NY: Dover.

Norman, S. (1991). I am a leatherfaerie shaman. In M. Thompson (Ed.), *Leatherfolk: Radical sex, people, politics, and practice* (pp. 276–283). Boston: Alyson.

Ritzer, G. (1996). *The McDonaldization of society* (Rev. ed.). Thousand Oaks, CA: Pine Forge Press.

Roquelaure, A. N. (1983). *The claiming of Sleeping Beauty: An erotic novel of tenderness and cruelty for the enjoyment of men and women.* New York: Plume.

Roquelaure, A. N. (1984). *Beauty's punishment.* New York: Plume.

Roquelaure, A. N. (1985). *Beauty's release.* New York: Plume.

Rubin, G. (1991). The catacombs: A temple of the butthole. In M. Thompson (Ed.), *Leatherfolk: Radical sex, people, politics, and practice* (pp. 119–141). Boston: Alyson.

Sacher-Masoch, L. von (1989). *Venus in furs.* New York: Blast Books.

Simon, W. (1996). *Postmodern sexualities.* New York: Routledge.

Spengler, A. (1983). Manifest sadomasochism of males: Results of an empirical study. In T. S. Weinberg & G.W.L. Kamel (Eds.), *S&M: Studies in sadomasochism* (pp. 57–72). Amherst, NY: Prometheus.

Stekel, W. (1965). *Sadism and masochism.* New York: Grove Press.

Steward, S. M. (1991). Dr. Kinsey takes a peek at S/M: A reminiscence. In M. Thompson (Ed.), *Leatherfolk: Radical sex, people, politics, and practice* (pp. 81–90). Boston: Alyson.

Thompson, M. (1991a). Erotic ecstasy: An interview with Purusha the Androgyne. In M. Thompson (Ed.), *Leatherfolk: Radical sex, people, politics, and practice* (pp. 284–293). Boston: Alyson.

Thompson, M. (1991b). Introduction. In M. Thompson (Ed.), *Leatherfolk: Radical sex, people, politics, and practice* (pp. xi–xx). Boston: Alyson.

Vatsyayana. (1962). *The kama sutra* (R. Burton, Trans.). New York: E. P. Dutton. (Original work published circa 450)

Weinberg, M., Williams, C. J., & Moser, C. (1984). The social constituents of sadomasochism. *Social Problems, 31,* 379–389.

Weinberg, T. S. (1983). Sadism and masochism: Sociological perspectives. In T. S. Weinberg & G.W.L. Kamel (Eds.), *S&M: Studies in sadomasochism* (pp. 99–112). Amherst, NY: Prometheus.

Weinberg, T. S. (1987). Sadomasochism in the United States: A review of recent sociological literature. *Journal of Sex Research, 23*(1), 50–69.

Weinberg, T. S. (1995). Sociological and social psychological issues in the study of sadomasochism. In T. S. Weinberg (Ed.), *S&M: Studies in dominance and submission* (pp. 289–303). Amherst, NY: Prometheus.

Weinberg, T. S., & Kamel, G.W.L. (1983). S&M: An introduction to the study of sadomasochism. In T. S. Weinberg & G.W.L. Kamel (Eds.), *S&M: Studies in sadomasochism* (pp. 17–24). Amherst, NY: Prometheus.

Discussion Questions

1. What examples does Westerfelhaus give to describe the relationship between BDSM and spirituality?

2. How does the reading support or challenge your assumptions about and perceptions of BDSM and its community of practitioners?

3. What do you think that Audre Lorde would think of Westerfelhaus's appraisal of BDSM as "soulwork and social critique"? Might the same argument be made for all forms of erotic play?

20

Menopause and Desire,
or 452 Positions on Love

MERCILEE M. JENKINS

INTRODUCTION

I began writing this piece with a poem about cleaning my refrigerator as a metaphor for dealing with the decay of past relationships. Gradually I realized that my theme was menopause and desire. I have never seen these two topics connected before and I felt it was high time they were. *Menopause and Desire* evolved in New York, during my sabbatical where I worked with Suzanne Bennett as director and Rae C. Wright as an actor interested in performing the monolog. Out of the work came the poems entitled "Bureau of Appropriate Self-Disclosure," "Civil Service, NYC," and "452 Positions on Love" which ended up in the final draft. A trip to Bourbon Street in New Orleans sparked my remembrances of all I went through after I had a mastectomy, so I started working on "Show Us Your Tits"

when I got back to San Francisco. I had written one other poem about having breast cancer ("What to Do When You Find Out You Have Breast Cancer") when I was asked to speak at a local gay church during Breast Cancer Awareness month a few years ago.

I was invited to perform at the San Francisco Fringe Festival in 2002, thanks to Stephanie Weisman, Artistic Director of The Marsh, a venue where I have presented several of my plays and performance pieces. I decided *Menopause and Desire* would be composed of interconnected prose poems and scenes dealing with such topics as sexuality in middle age, how to admire the post-mastectomy body, and whether or not it is possible to learn anything about love, even if you live to be a hundred. "You Made Me Love You" was edited and revised from an earlier prose monolog into poetic form. I use the poetic form because it

SOURCE: This chapter was originally published as a part of "Menopause and Desire or 452 Positions on Love" in *Text & Performance Quarterly* (July 2005). Copyright © 2005 National Communications Association. Reprinted by permission.

offers an economy, rhythm, and imagery I don't evoke when I write in prose. I've written poetry since I first started keeping a journal at age eighteen, and my poems always seem to be the place where my truest feelings take shape.

The rest of the pieces were written during the summer of 2002, as I began to prepare for my upcoming performances. I was not only writing for performance but, through the act of performing, my writing was being tested and refined. Poems I loved were cut, as a cohesive script began to emerge from the juxtaposition of the parts. During this process, I recruited a male director because I wanted to include men in the audience, even though the M-word might scare them away. Ron Pelias served as dramaturg and director, and, as a fellow poet, encouraged me to bring out the sensuality of the writing in my performance, along with the sadness and humor.

When it comes to poetic traditions, I am inspired by the poets of the everyday conversations we have in our heads, such as Frank O'Hara (*Lunch Poems*) and the feminist poets I grew up on—Diane Wakoski (*Motorcycle Betrayal Poems*), Jessica Hagedorn (*Dangerous Music*) and Susan Griffin (*Like the Iris of an Eye*). They know how to look at a life, slice it up, and serve it on the best china. Here I offer up a slice of my own life for you to taste.

Menopause and Desire was first performed in its entirety for the 2002 San Francisco Fringe Festival and shortly thereafter at the Lake Superior Festival in Sault Ste. Marie, Michigan thanks to Gary Balfantz. In 2003, I presented the show for International Women's Day at Skyline College in San Bruno, California and most recently as a Distinguished Visiting Artist at California State University at Northridge and at the National Communication Association annual meeting in Miami. My ambition was to write a text that could be appreciated in performance and in print. I hesitated to add many stage directions or performance notes that might interrupt the lyric flow and interconnection of the pieces, which do reference each other at times. I will, however, sketch in some of the staging to help the reader visualize my performance. I do hope that there will be other performers of *Menopause and Desire* and that they will feel free to make it their own.

There are three major segments or scenes, which contain separate prose poems that are variations around the themes indicated by the scene titles. Each scene is introduced by a musical interlude during which I move matter-of-factly around the stage setting up the next scene, changing costume pieces, picking up props, etc. I think of the whole piece as being like a musical composition with the theme of menopause and desire and sub-themes concerning destiny, body image and secrecy reflecting and resonating with each other as they recur. (Note that only selected segments appear in this chapter.)

Scene 1: Destiny & Desire
"Civil Service, NYC"
"You Made Me Love You"
"Dialogue with Menopause & Desire"

Scene 2: Geography of Desire
"452 Positions"
"What to Do When You Find Out You Have Breast Cancer"
"Show Us Your Tits"
"Bureau of Appropriate Self-disclosure"

Scene 3: Secrets of Desire
"A Sign"

"Dyke March 2002-2003"
"Cleaning the Refrigerator"

SCENE 1: DESTINY & DESIRE

[*The stage is set with a small square table and a chair mid-stage left and a bench arranged diagonally mid-stage right. There are strands of Mardi Gras beads hanging along the back wall of the stage and a bright colored paper parasol, which is covering a bucket of props. A bright colored feather boa hangs on the back wall stage right*]

[omitted: "Civil Service, NYC"]

[*I leave the post office area and walk to the table and chair as if I have come back to my office. I begin speaking standing behind the chair, which is facing the audience. I sit at the desk when talking with David in my office. I use stage right for our rehearsals and center stage for the lobby of the hotel. Intermittently I sing phrases from the song "You Made Me Love You"*]

You Made Me Love You

If I were being honest with myself,
I'd have to say that before I met David,
I didn't like my students to get too close to me.

(sings) *"You made me love you.*
I didn't want to do it."

He was very good looking—
tall, dark hair, coal button eyes
and cheekbones for days.
Native American—Osage tribe.
He claimed that's why he had "attitude."
I didn't mind. Everybody's got something
you have to contend with.
He was smart, laughed at my jokes,
but we argued about who was funnier.
He could always get me
with some stupid joke.
Like his Xerox® allocation was bigger than mine,
and I, a professor, and he
a mere graduate teaching assistant.
He'd change the numbers on his memo,
casually leave it on my desk.
"How did you get 400 copies
and I only got 200?"
Midwestern gullibility
after all these years in California.

*"I didn't want to do it.
You made me love you."*

He was just a student in one of my classes
who kept coming to my office.
He said he wanted to be like me—
do theater and academics,
study gender and communication,
sexual identity—he was gay.
Then one day he announced that he had a crush on me.
I found that very endearing.
Here I'd been trying to write plays,
do research and teach all these years
and I just thought I was crazy.
Now I had a protégé.

*"And all the time you knew it.
I guess you always knew it."*

I woke up sick one morning
and called him to take over class for the first time.
He said, no problem. He'd love to do it.
He was never shy about speaking in public.
I fell right back to sleep which isn't like me
Usually I'd worry. I woke up and realized
I loved him. I trusted him.
At that time, I shared an office
with two other colleagues,
so David sat at my desk with me for a year.
Being a workaholic, I don't think I ever spent so much time
with anyone in such close quarters while awake.
We used to joke about getting married,
except we didn't think my girlfriend, Kay,
would approve, but we were noticeably a couple
parading up and down the hallways
always doing something, going somewhere together.
I knew he had AIDS, but then
he walked so fast.
I used to have trouble keeping up with him

"You made me happy sometimes. You made me glad."

That fall, we were rehearsing a few scenes
to perform at the conference in Atlanta
from my play, *Dangerous Beauty*.
It's a love story about a gay man

and a bisexual woman
that starts in the 70's and resumes after the earthquake in 1989. That second part was
mostly fiction,
until we started doing the play together.
Life and art intermingled
and I never could separate them after that.
We worked on every scene, but the love scene.
We joked that our director
wasn't ready for that.

"But there were times, dear, you made me feel so bad."

He arrived late the morning of our performance
in Atlanta, and we missed connections.
I was pacing the lobby and phoning him every 15 minutes.
Finally, we found each other, but I was furious.
So we go to my hotel room to have it out and rehearse,
but by the time we got into the elevator
I was over it and he was upset.
He started to cry and said,
"I'm only doing this for you."
I thought of the hours of rehearsal,
the long plane flight,
he had chosen to spend the time he had left
working with me.
I didn't know how sick he was.
He didn't want me to know.
It was my job to make sure he always had a future.

"You made me sigh 'cause.
I didn't wanna tell you. I didn't wanna tell you.
I think you're grand. That's true. Yes, I do, 'deed I do, you know I do."

During the rest of that conference,
people would stop us and compliment us
on our performance.
We were always going up and down escalators
in our dress-up clothes, getting lost in the hotel.
I chided him for being Native American
and having no sense of direction.
He said it was because we were so enamored
with ourselves and each other.
We even found time to get
the right blouse for my outfit.
A tunnel went from the hotel to Macy's.
We emerged amidst all this merchandise.

I stood there stunned but he swooped
down on the racks of clothing and found me
exactly the right shade blouse.
And we were off again
to hear another panel of speakers
taking notes on the same pad of paper,
an intertwining dialogue on all that we saw and heard.
I hate these conferences, and here I was
having the time of my life.
When we got back
sitting in the courtyard at school
I told him I'd never be the same without him.
I knew they would invent a drug to save him.
It just came too late.
By next fall he was gone.

*"I can't tell you what I'm feeling.
The very mention of your name sends my heart reeling."*

And he did make me love him.
It was really all his fault.
It all started when he said
he had a scholarship to pursue an M.A. at Arizona State,
but he was thinking of staying in San Francisco because of me.
Normally, I would have recommended
that he go to a new school,
tap into new resources and teachers.
But as it happened we were walking down the street
after a class dinner, and I just took his arm and said,
"I think you'd better stay here with me."

"You know you made me love you."

[*Song "You Made Me Love You" sung by Judy Garland comes up as I shift from the table and chair to the bench. I pick up the feather boa and hold it in my hands as the music fades out.*]

David always said he didn't want to be around when I went through menopause. Now I know why.

Dialogue with Menopause & Desire

[*Throughout this piece I sit, lie down, and move around on the bench striking various poses. The feather boa is draped seductively around Desire but hangs limply around Menopause*]

Menopause: Desire, you're back?
Desire: Yeah, Menopause, I'm here. How you doin'?

Menopause:	OK, I guess. I've got my symptoms—hot flashes, headaches, my head feels like it's full of cotton batten, I think my hair is falling out, and I've got a vagina like the Sahara.
Desire:	Please, don't bore me with your medical history. That's not why I'm here.
Menopause:	OK, OK, sorry. Why are you here?
Desire:	You know. Don't you feel anything yet?
Menopause:	Well, let's see. I am feeling a little restless, unsatisfied, I haven't been sleeping that well.
Desire:	Yes, yes, anything else?
Menopause:	I don't know. I always seem to want something, but lately. . . .
Desire:	Yes?
Menopause:	I want sex.
Desire:	It's about time.
Menopause:	Why now, when most women my age have sworn off sex, relieved to be done with it all, not so dependent on having a mate.
Desire:	Everybody's different. Some people go through periods when they are too busy for passion. Know what I mean?
Menopause:	So I was busy still, why now?
Desire:	Let's see, your horoscope says, and I quote: "You know you're not happy when you get what you want. You need something to long for."
Menopause:	That's not true. I do so like getting what I want. I've just been a little moody lately. Do you think I've gained weight?
Desire:	You can't blame your whole personality on hormones.
Menopause:	Shut up. I have drive, that's all. OK, I'm driven.
Desire:	Face it, you're an incurable romantic. You are all about desire.
Menopause:	Maybe, but that doesn't mean I want desire now. Not for that.
Desire:	Why not? You're bisexual. You've got the whole world to choose from.
Menopause:	Not that that ever did me any good. I still managed to fall in love with the wrong person, at the wrong time, in the wrong place. And even when I do really love someone who loves me, it never lasts very long. Something bad always happens—we break up, they die, etc.
Desire:	You are so tragic. So you want me to go away, is that what you want?
Menopause:	Well, I didn't say that.
Desire:	Because I'm inconvenient?
Menopause:	It's not just that. Who's gonna want me, male or female, at this point in my life? Men like younger women. Women like younger women. It's not fair. Society is still sexist.
Desire:	Remember the little old lady in the post office. She got what she wanted.
Menopause:	Oh, please. That's not what I want. (*pause*) I'm into S & L relationships: sincere and lasting.
Desire:	Good. See, that wasn't so hard.
Menopause:	But it's too late for that now.
Desire:	I don't see why.
Menopause:	If I haven't been successful by now, what are my chances?
Desire:	You know better than to believe in percentages. (*pause*) But I could leave right now and you'll be stuck in your head intellectualizing like always.
Menopause:	No, no, don't leave, even though you are in my head. I like feeling desire, wanting someone, longing for him (*pause*) or her, imagining what it could be like.
Desire:	Then what are you going to do about it?
Menopause:	I don't know. Got any ideas?
Desire:	Yes, start with yourself. Get in touch with me and all I have to offer.
Menopause:	You mean masturbate?
Desire:	Not just that. Use your imagination. That's what you're really good at.
Menopause:	Yeah, I am good at that.

Desire: Go ahead, let yourself go. Dare to love whomever you want in whatever way you want. What have you got to lose? We'll get back to reality—

Menopause: —later.

[The song "Drift Away" by Dobie Grey fades up as I get ready for Scene 2. I hang the feather boa back up on the wall and go to the table and pick up a set of Xeroxed pages stapled together. When I am ready I move downstage center and the lights come up as the music fades and I begin.]

SCENE 2: GEOGRAPHY OF DESIRE

[omitted: "452 Positions on Love"]

[I deliver this piece as if I am making an impassioned speech to the audience, looking at individual audience members in different locations around the theatre every time I offer instructions on what you should do.]

What to Do When You Find Out You Have Breast Cancer

Call all your friends and ask them to help you.
Get mad as hell and rage at the medical industrial establishment
for not taking better care of you.
Blame the government for not taking better care of all women
and this planet.

If someone says,
What did you do to get this?
Say, I was born after World War II
during the time of above-ground nuclear testing.
All my life, I drank the water and breathed the air
that has been polluted by industry.
I worked too hard for the money I needed to live
and my heart has been broken because too many of my friends
have died of AIDS.
And no, breast cancer doesn't run in my family
but it's running like crazy through the family of woman.
Thirty years ago it was 1 in 20.
now it's 1 in 8.
But we're told there's no cause for concern.

Maybe it's our diet
we should eat less fat
until we disappear
no breasts to speak of
no flesh to nourish this disease.

If someone gives you the book
Love, Medicine and Miracles
(And they will)

first throw it across the room
because you don't want to hear about
how you are responsible for your own healing.
Then pick it up and read it
and find out the author thinks it's good to be a troublesome patient
and realize you are well on your way.

Do whatever you need to do
to make yourself feel whole again:
walk on the beach,
go dancing,
prune the garden with a fury,
have secret ceremonies by moonlight with witchy friends,
or rent a lot of old movies and cry as much as you can.

Go to the doctor.
When he pulls the drain out of your side
get a good look at your mastectomy scar,
then go out and get drunk.
When your doctor surprises you with the news
that now you are going to have chemotherapy,
go home
and ask your partner to cut off all your hair
because you're going to lose it anyway.
If the diagnosis doesn't kill you,
the cure sure feels like it will.

Tell the newspapers to ban all lingerie ads
since they only make you jealous
of women with two breasts of any size.
Tell your doctors and your well-meaning friends
you are not cheered up by the idea
that now you can get perfect fake breasts
to replace your middle aged natural ones
which you like just fine, thank-you-very-much
because they respond to sexual stimulation
and fake ones don't.
Funny we never seem to talk about that.

And you will find out things you don't want to know
like who your real friends are,
the ones who offer to help and mean it.
Or what your love relationship is all about.
Fifty percent of relationships break up
and not because you are abandoned
but because you can no longer afford to love people
who don't nurture you.

Find out how spiritual you really are.
Don't be afraid to pray
and ask whoever is "in"
as you see it—that great being in the sky—
to lift you up to where you belong
and carry you on a dove's breath
away from all this
'cause you certainly don't belong here.

And tell yourself you love yourself
even if you don't mean it.
Tell yourself that every day
until you do.
That won't make up for the loss
but it will take you to
the next person you're going to be:
wiser, more beautiful,
capable of kicking ass and taking prisoners.
And when they call you a
"Cancer Survivor"
tell them no
you're much more than that.
You're a whole woman inside out.
You're a self-made woman
and you celebrate life
every time you think of it
and you feel lucky
and you bless your body and honor those who have died
because that's what eventually happens to one out of three of us.
So you tell that person
that it's about so much more than surviving.
It's about defining yourself by new rules
even if you don't know
how it's all going to end.

Show Us Your Tits

[New Orleans style music comes up during the segments on Bourbon Street, along with a change in lighting, which includes a disco ball rotating. I use the entire stage, picking up Mardi Gras beads and putting them on along the way as I move under the imaginary balconies and walk along the street. These segments alternate with my self-reflections on my decisions about what to do after I had a mastectomy.]

They are chanting from the balconies
"Show us your tits."
People who might otherwise
run offices, invest your money or fix your car

are asking for such a display
in exchange for Mardi Gras beads.
[Put on strand of beads]
This is Bourbon Street in New Orleans
as it rises to its full height
of cocktail induced merriment
so they feel entitled.
I am shocked.
I thought this sort of thing only happened
during Mardi Gras.
This is an ordinary Tuesday night.
My companion looks up and
beckons for beads
so they wave and point to me,
"Show us your tits."
"Don't laugh and encourage them.
Thank you so much.
What are you going to show?"

We walk on
but I start to think of all the times
I have been asked to do just that
to demonstrate my womanhood.

First as a kid, "I'll show you mine, if
you show me yours" grows into the desire
for a bra, despite the lack of physical need.
I simply could not go on wearing
an undershirt in seventh grade.
I had to have the outline of a bra
underneath my blouse
So boys could say, "Are you a turtle?"
"No." "Then why do you snap?"

The same scene is taking place
under another balcony.
Here two young women egg each other on.
"Come on, go on. I will, if you will."

I see myself as a teenager on the swimming team
wearing an old-fashioned black nylon tank suit
made of filmy layers that cling
like transparent kelp when I emerge from the pool.
My teammate, Jenny, ascends the ladder with
her big beautiful breasts streaming with water
and threatening to escape their nylon second skin
but I notice I am sleek as a seal.

The young women cruising the strip seem prepared
for this venture, wearing nothing underneath
their tight stretchy tops.
Am I the last woman on Bourbon Street wearing a bra?
That's so ironic because I hate wearing one.

Through my teens I struggle with
various models, shapes, sizes, padding or not.
but the bra I remember most
is the Merry Widow,
a strapless white one like a corset,
padded on top to give you cleavage.
My breasts ignore this idea.
The bra and I seem to move independently
one trying to catch up with the other.
Meanwhile, the boys grin and exchange glances
and are more interested
in talking to me.
Is even the appearance of boobs
so appealing?
Fake or real doesn't matter.

I stopped wearing one in the 1970's.
Thank heavens for the feminist movement.
Bras are so uncomfortable
and the straps always fall off your shoulders
which makes you do this
[mimes pulling up straps]
so you look unkempt and pathetic
like you can't keep your clothes on.
It's hard to make a serious point
when you're doing that.
I kept one dull white one
for modesty's sake.
Otherwise I wore nothing
under my tight stretchy tops
until I had a mastectomy.
[Pick up strand of beads]

"Show us your tits."
another balcony full of revelers
draws a crowd on the street
waiting for someone to heed the call.
Most flashers are young women
but a few middle-aged women bare their
well-preserved wares.
The ritual is the same.

Their male companions merely hold their coats
and drinks and pick up the beads that hit the sidewalk
placing them carefully over their heads in tribute.
[Put on beads]
"Show us your tits."
I consider the possibilities.

During my political phase,
I firmly believe that no breast cancer survivor
should have reconstructive surgery.
[Hang beads over left breast]
We should proudly display
our lopsided chests so the world won't forget
how many of us there are.
My then girlfriend, Kay, says, "It doesn't matter to me."
But we weren't having sex anyway.
"Who can tell?" Another dear friend says,
"Your breasts weren't that big to begin with."
My straight friend, Richard, whose opinion
I solicit, says, "Well, it's not for everybody,
but on you it looks good."
I show my friend Sara,
in a restroom at a local dive after a few drinks.
She says it doesn't look so bad
but something flashes across her face
and what she says is not what she sees.

Bourbon Street is becoming almost impassable
for all the people walking along
with a drink in their hands. You feel naked without one.
Everyone seems to be genuinely having a good time
in this manufactured world
but it's too noisy to talk to each other.
So, we take refuge in a sex shop.

All along the wall hang translucent sex toys
dildos and vibrators in amazing shapes, sizes, colors
and compositions with variable speeds, battery or plug in.
Inflatable dolls with vaginas and plenty
of leather whips, collars, and handcuffs.
French ticklers and other condoms that
promise more than just safer sex.
Lubricants of all flavors. Nipple clamps.
Later we regret not buying the orgy kit.
What were we thinking? We'd just pick one up
at the local drug store?

Suddenly I am reminded of the aquarium
we visited earlier that day. The fish swimming over us
in the archway, the leafy gold dragon seahorses,
the shark with dual torpedoes protruding underneath
his smooth belly, the sensuous jellies
delicately engulfing their prey with lacy transparency.
The way it feels to pet a starfish
sometimes firm, sometimes soft.
"Look at that!" you say in your demented way
in both places. "Look there's a pussy in the window"
and I am surprised to see it is just a cat.
This is what you and New Orleans have done to me.
As we head for the door
we overhear a woman at the counter ask:
"Do you have some thing for the ass?"

Outside the street scene escalates.
"Show us your tits."
Two young women above us kiss
and one rubs the other's nipples
simulating lesbian sex in a way that says
we are not really lesbians. This is a man's fantasy
of having two women. The crowd cheers and beads
are thrown up to them. But still there's something sad
about that gesture. I wonder why
no woman shows her tits and then kisses her man.

I also consider getting a tattoo
along my scar
[Arrange beads around scar]
something feminist and faintly Native American
and symbolic of the Solstice or something.
Just like Deena Metzger did.
She looked magnificent naked
arms and legs spread wide
on the cover of her cassette:
"This Body, My Life."
But that still leaves me flat chested
since my other breast seems to disappear
without its mate
and who was going to see it anyway?
[Pick up beads]

A conservatively dressed matron
who must have just removed her convention badge
is dangling beads over her balcony

to entice young female flashers.
Why do women participate in this as much as men?
Is it objectification or desire?
This street offers every sort of enticement
for the body—food, drink, dancing, the erotic.
Everywhere the drums beat
the voodooienne's shop is on the corner
young Christians pray for us around a large cross
as we peek through a doorway at a naked woman
then admire a shapely silhouette in shadow play before a window.

I want my boobs back.
So I go to Nordstrom's
to be fitted for a bra and prosthesis
or fake boob, as I like to call it.
Wearing my bra with the silicone mound inside
you can't tell I'm missing one.
It warms to skin temperature, the helpful clerk says.
But not to the touch, I think.
What will happen if I ever
have a date again? What will I say?
When should I broach the subject?
Oh by the way, one of these is fake.
[Point to chest]
No, darling, the whole thing.
I'll let you guess which one.

"Show us your _____" what?
Some of the women on the balconies
beckon the men to reciprocate
and showing their chests won't do
they have to drop "trow" or moon the crowd
but only the very drunk will comply.

I'm not satisfied with this bra stuffer for long.
There are so many clothes I can't wear
and I worry it will fall out and some dog
will run away with it. It's happened, I'm telling you.
So, next I try a stick-on boob.
attachable to the skin on the chest.
[Demonstrate]
First, mark the right spot with a white pencil
then apply surgical glue
and press a V shape form onto this spot.
Wait a few minutes and then apply the boob
which attaches via Velcro strips.

Thus in place, you can proceed without a bra
to wear a spaghetti strap top or even a bathing suit.
I'm delighted with this new extension of my body
until one day when I'm seated on a bar stool
wearing a tank top
with one arm leaning on the bar
like so
having a drink with an attractive woman
when I realize that my boob is no longer attached
to my chest
and instead is gently resting on my arm.
I quickly put on my shirt and say:
"Gee it's getting colder, guess the fog came
in I've got to run, see you later."
'Cause I'm a big phony with only one tit.
[Pick up beads]

We retrace our steps and see the same women
flashing for new onlookers. To me the spontaneity is lost
[Put on beads]
but you never seem to grow tired of this scene.
Later you explain, it's not the breasts
but the interaction of the crowd
that holds your attention.

I decide to have reconstructive surgery.
So I go to see a famous male plastic surgeon
who gives me three options:
[Said as doctor]
"Silicone implant, saline implant or
trans-flap procedure
where we take flesh from your stomach
giving you a free tummy tuck
then tunnel it up to your chest
and make a breast of your own tissue,
a more extensive operation—seven or eight hours.
We have to cut the stomach muscles
so the recovery is longer
but the results are very promising.
I've got someone here now I'd like to show you.
She had large breasts but now she has
lovely small ones, very natural looking."
So I'm ushered into an examining room
and she *"shows us her tits!"*
very nice and even smaller than mine
but she is over 6 feet and I'm 5'2"

They don't match the rest of her body.
He doesn't see the whole picture
only his creation, Dr. Frankenstein.
[Dr. Frankenstein accent]
"I will make you the most glorious tits."
I leave almost as quickly as I left that bar.

There has to be another way,
so I find a female plastic surgeon.
She understands my need
to leave the other breast intact.
Male physicians are always offeringto
give you two perfect C's while they're at it,
by jacking up the other one with an implant.
I also want my hair left in place.
The one growing in the spot where
my left nipple was.
She agrees this is a nice "natural" touch.

After three operations, I now have
a new left breast which I like very much
although it's not quite the same as the old one.
At first I thought it was just decorative
but gradually the feeling is coming back
because after all those connections
are mostly in our heads.

"Show us your tits."
We are getting tired and this might be my last chance.
But one breast is sort of old and the other one is new.
I wonder if the revelers would notice the difference
between nature and plastic surgery.
Has any woman with a mastectomy been so brave
as to show her scar, her tattoo, a rebuilt boob
on Bourbon Street?
Would jewelry or despair rain down on me? Or would everyone
pretend not to see, turn away and have another drink.
Maybe tomorrow, I think as we saunter down the street
arm in arm. Maybe tomorrow this sinner won't be saved
and I'll do it.

[Music gets softer as I turn the chair around and sit backwards in it]

Back at the hotel
I unhook my bra.
You say they are just right
a champagne glass full.

I do like to drink champagne
and so do you, we celebrate.
You know how to excite me
finding that magical current running
between my breasts and the rest of my body
sending shock waves through me
and afterward the tingling of every nerve
my skin glowing.

REFERENCES

Griffin, Susan. *Like the Iris of an Eye.* New York: Harper & Row, 1976.
Hagedorn, Jessica Tarahata. *Dangerous Music.* San Francisco: Mono Press, 1977.

O'Hara, Frank. *Lunch Poems.* San Francisco: City Lights Books, 1964.
Wakoski, Diane. *Motorcycle Betrayal Poems.* New York: Simon & Schuster, 1971.

Discussion Questions

1. The first excerpt explores a close relationship between a teacher and student. This topic is rarely openly discussed. How do you feel about student-faculty friendships, and how do sexual identities play a part in them?

2. The dialogue between Menopause and Desire illustrates how we are sometimes of two minds about our bodies and sexual desires. Have you ever felt that way?

3. The last excerpt deals with society's obsession with breasts from the perspective of a breast cancer survivor. Can you relate to any aspects of this? How does this piece relate to sexual identities and communication?

21

"Quare" Studies, or (Almost) Everything I Know About Queer Studies I Learned From My Grandmother [Part II]

E. PATRICK JOHNSON

BRINGIN' IT ON "HOME": QUARE STUDIES ON THE BACK PORCH

While there is intellectual work to be done inside the academy—what one might call "academic praxis"—there is also political praxis outside the academy.[1] If social change is to occur, gays, bisexuals, transgendered people, and lesbians of color cannot afford to be armchair theorists. Some of us need to be in the streets, in the trenches, enacting the quare theories that we construct in the "safety" of the academy. While keeping in mind that political theory and political action are not necessarily mutually exclusive, quare theorists must make theory work for its constituency. Although we share with our white queer peers sexual oppression, gays, lesbians, bisexuals, and transgendered people of color

also share racial oppression with other members of our community. We cannot afford to abandon them simply because they are heterosexual. Cohen writes that "although engaged in heterosexual behavior," straight African Americans "have often found themselves outside the norms and values of dominant society. This position has most often resulted in the suppression or negation of their legal, social, and physical relationships and rights" (454). Quare studies must encourage strategic coalition building around laws and policies that have the potential to affect us across racial, sexual, and class divides. Quare studies must incorporate under its rubric a praxis related to the sites of public policy, family, church, and community. Therefore, in the tradition of radical black feminist critic Barbara Smith ("Toward"), I offer a manifesto

SOURCE: This chapter was originally published as a part of "Quare" Studies, or (Almost) Everything I Know About Queer Studies I Learned From My Grandmother, in *Text and Performance Quarterly* (vol. 21, no. 1, pp. 1–25). Copyright © 2001 National Communication Association. Reprinted by permission.

that aligns black quare academic theory with political praxis.

We can do more in the realm of public policy. As Cohen so cogently argues in her groundbreaking book *The Boundaries of Blackness,* we must intervene in the failure of the conservative black leadership to respond to the HIV/AIDS epidemic ravishing African American communities. Due to the growing number of African Americans infected with and contracting HIV, quare theorists must aid in the education and prevention of the spread of HIV as well as care for those who are suffering. This means more than engaging in volunteer work and participating in fund raising. It also means using our training as academics to deconstruct the way HIV/AIDS is discussed in the academy and in the medical profession. We must continue to do the important work of physically helping our brothers and sisters who are living with HIV and AIDS through outreach services and fundraising events, but we must also use our scholarly talents to combat racist and homophobic discourse that circulates in white as well as black communities. Ron Simmons, a black gay photographer and media critic who left academia to commit his life to those suffering with AIDS by forming the organization US Helping US, remains an important role model for how we can use both our academic credentials and our political praxis in the service of social change.

The goal of quare studies is to be specific and intentional in the dissemination and praxis of quare theory, committed to communicating and translating its political potentiality. Indeed, quare theory is "bi"-directional: It theorizes from bottom to top and top to bottom (pun intended!). This dialogical/dialectical relationship between theory and practice, the lettered and unlettered, ivory tower and front porch is crucial to a joint and sustained critique of hegemonic systems of oppression.

Given the relationship between the academy and the community, quare theorists must value and speak from what hooks refers to as "homeplace." According to hooks, homeplace "[is] the one site where one [can] freely confront the issue of humanization, where one [can] resist" (42). It is from homeplace that people of color live out the contradictions of our lives. Cutting across the lines of class and gender, homeplace provides a place from which to critique oppression. I do not wish to romanticize this site by dismissing the homophobia that circulates within homeplace or the contempt that some of us (of all sexual orientations) have for "home."[2] I am suggesting, rather, that in spite of these contradictions, homeplace is that site that first gave us the "equipment for living" (Burke 293) in a racist society, particularly since we, in all of our diversity, have always been a part of this homeplace: housekeepers, lawyers, seamstresses, hairdressers, activists, choir directors, professors, doctors, preachers, mill workers, mayors, nurses, truck drivers, delivery people, nosy neighbors, and (an embarrassed?) "etc." SNAP!

Homeplace is also a site which quare praxis must critique. That is, we may seek refuge in homeplace as a marginally safe place to critique oppression outside its confines, but we must also deploy quare theory to address oppression within homeplace itself. One might begin, for instance, with the black church, which remains, for some gays and lesbians, a sustaining site of spiritual affirmation, comfort, and artistic outlet. Quare studies cannot afford to dismiss, cavalierly, the role of the black church in quare lives. However, it must never fail to critique the black church's continual denial of gay and lesbian subjectivity. Our role within the black church is an important one. Those in the pulpit and those in the congregation should be challenged whenever they hide behind Romans and Leviticus to justify their homophobia. We must force the black church to name us and claim us if we are to obtain any liberation within our own communities.[3]

Regarding ideological and political conflicts in gay, lesbian, and transgendered communities of color, quare praxis must interrogate and negotiate the differences among our differences, including our political strategies for dealing with oppression and our politics of life choice and maintenance. Consequently, quare studies must also focus on interracial dating and the identity politics such couplings invoke. Writer Darieck Scott has courageously addressed this issue, but we need to continue to explore our own inner conflicts around our choices of sexual partners across racial lines. Additionally, quare studies should interrogate another contested area of identity politics: relations between "out" and "closeted" members of our community. Much of this work must be done not in the academy, but in our communities, in our churches, in our homes.

Unconvinced that queer studies is soon to change, I summon quare studies as an interventionist disciplinary project. Quare studies addresses the concerns and needs of gay, lesbian, bisexual, and transgendered people across issues of race, gender, class, and other subject positions. While attending to the discursive constitution of subjects, quare studies is also committed to theorizing the practice of everyday life. Because we exist in material bodies, we need a theory that speaks to that reality. Indeed, quare studies may breathe new life into our "dead" (or deadly) stratagems of survival.

NOTES

1. I do not wish to suggest that the academy is not always already a politicized site. Rather, I only mean to suggest that the ways in which it is politicized are, in many instances, different from the ways in which nonacademic communities are politicized.

2. For a critique of the notion of "home" in the African American community vis-à-vis

homophobia and sexism, see Clarke, Crenshaw, hooks, and Simmons.

3. For a sustained critique of homophobia in the black church, see Dyson 77–108.

WORKS CITED

Burke, Kenneth. *Philosophy of Literary Form.* Baton Rouge: Lousiana State UP, 1967.

Clarke, Cheryl. "The Failure to Transform: Homophobia in the Black Community." *Home Girls: A Black Feminist Anthology.* Ed. Barbara Smith. New York: Kitchen Table, 1983. 197–208.

Cohen, Cathy. *The Boundaries of Blackness: AIDS and the Breakdown of Black Politics.* Chicago: U of Chicago P, 1999.

———. "Punks, Bulldaggers, and Welfare Queens: The Radical Potential of Queer Politics?" *GLQ: A Journal of Lesbian & Gay Studies* 3 (1997): 437–465.

Crenshaw, Kimberlé Williams. "Mapping the Margins: Intersectionality, Identity Politics, and Violence Against Women of Color." *Stanford Law Review* 43 (1991): 1241–99.

Dyson, Michael Eric. "The Black Church and Sex." *Race Rules: Navigating the Color Line.* Reading, MA: Addison-Wesley, 1996. 77–108.

hooks, bell. *Yearning.* Boston: South End, 1990.

Scott, Darieck. "Jungle Fever?: Black Gay Identity Politics, White Dick, and the Utopian Bedroom." *GLQ: A Journal of Lesbian & Gay Studies* 3 (1994): 299–332.

Simmons, Ron. "Some Thoughts on the Issues Facing Black Gay Intellectuals." *Brother to Brother: New Writings by Black Gay Men.* Ed. Essex Hemphill. Boston: Alyson, 1991. 211–228.

Smith, Barbara. "Toward a Black Feminist Criticism." *All the Women Are White, All the Blacks Are Men, But Some of Us Are Brave.* Eds. Gloria T. Hull, Patricia Bell Scott, and Barbara Smith. Old Westbury, NY: Feminist Press, 1982. 157–175.

Discussion Questions

1. What is the goal of quare studies?

2. Johnson argues that there are social issues with potential impact across race, class, and sexuality divisions and says that quare studies need to promote more coalition building around these issues. What are some specific examples he offers? What other ones can you think of?

3. How do we go about "theorizing the practice of everyday life"? Why is this important?

22

Activism and Identity Through the Word

A Mixed-Race Woman Claims Her Space

WENDY M. THOMPSON

When I first heard that *Restoried Selves* (Kumashiro, 2004) was being assembled, I felt compelled to write about my own experience and create a voice for myself and for people like me who struggle within margins. I wanted to reserve a place for myself within this space we call Asian/Pacific America. I wanted to speak out as a bisexual woman, a poor woman, a young woman, and a mixed-blood woman who has survived sexual violence. And I do so knowing that, for the most part, I cannot represent and will not fully be accepted by APA communities or queer communities because, within them, I often fall out of the boundaries for not being obviously either.

My skin color and appearance betray my Asian American identity. My identification as a bisexual person invites assumptions that I cannot make up my mind or that I am still questioning and will one day find my true sexual identity as either gay or straight. A certain stigma is attached to being both queer and Asian American: It just doesn't happen, or when it does, it's because the person has been Americanized and has adopted this freestyle form of "American" sexuality.

When identifying racially, I say that I am Afro-Chinese American. I may not be Chinese enough to compete for the title of Miss Chinatown, I may only be half-Chinese and exist without the super-Asian stereotypes and model-minority status, but I am an Asian American and no one can take that away from me. This is part of my activism: claiming my own agency and naming myself. I know it has been difficult for my mother, an immigrant who has lived throughout the Asian continent, to know herself and come close to claiming her own agency. It has been difficult for my African-American father who, in his own self-hatred and desire to become detached, raised his three daughters as Asian daughters, disregarding their brown skin.

I was born in Oakland, California, in 1981. It was an experimental time for all of us. My father was living post-Black Power Movement, struggling with menial jobs, with being a new father, and with trying to be a better father than his own abusive, alcohol-dependent dad. My mother was still learning what "America" was all about. She had been disowned for dating my father. With nowhere left to go, she married him and became pregnant with me. They raised me to be moral and religiously righteous. They raised me in hopes that I would not grow up to mimic the bad habits they had inherited from their parents. I was taught to be an obedient Chinese daughter because, at this time of urban, social, and economic decay, being black was more a burden than something to be proud of.

Growing up, I was reprimanded when I spoke of sex. My parents told me never to touch myself "down there" and raised me to reflect all aspects of what it meant to be a good woman who would someday become some man's wife. I never told anybody about my sexual explorations or how I felt about girls. Psychologists say it's normal for little children to experiment with the same sex while growing up, but at what age do they expect the child to grow out of it?

In school, I was called names and picked on for not acting like a regular girl. I remember being curious about pornography after sneaking looks at my father's *Playboys*. I told a girl friend about these girl-on-girl spreads and after recess had found that she had blabbed about it to the entire fifth-grade class. I was shamed and ostracized by the kids at school for being attracted to women and women's bodies. I had assumed that the boys disliked me so much and ridiculed me because I was ugly, weak, and wore secondhand clothes, not because I posed some kind of sexual threat to them. The girls avoided me altogether, afraid I'd try something on them. It was hard being branded a "lesbo" or "pervert" by my classmates, and being one of the few mixed-race

people at my school only further complicated things.

The first time I ever knew of any girl who self-identified as a queer was in high school. There was a biracial girl I had known since tenth grade. From day one, she had always dressed like a tomboy, wearing basketball jerseys and baggy "boys'" clothing. The girls she hung out with talked about her behind her back, gossiping that there was something wrong with her and she must be gay because of her nonfeminine mannerisms and lack of attraction toward boys. At the beginning of school the following year, when everyone was busy talking about their vacations, their new boyfriends, and other random happenings, she showed up in the leather pants, combat boots, spiked collars, and her curly hair shaved off. The fashion statement was one thing, but she also made it verbally known that she was out. Once this happened, she was immediately ostracized by her old friends but quickly made new ones—the Goth kids who hung out alone for the same reasons—and began a new trend of experimental sexual encounters with some of the younger female students at school.

Watching her become brave and come out, I felt that there was no reason I should deny part of who I was. It was as if in the past I had been living a secret life, or two secret lives: one as an undercover Chinese American girl and the other as an undercover girl who loved girls (and boys occasionally). In coming out sexually and coming to terms with my identity in a society obsessed with labels and categorization, there was always some kind of backlash from men who thought I was "not woman enough"; from (white) feminists who rejected my theories of having a feminism that was geared toward the "agenda" (that is, the mere survival and education) of women of color and poor women; from GLBTQ community organizations inside and outside of school that seemed to be dominated by white queers and in which I could never really feel accepted, only seen/treated as a token; and from my mother, whose sole want was for me to have a good life and to be a normal girl.

My activism springs from my own experiences with racism, with sexual and physical violence, and with sexism and homophobia. It springs from years of wanting but never feeling brave enough to combat these issues, and of putting off these encounters until I had gotten bigger, older, and wiser. But you can never put off these experiences. You get hurt, you bleed, you get angry, and you move on, but you never forget.

As a writer, an artist, and an activist, my identities and personal political beliefs are always infused into my work. I write and create mainly from the perspective of a queer mixed-race woman who is navigating her way through a world that criminalizes and incarcerates youth at increasingly higher rates (while youth crime rates are steadily dropping), that teaches girls to value and adhere to sick sexist gender roles, and that is unsafe for anyone existing publicly outside of the heterosexual mainstream.

I could march to city hall with placards in my hands chanting catchy slogans, but I believe that, for me, the best way to actively bring change is to carve it from the inside out. Through art, through writing, through other sources of media, my voice and agenda can be more effectively visualized and absorbed by those beyond my immediate community. I want people to experience my activism in ways other than by watching it televised on the evening news or reading about it in the newspaper. I want them to walk into a gallery or open up a book and feel captivated by the images. I want them to reflect on what they encounter, I want them to critique it, I want my visions and words to permeate their minds and make them really question their positions regarding gender, sexuality, class, and ethnicity.

The main goal of my art and activism is to steer marginalized people toward finding their voices, toward finding their places or creating a space in this society that they can call their

own. I would like to see more queer/poor/urban/surviving youth and people of color representing themselves with media, literature, and the arts. Just because we see Lucy Liu's face in theaters and see Amy Tan's writings neatly shelved in bookstores doesn't mean that we—particularly in APA communities—have succeeded and the job is done. There are a select number of sexual and ethnic representations out there but are they accurate? And if they're not, why not create our own?

I feel that I will always exist at the fringes of society. In being racially mixed I will never be assumed to be an Asian but always something else. In believing that sexuality is fluid and that no one should be forced to deny love for a person because of their physical sex, I will constantly be regarded as a sexual rebel, a loose and dangerous woman. Being queer is being anything but normal, and being queer is what I would prefer to be, seeing that normality in this society comes at a painful price. I don't want to limit myself in any area. I want to love myself and other women the way I choose. I have the right to choose my community and home. I will cross borders and break boundaries because I was never an obedient girl to begin with and was always much too curious to "stay inside the lines."

Many people ask me, "Who are you and what are you doing here?" They want to know who I am: What is my racial, ethnic, socioeconomic, sexual background?

And what I am doing here: Where am I from? Whose side am I on? How far do I intend to go?

My answer is that I am a complex individual who is simply trying to change the world. I am a woman yelling from the sidelines, creating new narratives, bringing forth a new experience, using her power to transform and fight and bring beauty to this society.

The following is a poem I wrote that describes the time around which I came out and the feelings of my community and family in response to this decision as well as my own feelings regarding my ever-shifting identity.

The first (culture fuck)

I saw her for the first time
Standing in front of a dressing-room
  mirror
Trying on a bathing suit that fit too loose
  over too small limbs
Her slant eyes bitter
Her mouth twisted down
It was no accident
The disoriented Oriental
Outgrowing her place
Like a wild untamable stalk of sugarcane
Japanese Godzilla made in the USA
Towering over buildings
Water towers
Overturning vehicles and corrupting
  freeways.
For the first time I was seeing me
It was a distorted reflection
The half-black Asian girl
The only person darker than the super-
  smart FOB kids in my English honors
  class
Stuck at home on Friday nights
Only to turn 18 one day and leave home
  with plans for the prom.
My mother standing in the doorway
My father behind her
His fists balled up
Her mouth in the shape of an O
A maddening scream in Mandarin
About
How dare I walk out the house wearing
  that
That!
They ache knowing that I am
  unstoppable
A little brown girl born out of broken
  English
Stuffing herself with *bao* and rice
While her immigrant mommy tells her:
be a good girl
be polite
study hard
and smile.

Yet I was not good enough
I was not polite
And I didn't study hard.
My aunts wanted me to be pretty
They fed me lies at my *po po's*
  (grandmother's) house about how
If I ate all the *bok choi* on my plate
I would one day be Miss Chinatown
With a diamond tiara stranded in my
  curly black hair
The sash covering a chest where big
  American breasts should be
I was never as good-looking as I should
  have been.
But I was the number-one daughter
No sons
Just three girls
Bad luck
And arguing.
Ma crumpling to the floor after daddy
  hits her in the head with the door of
  the freezer
I hated that refrigerator ever since.
Black daddy yelling at yellow mommy
  about not understanding English
Stupid motherfucker, he says
I act like I don't hear it.
I don't hear a lot of things
The way my father is disappointed for
  not having a son
And in my act to appease him
He calls me stupid
Confused
He says I am needing therapy
Because I act like a man (dysfunctional)
All macho
Pretending I do not know how to cry.
I talk loud and mask my body with XXL
  clothes
I make myself look bigger than I am.
Act like the tough guy and challenge
  boyfriends to fights
Coming home with a smashed nose
Bloody black eyes.
I do not report it when they rape me
The first and the next

Proving that they are real men
Realer than my fake acts of survival.
They get offended when I say I like girls
They feel threatened
And establish the boundaries by saying that I will never have a dick to please her with.
My sesame-seed girl on top of my brown-rice body.
They say she won't fall for it,
Bullshit.
But still we act it out
Like genderfucked Barbie dolls
Me being the man-woman
And her
This girl with the Sanrio fetish who likes to buy tapioca drinks from Chinatown
Her round moon face
Her body twisting like a root inside and outside of mine
Bending out of tradition.
She is not straight but won't admit that she's gay either
Her sex split in halves like her culture
1.5 Korean American female sexed with laced thoughts of me
Undercover from her immigrant mother who can't quite roll the R's.
And I remember it like the first day we met
Or the first day I looked at her and we kissed.
She wasn't like the other girls,
She didn't pull away.
I remember how we faked it
Told her mom we were going upstairs to try on a new dress
When her mother suddenly burst into her bedroom and found me *doing that*
That!
To her daughter

Spread-eagled and naked from the waist down
That!
It was no longer funny
The language had ceased
Our little fling ended with the shunning of my disloyal identity.
I had ruined that chance to prove my Asianness
To disown the part of me that was rotten
The apple that Buddha never blessed.
Turning mute
The eyes growing accustomed to the dark
Her two eyes never seeing that way again.
And after her disappearance they all became white
Like white walls and white sheets
White lovers like buttered popcorn and candy apple number my tongue,
Scarring my taste.
No more fish balls snapped up in cross-legged chopsticks rubbing together like lovers
The dim sum passed up for a meal of fast food burgers and fries.
I walk this world alone
Seeing signs in Spanish that hang in the greasy windows of Little Asia Chinese Take-Out
Now serving American cuisine
Curtains browned and shut
Like her legs
And her mind.
A whispered reminder of how
English was never spoken here.

REFERENCE

Kumashiro, K. K. (Ed.). (2004). *Restoried selves*. Binghamton, NY: Harrington Park Press.

Discussion Questions

1. Thompson refers to her "ever-shifting identity." What does she mean by this and what examples does she give?

2. Do you see your identity(ies) as relatively stable? Relatively fluid? Can one aspect of identity shift without affecting the others?

3. Thompson explains that her "identities and personal political beliefs are always infused into [her] work." Do you feel this way about what you do? Is it possible to entirely separate one's work, identities, and politics? Do you see that as desirable? Why or why not?

23

Making Alliances

GLORIA E. ANZALDÚA

IDENTITY: THE POWER OF SELF-INVENTION

Jamie Lee Evans: Can you talk a little bit about lesbian alliances? What are some major issues that come up for you, not just within the Latina/Chicana community but mainly with other communities?

Gloria E. Anzaldúa: Identity is one of the major issues. What you call yourself or what other people call you, makes you; it's an aspect of identity formation, a process that constructs or invents you. You can take your identity into your hands recognizing that you don't need a white person or a Chicana middle-class person to tell you who you are. You have some say in it. Constructing identity is a collaborative effort. What you name yourself comes up—you know, do you call yourself "dyke," "lesbian," "marimacha," "jota"?

You can decide what to label yourself. What does it mean when a Chicana calls herself "lesbian"?

When discussing identity you get into the controversy of the social constructionist verses the essentialist. What do you think—was I born a queer or was I made a queer? Is there something in my genetic makeup, a queer gene? Why are some people in the family queer and others not? There may be a third or a fourth way of conceptualizing identity. What is the history behind your identity?

I explored what queerness was in Native cultures, how they treated same-sex orientation or whatever you want to call it. (The vocabulary changes every day.) The Nahuatl word for a dyke is "patlache." Queer sexuality was prevalent in some Indian societies, taboo and punished by strangulation or stoning in others. I could connect my queerness to my Mexicanness. So now I have the white

SOURCE: This chapter was originally published as part of "Making Alliances, Queerness, and Bridging Conocimientos: An Interview With Jamie Lee Evans" (1993) in *Interviews/Entrevistas* (AnaLouise Keating, Ed.). Copyright © 2000 Routledge. Reprinted by permission.

307

traditions but I also have my own. When I think of myself as a queer woman, my queerness is not just white, but Indian, Mexican, Chicano, a regional queerness, a working-class queerness of my growing up in South Texas. Kids of color growing up now don't have a sense of roots. Their identities are secondhand—derivative from the white—so they're floundering. They know they're not white, and the issues of language keep coming up.

Agreeing on what to call ourselves as queer women is one of the hardest things to do. The world "lesbian" has different meanings to different people. Adrienne Rich defines it in one way, Pat Califia defines it another. So what is a lesbian? Is a lesbian identified by sexual activity or by cultural orientation or by political view? Take the word "queer"—What is queer? The word "queer" has been taken over by the academy, queer theorists have borrowed this working-class word.

JLE: Have they borrowed it?

GEA: Taken it over. Stolen it. For you "queer" means something, for Lisa it means something else, for me it means growing up in South Texas where the word was used for somebody who was different sexually. It was a working-class word, a world I feel more comfortable with than with "lesbian" or "gay" or "homosexual" or "invert." So language becomes an issue that accompanies identity. As does one's economic station. Money and sex are the two main issues in alliance work. Who has control over what, who has the resources? Who has the power, who has the big club? And how is that club being used—to shuttle resources to people who have need of it? Or to hit people over the head to keep them in their place? Issues of class ultimately have to do with money. Money is energy and people with money have the means, energy, and resources to get other people to do things their way. People who don't have money are expected to give their energies, resources, to the power holders who siphon them of their life's blood. The three major issues are: who I am, what language I speak, and how much money I have. Money, sex, and identity.

JLE: So when you say "sex" you mean female or male? You don't mean how much sex you have—say, four times a week?

GEA: No. And heterosexual sex is always a power thing, who is bottom and who is top. I shouldn't use those terms.

JLE: No, that's fine. I think that there could be a lot of disagreement.

GEA: In sexual relationships there's always a stronger person, the one with more power. The person who's more needy will make concessions to the person she loves because of that need, which gives the other person more power. It may not matter who's on top and who's on bottom. The bottom can be in control.

JLE: You've been reading too much psychology!

GEA: Whether in a homosexual, a lesbian, or a bisexual relationship, the power issue is still there. Somebody needs or loves the other person more. It's never equal. I think it comes closest with lesbians because they kind of take turns. But in your average relationship there's always a stronger party. The controller. Isn't it awful?

JLE: Of course my lover is sitting here. I have no comment. I'll call you later.

GEA: If the relationship breaks up it's because of the sex, which is actually about power, and that power can be about money or it can be about class which adds up to identity.

JLE: So you're saying that sex is all about power and money and class?

GEA: No. I'm saying that when a sexual relationship doesn't work, when it falls apart, the straw that broke its back is money, power, class issues of identity. If something goes wrong in your relationship, you can look back and it will be one of these: sex, money issues, or class which is language. Maybe I'm totally off the wall.

JLE: We could have a long conversation on this; it's very interesting, I don't know that I would agree. Do you consider the basic relations of love—two lovers—as being in alliance?

GEA: Yes. That's why the issues I'm talking about in speaking to Latino Heritage Week about identity are the same kinds of issues I'd be talking about to two dykes who were breaking up or trying to work the relationship. You just take the microcosm and expand it to the macrocosm, and you're doing the same thing. What I see happening between two lovers is what's happening between two or three different groups of people, nations, continents. It's no longer a house of two people but all the different communities trying to work together, the United States, the planet. But I may be generalizing.

JLE: You said a lot.

GEA: What I'm saying is that when you're doing process work on yourself or facilitating somebody else's healing, it's the same mechanisms that would be at issue and talked about in couples' counseling, and the same kinds of things I'd be talking about to these groups of people in alliances. I say "I" because other people would not be addressing this issue. That's my hit on it. Like I said before—activists want to divorce their personal feelings from their organization. They want to work in a reasonable, cool, collected manner. But I say that all of those problems and issues—the origin goes back to particular feelings and experiences that these activists have had when they've been one-on-one with their parents, with their boyfriends, with their friends, with their classmates. So the two of you are, in miniature, this country.

JLE: And all of the oppressions and power struggles.

CONOCIMIENTOS

GEA: But the two of you can work together and be allies. People bond because they want to work together. I'm hopeful because to be human is to be in relationship; to be human is to be related to other people, to be interdependent with other people. So that's what we have to work at. Sometimes in order to be human and to relate to other people we have to cut ourselves a little slack—separate out, regroup, and recharge our batteries so that we can continue the work. That's where my model of the bridge, drawbridge, sandbar, or island comes in. My model is conocimientos. My pictogram for it is la lengua, los ojos, y las orejas en la mano surda. At the end of the tongue is a pen. "Conocimiento" is the Spanish word for knowledge and skill. It has to do with getting to know each other by really listening with the outer ear and the inner ear. Really looking at each other and seeing with our eyes and communicating orally or with the written word. It means always putting ourselves out on the line by raising our hands. The hand is the symbol for activist work, for doing. You raise your voice, you raise your hand. Because it's not enough to see and to understand. You have to go out there and take action. Whether it's to write a book, make an anthology, attend meetings once a week, mail flyers, or picket—it has to be done. Con la mano. With the hand. Activism. Writing is a form of activism, one of making bridges.

JLE: So when you talk about being a bridge. . . .

GEA: One of the drawbacks to being a bridge is being walked on, but one of the pluses is that it's two-way—oncoming and outgoing traffic. It's being in different worlds and getting the best from those worlds—white and colored, gay and straight—and benefiting from those connections. But you also get damaged in some ways. This work bends a person, wastes a person; the wear and tear is stressful. Stress makes your body ill. I got diabetes. I have to watch that I don't get stressed out and overwhelmed. With the job of being a bridge comes another perk—of getting my name out, of people buying my books and believing in my work. I don't know if there's a balance.

JLE: You've made a career out of being a bridge?

GEA: Yeah, of extending my identity. It's not enough for me to be just a chicanita farm worker from South Texas. I have to see other worlds, experience other things. It's not enough for me to be a Chicana dyke. I am also a writer, an intellectual, an artist; I am also middle class, or will be.

JLE: Can you talk about the risks involved in being an ally?

GEA: The biggest risk is betrayal. When a person is betrayed she feels shitty, feels stupid: "Why did I trust this person and allow her to stab me in the back? It's all my fault." You know—the victim syndrome. I beat myself up over the fact that this person betrayed me. With Chicanas, betrayal is a big thing. We were betrayed as women, as Indians, and as a colonized group in this country. Along with the betrayal, you feel less of a person, you feel shame. Feelings of betrayal make you a smaller person, reduce your self-esteem. Betrayal is politically deadening. It's dangerous. It's disempowering. When you lose that self-esteem you no longer trust yourself to make value judgments about other people. "If I instinctively trusted this

woman for over a year and she stabbed me in the back, what's to say I'm going to be right about this other person? What if I'm wrong? What if my gut feeling is wrong again?" So I lose confidence in myself and my values. The whole person is slowly destroyed, and this is what women of color are suffering from: Their personhood is chopped off at the knees by these wounds.

JLE: What about betrayal in the lesbian community or with lesbians of color? Is it a problem there also?

GEA: Well, it depends on what stage of coming out you're in or how long you've been out, how much experience you've had in the greater lesbian world or whatever. At first I felt really good belonging to the lesbian community, even though it was mostly white. Before I'd had no home; I now had this new home. But after a few years I started looking at the power dynamic, at who had power, and who was trying to define for me what I was as a Chicana lesbian. I saw that my voice was silenced and my history ignored. Those issues drove me into looking at my queer roots. I had to get a positive sense of being queer from my culture, not just from the white culture. Now I can look at both the white lesbian community and my own culture beginning to have groups of lesbians organizing. Chicana dyke organizations are beginning to form, are beginning to come into their power. So now I'm trying to position myself, looking not just at my culture and the white culture, but at the whole planet. I'm looking at other nationalities and how they deal with their queer people. I'm trying to get a global perspective on being queer. Sometimes I feel very comfortable with a bunch of white dykes and other times I feel totally invisible, ignored. I feel that they only see the queer part of me and ignore the

Chicana and working-class parts. As long as I leave my class and my culture outside the door when I walk into the room I'm OK. But if I bring in my race or my class, then education starts.

JLE: You're not as welcome.

GEA: I think that the white dykes really want a community that's diversified. Sometimes they want it so badly that they want to put everybody under this queer umbrella: "We're all in this together and we're all equal." But we are not equal. In their thirst and their hunger for this diversity, the issues of class and race are issues that they don't even want to examine because they feel those issues can be divisive. So they're hungry for being politically correct and having women of color in their organization and women of color lovers and women of color in their syllabi and women of color performers, singers, writers, or whatever. The greater our numbers the more power we have as queers. Bringing us under this queer umbrella is a kind of survival tactic. But often in order to bring us under the queer umbrella they ignore differences, collapse the differences, not really deal with the issue. Just sort of pay word of mouth attention to the issue and when it comes down to the numbers of who has power and how many women of color are in this anthology—in terms of the real work, they fall short. The vision is good—the greater numbers, the greater strength kind of thing— but they want us to leave our rage and our class in the checkroom when we walk in. I wrote an essay called "To(o) Queer the Writer" that deals with these concerns.

JLE: Do you think they really want a multicultural world or do they just want to stop being called racists?

GEA: They really want a multicultural diverse world. As a group, dykes are more progressively political than any other group. Because they've been oppressed as dykes and because of feminism they're more apt to see the oppression of women of color. There are always the false ones, of course. Dykes' politics are more progressive than most other groups, but they have a lot of work to do because of that very assumption: that they're enlightened and politically progressive. This assumption blanks out the trouble spots. Some don't want to really look at race or class issues. But I see some honest motivation about wanting to be allies. Sometimes they don't contend with their *unconscious* motivation, that they're doing it out of guilt or whatever. As a group, white dykes do a lot of therapy and therefore are always questioning their motivations; I think they really do want a multicultural diverse group and world. I am very hopeful. I think I'm one of the few people who are hopeful. Most people my age or younger have burned out and become disillusioned. It's the pits right now. Many young people of color have no hope, do not see alliances working, do not see white people reaching out, and do not see the possibility of white people changing perspectives or allowing change to come into their lives, but I do.

Discussion Questions

1. What is *conocimiento*?

2. What concerns does Anzaldúa raise about the term *queer*? Do you agree with her concerns? Why or why not?

3. In what senses does Anzaldúa describe herself as being a bridge?

4. What are the benefits and risks of forming alliances across sexual identity, gender, class, and race? Who do you tend to see as your own allies? What kinds of alliances have you found most rewarding? Most challenging? What have you learned about what it takes to be an effective ally?

Index

About the Editors

Karen E. Lovaas (Ph.D. American Studies, University of Hawai'i) is Associate Professor of Speech and Communication Studies at San Francisco State University. Her recent publications underscore her interest in sexualities, gender, communication, and pedagogy. *The Contested Terrain of LGBT Studies and Queer Theory* (with John Elia and Gust Yep, in press) is a follow-up volume to *Queer Theory and Communication: From Disciplining Queers to Queering the Discipline(s)* (2003). She has authored encyclopedia entries on "gender roles" and "sexism" for *Youth, Education, and Sexualities: An International Encyclopedia* (J. T. Sears, Ed.; 2005), and glossary entries on "cross-dressing," "free love," "liberation," and "sexual assault" for *Sexuality: The Essential Glossary* (2004). "A Critical Appraisal of Assimilationist and Radical Ideologies Underlying Same-Sex Marriage in LGBT Communities in the United States" (with Yep and Elia, 2003) and "Sexual Practices, Identification, and the Paradoxes of Identity in the Era of AIDS: The Case of 'Riding Bareback'" (with Yep and Alex Pagonis, 2002) were both published in the *Journal of Homosexuality*, and "Transcending Heteronormativity in the Classroom: Using Queer and Critical Pedagogies to Alleviate Trans-anxieties" (with former undergraduate students Lina Baroudi and S. Collins, 2002) was written for the *Journal of Lesbian Studies* and was simultaneously published in *Addressing Homophobia and Heterosexism on College Campuses* (E. P. Cramer, Ed.; 2003). Her chapter "Communication in 'Asian American' Families With Queer Members: A Relational Dialectics Perspective" (with Yep and Philip Ho) appears in *Queer Families, Queer Politics: Challenging Culture and the State* (M. Bernstein, R. Reimann, & R. Bartsch, Eds.; 2001). Her ongoing projects use critical, queer, and feminist approaches to communication research and pedagogy.

Mercilee M. Jenkins (Ph.D. Speech Communication, University of Illinois) is Professor in the Department of Speech and Communication Studies and a core faculty member in the Human Sexuality Studies Program at San Francisco State University. Her publications include her solo performance texts, poetry, and scholarly articles on women's small group communication, the performance of personal narratives, and communication in the college classroom. She was Associate Editor for *Queer Words, Queer Images* (R. J. Ringer, Ed.; 1994). Her ethnographic research on gender, sexuality, and relationships has resulted in several produced plays, including *A Credit to Her Country*, based on the oral histories of lesbians in the U. S. military, and *She Rises Like a Building to the Sky*, about the founding of the San Francisco Women's Building. She received two Horizon Foundation grants for *Credit* and a San Francisco Arts Commission Cultural Equity Grant for the development of *She Rises*. Her solo performance piece, *Menopause and Desire*, premiered at the San Francisco Fringe Festival in September 2002 and was published in its entirety in *Text and Performance Quarterly* in July 2005. She received the Leslie Irene Coger Award for Distinguished Performance from the National Communication Association in 2004.

List of Contributors

Gloria E. Anzaldúa
deceased

Myron Beasley
Brown University

Elizabeth Bell
University of South Florida

Christopher Castiglia
Loyola University Chicago

Lisa M. Diamond
University of Utah

John P. Elia
San Francisco State University

Michele J. Eliason
San Francisco, CA

Cathy B. Glenn
St. Mary's College

Mercilee M. Jenkins
San Francisco State University

E. Patrick Johnson
Northwestern University

Jonathan Ned Katz
Independent scholar

William Leap
American University

Audre Lorde
deceased

Karen E. Lovaas
San Francisco State University

Christopher Reed
Lake Forest College

Sara Salih
University of Toronto

John M. Sloop
University Vanderbilt

Terry Tafoya
Taos and Warm Springs, New Mexico

Wendy M. Thompson
Independent video artist and poet

Jennifer Tuder
Saint Cloud State University

Paul Turpin
Willamette University

John T. Warren
Southern Illinois University

Jeffrey Weeks
London South Bank University

Robert G. Westerfelhaus
College of Charleston

Gust A. Yep
San Francisco State University

Nicholas A. Zoffel
Bowling Green State University